HOW JESUS BECAME CHRISTIAN

HOW JESUS BECAME CHRISTIAN

BARRIE WILSON, PH.D.

RANDOM HOUSE CANADA

Random House Canada and colophon are trademarks.

www.randomhouse.ca

Library and Archives Canada Cataloguing in Publication

Wilson, Barrie, 1940–
How Jesus became Christian / Barrie Wilson.

Includes bibliographical references and index.
ISBN 978-0-679-31493-6

1. Jesus Christ—Person and offices. 2. Christianity—Origin.
3. Christianity and antisemitism. I. Title.

BT198.W47 2008   232.9'08   C2007-907345-X

Printed and bound in the United States of America

10 9 8 7 6 5 4 3 2 1

To Linda

who taught me life's hardest lesson,
that one can disagree with someone and still love them

CONTENTS

ACKNOWLEDGMENTS

In the course of writing this work, I discovered it takes a village to create a book, and I owe a debt of gratitude to family, friends, colleagues, and students for helping to make these ideas a reality.

Special recognition goes to my children and their spouses—Jamie and Erin Wilson, David and Sarah Wilson, Michael Wilson and his friend Julia Tedesco, Dorothy Wilson and Jack Mailloux—as well as my in-laws, Karl and Phyllis Reeser. Along with other family members—Ted and Elizabeth Reeser, Joyce Forster, Martin Traub-Werner, Tamara Kronis, and Marion Wilson—they provided ongoing support and encouragement.

A wonderful group of friends acted as cheerleaders along the way. I owe an important debt of gratitude to them for being so supportive—Lani and Byron Alexandroff, Elaine and Jack Barkin, Shira Benson, Joan and Zane Cohen, Rena and Len Gill, Kathy and Saul Glober, Linda and Arnold Gordon, Judi and Aron Kohn, Marian and Declan Magrane, Zelda and Tony Reich, Donna Shoom-Kirsch, Jenny and Julio Szmuilowicz, Lynn and Witold Szytkiel, and Marlene and Robbie Zeldin. They never failed to ask, How is the book coming along? Their interest clearly indicated that a history of early Christianity, told in nontechnical language, would resonate with a wide audience.

Many thanks also to my good friend, Suresh Chawla, who always insisted on clarity of thought and precise expression when presenting ideas.

I owe my colleagues at York University a debt of gratitude, especially Patrick Gray who epitomizes the meaning of a true colleague. We frequently taught a course on the Bible together, and, as we exchanged views in class, students often witnessed what was hopefully an intriguing scholarly debate. I am indebted to him for these "high points" in my teaching career as well as for his support at key stages in the publishing process. Another colleague, Joan Gibson, upon hearing the focus of my research, blurted out, "What you're really tackling is how Jesus became Christian." That insight stuck as the title of the work, and I am very grateful to her for that contribution.

Lani Alexandroff, Carla Ionescu, and Tamara Kronis reviewed an early draft of this work. Their perspectives and useful comments helped me recognize what typical readers are apt to bring to the book by way of background knowledge.

A special salute goes to my literary agent—Joëlle Delbourgo of Joëlle Delbourgo and Associates—who saw the merits and potential of my ideas and who was instrumental in bringing the proposal to the attention of St. Martin's Press. David Sobel, an experienced independent writer and editorial consultant, helped me write the initial book proposal and an early segment on Paul. To my editors—Michael Flamini of St. Martin's Press, New York; Nick Garrison, Marion Garner, and Kendall Anderson of Random House, Canada; and Ben Buchan of Orion Publishing Group, London—many thanks to all of you for your critical eye and keeping my focus on the central story. Thanks also to the production personnel at St. Martin's Press for a thoughtful and thorough review.

I have worked with thousands of students over the years from many different backgrounds. We have probed biblical texts together, studied their historical contexts, and questioned some of the things that faith leaders and scholars say about these important writings. To them I am grateful. Their interest, enthusiasm, and willingness to explore have made the study pleasurable. In particular, Dianne Cole, Jonathan von Kodar, and Janice Meighan challenged my thinking and helped sharpen my thesis.

I owe an enormous debt of gratitude to my wife and companion on life's journey, Linda. She not only provided astute observations along the way, but also forced me to tell the story clearly, in "normal language"—to bring biblical scholarship out of academia into the mainstream in an interesting and engaging fashion. This I have tried to do—but you, reader, will have to be the judge of whether I succeeded.

PROLOGUE

A PERSONAL NOTE

How Jesus Became Christian is intended for general readers who are curious about the origins of Christianity, who are interested in the big picture, and who are perplexed by some of the same mysteries that have intrigued me over the years. How did the Jewish Jesus of history become the Gentile Christ of faith? How did early Christianity become a separate religion from Judaism? What really accounts for Christian anti-Semitism?

I first became aware of the Jewishness of Jesus in high school. A visiting speaker, a rabbi by the name of Dr. Joshua Stern of Temple Emanu-el in Montreal, introduced himself to a mixed Protestant-Jewish audience as, "My name is Jesus [Joshua]. Jesus was Jewish." That was a new and interesting thought—both that Jesus's name was really Yeshua (Joshua in English) and that he was Jewish. I hadn't realized that before, and it is one of the few things I remember from my entire high school education. I don't think anyone intentionally hid that truth from me: Jesus's Jewishness just wasn't spoken of. Then or now.

This insight stuck with me as I worked through my academic studies in the Philosophy of Religion as well as Biblical Studies. I completed my Ph.D. at the University of Toronto, after an M.A. from Columbia University and a B.A. in Philosophy and Psychology from Bishop's University in Quebec. Along the way I studied at Union Theological and General Theological Seminaries—both in New York City—and completed a degree in Religious Studies at Trinity College, Toronto. I was privileged to study with two of the world's leading Anglican theologians of the time—Eugene R. Fairweather and W. Norman Pittenger—as well as with a prominent Anglican New Testament scholar, Frank W. Beare.

My dual education in both Philosophy and Biblical Studies has helped to shape my perspective on texts. As a philosopher and historian of religion, I seek evidence and support for positions. Consequently, I approach the study of the Bible with a critical eye. What is the claim being made? What is its social and political context? What motivates the author of the individual biblical texts? Do the claims make sense? What's *not* being said?

This book builds upon contemporary scholarship. Along the way, I have put into the notes (at the end of the book) references to scholars who have helped me in my quest to understand the New Testament and early Christian origins. I am highly indebted to many of these thinkers, but I have taken a somewhat independent stance with the formulation of what I call the **Jesus Cover-Up Thesis**. This contention represents a more forthright claim than one will find in the current literature.

Most of my publications hitherto have been for scholars, and I've published articles on biblical writers, ancient Greek authors, as well as theorists of textual interpretation.[1] It has been in teaching Biblical Studies over twenty years, however, that I gradually came to realize that a lot of things do not add up when we examine New Testament and early Christian writings from a critical, evidence-based perspective. These interpretive puzzles prompted me to probe further and to go beyond the superficial story line embedded in the New Testament documents.

AN INVITATION TO EXPLORE

This book is the result of some two decades of reflection. I invite you to share in this investigation and to see afresh the origins of Christianity as we know it. Along the way, several varieties of early Christianity will be explored. We will gain a new appreciation of how Jesus himself was originally perceived by his family and, after his death, by his earliest followers, the Jesus Movement in Jerusalem, under James. We will discover who Paul really was and why his message was so radical . . . and disruptive. His impact upon "what eventually became Christianity" can hardly be underplayed. We will also see, decade by decade, how the new religion departed from Judaism and repackaged Jesus in an interesting and extremely successful way. We will come to understand why it emerged with anti-Semitic attitudes well entrenched.

I encourage readers to think through the origins of Christianity and to ponder the new perspective presented in this work. The intended reader is one who asks questions, likes challenges, and seeks to learn. I have met many such people teaching a generation of students at York University, a multicultural secular university in Toronto. With over fifty thousand students and seven thousand faculty and staff, York is Canada's third largest university. Students come from many different backgrounds—all varieties of Christians, Jews,

Moslems, Zoroastrians, Hindus, Buddhists, and those with no current religious affiliation. They have been open to historical and philosophical questioning and relish the search for answers. Their questions and findings have enriched my own thinking with their perspectives. I am grateful that I have had the opportunity to teach within a secular institution, giving me the liberty to probe uncomfortable questions with students who have enjoyed the freedom not to be defensive about faith positions and to discern anew what could have happened "back there then."

Over the years, I have traveled many times to Israel, Egypt, Jordan, and Turkey, to see firsthand the places to which the Bible refers. In 1994, we enjoyed a wonderful family adventure in Israel on the occasion of our son, Michael's, bar mitzvah at Masada. Along with his brothers, Jamie and David, we toured Israel from the Negev in the south to the Galilee in the north and back down into Egypt, visiting many historic and archeological sites along the way. Israel, however, is not just a museum of antiquities: it is also the land of the living Bible, and we explored contemporary Israeli sights and sounds as well.

In 2001, I took twenty-nine students from York University on a course trip to this region, aided by my colleague, Patrick Gray. We walked, hiked, talked, sang, and roamed the historic haunts of Jerusalem, the lush Galilee, and the arid Dead Sea area where the Dead Sea Scrolls were discovered. We took the cable car up to the top of Masada to see Herod the Great's magnificent palaces. As we later hiked down the steep incline of Masada, I recall the group singing "Amazing Grace." I wondered at the time what its original Zealot inhabitants would have made of these sentiments.

Most of us climbed up what is alleged to be Mount Sinai over a four-hour period in the late afternoon, to see the sunset from the summit and to gain a sense of the splendor that Moses himself might have experienced. Whether it was on this mountain—or one close by—it was an overwhelming experience. We descended in the dark with a brilliant canopy of stars overhead—the brightest sky I have ever seen. With our increasingly dim flashlights showing us the way, we bumped into camels trekking silently up the pathway. We all wondered, how can such huge animals move so quietly in the dark? We came back, late for the dinner that our gracious Egyptian hosts had arranged, and we were quickly brought back down to earth.

They were a remarkable group and it was a unique experience. They were all searching for something about their heritage that would resonate with them today. The experience we underwent was very similar to the sense of wonder and history that Bruce Feiler writes about in *Walking the Bible*. He wrote that book in conversations with a prominent Israeli archeologist, Avner Goren. I was later privileged to trek through many of the temples and tombs of Egypt with Avner as my insightful guide. Feiler writes movingly of his experience, much of it tracing the probable path the ancient Israelites under Moses would have taken through the Sinai, Jordan, and Israel. Members of our group had much the same experience he did tracing their roots.

Feiler's book was published in 2001, around the same time as our trip through Israel and the Sinai. I was amazed to read that he and Avner had read passages from *Egeria's Travels* while visiting Mount Sinai. This account was written by a fourth-century nun or wealthy patroness who had traveled throughout the Middle East, visiting biblical sites. We, too, had read her descriptions of Mount Sinai and its surroundings.[2] We could stand where she had stood and see what she had witnessed in the 380s. It was remarkable how many of her observations were accurate after a span of over sixteen hundred years. Not much has changed in the harsh rugged Sinai.

Many of my students have been on a journey, taking elective courses in Biblical and Religious Studies as part of their own exploration and using their own faith perspective as a launching pad for making sense of their personal stance. We all customize religion, based on our own experiences and sense of what is of ultimate importance in life. In my own case, my journey has taken me from Episcopalianism into Judaism. I find that a religion focusing primarily on behavior rather than on belief fits better with my sense of what religion should be. Oddly enough, I also find that approach closer to the religion *of* Jesus than the one that developed *about* him. In particular, I like the Jewish concept of *tikkun olam,* in which people are called to work creatively with God in repairing the world. Within early Christianity, my sentiments are with the Ebionites, not with Paul, and I regret that Christianity did not develop along the lines of their beliefs and practices. But that's only my journey. Others have different routes to follow as they make out their own destiny.

This book is written for readers who are curious, who possess an open mind, and who like to savor different possibilities about the way history may have unfolded. In particular, it is not written for those who are plagued by an absolutist spirituality, who claim that they and they alone possess the one and only one correct interpretation of their particular brand of religion. Such a stance represents the enemy of dialogue and discourse and it's a pathology that unfortunately runs throughout many contemporary religious faiths. This book is also not written for scholars who have probed minute portions of the development of early Christianities in great detail. They are rightfully concerned with micro issues. My focus, however, is macro—the bigger picture of early Christianity—and I have built upon contemporary research in my own investigations. The Jesus Cover-Up Thesis, which I will explore in this book, is mine and mine alone. I'm aware that it pushes the boundaries of contemporary scholarship but in a direction, I think, that best fits the evidence.

A Timelines section is included at the back of this book, providing dates of major movements and writings. A Terminology section is also provided, but technical terms, the sort that scholars are fond of, have been kept to a minimum.

HOW JESUS BECAME CHRISTIAN

THE COVER-UP

Jesus was thoroughly Jewish. Mary, his mother, was Jewish, and Judaism was the religion he practiced throughout his life. Jesus' teachings focused on the important Jewish issues of the day—how to interpret the law correctly, when the Kingdom of God would appear, and how to behave righteously. He was executed as "the King of the Jews," a political claim that the Roman authorities could not have tolerated. His earliest followers in Jerusalem were Jewish, and they, too, observed Jewish law. They thought of him as a teacher and as a Messiah figure.

But all this exploded. Within a few years of his death, around A.D. 30[1], Jesus began to be thought of as much more than a teacher and possible Messiah. He came to be spoken of as a Christ, a divine being—a God-human, in fact, who had preexisted his earthly life and who had become human in order to save humanity. What happened? How did Jesus the Jew become a Gentile Christ? That's one of the questions this book explores.

TWO DISTINCT MOVEMENTS

In the course of some twenty years studying and teaching early Christian writings, I have come to some startling conclusions. For one thing, I contend that the religion of Jesus no longer exists. The movement that emerged out of Jesus' teachings and practices, the Jesus Movement, was led by Jesus' brother, James, in Jerusalem. It honored and treasured what the Jesus of history stood for and proclaimed. That original religion, however, was replaced, in time, by a much more successful movement. Paul, in the Jewish Diaspora around the

Mediterranean, forged a new religion, the Christ Movement. We tend not to notice how truly distinctive this movement was. Part of the excitement of this book consists of exploding the commonplace notion that Paul was somehow a faithful disciple of Jesus. He wasn't. While Paul's innovative Christ Movement offered its members many advantages over Judaism and the Jesus Movement, it was something quite different. It was much simpler and easier to follow, and it focused on a familiar figure known throughout the Mediterranean world, that of the savior. This Christ Movement came to cover up the original teachings of Jesus. "Christifiers," as I call them—leaders who packaged Jesus into a Christ—took charge of the early Christian movement. The original followers of Jesus—members of the Jesus Movement—faded away, being overshadowed by the more popular Christ Movement. But that process took time, some five or six centuries, before the Jesus Movement disappeared entirely.

While developing a robust theology of the divine-human Christ and creating an impressive infrastructure, the Christ Movement angrily steered its members away from Jewish practices. Why did early Christianity think it had to attack Judaism? Why was it the focus of attention, so much so that anti-Semitic sentiments are ingrained in the pages of the New Testament? There's much more to this aspect of the story, however. As we investigate some of the writings of Paul's religion, reflected in the New Testament and second-century Christianity, we will make a remarkable discovery. We will come to see the real roots of Christian anti-Semitism.

THE JESUS COVER-UP

Looking ahead, you will discover that I contend the tradition "miscarried," that Christianity became over time something radically different from what its originator intended. The faith that emerged was not the religion practiced by its founder. There was a switch. I call this the Jesus Cover-Up Thesis. This stance has three components.

First of all, the Jesus Cover-Up Thesis contends that the original message of Jesus and the Jesus Movement, Jesus' earliest followers in Jerusalem, became switched for a different religion. This other religion, one that in *origin, beliefs,* and *practices* differed from the Jesus Movement, was the Christ Movement developed by Paul in the Diaspora. A few decades after the death of both Paul and James in the 60s, the religion of Paul became grafted onto the original religion led by James. This was the impressive accomplishment of the author of the Book of Acts around the turn of the second century. The Christ Movement replaced the original Jesus Movement at least in the popular imagination as the dominant expression of the new religion.

Second, according to the Jesus Cover-Up Thesis, there was an important shift away from the teachings **of** *Jesus to those* **about** *the* **Christ.** That is, beliefs about the person of Jesus conceived of as a Christ came to obscure what he said and did. Thus, the religion *of* Jesus, the one Jesus practiced and taught, became transformed into a cult *about* the Christ. Speaking of Jesus as a Christ had a tornado effect. Much like the bewildering effect of *The Wizard of Oz,* the Christ Movement swept Jesus up out of his Jewish context and landed him down right in the midst of a new, strange Gentile environment. That changed everything, since the Christ figure is not a Jewish Messiah. The whirlwind caused by Paul has had a profound effect on how we understand the Jesus of history, his teachings and his mission. Everything is now seen through the eyes of Paul and his new landscape.

Early Christianity separated from Judaism, but it did so in an exceptionally angry fashion. Over and over again, leader after leader lambasted Judaism. Why they felt they had to do so represents an interesting story that we will come to in due course. In fact, as you will see, **the third component of the Jesus Cover-Up Thesis is this: it proposes a new way of understanding Christian anti-Semitism.** Early Christians were very much aware that they had created a shift in the religion and had substituted the Christ of experience for the Jesus of history. They were also conscious of the fact that the Jews were witnesses to this event. Jewish leaders recognized and understood how dramatically Christianity had changed since leaving the fold. We will discover how this dynamic plays out and what it means for how Christianity traditionally views Judaism.

My intent in this book is positive. It is simply to understand the roots of Christianity better. I am aware that there are ideas in this book that may startle or even shock some readers. You will find I argue the following:

- Paul's religion was not the religion of Jesus.
- There was a cover-up. The divine Gentile Christ was switched for the human Jewish Jesus. A religion about the Christ was substituted for the teachings of Jesus. Moreover, the religion of Paul displaced that of Jesus.
- The New Testament is not a neutral collection of early church writings. It was produced, selected, and approved by one—but only one—faction of early Christianity, the very group that endorsed the cover-up.
- The Book of Acts presents us with a fictitious history of early Christianity and represents an unreliable source of information.
- Anti-Semitism is rooted within New Testament writings and is the result of the cover-up.

Some things I say about Paul and the Book of Acts are not run-of-the-mill observations. I point out, for example, how Paul's religion emerged out of a *separate* revelation, not from the religion of Jesus as is often assumed. That is new. I also argue that the Book of Acts glued Paul's Christ Movement onto the earlier Jesus Movement, switching the Christ for Jesus. That also is new, and I contend that this represents historical fiction on the part of whoever wrote the Book of Acts. Why the author of this work felt he had to invent this linkage is interesting and we will probe his probable motivation.

So, who killed off the historical Jesus? And why? How was the switch made? Who covered it up? What does it mean for us here today? The Jesus Cover-Up Thesis helps us unravel a mystery. *How Jesus Became Christian* is a detective story, using the results of modern scholarship, to uncover a "crime" committed close to two millennia ago.

Religion then, and I suspect now, was thoroughly political, as well as spiritual. Jesus in particular made strong political statements and claims. His followers did so as well, seeing him as a Messiah claimant. That staked out a very important political role for their rabbi. On its journey from being a small struggling group into becoming the official religion of the Roman Empire in the fourth century, Christianity was politically engaged. Power struggles erupted in early Christianity as groups fought for supremacy over their rivals. So we will examine the contest between the religion of Jesus and that of Paul—the Jesus Movement versus the Christ Movement—as each strove to achieve a place of prominence within the Roman world against all their competitors, Judaism and the mystery religions included.

LOOKING AHEAD

The story is organized historically. It covers three hundred years, from roughly 150 B.C. to A.D. 150. These were exciting and confusing times as Judaism reshaped itself and Christianity was born. People were faced with many different choices, not only because they lived in a multicultural world that offered many religious options, but also because, within each religion, there were so many varieties. There were, for instance, many ways of being Jewish and Christian. Neither religion was monolithic.

Our story starts in the Hellenistic world with the religious and political realities that Judaism faced in the second and first centuries B.C. We then move into the time of Jesus, James, and Paul in the early decades of the first century A.D. This will allow us to see the challenges that the Jewish people at that time faced, and the problems they tried to solve, being a small colonized minority within a much larger world. Jesus did not exist in a political vacuum and the New Testament writings do not always fill us in on the policies and players of his place in history. Without these background nuances, understanding Jesus is much like trying to make sense of a presidential State of the Union address without knowing current foreign and domestic policies or the stances of Republicans and Democrats on key issues at the time. Understanding the religion and politics of the period places Jesus in his historical context. That way, we can better appreciate the vitality of his message to his audience. More importantly, we can recognize the powerful and radical solution he put to the people of his generation.

Growing out of the teachings and practices of Jesus was the original religion of Jesus, led by his brother, James. We will profile this movement and contrast it with the dramatically different religion of Paul. Today we tend to think of Paul as a faithful follower of Jesus, one whose organizational genius led to the formation of what became Christianity. We'll learn more about Paul, how he emerged on the scene *after* the death of Jesus, never having met him in person, and how he cleverly crafted a new religion that succeeded in capturing people's imaginations.

Key discoveries will be made along the way. For one thing, how and why Paul's Christ Movement had so little to do with the religion of Jesus will be uncovered. We don't normally see that and that's because we're not supposed to see the differences between Paul and Jesus. This is part of one of the most effective cover-ups of all times. It is much more significant than the current popular hypothesis that Jesus was married to Mary Magdalene and that they had children together whose offspring survive to the present day. For *that* cover-up there is little evidence even of marriage, let alone children. The meager support for that hypothesis are just generalities—that rabbis of that era typically married, that Mary Magdalene went to the tomb to claim his body (and so acted as wife), and that she was highly regarded by a faction within early Christianity, the Gnostics. While Mary Magdalene was evidently an important person within early Christianity, the evidence for the Jesus-as-family-man hypothesis is slim, and that's not our story here.

But there was an important cover-up. By examining the evidence— writings from New Testament times—we will reveal how the real deception actually happened. It was a huge switch—the Christ for Jesus, Paul's religion for Jesus', and the Christ Movement for the Jesus Movement. Unraveling this shift clarifies some of the most powerful mysteries of early Christianity and explains how Jesus became Christian. Much of the confusion of Paul's religion with that of Jesus, for example, is traceable to the fictitious history invented by the Book of Acts, around A.D. 100 . . . But that's getting ahead of our story.

The new Christ Movement came on the scene angry. As it evolved its own institutions in the late first and early second centuries, it turned on Judaism with a vengeance. That anti-Jewish hostility represents a curious feature of early Christianity. It was not, for instance, content to ignore Judaism. Instead it ransacked and hijacked from Judaism what it thought useful while simultaneously demonizing Jewish leaders and the Jewish people. If we were to take these writers at their word, there was no point in Judaism—or the Jewish people for that matter—continuing to exist. That's a powerful message that has had dreadful repercussions throughout subsequent history. This will enable us to discover the real reason for Christian anti-Semitism, buried for so long in the hidden history of early Christianity. The cover-up had much to do with these destructive attitudes.

The Jesus Cover-Up Thesis suggests that Christians need to put into perspective the dynamics that shaped the early years of this religion. These still have a tremendous influence today. Most Christians look at the New Testament through the eyes of Paul. In my judgment, this is not helpful. Paul's image of the Christ obscures much of the real Jesus of history. Simply put, Jesus got upstaged by Paul. In recovering more of its Jewish roots, the message of the human Jesus of history will become more prominent. This means moving Paul off center stage.

So step back with me into the world of Jesus, James, Mary Magdalene, and Paul. The first century A.D. was an exceptionally confusing time. Jewish people found themselves to be a small, colonized minority within a vast empire controlled first by Greece and then by Rome. The challenge every Jew faced then was how to retain Jewish identity in the face of constant and overwhelming pressures to assimilate into the larger, more cosmopolitan culture.

2

CULTURES IN CONFLICT

They were turbulent times, those two centuries before the time of Jesus. A flood of new ideas had swept across the Mediterranean, throwing local cultures into huge turmoil. Radically different ways of looking at the universe crept in from Greece, Egypt, and from farther east, Persia. Novel views concerning human nature and religion took people by storm as traditional religious moorings were challenged, questioned, and undermined. A vast cosmopolitan world order around the Mediterranean had become a reality, opening up tremendous trade, economic, and cultural opportunities. Some people, however, found these new ways of thinking about society and the world threatening. These were uncertain times, and, as with all such times, some people wondered what they could count on.

Especially vulnerable was the one monotheistic religion of the eastern Mediterranean, Judaism. Things were much simpler for polytheists. After all, they had the advantage of "intertranslatability" from one religion to another—supreme male god for supreme male god; goddess for goddess; divine being for divine being. Thus Zeus was Horus or YHWH or Ba'al. A polytheist had no problem with many deities and interchangeable names. The name did not matter. Gods and goddesses were as intertranslatable as menus that we can shift from English to Spanish to Chinese to Arabic. For a Jewish monotheist, however, those easy transfers were not an option. They simply could not be made. The Jewish God was the one true God, they thought. For a true believer, the Jewish God was not Horus, Ba'al, or Zeus, or any of the other chief male divinities. All of these other "divinities" lacked substance and power and so could not qualify as the one Supreme Being, the creator of the universe . . . and of humanity.

The problem was even greater when it came to female supreme beings—Anath, Isis, Artemis, Athena, and many other goddesses. A goddess could not easily be introduced into Judaism, which lacked a pantheon or lineup of deities. That would corrupt the prime directive of the Ten Commandments: have no other gods. For Judaism, God did not have a wife or consort and wasn't conceived of in those terms at all.

Much as Jewish people today live in the shadow of the Holocaust, Jews of the first centuries B.C. and A.D. were haunted by the possibility of annihilation. They lived with the possibility that their religion and separate identity as the people of the covenant might be extinguished. Hanging over all that they thought and did was this sense of dread. Perhaps their unique community and unusual monotheistic religion could come to an end with everyone assimilated into the common culture either by gentle persuasion or by force. The cosmopolitan world in which they lived was under the firm grip of a new dominant society and social order—that of the Greeks and subsequently the Romans. These foreign occupiers entertained no illusions about *their* cultural superiority.

In these troubled times, the Jewish community faced two cultural conflicts. One was simply a pervasive fact of life. Pluralism was all around them, offering choices and opportunities but also creating confusion over religious practices and beliefs. The other one was very specific and it was aimed right at the heart of Judaism. It originated from an aggressive policy on the part of one ruler who prohibited the practice of Judaism upon pain of death. That threat generated the greatest fear. Its impact reverberated throughout the Jewish community in the centuries that followed.

HELLENISTIC PLURALISM

The fourth century B.C. conquests by Alexander the Great in the Middle East started a process throughout the eastern Mediterranean that would last long after formal Greek rule. We call it Hellenization—making the world Greek in terms of culture and thought. It spread quickly and invasively through language, religion, politics, law, theater, education, philosophy, cultural centers, trade, government, and, most importantly, through local Greek city-states.[1] From the death of Alexander the Great in 323 B.C. onward, Greek culture was simply a brute fact of life for minorities such as the Jews. Foreign rule was present everywhere. It touched peoples' lives in the taxes they paid, the decisions of the law courts, the conversations they heard, the strangers they met along the highways and in their villages, work opportunities, and the goods they bought. It spurred the development of service industries to provide shelter and food for foreigners. With foreign troops passing through the towns and villages, it meant rape and confiscation of property. New cities built on Greek and Roman models provided much-needed work, but also social interaction, new customs, intermarriage, and different demands. No one could escape becoming, to some extent, Hellenized. It was an "in your face" phenomenon—part of the landscape of everyone's day-to-day existence.

Greek rule in Israel ended in 63 B.C. when Roman troops under the leadership of Pompey conquered Jerusalem. The last bastion of Greek power in the Middle East—Egypt—succumbed to the advancing Roman army some thirty years later. Gone was Greek rule, but not Hellenization. That process continued unabated, but it assumed another form. The Greek gods and goddesses were simply given Roman names. For instance, Zeus became Jupiter, Artemis became Diana, Ares became Mars, and Poseidon became Neptune. Greek remained the language of the eastern empire for centuries. Cultural conflict and assimilation remained a problem for minority groups, which continued to be confronted with religious pluralism. So Hellenization held everyone in its clutches. With its Graeco-Roman beliefs and values, it constituted a powerful cultural presence no one could escape. It lasted for almost a thousand years, well after Christianity became the official religion of the Roman Empire. It was not until the sixth century A.D. that the Christianized Roman emperors began to close the Greek schools of philosophy and the temples of non-Christian religions.

For the most part, Hellenization was part of the background to everyday living, and usually the threat was one of soft assimilation, the gradual adoption of at least some foreign practices. Greek and Roman government, law, schools, entertainment, festivals, civic ceremonies, and culture dominated the Mediterranean world. Much in the same way as it is advantageous for many in today's world to speak English, those who wished to get ahead had to speak Greek and to adopt some of the practices of that culture.

Many Jews of the time took advantage of learning Greek. It broadened horizons and opened up a wealth of literature to inquiring Jewish minds—philosophy, drama, mathematics, astrology, astronomy, and many other branches of study. Some grasped the opportunity to use the new common language to inject Jewish ideas into the Mediterranean basin. Alexandria in Egypt, boasting the treasure trove of the world's greatest library of the time, became a hub of such activity. Its vibrant Jewish community witnessed the translation of the Hebrew Bible into Greek.[2] This was the Septuagint that rendered the Law, Prophets, and the Writings accessible to non-Jews . . . as well as to Jews who no longer read or understood Hebrew. In time, additional writings would be added to this collection of texts. Unlike previous sacred writings, these new scrolls were written originally in Greek. The Septuagint included such influential books as the story of the heroic Judith who single-handedly saved her people against overwhelming odds as well as the various books of the Maccabees. The latter outlined the drama that unfolded in the midsecond century B.C. as pious Jews defended their autonomy by military and political power. Books of Wisdom were developed as well, which introduced philosophical ideas into Jewish thinking. Wisdom became regarded as a creature, female in gender, a manifestation of God. Wisdom was conceived of as a creative being close to God yet not quite God—divine yet not quite a goddess. As the Wisdom of Solomon put it referring to the figure of Wisdom,

> ". . . she is a breath of the power of God, and a pure emanation of the glory of the Almighty . . . she is a reflection of eternal light, a spotless mirror of the working of God" (Wisdom of Solomon 7:25–26).

This is the closest ancient Judaism came to recognizing the female aspect of the divine.

These were truly exciting times that offered opportunities for expanding Jewish thought both among its own adherents as well as to others on the world stage. On the eve of the new millennium, in the few decades toward the end of the first century B.C. and the early decades of the first century A.D., the Jewish philosopher, Philo, wrote scores of books in Alexandria. Many still survive. There he attempted to build bridges between biblical and Greek thought. A mutual exchange, he must have thought—Torah made accessible to the Greeks while Greek thought would enrich Torah study. Parallels, he contended, could be drawn between Moses and Plato. The Hebrew prophets could be seen as powerful social critics comparable to some of the best Greek philosophers. Perhaps, some dared to speculate, the wisdom of the Greeks originally came from Moses, an audacious thought that would be repeated over the centuries. One Jewish writer, Ezekiel the Tragedian, even attempted in the second century B.C. to write a tragic drama along the lines of Greek models concerning Moses and the Exodus.[3]

Some non-Jews—Gentiles—found the high ethical principles and monotheistic stance of Judaism attractive and began to associate themselves with Jewish synagogues. They were the "God-fearers," and they were crucial to early Christian success. So Hellenization offered multiple opportunities as well as serious threats.

In *The World Is Flat*, Thomas L. Friedman observes how connected the modern world is, through trade, technology such as the Internet, as well as the reduction of political barriers. This "flattening of the world" makes it possible now for individuals and business people to contact others instantaneously around the world.[4] This represents a dramatic new development.

Well, perhaps not so new. Hellenization had the effect of flattening the cultures of the Mediterranean world . . . but without the Internet. Never before had it been possible for people to communicate so easily with one another, through trade routes, a common language, and a simplified network of nations governed by Greek and Roman rulers. Some were receptive to reaching out from within one's own culture to what was good and valuable in that of others. Those less courageous or self-confident turned defensively inward, shunning exposure to foreign ideas or alternative practices.

It should not be supposed that Hellenization was something remote, lurking far off, hundreds of miles away in Greece, for example. It lodged on everyone's doorstep, especially in the Middle East. Greek-speaking cities were established throughout the empire, including ten cities within what is today northern Israel and Jordan. These bastions of Hellenization included one major cultural center just a few miles south of the Sea of Galilee on an important trade route. Beth-Shean (Scythopolis) was a large, impressive city that has been excavated in modern times. Today we can still walk down the broad Roman streets that survive amidst the ruins and admire the huge columns on either side of the main avenues. Its splendor reflected the best that the world's most advanced civilization of the time had to offer. This sophisticated city embodied planning for both individual and communal needs. In time, a large theater would be built, as well as communal bathhouses. Temples were constructed to honor the gods and goddesses of the Mediterranean world—the magnificent Temple of Zeus and the Round Temple, which was probably dedicated to Dionysus.

Ten Greek cities were established, nine of them to the east of the Sea of Galilee. Called the Decapolis (ten cities), this league of cultural centers had its administrative head in Scythopolis. It, along with such cities as Gerasa (Jerash), Pella, and Philadelphia, provided the backbone for the spread of Greek culture throughout the Galilee. Philadelphia would later become the capital of modern-day Jordan, Amman, where the large ancient amphitheater can still be visited in the downtown area.

Like Beth-Shean, Jerash has been excavated and is one of the archeological wonders of modern-day Jordan. With colonnaded streets, this modern city featured a hippodrome for the races with capacity for fifteen thousand spectators. A magnificent Temple of Zeus stood high on a hill commanding an impressive vantage point over the area. Another prominent temple was dedicated to Artemis (Diana), the deity who protected the city. Three Roman theaters dotted the city, the largest one capable of holding three thousand people with perfect acoustics. These intersections were places for sharing ideas. Here people would meet and talk on their way to other places within the city. Plays, government decrees, public announcements, and festivals would all be carried out in these theaters in honor of the Greek and Roman deities.

From these civic centers, merchants, residents, soldiers, teachers, and priests all pursued their livelihood throughout the region, connected through major highways that reached out as well to other parts of the empire. People were rightfully amazed at what civilization had wrought and how small the world was getting. Progress, a wealth of new ideas, and peace were everywhere in evidence.

The flood of new ideas may have seemed somewhat overwhelming, but these were offset by technological advances in construction and military might, and by the sophistication of Roman law. They experienced then what we, too, are immersed in today: a cosmopolitan, multicultural world.

A RELIGIOUS SMORGASBORD

On the religious side, movements like Olympian religion made their way throughout the empire, backed by its theological arsenal, the *Iliad* and *Odyssey* of Homer, and the *Theogony* and *Works and Days* of Hesiod. Homer's stories were delightful adventure tales, vividly recounting the siege of Troy in today's western Turkey and the return to Greece of its most famous heroes of antiquity. These poems, however, also served as seductive religious texts. Through engaging stories, they trumpeted Zeus as the father god, delineated the role of many other deities—Poseidon, Apollo, Athena, Aphrodite, and Ares—and explained the world in terms of their interactions with one another and with humanity.

Olympian religion injected a different view of divinity into the religious landscape of the Middle East. Their gods were not immortal: they were created. They could also be destroyed, as evidenced by the demise of the gods before the Olympian deities, the ancient Titans. The mortality of divine beings represented a startling new thought. It challenged a religion such as Judaism, which thought of God as eternal, without a beginning or an ending.

Moreover, the Greek gods and goddesses were not guarantors of justice, morality, or fair play. These amoral beings created conflict within the world, accounting for much of the chaos of our everyday lives. They were fickle, and they devoted a considerable amount of energy into tricking, cheating, robbing, seducing, and raping humans. Homer's *Odyssey* is a story of how various gods constantly conspired to thwart the plans of Odysseus to return home. True, he had many remarkable adventures along the way, but god after god frustrated this leader's wishes. They were so successful in distracting him that it took him ten years to reach home. According to this religious perspective, gods, goddesses, and other divine beings placed obstacles in the path of humanity. They were responsible for much of the uncertainty of the world, depriving it of order and stability. The *Odyssey* provided a powerful message for what humans could expect in a world ruled by such deities.

This view of deity offered some advantages. Olympian religion had the merit of easily accounting for why there is evil and wrongdoing in the world. It was simply the result of some god or goddess stirring up trouble. The world had become the stage for divine entertainment, we humans representing the unwilling players in the cosmic drama of our times. Thus the problem of suffering, so difficult for monotheistic religions to explain—especially when coupled with the belief in one supreme loving being—was not an issue for this religion.

But there were disadvantages as well. A devotee of Olympian religion could not have confidence or trust in God. He could not, for instance, have ever uttered that great Jewish psalm, "The Lord is my shepherd" (Psalm 23). That song exudes a personal trust in a God who leads people on paths of righteousness. The Lord heals, comforts, and ensures goodness and mercy. He provides calm and refreshes the human soul. God reassures his people that they will dwell "in the house of the Lord" forever. Those thoughts were not part of Olympian religion.

Curiously, unlike Judaism in particular, the Greek gods and goddesses did not issue a code of morality. There was nothing like the Ten Commandments or Torah within this religion. Unlike most religions that make it clear how members are to behave, part of its appeal lay precisely in the fact that Olympian religion made so few demands on its adherents. No rules. No regulations. No prescribed path to follow . . . but also no certainty and no order. The gods did not reinforce morality, nor did they encourage it. They were amoral beings. People were on their own when it came to reason and rationality, striving to ascertain what is true or reliable in a world in which chance and fate all play a role. Plato criticized the gods in his ideal society, *The Republic,* on this very basis. There he proposed abolishing the traditional stories of Olympian religion within his educational system. The gods, he argued, were simply poor role models for humanity and should be dispensed with.

Where was order and certainty to be found? What can humans do when confronted with such a universe? Sophocles's powerful play, *Oedipus the King,* exploited these all-too-natural fears, pitting Oedipus against the Chorus. This skillful dramatist called upon the audience to take a stand: who was right—Oedipus or the Chorus? Should we side with Oedipus, with his rational, slow, plodding discovery of the truth via reason and evidence? Like a modern detective, Oedipus was the trial attorney who eventually found out the truth. He called witnesses and built up a case concerning the identity of the person responsible for the devastation that was afflicting Thebes, his city-state. The process was gradual and impressive, with Oedipus inquiring and asking the right questions. But what was that dreadful truth that he found out? Nothing less than that he unwittingly had fulfilled his preordained destiny—that he had in fact killed his own father and married his own mother. Is this what reason leads to? Sophocles asked us to consider. But there is an alternative. Perhaps fate really does rule, in spite of rational inquiry. Should we therefore side with the Chorus, which rejected the path of reason? The Chorus was confident throughout the play that the gods had a hand in everything that Oedipus did. Thus the gods rule human destiny secretly behind the scenes. For the Chorus, the events as they unfolded demonstrated that the gods were vindicated and that Oedipus freely chose his own fixed destiny. Does reason stand a chance in such a universe? How do reason and Olympian religion interrelate? Sophocles inquired.

The gods stirring up trouble? Acting like badly behaved kids? Placing obstacles before human beings? Not helping people achieve their goals? Not making ethical demands on human behavior? People ruled by chance and by fate? Pernicious, powerful, amoral, rambunctious beings pursuing their own agendas in interaction with one another? These were extremely unsettling new ideas for the average Jewish person of the time. That's certainly not how Torah or the Jewish law functioned. Nor were the Olympian gods arbiters of justice or the conveyers of mercy. These were truly disturbing thoughts that shook the foundations of religion. What if Olympian religion was right? What then was to be made of the God of the Hebrew Bible, who gave Torah and who rewarded its faithful practitioners with righteousness and blessings? What value was there in the daily struggle to make choices reflective of the demands of the law? There was no escaping the presence of Olympian religion within the Middle East. Their representatives ran the civic ceremonies and their deities were honored in the Greek city-states scattered throughout the region.

The cult of Dionysus added another crucial dimension into the exotic religious mix of the first centuries B.C. and A.D.: the personal experience of immortality. Dionysus was a divine-human. Zeus was his father and Semele, an ordinary mortal, was his mother. As a God-human, he became the object of worship and a role model for humanity. Shrouded in mystery, his religious rites involved ecstatic participation on the part of the worshippers. Through chanting, dancing, sexual activity, and drinking they became one with his being. This was a religion of joy, ecstasy, wonder, and liberation. Even more importantly, by participating in his nature, Dionysus freed the soul from the confines of mortality. People lost themselves in this God-human, and, for a moment, glimpsed the possibilities of eternity.

The cult of Dionysus exercised a powerful dual appeal: a fabulous liturgical experience as well as personal immortality. No wonder it attracted followers around the Mediterranean. Its appeal was totally experiential—a highly participatory, engaging religious rite. This rich experience provided a sharp contrast to the stern, serious Temple sacrifices in Jerusalem with its cattle, grain, and oil offerings given to God to be shared by the priests and by the people making the offerings. Nor did the cult of Dionysus make demands on behavior. No code of ethics. No dietary laws. No circumcision. Just fun, seductive joy and the taste of personal immortality.

In the religious smorgasbord of the time, with different temples and shrines everywhere in evidence, religious fidelity was threatened. For religious followers, no longer was it the case that a person should be identified with one and only one religion. Those who shared in the enthusiastic celebrations of the cult of Dionysus could also participate in the civic religious ceremonies in honor of the Olympian deities. Devotees of Artemis could show up at temples dedicated to Isis. There was no problem with multiple religious allegiances, for exclusivity was not a religious virtue. Some Jews toyed with the idea that it might be possible to worship in the Temple of Judaism and also at those of the Greek gods. Could one, for instance, combine Temple worship with participation in the cult of Dionysus? Or, perhaps, even in a temple of a goddess? Why not? Where was the harm? they asked.

On a more sober side, philosophers set up branch schools around the Mediterranean. Pythagoreans, Platonists, and Aristotelians carried out their demanding investigations. The Pythagoreans studied mathematics as a way of detecting order within the universe. They thought that through mathematics, they could discern the right balance within the human personality as well as the social order, the city-state. Plato, too, studied the structure of the city-state while musing on whether the world as we perceive it represents authentic reality. Perhaps experience itself was deceptive and reason disclosed a higher, truer reality. In a dramatic allegory—that of the cave—Plato takes us on an ascent to highest understanding, to the knowledge of ultimate reality itself, the pursuit of which should shape our daily quest, our souls and our societies. Plato's academies spread throughout the Mediterranean as people eagerly sought this higher knowledge. The Jewish philosopher Philo, in particular, was heavily influenced by the thinking of Plato, as were many early Christian writers.

Aristotelians went in a different direction. Through their centers of study, they investigated the nature of reasoning, developing the world's first system of logic—the syllogism—and proposing categories for understanding the world of nature, the concepts we need to make sense of our universe of time and space. In addition, they probed the movements of the sun, planets, and stars to discern regularities and to make predictions. All these philosophers provided schools for the elite and attracted a large following in many locations around the Mediterranean. They lasted for a thousand years.

On a more popular level, however, Stoics moved from city to city dispensing practical "self-help" wisdom on a wide variety of topics to those who would listen. Their focus was on how to take control of the self—how to achieve mastery over conflicting emotions and so liberate reason and self-discipline. There existed an overwhelming need for these practical thinkers. One simply could not count on religion to provide an insight into understanding the nature of the universe, the civic state, or practical ethics.

In a world of tremendous uncertainty and suffering, taking control of the self became important. How should we *choose* to respond to tragedy? How should we cope with the ravages of being human—death of family and friends, sickness or injury? Should we succumb to emotion, bewailing loss, or becoming sad, depressed, or mournful? Or should we decide to respond differently, perhaps by refusing to allow these events to disturb our equanimity? These philosophers made an important distinction. While we may not control the events that impinge on our daily lives, how we respond to them is within our power. Difficult though it may be when faced with crippling illness or a sudden death, we can choose how we react, they contended. We can decide not to give way to irrationality or emotionality. The Stoic practitioners promised to show us how, and, perhaps, we might speculate, set up workshops to help us practice using reason to control what is within our power.

All these philosophical movements questioned the nature of Olympian religion and tried to work out rational approaches to the uncertain world in which we live. Some writers criticized the validity of Olympian religion, wondering about the place of the divine in the universe when the gods seemingly bore no relationship to order within the world. What were the grounds for right living? Or for developing social policy? Or for contemplating model ideal societies in which justice and fair play would rule? Along with many others, Plato investigated these matters in several of his dialogues—*Euthyphro, The Republic, Statesman,* and *Epinomis.*

Within this marketplace of ideas, non-Greek religions seized the opportunity to enter the Mediterranean world. Originating in Persia, the secret religion of Mithras spread throughout the empire, appealing primarily to members of the Roman army. Mithras, like Dionysus, had had a strange divine-human birth. It was a virgin birth, with Mithras born of a human mother and a divine father in a cave. Like Dionysus, this religion was based on experience and demanded participation. It also offered salvation to worshippers who became caught up in its ecstatic rituals. The worship of Mithras took place in a temple or "Mithraeum," a cavelike structure reminiscent of Mithras's birthplace. Mithras is typically depicted as struggling valiantly against a bull, eventually succeeding. He's the savior God-human, the superhero who conquers the forces of cosmic evil. Religious ceremonies involved eating a common meal, interpreted as sharing in the life force of their founder who was worshipped as a savior. Viewing life as a struggle between good and evil, followers of Mithraism were encouraged to lead a life of virtue and self-control, a path that would result in everlasting life. Here was a religion that related theology to ethics: behavior actually mattered.

A rival cult, the ancient Egyptian religion of Isis, was newly transformed to suit the needs of non-Egyptian worshippers throughout the Roman Empire. It attracted devotees attracted to its rich, inspiring theology. Isis's son Horus, as the incarnation of God, was said to be the Son of God. He conquered the power of evil and triumphed over death. Thus he, too, was a savior of humanity. Through participation in his life and death through the rituals of the religion, members of this cult were promised immorality.

Both cults—Isis and Mithras—offered followers a heroic figure who did battle with cosmic forces. The hero of both religions had a special birth. He was also a dying-rising, divine-human savior who gave members eternal life. Many features of these two religions bore remarkable similarities to Christianity later on—the virgin birth and Jesus as a divine-human who was the savior of humanity and who defeated the power of evil and death. Visually Isis is also depicted as nursing her son, Horus, in the same posture and pose that later Christians would use to portray Mary holding Jesus.

For once, people had a wide choice of religions, very much like our own pluralistic society. There were religious options everywhere, and communities were riddled with people who shared different opinions about God, the world, and human destiny. No longer had they to remain in the ancestral religion. There were choices. Each religion was engaged in a life-or-death public relations battle with the others. People rightfully wondered which one was right or could really offer the way to salvation.

Judaism was put somewhat on the defensive. It did not possess a robust sense of an afterlife, unlike the religion of Dionysus or the philosophies of Pythagoras or Plato. There was no mention of eternal life in the Books of the Law, and belief in an afterlife only appeared within Judaism much later, in the midsecond century B.C. Even then, eternal life was not thought of as a movement of an immortal soul from this plane to another one as was the case with Plato, Pythagoras, and many of the Egyptian cults. And so, as religions go, Judaism lacked strong support for the greatest spiritual reward, the continuing of life after death.

Also, Judaism lacked an experiential, ecstatic component, unlike the hugely attractive, highly participatory mystery religions of Dionysus, Isis, or Mithras. True, it memorialized specific historical events—the escape from Egypt and the trek through the desert, for instance. But that was a "back there then" commemoration somewhat removed from present experiences. Above all, it was a demanding religion, one that stressed fidelity toward the law God had given Israel. Ethical, social, and religious monotheistic obligations were inescapable. By comparison, the Greek, Egyptian, and Persian cults offered pleasure, escape, and enjoyment—powerful alternatives to a path of uncompromising rigor.

HELLENIZATION IN ISRAEL

We begin to see evidence of soft assimilation within Jewish culture of the second century B.C. The Book of 2 Maccabees, for instance, shows that many leaders during this period had come to adopt Greek names.[5] High priests, for example, were named Jason and Menelaus. But that was only the start.

In 175 B.C., a ruler by the "modest" name of Antiochus Epiphanes—"the

Manifestation of God"—came into power in the Middle East. Things immediately started to change for the worse for the Jewish people. With the support of Jewish religious leaders, an attempt was made to convert the Jewish state to Greek ways. 2 Maccabees noted that around 174 B.C., Jason secured the office of high priest through bribery and corruption. He immediately began a program of Hellenization, introducing new customs that violated Jewish law. These were radical departures. The actions Jason undertook were not just optional add-ons to Jewish culture: they were designed to supplant traditional Jewish practices.

With the approval of Antiochus, Jason the high priest made attempts to convert Jerusalem itself into a Greek city. Politically, citizens of Jerusalem were cross-registered with the Greek city of Antioch and thereby entitled to share in its benefits. As Jason and other Hellenists saw it, this afforded everyone tremendous advantages. Jerusalem and the Jewish people could become visibly part of the new global world order. It would serve to bring Judaism and the Jewish people onto the world stage, foster international trade, encourage tourism, and give the elite of Jerusalem greater prominence within the empire.

Jason also set up a gymnasium in Jerusalem, a conduit for the spread of Greek political, social, and educational values as well as for athletic competition. We think of gyms and sports clubs as neutral, as places to work out and get in shape. Not so in antiquity. Much more was involved. For one thing, games were played in honor of the Greek gods. Processions carried emblems of Greek deities. Competitions also involved nude male athletes, thus exposing circumcised athletes to the displeasure of the crowds and the ridicule of other athletes and the Greek officials. Greeks viewed circumcision as gross mutilation. Some Jewish athletes even went to the extreme of undergoing the painful procedure of reverse circumcision in order to fit into the dominant culture and be accepted into the sporting competitions.

Jason induced athletes to wear the hat of the Greek god Hermes when competing. 2 Maccabees seethed with anger at the official sanctioning of Greek customs:

> *There was such an extreme of Hellenization and increase in the adoption of foreign ways because of the surpassing wickedness of Jason, who was ungodly and no true high priest, that the priests were no longer intent upon their service at the altar.* (2 Maccabees 4:11–14)

This is tantamount to cutting short attendance at the Mass or the Sunday morning service in order to see "the game."

The real threat, however, was aimed specifically at the heart of Judaism. In 167 B.C., Antiochus Epiphanes launched a major attack on Judaism. He outlawed it, by fiat. The reasons for this move are not clear, but the steps he took were very evident to the author of 2 Maccabees. Antiochus forbade Jews to remember the Sabbath, observe festivals, keep the dietary laws, or practice male circumcision. The observances of Judaism were banned upon pain of death. The Temple in Jerusalem was renamed "The Temple of the Olympian Zeus" (2 Maccabees 6:2). This ancient center of Jewish worship was further desecrated with prostitutes cavorting within the sacred precincts and pigs used for sacrifices on the altar in the Temple. Antiochus's actions represented one of the most serious assaults on the survival of the Jewish people ever undertaken in history.

There had been other times when the survival of the Jewish people had been at stake. The enslavement in Egypt centuries before, along with liberation in the form of the Exodus, was an ancient time-honored memory. So, too, was the threatened persecution of the Jews in the Persian Empire, led by the evil Haman. The Book of Esther described his outlook when speaking to the Persian ruler, Artaxerxes: "There is a certain nation scattered among the other nations in all your kingdom; their laws are different from those of every other nation, and they do not keep the laws of the king" (Esther 3:8). The Jews were just different and therefore should not be tolerated, was Haman's complaint. Whether the Book of Esther described an actual event or was a work of fiction, this writing probably recorded the first instance of anti-Semitism: the Jews are different and have their own set of laws. Haman's plot was foiled, however, and the Book of Esther described her bravery in confronting her husband, the absolute monarch of Persia, to set aside his edict condemning the Jews to death. She succeeded and Haman was executed instead.

Antiochus Epiphanes's actions in 167 B.C. were designed to wipe out Judaism. The objective of his assimilationist policy was clear: "kill those who did not choose to change over to Greek customs" (2 Maccabees 6:9). It was directed against Jews individually as well as the religion of Judaism. Passive resistance was not an option. Antiochus compelled everyone actively to take part in sacrifices to Greek gods. In particular, they were required to observe the festival of Dionysus. Here they were forced to don wreaths of ivy and to walk in the procession honoring the god. While some welcomed or succumbed to Antiochus's ways, many did not. Those who refused to adopt Greek ways were simply killed. Antiochus was ruthless in his campaign.

2 Maccabees provided grim details of persecution against those who stubbornly resisted. Two devout women, for instance, who had had their babies circumcised, were paraded through the city, seminaked. Then they were thrown to their deaths from the top of Temple Mount onto the hard stone pavement below. Others who had hidden in a cave to observe the Sabbath were burned as they stood passively, refusing to defend themselves on this holy day. Eleazar, a noted scribe of high standing and advanced age, was slaughtered when he refused to eat pig meat. Seven brothers and their mother were also martyred for the same offense. The mother saw her children tortured and slaughtered in a gruesome fashion before her eyes. Yet she confidently reassured them, "the

King of the universe will raise us up to an everlasting renewal of life, because we have died for his laws" (2 Maccabees 7:9). This represents one of the earliest references in Judaism to a belief in eternal life and it was born out of desperation. Surely there had to be a life beyond this life. If God truly is a God of justice, then there has to be an afterlife in which he makes good on his promises that the righteous will be blessed. Otherwise, why cling to this religion? Why pay the supreme price for living a life of righteousness?

But was there an afterlife? Was following the law and honoring the God of Israel as the sole God of the universe truly the way of obtaining it? Or were the cults of Dionysus, Mithras, and Isis equally valid ways of attaining immortality? Was there, perhaps, a spiritual equivalence among all religions? These were unsettling thoughts for a Torah-observant Jew cognizant of alternatives in the religious lineup of the time.

Judas Maccabeus led a revolt, along with a number of Torah-observant Jews. He and his followers escaped into the wilderness of Judea and, from there, mounted a series of lightning strikes against Antiochus's troops. In 164 B.C., three years after Antiochus's edict outlawing Judaism, they succeeded in capturing Jerusalem and the Temple. The Temple was cleansed and rededicated in a beautiful ceremony. Thus the festival of Hanukkah was born: "Therefore, carrying ivy-wreathed wands and beautiful branches and also fronds of palm, they offered hymns of thanksgiving to him who had given success to the purifying of his own holy place. They decreed by public edict, ratified by vote, that the whole nation of the Jews should observe these days every year" (2 Maccabees 10:7–8). While Hanukkah has added other stories to its narrative, at its heart, Hanukkah is a wonderful, warm celebration of Jewish survival. It commemorates the victory of Judas Maccabeus over Antiochus, a triumph over enforced Hellenization against tremendous odds.

The intent of Antiochus Epiphanes was clear: to eliminate Jewish worship and practices and to convert the people forcibly to Hellenistic ways. He did not succeed, although there was massive pain and devastation during the three years of his edict until Judas Maccabaeus could drive him from Jerusalem. This enormous threat cascaded throughout Judaism for several centuries, much in the way the Holocaust overshadows Jewish thinking today. The challenges of assimilation and loss of identity were very much on people's minds in the first century A.D. when Jesus, John the Baptist, James, Peter, and Paul were proclaiming their teachings. The threat of cultural assimilation some 175 years later had not diminished. Hellenization remained a constant powerful force all Jewish leaders had to contend with.

Whether by overt persecution or, more subtly, by relentless, daily cultural pressures, Jewish identity was severely shaken by the prospects of Hellenization. What was at stake was nothing less than the historic covenantal relationship the Jewish people shared with God. Hellenization provoked Judaism into debating the question, How should this ancient covenant be honored in modern, progressive times? Did it have a place in a cosmopolitan world? Jewish thinkers of the era—the Dead Sea Scroll community's Teacher of Righteousness, Hillel, Jesus, John the Baptist, James, Paul, and many others—all had to identify themselves in terms of how they understood keeping Jewish law in light of the new world Greece and Rome had created. It was the most important issue of the day.

COVENANT AND LAW

The fundamental premise of the Hebrew Bible or Old Testament is that God has made a deal, an agreement with his people, Israel. This agreement—called in more formal biblical terminology a covenant—is expressed in terms of contract law. There are two parties to the deal: God and the people of Israel. Each has obligations to the other as expressed through this covenant. This represents an astounding concept: the human-divine relationship is conceived of as a bargain. God has freely chosen to bind himself to a people and will deliver on promises, so long as they uphold their side of the agreement.

The details of the contract are to be found in the Books of the Torah, namely the first five books of any Bible: Genesis, Exodus, Leviticus, Numbers, and Deuteronomy. These books have been viewed historically as containing the instruction—the laws and rules—that God set before the Jewish people through Moses and that the people themselves agreed to (Leviticus 26:46; Deuteronomy 6:1). In fact, because of its importance, the ratification by the whole nation is mentioned three times in the Book of Exodus—Exodus 19:8; 24:3, and 24:7.

The covenant itself is regarded as a perpetual agreement, throughout all generations. The imagery used to describe the agreement is intimate, as in one spouse to the other, or as indissoluble, as in the relationship between parent and child.[6] There is more to the covenant and law than just a contract, however. It involves the whole human personality—the will to commit and a wholehearted attitude to carry out the law as a way of life. The Torah is the means by which a relationship with God is worked out and expressed.

Perhaps nowhere are the terms of the deal made more explicit than at the end of the Book of Deuteronomy. There Moses had put forward all the commandments, decrees, and ordinances of God before the people. He urged them to love the Lord and to walk in his ways. The concept advanced in Deuteronomy 30:13–20—the Model of the Two Ways—lurks behind the message of many biblical books. This influential model presupposes that we have a choice in life, either to follow the law or to not follow the law. One is the way of life, the other, the way of death. The choices are stark, but, nonetheless, they represent a choice. At a time when Greek religion and philosophy were stressing fate and determinism, the Book of Deuteronomy proposed human freedom. It is the first document we have in Western civilization that advances this point of view.

As Deuteronomy portrayed, it the choice before us is clear. By deciding to keep the law, a person has chosen the path of righteousness. This choice has beneficial consequences, as God fulfills his part of the deal. Collectively, God will ensure that the people have the land of Israel. Individually, righteous people will enjoy such blessings as long life, health, and happiness. This is positioned as the way of life and prosperity.

On the other hand, there is the way of death, a path taken when a person decides not to observe Torah, failing to love the Lord God, declining to walk in his ways, and not observing his laws and rules. This decision has profoundly negative consequences. As the nation of Israel fails to live up to its promises, God can opt not to fulfill his side of the bargain. Hence, as a result of this choice, collectively there will be no guarantee of land and individually there will be loss of blessings. This is the way of death and adversity.

The Model of the Two Ways was used by the prophets to understand history. Moses, for example, toward the end of Deuteronomy, was shown envisaging the future course of Israelite society.[7] He "foresaw" a time when the people would abandon the covenant. Ignoring Torah, he said, they would be conquered by a "grim-faced nation" and would lose the land (Deuteronomy 28:49, 50). This shows us how a prophet deftly employed the Model of the Two Ways to make sense of history. In this instance, Moses provided us with a theological context for understanding the Babylonian Exile (587/586 B.C.)— an event that happened long after his time.[8]

In the mideighth century B.C., the prophet Amos roared that people had abandoned the covenant with God. He provided concrete evidence. His fellow countrymen were cheating people, oppressing the poor, and enjoying a decadent luxurious lifestyle high on the hillsides with their expensive mansions and state-of-the-art décor made from precious metals. It was a society riddled with corruption. They had forgotten their history and what God had done for them. In particular, he was outraged that many were engaging in Canaanite religious practices. Canaanites were the nearby ethnic group that shared the land with the ancient Israelites. Their religious rites were often of a sexual nature: male intercourse with the priestesses was permitted and, in fact, encouraged as part of religious duty. In this nature-based religion, sexuality represented an important part of worship. Humans participated in the divine, and sexuality was viewed as prompting the goddess Anath to restore the god Ba'al to life in the springtime. Hence male worshippers would have sexual relations with the priestesses, joining in the power of the goddess to awaken the sleeping male deity. It was a nature-based religion, organized around the annual cycles of planting and harvesting, not a history-based religion as was Judaism.

In Canaanite religion, too, the major deities involved worship of the goddess. That is something that would have really rankled Amos. With their religious shrines only a mile or two away from Israelite villages, this alternative culture exercised a powerful influence on Jewish practices. As Amos and other prophets make abundantly clear, the path of assimilation was from Israelite to Canaanite, not the reverse. In the battle of hormones versus history, the Canaanites often won out.

Applying the Model of the Two Ways, Amos outlined dramatically what would happen. By failing to live up to the requirements of the law, the people would lose the land and individual blessings. He described the consequences in graphic terms: Assyria would likely invade, costing the Israelites life, property, and political freedom. Leaders would go into exile in Assyria. Amos's was an uphill battle, however, and his people did not listen. Even then, no one liked bad news.

For Amos, world events vindicated the covenant: choices have communal consequences. One day in 721 B.C., had there been a secular newspaper, the lead article would have read:

ISRAEL FALLS

Overwhelmed by superior military might, Assyria tonight conquered the Northern Kingdom (Israel) and, with it, all the cities and towns. Looting, plundering, and rape continue unabated as military leaders fail to contain their troops. The king and the political/religious elite of Israel are holed up, wondering what will befall them.

This account views history, as we might, as a military confrontation between opposing armies, with the vastly superior Assyrian force winning. But that is not how Amos understood history at all. He saw historical dynamics in radically different terms. Had Amos a blog, he would have written something like the following:

ISRAEL COLLAPSES
Beset with internal corruption and having abandoned the covenant, Israel has collapsed. Because the people failed to keep their part of the deal, God has allowed the nation of Assyria to storm the land and devastate the population. Exile is likely.

The difference in perspective is remarkable. For Amos, the small independent Jewish state was not conquered because it stood in the way of Assyria's southward march toward Egypt. Nor did it fall because its puny armed forces were many times smaller than the huge Assyrian army. Rather, the kingdom fell because of internal religious failings. Like the prophets generally, Amos's version of events represented a unique and fascinating way of viewing history: the covenantal agreement with God. Israel would prosper when it honored the covenant by observing Torah. Otherwise it would fail, and failure entailed loss of land.

Bad choices, therefore, result in disaster, both communally and individually. The future, however, is not fixed. As with most prophets, Amos hoped that his searing message would awaken people as to the full consequences of their choices and encourage them to change quickly. An alternate outcome would be for the people to return to observing Torah as an expression of covenant, and thus avert disaster. While his best lines are centered on denunciation, Amos did at times urge the people to return to the covenant by following the path of righteousness, that they may live long in the land promised to them (Amos 5:14).

The covenant, therefore, provided a way the Jewish people could understand the dynamics of history. Hellenization threatened this basis for historical understanding. If the Jewish people were to abandon the covenant, what would replace it as a means of making sense of their world?

In its original form, the reward for following the Torah was not eternal life: it was real estate. The people were promised that they and their descendants would live in the land of Israel in perpetuity if they followed the law. The reward consisted of the satisfaction of knowing that one's grandchildren and their grandchildren would have a safe and happy life, secure in the land. By the mid-second century B.C., however—centuries after the Book of Deuteronomy—some segments of Judaism came to believe in an afterlife. Some of the martyrs of Antiochus's persecutions had advanced such a hope. So, too, did the members of the Dead Sea Scroll community. One of their major writings envisaged these blessings for the truly righteous:

> *healing, great peace in a long life, and fruitfulness, together with every everlasting blessing and eternal joy in life without end, a crown of glory and a garment of majesty in unending light.*[9]

Conversely, those who refused to follow the path of Torah could expect an extremely unpleasant afterlife consisting of

> *a multitude of plagues by the hand of all the destroying angels, everlasting damnation by the avenging wrath of the fury of God, eternal torment and endless disgrace together with shameful extinction in the fire of the dark regions.*[10]

Here in the first century B.C., this writer upgraded the Model of the Two Ways to include the promise of eternity within its overall framework. Now the reward for following Torah consisted not only of land and blessings, but also of eternal life.

In the Books of the Torah, however, typically long life, good health, and happiness were the blessings that were cited as the rewards for being righteous. The image was one of a rich and rewarding life, seeing not only one's children grow up but their children as well, living in the land God has given. While this came eventually to include eternal life for the righteous, the expectation was *this-worldly*: eternal life would take place on this planet. As they saw it, the reward for being righteous was eternal life on a re-created earth, at some time in the future. So the concept was *temporal*—eternal life occurring at some future point in history. It was not an *otherworldly* view that would involve the soul's relocation to a supernatural place or dimension—to a heaven or a hell, for instance—upon death. That is, the Jewish view of eternal life did not represent a *spatial* notion. The idea was fundamentally different. When God brings about his rule upon earth, and all humanity comes to worship the one God in purity and truth, then at that point in time, those who are righteous will receive the divine gift of remaining alive. At the same time, the righteous dead will be resurrected by God and will live eternally. So, eternal life does not occur immediately. It will occur at the end of history as we know it in a much different, highly transformed universe.

There's another important difference between Jewish and Hellenistic views regarding the afterlife. Only God can grant life to the dead. That was the Jewish belief. People are not naturally immortal as Greek philosophers such as Pythagoras and Plato thought or as Egyptian religion maintained. The biblical view was not that people have an immortal soul that continues on, immediately upon death, into another realm. On the typical Jewish view expressed in the Bible and related writings, the dead are truly dead. God alone will determine who gets resurrected . . . and when.

Hellenization threatened all these outcomes—land, happiness, and eternal life. If the Jewish people were to assimilate and join the larger emerging world culture—whatever the supposed advantages—what would happen to their assurances of keeping the land of Israel, enjoying long life, and all the other rich blessings that were conditional upon observance of Torah? What would be gained? What could possibly replace these promises if the bargain with God were forfeited? Could the promises of Hellenization compete with the rewards of Torah? Did Hellenized Jews of the period experience guilt at leaving the covenant and forfeiting all its blessings? Or did they just succumb to the siren call of Graeco-Roman thought with its assurances of the personal immortality of the soul?

The Torah, we will recall, was rooted in the relationship between God and Israel. It encompassed a whole lifestyle—choices, actions, and attitudes. In essence, it expressed the human side of the relationship with God, specifying what people must do individually and collectively to honor and uphold their end of the deal. There are some 613 commandments, laws, and rules covering all aspects of life. Prominent among these laws are the Ten Commandments, which command obligations toward God as well as to other human beings. Observing the Sabbath, honoring parents, not committing adultery, not bearing false witness against other people, and not coveting others' possessions or relationships were lumped in with such considerations as worshipping only one God and not murdering.

Other laws had to do with the major festivals, such as Passover, Shavuot, and Succoth. These constituted important time markers throughout the year for the community, providing pause and an opportunity to reflect on historical experiences. Observant Jews throughout the land and across the Mediterranean were expected to make the pilgrimage up to Jerusalem for these holy observances. This represented a major commitment. From the Galilee region in northern Israel, it would have been a two- or three-day trip each way in ancient times, with people walking on foot or using a slow-moving donkey. From points farther away, from around the Mediterranean or from Babylonia, the arduous journey might have taken weeks. These festivals recounted the historical stages of Jewish liberation centuries before and created a "we were there" type of experience for present-day Jews. Passover, of course, commemorated the Exodus out of Egypt. Shavuot marked the giving of the Torah. Succoth provided a time to reflect on the experiences the ancient Israelites underwent on their journey through the desert for forty years prior to entering the Promised Land. These were important annual events and the way the people connected with the roots of their religion.

In addition, there were many other laws that governed all forms of social interaction—worship, dietary holiness, the administration of the courts, protection of the poor, remission of debts, property rights, warfare, marriage and divorce, animal well-being, criminal law, marital and sexual conduct, and the treatment of strangers. Every aspect of life fell under the domain of Torah, with duties toward God and fellow human beings being implicated in all of personal conduct.

All these constituted Torah. It was presented as a complete package, the embodiment of a distinctive lifestyle. The agreement called for the observance on the part of the people of Israel of all the laws, all the time, not some of the laws some of the time. It was, in fact, the Jewish constitution. It expressed high ethical ideals to live up to, and an annualized ritual for forgiveness—the Day of Atonement, Yom Kippur—when they failed. It was a challenging religion that demanded daily lifestyle choices.

The comprehensiveness of "the Torah package" can be dramatically illustrated by considering four major types of laws. Torah, for instance, included religious laws, issuing prohibitions against worshipping other gods and summoning people to heed the call: "Hear, O Israel, the Lord our God, the Lord is one" (Deuteronomy 6:4). It also supported healthy sexuality being neither ascetic nor licentious. Interestingly enough, the first commandment we encounter in Torah, in the first chapter of the Book of Genesis, is to be fruitful and to multiply. At the same time, other passages in the Torah prohibited participation in improper sexual relationships that would corrupt family ties. Additionally, Torah required observance of specific dietary laws that the Bible positions as characteristic of a holy lifestyle. This included not eating specific kinds of animals, fowl, or shellfish. There was no claim that these laws were healthier, better for the heart, capable of promoting weight loss or reducing cholesterol, or simply necessary because of the time's lack of refrigeration. The Torah simply stated that it was a holiness requirement (Leviticus 11:44–45). Finally, Torah required observance of time, ceasing to work on the Sabbath and participating in such festivals as Passover and Succoth.

Put these different laws together and a pattern of comprehensiveness emerges: religion, sexuality, food, and honoring time. All are an integral part of a relationship with God, for the role of God is acknowledged and included in what we do. A strong relationship with God, then, is not just a cozy feeling, an ecstatic out-of-body experience, a mental state, or an inner faith. It is much more demanding: choices, decisions, attitudes, and actions are required.

Concern with Torah observance has sometimes been caricatured as legalism, as an obsession with rules and regulations. Christian writers sometimes stereotype Jewish observance of Torah as onerous and legalistic. It can become that, especially when preoccupation with ritual or purity matters trump ethical ones. But that was not the way Torah was portrayed in biblical times. Nor was it likely experienced as such, keeping the dietary laws and observing the Sabbath being relatively easy injunctions to follow in a society that tended to honor these requirements, although, as we have noted, there would have been strong temptations to defect.

Two of the most remarkable passages in the Bible are to be found in the Book of Psalms, the hymn book of ancient Israel. There we find two songs that praise Torah for the happiness it creates. Psalm 1, for instance, rejoices in Torah:

> "Happy are those who do not follow the advice of the wicked, or take the path that sinners tread, or sit in the seat of scoffers; but their delight is in the law of the Lord, and on his law they meditate day and night" (Psalm 1:1–2).

A much longer song of some 176 verses, Psalm 119, reiterates this theme. That the law is described as "a delight" and that its observers are presented as "happy" indicate that much more than law in our sense is being described here. This is truly exceptional. Our society does not have songs in praise of the law. No one today would compose a song about our laws. Could you imagine singing songs today about the income tax laws? the constitution? highway regulations? the first amendment?

It is clear, then, that the word "Torah" has a considerably different conno-
tation than our word "law." A "teaching" or a "way" might be a more appropriate translation of the term, given its comprehensive nature. Perhaps it might
be better to think in terms of a Torah lifestyle—an all-inclusive way of living
that combines right behavior, right attitudes, and right beliefs all manifested in
a way of life that results in fulfillment, satisfaction, and contentment.

While the Torah is primarily focused on practice, it also includes attitudes
toward God and other human beings. This is expressed in the Shema prayer:

> *Hear, O Israel: The Lord is our God, the Lord alone. You shall love the Lord*
> *your God with all your heart, and with all your soul, and with all your might.*
> *Keep these words that I am commanding you today in your heart. Recite them*
> *to your children and talk about them when you are at home and when you are*
> *away, when you lie down and when you rise. Bind them as a sign upon your*
> *hand, fix them as an emblem on your forehead, and write them on the door-*
> *posts of your house and on your gates.* (Deuteronomy 6:4–9)

God is to be loved, but love is expressed through behavior that emanates from
a "right attitude." In this case, belief in God as one and the love of God goes
beyond a mere mental dimension. It involves actions—for example, telling
children about the law, and binding passages from the law as an emblem on the
forehead (*tefillin*) and on the doorposts of one's house or gate (*mezuzah*) as reminders of commitment.

In another passage, the Book of Deuteronomy noted:

> *So now, O Israel, what does the Lord your God require of you? Only to fear*
> *the Lord your God, to walk in all his ways, to love him, to serve the Lord your*
> *God with all your heart and with all your soul, and to keep the command-*
> *ments of the Lord your God and his decrees that I am commanding you today,*
> *for your own well-being.* (Deuteronomy 10:12–13).

This succinct summary indicates five requirements: to fear God, to walk in his
ways, to love him, to serve him, and to keep his commandments. It grounds
well-being in "right attitudes" (to fear, to love) that result in "right behavior"
(to walk, to serve, to keep). The prophet Micah later refers to this passage
(Micah 6:1–8).

Above all, the Torah presupposes the view that people are decision makers
and can choose their path in life. These choices, however, have consequences.
Unlike the view propagated by many Greek thinkers of the time, for the Jewish observer of Torah, life is not fatalistic, and history is not determined by unalterable causes. The decisions that people and communities make affect the
outcome of history. People are called upon, through Torah, to work with God

to create a better world. It's a partnership of people with God in creation. Decisions, choices, envisioning consequences—all this is involved in "following" or "observing" Torah.

That was the historic heritage of Judaism that was thrown into question by Hellenization. The path of the righteous was demanding, exact, and all-encompassing. Every aspect of Jewish living came under Torah. And the consequences were enormous, both individually and collectively—blessings, land, and, as many began to believe, eternal life.

THE CHALLENGES OF HELLENIZATION

Cultures in conflict. This was the reality on the ground in the first two centuries B.C. and A.D. as Jews everywhere experienced the complicated world of religious pluralism. To be sure, Hellenization lured people with the promise of many powerful economic and cultural advantages. The elite of Israel sought expanded trade opportunities and new business enterprises to service the complex needs of foreign troops and their families. The impressive literature of the Greeks, and eventually of the Romans, opened up exciting and adventurous intellectual pursuits and visions.

But Hellenization also threatened the social, religious, and ethical fabric of Jewish society. Foreigners were in their midst, as rulers in Jerusalem and as nearby inhabitants of Greek cities all around the Galilee. Troops were on the move, creating the kind of social problems that ancient armies left in their wake—rape and prostitution along with theft of food and goods from local defenseless people. Foreign temples had sprung up, creating myriad religious alternatives for Jewish youth interested in investigating new ways of viewing the world and human destiny. Even within the Temple in Jerusalem, religious leaders were under pressure to admit non-Jews, to allow Gentiles to offer sacrifices, and to use copper vessels in the sanctuary created by non-Jewish workmen. We know this from objections the Dead Sea Scroll community raised to Temple practices.

How much social interaction was permitted? Talking together and doing business was one thing. But families would have been at odds about eating together, Jew with Gentile. There would have been concerns. Could we eat off plates, they probably asked, when these did not meet purity requirements, likely having come into contact with forbidden meats? And what if a forbidden food was served, such as pork or shellfish? It also raised many issues. For example, they may have wondered, could Torah-observant Jews work on pig farms? We know from the New Testament that these existed—one of Jesus' miracles was driving a herd of swine into the Sea of Galilee. More generally, to what extent could Jewish workers come into contact with such animals whose flesh constituted forbidden meat? Could one butcher them, for instance?

Transport them to Roman troop headquarters? What should one do about acceptable meats that had been slaughtered differently than prescribed by Jewish law, likely in a temple dedicated to a Greek, Egyptian, or Persian deity? Where to draw the line was a question many faced frequently as they sought to make accommodations with social realities of the time.

What about the law generally? If accommodations were to be made, how radical a reinterpretation was necessary? In addition to the dietary laws, what changes should be made to the time markers—the routine of Sabbaths and festivals? Should we work on the Sabbath, they may well have asked, to supply and service the occupying forces? Should we take a day off that they did not? What should happen to the practice of circumcision, which the Greeks and Romans detested as barbaric and openly ridiculed? What should be made of one of the central tenets of the Ten Commandments, not to worship other gods? Could compromises be made there? After all, the Greeks and Romans found no problem going to various temples, to honor different deities.

For some Jews of the time, there was no problem, and, making compromises, they assimilated into the general population. For others, however, it was important to hold fast to ancient practices, to be a minority holding different beliefs and values in the face of a majority culture. How tolerant and accepting would those within the dominant culture be toward this strong minority? What would stretch the limits of their patience? Even more radically, were there opportunities for trying to convince the Greeks and Romans that Judaism had merit and was worth their consideration?

Hellenization with its implied necessity for assimilation into the common culture unleashed a powerful new dynamic into Jewish life. A new question was born: How could covenant and Jewish law coexist with the challenges and realities of the modern world? That was by far the most important question of the day. Every Jewish leader of the time—and well into the New Testament period—wrestled with this complex issue and developed different strategies for dealing with the threat of Hellenization. Everything of value was at stake—ethics, social behavior, eating practices, holidays, and festivals, as well as the basis for understanding history and human existence. Even sheer survival as a distinct people and a religious community was at issue, for Antiochus's harsh edict was a recent bitter memory.

If Hellenization was the problem, what was the solution? As we shall see, Jewish leaders of the time, Jesus and Paul among them, developed different answers to this soul-searching question. Jews of this turbulent time experienced religious pluralism not only *between* competing religions but also, we shall discover, *within* the religion of Judaism itself. There were competing strategies within Judaism for dealing with the problem of Hellenization.

Truly these were exceptionally bewildering times.

3

BEING JEWISH IN
A COSMOPOLITAN WORLD

Jesus, John the Baptist, Mary Magdalene, Peter, James, and Paul—all were Jews of the first century A.D. But what did it mean to be Jewish at that time? A topic on everybody's mind was how to relate Torah to the times, how to blend Judaism with the demands of a new modern international civilization. Prior to these New Testament individuals coming on the scene, Jewish leaders had been working creatively to devise strategies for coping with Hellenization. Over time, four distinct factions had arisen, chiefly in response to the serious assault on Jewish survival posed by Antiochus Epiphanes. His dire threat served to galvanize the Jewish community into action. Factious groups—all within Judaism—offered various paths to ensuring Jewish continuity.

These different approaches to the problem contributed to the confusion. For the first time, ordinary Jews had choices *within* Judaism. By exploring these factions, it's possible to have a better vantage point from which to view the unique contributions of Jesus and the alternative he proposed to the political and social messages then current. It will also set the stage for understanding the radical Hellenized nature of Paul's message and why it so offended traditional Jews.

FOUR WAYS OF BEING JEWISH

THE SADDUCEES

The Sadducees were the "country club" faction of Jewish society: wealthy, connected, and firmly in control of business and religion. They arose shortly after the time of Antiochus Epiphanes, in the midsecond century B.C., forming the Temple and political elite. They lived, for the most part, in the better residential sections of Jerusalem—on the prestigious western ridge connected by a private causeway to Temple Mount. Thus they were able to avoid life in the congested lower city of Jerusalem and did not have to mingle with the vast throngs of pilgrims wending their way up the huge staircases to present their offerings. They were the priests and high priests in charge of the Temple and its sacrifices. They held this exalted position throughout the decades of the first century B.C. right up until A.D. 70. The only exception was during the brief reign of Queen Salome Alexandra (76–67 B.C.), when the Pharisees exercised control for a decade.

In antiquity, a temple was a much larger enterprise than what we understand by a church or synagogue today. For us, religious centers—even the new "megachurches"—tend to have only a few clergy and perhaps a paid education director, choir master, choir, cantor, organist, and office staff all supported by dozens of volunteers. Even the largest of our churches and synagogues do not measure up to what constituted an ancient temple.

We need to visualize the Jewish Temple as by far the largest industry within the country, the focal point of agriculture, worship, local government, law, and tourism. People would come to Jerusalem for major festivals—Passover, Shavuot, and Succoth—and they had to be accommodated. Those who wished to offer sacrifice would bring their best animals or produce, to offer it within the Temple and to share in the food with the blessings of God and the participation of the priests. Unlike modern religious institutions, the Temple engaged the services of tens of thousands of individuals. It was a massive economic enterprise, being a religious center, butcher shop, restaurant, law court, and civil administration all wrapped up into one huge complex.

Herod the Great vastly extended Temple Mount before he died in 4 B.C. He rebuilt the Temple, making it and its platform into one of the largest religious complexes the ancient world had ever seen. It stood high on the highest point of the eastern ridge of Jerusalem, splendidly reflecting the light of the sun in all directions. Priests, Levites, animal inspectors, judges, and scribes all worked there, each with their specific tasks prescribed by tradition. Establishments such as foreign currency exchange kiosks, clothing stores, food shops, ritual baths, as well as housing for visitors were in evidence. So, too, undoubtedly, were the souvenir stands. By the early part of the first century A.D., Jerusalem and its magnificent Temple had become a showcase city . . . and one of the Roman world's prime tourist destinations. It truly was big business.

Later rabbinic tradition would wistfully look back on these glory days with pride and yearning. One text boasted that whoever had not seen Jerusalem in its glory had never seen a beautiful city in his life. The text nostalgically went on to say that whoever had not seen the Temple while it was still standing had never seen a beautiful building in his life (Babylonian Talmud, Sukkah 51b). It was an impressive sight that drew hundreds of thousands of pilgrims annually.

The Sadducees benefited from this rich economy and were wealthier than most. Their luxurious villas were opulent. Today we can walk through the ruins of homes of wealthy priests that have been unearthed beneath the modern dwellings of the present-day Jewish Quarter of Jerusalem. These "Herodian mansions" furnish eloquent testimony to their owners' participation in the best that their world had to offer. Their homes were spacious and boasted beautiful floor mosaics, ornate wall designs, and large rooms. We can imagine the inhabitants routinely immersing themselves in the ritual baths set inside the houses. They must have entertained lavishly, for huge jars of provisions such as oil and wine have been found, along with finely crafted dishware.[1]

These elite members of society were more open to Hellenistic thought, culture, and practices than were other sectors of the community. The reason was simple: their livelihood depended on getting along with their political masters—Greek and, later on, Roman. They had to make arrangements work. Hence they were more cosmopolitan in outlook than other Jewish groups, provided that their livelihood and the Temple sacrifices were not compromised. For the most part, they worked out a modus vivendi with the occupying power. They looked after the Temple, its rituals, commerce, government, and trade, while the troops remained garrisoned in a not-too-distant corner of Temple Mount to ensure the peace. More than most factions, they were sensitive to troublemakers and rebels. Messianic claimants to the Jewish throne fitted into this category, for they had the potential to disturb the peace. The Sadducees had the most to lose should rebellion occur, and they did their utmost to help keep the peace for their foreign masters. *Accommodation* was their strategy for dealing with Hellenization.

In terms of religious beliefs, the Sadducees favored the first five books of the Bible, the Torah, as the authoritative texts. They gave little weight to the two other divisions—the Prophets and the Writings—that came to make up the Hebrew Bible. They also did not believe in an afterlife, since there is no mention of that topic in the Books of the Torah. So making the most of this life was vitally important. Rejection of an afterlife brought the Sadducees into major disputes with other forms of Judaism, whose followers by the first century B.C. had come to believe in eternal life and the resurrection of the dead.

As described in the New Testament, early members of the Jesus Movement typically ran afoul of the Sadducee high priest over this very issue. So, too, did the Pharisees, who, like early followers of Jesus in Jerusalem, affirmed belief in eternal life. In one of the most amusing incidents in the New Testament, Paul was depicted being in Jerusalem and talking about resurrection before the Sanhedrin, the Jewish council (Acts 23). Noting that there were Sadducees and Pharisees in the room, Paul cleverly observed that he was on trial because he believed in the resurrection of the dead. Needless to say, this set off a huge ruckus and sparked a shouting match between the Sadducees and Pharisees. Paul was almost forgotten in the fray.

The Sadducees did not survive the destruction of Jerusalem and the Temple in A.D. 70. As economic and religious leaders in Jerusalem, they were targeted by the Roman troops for elimination, and, for the most part, they were. They perished along with the Temple in which they had performed the required sacrifices.

THE PHARISEES

The Pharisees were the faculty of ancient Judaism. They functioned as scholars and teachers, focusing on teaching people Jewish law. For them, *education* constituted the most effective bulwark against Hellenization. They ran schools, not the Temple sacrifices that formed the focal point of Jewish worship in the ancient world.

The New Testament often mentions the Pharisees. In the gospels, they are typically portrayed as opponents who shadowed Jesus. In the Gospel of Matthew, for instance, Jesus is depicted as denouncing the Pharisees for hypocrisy. This may represent an unfair portrait, however, for they were highly popular teachers and their scholars attracted huge crowds. The Book of Acts, in fact, presents a different picture of the Pharisees than the Gospels do, seeing them as defenders of the Jesus Movement. In one instance, the leaders in Jerusalem are arrested by the Sadducee high priest and hauled into court. The leader of the Pharisees, Gamaliel, "respected by all the people," spoke in their defense. He noted that there had been many messianic claimants—Theudas and Judas the Galilean, for instance—and he urged the Jewish Council, the Sanhedrin, to let these leaders alone. His rationale was that if the movement was "of God," then it would be futile to oppose them. Conversely, if the movement did not come from God, then it would wither away like the other messianic movements (Acts 5:17–39). The Book of Acts also mentions that some Pharisees had become members of the Jesus Movement in Jerusalem. So who were they, really?

Like the Sadducees, the Pharisees arose as a group after the persecutions of Antiochus Epiphanes, although their beginnings are somewhat murky. They may have emerged out of a group of ultraorthodox supporters of Judas Maccabeus called the Hasidim, or they could have had a separate origin. They resisted the intrusion of Hellenization into Jewish life by teaching the traditions, anchoring the people in the covenant and the observance of Torah.

However they originated, by 100 B.C. they were clearly a force to be reckoned with. So much so that by the early decades of the first century B.C., they were thrust into a civil war with the Sadducees over the direction of society. Alexander Jannaeus, the king and high priest who governed Israel from 103 to 76 B.C., was a ruthless ruler who slew six thousand of his citizens, including Pharisees and their supporters, during a Succoth festival. Apparently, as a Sadducee, he had not carried out the rites properly. He poured water on his feet rather than on the altar as the Pharisees preferred. This incident sparked an ensuing revolt during which Alexander slaughtered fifty thousand of his subjects. Later on we find Jannaeus crucifying eight hundred Pharisaic leaders as their wives and children were killed before their eyes.

As these events indicate, disputes between Pharisees and Sadducees were bitter and often deadly. These were not just religious in nature but, as so often happens with religion, they were fierce political battles as well—so much so that virtual civil war erupted from time to time between the Sadducees and Pharisees.

After his death, Jannaeus's wife, Salome Alexandra, ruled as queen from 76 to 67 B.C. She switched sides and placed the Pharisees in control of the Temple. The reasons for this abrupt turn of events are not clear, but it may have reflected growing popular approval of the Pharisees among the people. It was only during her reign, however, that they ever enjoyed such political power in Jerusalem. Now it was the turn of the Sadducees to feel persecuted. Some Sadducees may have left the unfavorable political climate of Jerusalem at this time for the relative safety and obscurity of the Dead Sea area.

The Pharisees were not the priestly political elite. They saw their mission quite differently. They were teachers of Torah, a position that required a two-year training program. Thus they taught biblical texts, explained them, and encouraged people to observe the commandments. We can visualize them going through the Book of Deuteronomy, for instance, outlining the laws and commandments and providing illustrations of what these meant for ordinary people in their day-to-day lives. For them, the Bible consisted of three parts: the five Books of the Torah, the Prophets, and the Writings. This is the same as the Hebrew Bible for Judaism or the Protestant Old Testament today.

Unlike the Sadducees, the Pharisees believed in an afterlife. They thought that in the world to come, God would raise up the righteous from the dead. Along with righteous people then alive, the resurrected dead would live eternally in a re-created world where there would be universal peace and all people would worship the one God. As the Pharisees and other Jewish groups of the time thought of it, "the world to come" represented that point in human history when God would act decisively to remake the world. So they looked forward to a re-created earth, populated by the righteous, worshiping the one God, eternally, the way creation was meant to be. Paul later built upon this view of resurrection in his letter, 1 Corinthians. Resurrection represents a very different view of the afterlife than is found in many Jewish, Christian, and

Islamic groups today. These build more upon an "immortality of the soul" concept popularized by Plato and other Greek philosophers as well as by ancient Egyptian religion.

The Pharisees possessed a powerful weapon, the "oral law," in addition to the "written law" found in the scrolls. Everybody else had access to the written law—but only the Pharisees had the oral tradition. This was a remarkably flexible interpretive principle, helping to illuminate passages from the Bible and making them applicable to daily life. They thought that along with the written text of the Books of the Law, this oral tradition went back to the time of Moses. Without the oral law acting as a guide, many parts of the biblical text would be difficult to act upon. For example, the meaning of the written commandment "to observe" or "to remember" the Sabbath would not be clear without reference to an oral tradition that interpreted the prohibited activities. What does observing the Sabbath require? people would have asked their Pharisaic teachers. What kinds of things could they do and not do on the Sabbath that would enable them to "keep it holy"? This was a practical question by homemakers, farmers, craftsmen, traders, and merchants scattered across the land who were concerned to take the precepts of the law seriously. But how should it be interpreted? Could they cook, for instance? Travel? Look after the livestock? Repair tents? Buy or sell fish? Do home repairs? Discuss business? Fetch water?

Moreover, when did the Sabbath start? When did it end? In the world before clocks, this was an important question. In time, Jewish groups would determine temporal markers—counting the number of visible stars in the sky Friday evening, for one thing, to mark the onset of the day of rest. In Jerusalem, people had an advantage. On the southwest corner of Temple Mount, there was a "place of trumpeting," that is, an area where a trumpeter stood to announce the onset and the close of the Sabbath. The stone sign for this location exists to this day.

The Pharisees used oral law to help answer these practical questions. Other groups were also addressing these issues, by different means. One surviving document of the Dead Sea Scroll community laid out its interpretation of what the commandment meant in actual practice.[2] The *Damascus Document* prohibited such activities as: making financial decisions, doing business, preparing food, taking things out of the house or bringing goods into it, walking more than two thousand cubits, spending the Sabbath in a place near to Gentiles, and so on.[3] These interpretations created the pattern for Sabbath observance at Qumran. The Sabbath there would have been a quiet, reflective time. Judaism had not yet established the thirty-nine categories of creative work prohibited on the Sabbath—that would come somewhat later—but groups were already moving in that direction.

The process of interpretation was greatly assisted by the efforts of two prominent Pharisaic teachers: Hillel the Elder and Shammai. Each founded a school—the House of Hillel and the House of Shammai—and they disagreed over Torah interpretation. According to later sources, there were over three hundred points at issue. Most, in time, became settled in accordance with the more liberal views of Hillel.

Hillel lived just prior to Jesus, from the midfirst century B.C. to about A.D. 20. Someone outside the Jewish religion approached him and asked him to summarize Jewish law, standing on one leg. He obliged, saying, "That which is hateful to you, do not do to your neighbor. That is the whole Torah. The rest is commentary. Go and study it," (Babylonian Talmud, Shabbat 3la). Somewhat later, Jesus, too, would speak of the Golden Rule in terms similar to that of Hillel but expressed positively: "Do to others as you would have them do to you" (Matthew 7:12). Hillel added an important last phrase: "Go and study it." Providing an encapsulation of the law did not replace Torah. Rather, it provided a starting point. It constituted the first step in understanding its meaning.

Later sources tell of Hillel standing in a marketplace in Jerusalem. People passed him going to and fro on their way to work. Hillel asked, "How much will you make today?" "Perhaps one coin," said one. "Two coins," said another. Hillel inquired, "And what will you do with the money?" One person responded that by working, he'd be able to provide for the necessities of life. Hillel then followed up with a zinger: "Why not come with me and make Torah your possession, that you may possess both this and the world to come?" (Avot de-Rabbi Nathan, recension B, 26). So the challenge was this: What's of greatest value? What should be our greatest priority?

Later on, Jesus would make much the same point in parables that tout the Kingdom of God as life's greatest treasure.

The oral law is often misunderstood as having been given, in its totality, on Mount Sinai along with the written law. Nor should it be pictured as a kind of secret lore that was passed on, person to person, whispered to select individuals throughout history from Moses on down to the present day. The Torah or written law is like *legislative law*: it sets forth the broad principles that are to be followed. It's like present-day constitutions and other foundational pieces of legislation that govern society. Oral law, on the other hand, is analogous to *judicial law*, the ever-growing body of interpretation of the law, with its cases, judgments, and precedents. This tradition of debating, interpreting, agreeing upon, or continuing to disagree about the meaning of the fixed text—that's oral law.

In time, the oral law became codified. Pronouncements by various rabbis, including Hillel and Shammai and many others, were collected and edited around A.D. 200 by Rabbi Judah haNasi (Judah the Prince). This writing is known as the Mishnah. Over the next three centuries, commentaries were produced on the Mishnah, providing further interpretation and examples, and this became known as the Gemara. The Mishnah and the Gemara together are referred to as the Talmud. This was the greatest blog ever created—debate, responses, as well as interpretive commentaries over the centuries: it was all there, like one gigantic electronic thread spanning hundreds of years.

The Pharisees survived the destruction of the Temple and Jerusalem in A.D. 70 in part because they were not concentrated just in Jerusalem. They assumed the leadership role in reconstructing Judaism after the destruction of the Temple, to take religious traditions into the home and the community. It is through the insights of these sages that we get Rabbinic Judaism, and, hence, modern Judaism.

In the gospels, Jesus was depicted as having conversations with Jewish leaders, chiefly Pharisees. Why primarily the Pharisees? For one thing, Pharisees were located throughout Israel, including the Galilee, where Jesus typically taught. More importantly, other than the members of the Jesus Movement who were then still part of the Jewish family, the Pharisees were the only major Jewish group to have survived the Roman onslaught of 70 with the destruction of the Temple and the city of Jerusalem. Gospel authors wrote after this event, and they would naturally depict Jesus talking and discussing matters with the religious leaders of *their* own time. Thus they typically used a Jesus-Pharisee dialogue to heighten the contrast between their movement and Pharisaic Judaism. Both were in transition, and it was important for writers during the latter part of the first century to pit the views of Jesus against those of the Pharisees. Whether he did so in real life, and whether he talked primarily with Pharisees, is hard to say.

THE DEAD SEA SCROLL COMMUNITY (THE ESSENES)

Had there been newspapers at the time, the members of the Dead Sea Scroll sect or Essenes would have expected to wake up one morning to read on the front page of the *Jerusalem Trumpet* the following headline:

EVIL ERADICATED, THE RIGHTEOUS REWARDED

Jerusalem. All evil rulers have disappeared. No more Romans occupy the land. Righteous people who have followed the law in its entirety are now in control. The righteous dead have, miraculously, returned to life—suddenly we have Abraham, Sarah, Moses, David, Solomon, Amos, Ezra, Esther, and many others in our midst who are shocked and bewildered by what has happened to them.

Israel has become the preeminent state in the world and people from all over the globe are beginning to flock to it. A new Davidic king—the long-awaited Messiah—has been installed in Jerusalem. All people acknowledge the sovereignty of God. Everyone who is righteous has eternal life. Peace reigns.

See details on p. 3. Interviews with Moses and David on p. 5.

This was their powerful vision—a wonderful new era in human history, a complete re-creation of the world as we know it. Much like messianic cults today, they thought they were living in the worst of times, that society was totally corrupt, and that the only way to escape God's wrath was separation from the rest of society. This they did, and they harbored no doubts that God was poised to act decisively within human history.

These end-time dramatic events would unfold during their lifetimes, they confidently asserted, although they were unsure how it would come about. According to one document, God would act, assisted by two Messiahs—one political and one priestly. Along with mighty archangels, God and his Messiahs would help the members of their sect wage war against all the unrighteous of the world. Then the righteous who had remained faithful to the Torah would be rewarded with eternal life. At other times, the scrolls talked of one Messiah. One remarkable document, 4Q521,[4] *A Messianic Apocalypse,* said that "the Heavens and the earth will obey His Messiah." This writing went on to affirm that God will glorify "the Pious Ones" on the "Throne of his Eternal Kingdom." Thus the righteous will be rewarded. God will then "release the captives, make the blind see, raise up the downtrodden." Then he (that is, God, or possibly the Messiah) will "heal the sick, resurrect the dead, and to the meek announce glad tidings." Whoever the agent of transformation would be, the members of this group were confident and excited to be living on the cusp of the most important years in all human history.

They thought they would never die.

So who were these visionaries who flourished during the first centuries B.C. and A.D.? In their writings, they veiled their identities, using such code words as "Teacher of Righteousness," "the Wicked Priest," and "the Liar." It would have been helpful to us had they inserted a few footnotes into their text telling us precisely to whom each of these epithets refer. But they did not. So we have to reconstruct the early history of this movement in light of what we now know of the second and first centuries B.C.

Some say that the Essene movement originated, as did the Sadducees and Pharisees, shortly after the time of Antiochus Epiphanes. This would place their origins in the midsecond century B.C., as yet another protest group against intense persecution and Hellenization in general.[5] On this view, a group of dissidents left Jerusalem and headed down to the shores of the Dead Sea to practice a life of dedication and extreme purity.

Another reconstruction locates their origin six or seven decades later, during the reign of Queen Salome Alexandra, 76–67 B.C. Perhaps this group arose out of disgruntled Sadducees who had become apoplectic with the Pharisaic takeover of the Temple and who, quite rightly, feared for their lives. It was payback time for the Pharisees, who had long suffered under the Sadducee yoke, and prominent leaders of this latter faction were by no means safe. In an interesting historical reconstruction, Michael O. Wise looks at the psalms that the Teacher of Righteousness wrote during a time of intense persecution.[6] It might well have been during this time that the Teacher of Righteousness fled Jerusalem, besieged by a wicked Pharisaic high priest. Over the decades, this renegade band of fearful Sadducees might have become transformed into the group that Josephus refers to as Essenes, an ascetic group living on the western shores of the Dead Sea, south of Jericho.

However they emerged as a distinctive group, their strategy for dealing with Hellenization was to *separate* from impurity and create a pure community of their own. To create a true community of the righteous—that was their ambitious objective.

We know more about the Essenes or Dead Sea Scroll community than the other groups because we now have their writings.[7] Following the advice of Isaiah, they "went out into the wilderness, to prepare the way of the Lord" (Isaiah 40:3). This setting in the wilderness of Judea provided an austere location for these dedicated and pious individuals to practice their religion, uncontaminated either by foreigners or by apostate Jews who had compromised their religion. Qumran, their headquarters, was located on a plateau overlooking the Dead Sea. Even today it is a strangely quiet place: no lapping of waves, not much traffic along the highway, and few birds chirping overhead. This settlement boasted a two-story tower and a walled settlement. Inside there were a number of rooms—a large multipurpose room for dining or for meetings, cooking areas and a pantry, a room identified as a "scriptorium" or place for writing, storage rooms, a stable, and many other rooms whose purposes cannot now be reconstructed. Inhabitants would have lived in tent shelters outside the main walled-in settlement.

Northward, on the rare clear day when the mist and haze of the Dead Sea lifts, we can see the settlement of Jericho and the Jordan River emptying into the quiet sea. Southward, behind a land mass jutting to the water's edge, lay the springs of Ein Gedi and, a few miles farther, the imposing fortress of Masada. A few springs near Qumran provided water, as did rainfall, which occurred only once or twice a year. Channels had been built by earlier inhabitants of Qumran to collect the rainwater from the cliffs above, directing it toward huge reservoirs interspersed throughout the settlement. Located about twenty miles east of Jerusalem, Qumran was just far enough away to be out of mind of the rulers, but not so far away as to prevent its members from keeping in touch with developments there. It would have been a two-day walk in antiquity up to the heights of Jerusalem from the floor of the Dead Sea, and one day back down the steep slope. While headquartered at Qumran, the members of this community had enclaves scattered throughout the land of Israel, including one in Jerusalem, entered through "the Essene Gate."

Their response to Hellenization was to live a righteous life according to Torah, strictly, as interpreted by their inspired leader, the Teacher of Righteousness. Their teacher's understanding of the biblical message represented, for them, the decisive meaning of scripture. They saw in ancient writings clear references to their times and events. An example from their commentary on the prophet Habakkuk illustrates how they applied scripture to their situation. Habakkuk was writing in the days just before the Babylonian Exile, around 600 B.C. When he wrote that the wicked are encompassing the righteous, Habakkuk had in mind the wicked of his own day—those who were not following the law and who were undermining the integrity of society, paving the way for Babylonian military success over Jerusalem and the Southern Kingdom. Sensing that disaster was again looming, however, the Teacher of Righteousness interpreted Habakkuk's words as applying to his own era some five hundred years later. Thus "the wicked" really referred to "the Wicked Priest," and "the righteous," to himself, "the Teacher of Righteousness."[8] Similarly, references by Habakkuk to the Babylonians on the move were interpreted by the Teacher of Righteousness as actually designating the Romans under whose sway the entire world would fall.

The Teacher of Righteousness was perceived by this movement as the one "to whom God made known all the mysteries of the words of His servants the Prophets."[9] This was their powerful weapon—an inspired teacher—and his words functioned very much like the oral law method did for the Pharisees. For his followers, the Teacher of Righteousness alone could ascertain the accurate interpretation of scripture and what it meant to be authentically Jewish.

Who was this influential Teacher of Righteousness? Amazingly—and frustratingly—we simply don't know. He would have been a priest, a writer, and an inspired leader who acted as a catalyst, bringing a group of individuals together who thought they were living in the last days. He taught, led, defended, and suffered on behalf of his community. He was not a Messiah, but he sought to prepare his people for life at the end of time when the Messiah would appear and God would transform the world. When he died, leadership was transferred to a "Master" supported by a council.

For the most part, other groups in society did not share their doom-and-gloom outlook. In particular, the Pharisees did not. Not everyone believed that the end of time was near or that the Messianic era was just around the corner.

The Dead Sea Scroll community parted ways with the Pharisees in other respects as well: a three-year training program (versus the Pharisees' two-year requirement) and sharing communal property. The Dead Sea Scroll group also vilified a movement they called "the seekers after smooth things" (4Q169, *Commentary on Nahum*), that is, those who sought compromise or accommodation. This is widely interpreted as referring to the Pharisees. If true, this would constitute another important point of difference. It is interesting to observe that whereas the Gospel writings present the Pharisees as strict interpreters of the law, the members of the Dead Sea Scroll community saw them as excessively lax and loose in their requirements.

The objective of the Dead Sea Scroll community was to create a community of the truly righteous who would uncompromisingly follow Jewish law. In a legal text referred to as 4QMMT,[10] they set forth more than twenty objections they had to the way sacrifices were being observed in the Temple by the Sadducees. They objected, for instance, to the use of Gentile grain in the sacrifices or vessels made from copper mined or fashioned by Gentiles. They contended that non-Jews should not be able to offer sacrifices in the Temple. Vessels made of the skins or bones of unclean animals should not be utilized in Temple offerings. Dogs should not be allowed inside Temple precincts. They rejected illicit marriages such as those between uncle and niece. Many of these laws had to do with preserving the sanctity and purity of the Temple and its rites, which they believed had been corrupted. Thus they very much detested the Sadducees and their policy of accommodating the foreign occupiers of the land.

Most importantly, these disputes show the extent of Hellenization within the Temple. Non-Jews were even permitted to offer sacrifices. Copper utensils for the Temple were manufactured by non-Jews. And the priests were using vessels made of pig skin. All of these practices represented illegal compromises as far as the members of the Dead Sea Scroll community were concerned.

We can imagine members of this pious sect devoting themselves to prayer, study, tending the goats and sheep, fetching fresh water, and writing. They were entirely certain they were on the right track, living life fully in accordance with God's instructions. They were contemptuous of their fellow Jews, whom they viewed as having abandoned the covenant, being co-conspirators with the occupiers, and placing in jeopardy all God's promises. For them, evil lurked everywhere—among the Romans, the Sadducees, the Pharisees, and ordinary Jews—and they had to be on their guard constantly. All these compromises had to be strenuously resisted.

By living at Qumran or in separate sections of towns and villages, the Essenes avoided many of the difficult problems caused by Hellenization. They did not have to meet or talk with the foreign occupiers. Issues of ritual purity, eating, or intermarriage did not crop up. Separation from the rest of society did not mean that the members of this community ceased from spiritual struggle, however. Rather, they saw themselves on the forefront of spiritual warfare, battling against the forces of evil that threatened the very fabric of society. The *Community Rule*, one of their writings, described how all humans are buffeted about by two spirits: the spirit of truth and the spirit of falsehood. People are called upon to make choices, to resist evil, and to choose the good. How a person decides through life determines his future. Those who have opted primarily for the spirit of truth throughout their lives have an amazing reward: "healing, great peace in a long life, and fruitfulness, together with every everlasting blessing and eternal joy in life without end, a crown of glory and a garment of majesty in unending light."[11]

Members of the Dead Sea Scroll community were prolific writers; manuscripts from over eight hundred different texts have been found and reconstructed. These comprise all the books of the Hebrew Bible (except the Book of Esther) as well as important noncanonical writings such as the *Book of Jubilees,* a treatise on understanding the phases of history. Their own writings included the *Community Rule,* a document outlining the procedures to be followed by this community; a *Temple Scroll,* which proposed modifications to the existing Temple in Jerusalem; a *War Scroll,* which envisaged a forty-year war against the unrighteous; a mysterious *Copper Scroll,* referring to huge deposits of buried treasure; along with many commentaries on biblical writings, psalms, and miscellaneous writings. They regarded themselves as living at the pivotal point in human history, and thus it was important to grasp the message of the Bible fully and completely. They thought they had this understanding.

The Dead Sea community did not survive the Roman onslaught, however. In A.D. 68, the Roman legions swooped down the Jordan Valley after having brutally crushed the Jewish rebellion in the Galilee. Qumran was destroyed, and presumably most of its inhabitants were killed. Some members may have fled to Jerusalem and others eventually to Masada farther south along the shores of the Dead Sea. Maybe some also escaped into Egypt. Prior to their demise, they hid their manuscripts in jar containers in a variety of caves around the plateau of Qumran.

There the scrolls remained until 1948 when the jars and their contents were accidentally discovered by a Bedouin boy. Gradually these manuscripts, along with others from different nearby caves, came to the attention of scholars. Whether all these manuscripts came from the Qumran community or whether some originated in Jerusalem is a matter of some scholarly dispute.[12] Many of the original members of the Scroll team were Roman Catholic, and they refused to share these documents with other experts in the field, notably Jewish scholars. Their secrecy and clandestine behavior gave rise to speculation that they were intentionally sitting on earth-shattering revelations that they wanted to hide. Perhaps, some speculated, they contained writings that would unseat Christian teachings. It was not until the early 1990s that the scrolls as a whole were made available to the public, and we can now see for ourselves what members of this ultraorthodox Jewish community were thinking.[13] Their importance—less startling than the conspiracy theorists would have it— lies primarily in helping us understand better the debates in Judaism in the first century B.C. and first century A.D.. That helps us significantly in making sense of the world in which both Rabbinic Judaism and early Christianity emerged.

THE ZEALOTS

Were they patriots? Or terrorists?

The Zealots originated later than the other movements. They emerged as a religious and political force as a result of taxation, in A.D. 6 under the leadership of Judas of Gamla (or, as he is also called, Judas of Galilee). Their response to Hellenization was straightforward: *fight*. Rid the land of foreign occupation and bring about the restoration of Israel as an autonomous state. Their focus was primarily political rather than narrowly religious. They probably lived in Jerusalem as well as throughout the land of Israel. Toward the end of their existence, they probably concentrated forces along the shores of the Dead Sea.

They looked forward to God acting decisively to bring about the end-time reconstruction of the world, whether directly through their efforts in military resistance or through the instrumentality of a Messiah. For them, the task of a Messiah was very clear: restore the fortunes of Israel and establish the Davidic king on the throne. Some Zealots may have formed an alliance with the members of the Dead Sea Scroll community. The aggressive *War Scroll* of the latter movement advocated many of the views Zealots would have approved of: the complete removal of foreigners from the land along with the complete eradication of the unrighteous from the face of the earth. Judas Iscariot, one of the original disciples of Jesus, may have been a Zealot. Probably other disciples of Jesus were as well.

The Zealots were eventually defeated by the Romans at Masada four years after Jerusalem was destroyed. According to Josephus's dramatic account, as the Roman armies encircled this towering mesa high above the floor of the Dead Sea, close to one thousand Zealots committed suicide rather than be taken captive by Rome. As Josephus expressed it in *The Jewish War* (Book 7, 386), Eleazar, their leader, urged his followers to live and die as free men. That was preferable to Roman enslavement and the rape of their wives and female children. After building a road from the ground level up to the heights of Masada, the Romans arrived only to find everyone dead. Only a couple of women and children lived to tell their tale.[14]

SURVIVAL STRATEGIES

So how did a subjugated, colonized minority tackle ethnic and religious survival? How could the covenant and Jewish law coexist with the challenges and realities of the Hellenistic world? As we have seen, the various factions within Judaism proposed different answers and sparred with one another over the correct strategy. Most of the differences had to do with how much of the surrounding culture one could appropriate without ceasing to be Jewish.

The Sadducees were probably the least threatened, favoring cultural interaction so long as Temple sacrifices were not interfered with by Roman authority. For them, accommodation and cooperation with the occupiers was the best policy, to ensure peace and maximize opportunities on the world stage. Putting down revolts and carefully containing would-be Messiahs were very much in their best interests. In their view, these precautionary activities also served the general well-being of the Jewish community as a whole, helping the Romans maintain peace and stability.

Pharisees, on the other hand, believed that the populace could be educated into observance and that this would form a barrier around Jewish culture, preventing assimilation and ultimate extinction. In a sense, this would build a fence around cultural assimilation, shielding the Torah-observant Jew from practices that would lead to eventual Hellenization. This was the start of a long-standing strategy that worked itself into Rabbinic Judaism, with education acting as a hedge around later pressures to assimilate.

By way of contrast, the members of the Dead Sea Scroll community simply separated themselves from close contact with foreigners and from nonobservant Jews, being intent upon preserving a pure community fully devoted to the observance of Torah without reference to the social and political dynamics of the larger world. They took seriously the injunction to prepare a way for the Lord in the wilderness, fully expecting that he would appear and act to bring about the new world order. They aimed at being the community of righteousness that would spark the time of the end.

For the Zealots, the strategy was much simpler: resist and fight the Roman occupiers.

All Jewish groups agreed upon keeping the law. No one had yet suggested that the Torah be abandoned—except Antiochus Epiphanes, who had tried to outlaw Judaism.

Four main strategies for dealing with the challenge of Hellenization had emerged by the first century A.D.: *accommodate and compromise* (Sadducees), *teach* (Pharisees), *separate* (Dead Sea Scroll community), and *fight* (Zealots). These strategies set the parameters that affected Jewish daily life with non-Jews, establishing the boundaries and rules for social interaction. A particularly sensitive area was eating—the types of permissible foods, whether Jews and Gentiles could eat together, using common utensils and plates—for these questions went to the heart of the dietary and purity laws.

Another pressing area concerned the observance of the Sabbath, especially in the larger towns and cities where Roman practice did not include this particular day of rest. There were constant pressures to cut corners, for merchants to engage in trade, for people to provide accommodations, food, and other resources for troops and families on the move. Intermarriage, too, was always a threat, as was loose sexual morality, which could affect the fabric of family life. Education also posed problems for the wealthier families who could afford this—to what extent should study time be divided between the study of biblical materials versus the literary productions of Greek and Roman culture? Would education lead to cultural assimilation?

Overarching everything was the whole question of Torah observance, including the belief in one God. What did this mean in a world dominated by an extremely powerful society and its occupying army? How was compliance possible? Indeed, in such times, how could a fair God in charge of world history expect such observance?

In time, three more strategies for dealing with a dominant powerful culture and the threat of assimilation were added. John the Baptist emphasized *rededication to Torah*. Jesus proclaimed an innovative two-fold strategy: *strict Torah observance* coupled with preparing for a *new world order*—the long-awaited Kingdom of God that Jesus thought would materialize soon. Paul adopted a different route, effectively affirming *assimilation* into the Gentile world without any pretense at Torah observance whatsoever. His solution was the abandonment of Judaism, giving in to Hellenistic pressures.

All Judaisms of the time were political. At stake was continued Jewish identity and survival in the face of unrelenting Hellenization. Debates were fierce. If a teacher were to come on the scene and say "Love your neighbor," that injunction was not neutral. It would immediately raise questions. Who is my neighbor? some might ask. Does "my neighbor" include the occupying Romans? others would pointedly and disdainfully inquire. The Zealots would certainly have disregarded such a teacher—their objective was to rid the land of hated foreigners, so they would not have accepted a message of loving one's neighbor if that included Romans. Leaders of the Dead Sea Scroll community also would have rejected this message—they urged hatred of enemies such as the Romans.[15]

There were probably many different kinds of submovements within each faction, much as there are within political parties today. Not all Sadducees were wealthy, for instance, and probably not all Pharisees were popular teachers.

There may have been many groups of Zealots, unaffiliated with one another, but sharing the same common objective. In this instance, we know of a sub-group of Zealots, the Sicarii, who used a small dagger to murder their opponents. And there may have been many other subsidiary movements among the other factions. These descriptions must be taken as true for the most part, as broad generalizations of complex movements over a two-hundred-year period responding to the pressures of Hellenization. The same would be true if two thousand years hence we were to characterize political parties of our time. Some nuances, important to us, might be missing.

But what of the mass of the people? To what faction did they belong? Probably most were unaffiliated, intent upon making a basic living, doing the best for their children, providing modest shelter, and having sufficient food to eat. These were preoccupations that would consume the waking hours for most families, leaving little time for religious reflection and social strategizing. Probably most were confused about but likely aware of the main positions of the Pharisees and Dead Sea Scroll community and, later on, the aggressive policies of the Zealots. They also knew who was running the show in Jerusalem— the Sadducees along with their benefactors, the Greeks and Romans. Never before in Jewish history had such an array of religious and political alternatives existed. There were choices among a variety of non-Jewish religions as well as options within Judaism itself. Most must have felt that they lived in confusing times.

So where was certainty to be found? Surely someone had to know "the truth." Did scripture perhaps contain *hidden* meanings?

4

THE SECRETS OF HISTORY

On the surface, everything seemed quiet. Beneath the facade of Judaism in the first century B.C., however, other groups were busily pursuing a very different agenda. The Sadducees were doing business as normal, making sure that the Temple establishment was operating smoothly and efficiently while keeping the Roman occupiers satisfied. While this was going on, however, others were deeply troubled about the state of the religion as a whole. The Pharisees, too, went about operating their schools, debating the meaning of Torah and interpreting it to accommodate new situations. But others wondered if they were focusing on the really important issues. We have no name for these "others" who functioned below the radar, but we do know their outlook and forecast for the future. These were the worst of times, they contended, and these searchers for certainty started advancing a doom-and-gloom scenario and developing a plan of action based on this pessimistic outlook. They were small groups, not connected and, from what we can tell, not well organized—virtually cults without much clout. They began to search the ancient scriptures for clues about the truth of the times in which they lived.

These disgruntled individuals were also beginning to move beyond the Model of the Two Ways, promoting a highly activist agenda. For them, what it meant to be Jewish in Hellenistic times had taken a radical new twist. They favored different writings, entertained much higher expectations, and above all, approached life with a fierce mind-set. They wanted change . . . and they believed that God was just about to act. These were never mainstream movements—most of the Judaisms of the time did not endorse their thoughts—and so it is not surprising that their ideas and writings did not make it into the Hebrew Bible in a major way when it became fashioned by the Pharisees.

Nonetheless, these cults developed a significant body of literature alongside the growing, more accepted, canon of the Torah, Prophets and Writings. Their titles included *1 Enoch, Jubilees, Testaments of the Twelve Patriarchs, Psalms of Solomon, Testament of Moses, Apocalypse of Zephaniah,* and dozens of other writings.[1] All these writings circulated within the two hundred years prior to the destruction of the Temple and survive to this day.

Devout people pored over writings such as these as they tried to discern God's likely actions during these dreadful times. Readers thought that they were gaining "the inside scoop" on history. Bizarre images, eclectic visions, and strange allusions abound in these works. We hear of weird dreams, opaque visions, various layers of heaven, and strange human-animal beasts. This unfamiliar imagery makes for difficult reading today because the dense language cloaks historical events and personages. We do not know much about the people behind these writings. Who were they? Did they collaborate or meet to discuss these ideas? Did they share a unified outlook on the future? How did they produce these arcane writings? How did these writings circulate and how extensively? How large a group were they and where were they concentrated? Did their subversive outlook boil over into overt anti-Roman activities?

Some contemporary mass media Christian preachers purport to provide followers with a timetable for God's actions, scanning the Hebrew prophets and the end-time portions of the New Testament for signs of our times. These teachers locate the end-time within our generation. Most view the formation of the State of Israel in 1948 with the return of the Jewish people from around the globe and the resurgence of Hebrew as a living language as indicators that redemption is at hand. They contend that we are about to experience tremendous world tribulation and awful disasters on a scale never before imagined. War will break out and nations from the North, East, and South will descend upon the tiny Jewish State of Israel, an area not much larger than the State of New Jersey. Some speculate on the identity of these marauding nations. Russia to the north and Iran to the east of Israel are among the top contemporary contenders. Some also predict when the armies of the nations of the earth will march on Jerusalem. Then, in the midst of horrible bloodshed, Jesus will return swiftly in glory to establish the Kingdom of God in perpetuity. This is the dramatic future these contemporary preachers envisage will happen on earth shortly.[2]

Like them, the readers of these ancient underground writings believed they were gaining insight into when God would decisively act to change human circumstances. Their favorite scrolls never entered anyone's Bible. But in their heyday—200 B.C. to A.D. 100—they were influential among groups of devout Jews who wished for something better than what the Hellenistic world had to offer: nothing less than God's sovereign rule over the whole earth.

KNOWING GOD'S AGENDA

Imagine an interview with a panel of these writers.

"And why do you think these are the worst times ever?"

They would probably have cited many indicators that the social environment had changed for the worse. The prevalence of Hellenization and its "in your face" presence reinforced daily the degree to which non-Jews were running the country. The threat of cultural assimilation was everywhere, from the ideas that were current to the food one ate. For many it meant having to speak or at least understand a different language, interfacing with foreign government officials or talking or socializing with people who shared a radically different perspective on life. These "superior" people did not follow—or understand—the mores of Jewish law and were contemptuous of it. The demands of Hellenization were part of the fabric of everyday life, annoying and causing dismay for those who thought that the world should be dramatically different.

"And why does this bother you so much?"

They might very well have pointed to the sacred Temple, with officials running this establishment with the connivance of foreigners whose troops were less than a block away, ready to put a quick end to any dissent. Gentiles fresh from the worship of other deities were evident in the sacred precincts, offering their sacrifices to God. This dripped with sacrilege, for they were equating the Jewish God with Zeus, Dionysus, and other deities.

In addition, in the background of their minds there lurked the constant underlying dread of yet another bout of enforced Hellenization that would ban the practice of Judaism. The specter of Antiochus Epiphanes had not been forgotten. Could it happen again? they asked. Would it happen again—to us, here, now?

"Is it just a matter of foreigners on your soil? If they were all to leave, would things improve for you?"

Probably not. It was not just a matter of foreign rule. There were also internal concerns, how to interpret the law correctly. A cold war between Sadducees and Pharisees had not helped the situation either, with members of these factions at one another's throats. Real civil war, of course, had occurred early in the first century B.C., in the time of Alexander Jannaeus. He massacred Pharisees and they had had their payback revenge during the time of Queen Salome. Times were brutal and far from what God intended for his people. The threat of enforced Hellenization had unleashed a powerful dynamic within Judaism: vigorous religious debate over the meaning of Torah.

"Is the solution, then, to follow Torah strictly?"

If this were to occur on a community basis, with everyone obeying all of the law all of the time, then perhaps everything would eventually be fine. A community of righteousness was a vision that some, like the members of the Dead Sea Scroll community, entertained. They recognized, however, that for all Jews everywhere, this solution was highly unrealistic. There had to be a different solution, and these underground biblical activists thought they had detected what it was. God needed a hand. There had to be a catalyst, something that would push God over the edge. They thought they had identified this catalyst: the period of time in human history when evil had reached its zenith—the absolute worst of times. Surely, they speculated, this would represent the tipping point. God would have cause to act. Moreover, they were confident that they were living at just that period in human history: the time of the greatest evil imaginable. There had been Antiochus Epiphanes' assault on Judaism and massive persecution of devout Torah-observant people. Then there had been brutal foreign occupation, political subjugation, religious confusion, behavioral compromises, and apostasy away from the covenant and the law. The catalyst had occurred, they speculated, and they would be front-row witnesses to world transformation. This gave them the inside track on understanding the era in which they lived. They knew what was about to happen.

"And what do you think the future holds?"

Terrible times, they would have answered—horrible wars, disease, famines, plagues, devastation, enormous pain and suffering on an unimaginable scale. But this was not cause for despair but for hope, that this was the catalyst for divine intervention. After this dreadful time, there would be a marvelous future for the truly righteous. God, they thought, would set things right.

This was their hoped-for solution, that God himself would re-create the world. These ancient activists rummaged around in the ancient sacred texts and found passages that they thought shed light upon their plight. They seized on these to discern the true nature of the times in which they were living and what it presaged. Here are some of the texts they would have found insightful.

CLUES FROM ISAIAH

Portions of the Isaiah scroll would probably have leapt off the pages. Writing toward the end of the Babylonian Exile, probably around 539 B.C., there was a prophet we now call Second Isaiah. His words are found in our present Book of Isaiah, chapters 40–55.[3] This prophet proclaimed a return of exiles from Babylonian captivity where they had been ever since the deportations some fifty years earlier. Declaring that Babylonian rule was about to end, he roused the exiles into action. A "Messiah," he declared, Cyrus the Great, was about to conquer the Babylonian Empire and allow captive minorities to return to their homelands, Jews included. He thought that the Jewish exiles would be overjoyed at the news and would leap into action, ready to pack their bags and return.

Well, not so fast. Cyrus the Great did issue a proclamation allowing the Jewish captives to return to Jerusalem. But some fifty years had passed. The exiles had made a life for themselves in the new land. Two generations had come and gone and very few old folks remained who could remember and reminisce about the "good times" back there in Jerusalem. Moreover, the exiles had not been slaves in Babylonia. They earned a living and had formed their own social institutions. We know from ancient Babylonian records—the Murashu texts— that some, in fact, had become wealthy by becoming involved in banking and financial institutions. The Babylonian authorities had placed no restrictions on their livelihood, just their movement. Up until the conquest of Cyrus, they were not free to return to Jerusalem. But did they really want to return to the land of their grandparents, or possibly even great-grandparents? How many Americans today would like to return to the land of their ancestors? Second Isaiah probably got the same reaction. Disinterest.

Nonetheless, Isaiah painted a marvelous picture of a great destiny, and it represents one of the most magnificent public relations releases in history. All nations, he said, will see the glory of the Jewish God. The desert will blossom, blessed by the Lord. People will return from all directions—from the East, the West, even from Egypt. Dispersed groups will eagerly wend their way back up to Jerusalem. It will be rebuilt, he said, its Temple, homes, and walls. It will be a glorious and prosperous time: the wealth of nations, he confidently predicted, will flow into Jerusalem. And, best of all, the whole world will come to acknowledge the supremacy of God.

Some exiles did return, and the Book of Psalms records a moving song as they euphorically approached Jerusalem: "When the Lord restored the fortunes of Zion, we were like those who dream" (Psalm 126:1). This was a glorious time, the first sight of Jerusalem high on its hill for the returning exiles who had spent many weeks or even months in transit from Babylonia. They were undoubtedly overwhelmed by emotion as they beheld the city their grandparents had romanticized. The returning exiles faced tremendous problems, however: a temple in ruins, protective walls and towers in shambles, former properties confiscated and used by those citizens of Jerusalem who had not gone into exile, a ruined economy, agriculture in disarray, and little by way of centralized authority to plan rebuilding. Tensions must have run high between the returning exiles and those who had remained in Jerusalem during this period. They had undergone different experiences for several generations, and those who had remained in Jerusalem probably did not welcome an influx of families who had been gone for decades. Many exiles, moreover, chose not to return but stayed in Babylonia and Egypt. They had made a life for themselves, albeit as resident aliens, and they probably could not envisage any compelling reason to abandon it for Jerusalem, much in the same way many Jews today in the Diaspora—in the United States, Canada, or Britain—cannot conceive of leaving their established lives to move to an uncertain future in Israel.

Slightly later, another prophet would look toward a new era in human history and a re-creation of the universe. His words are also attached to the Book of Isaiah (chapters 56–66) and scholars refer to him as Third Isaiah. On behalf of God, he speaks movingly of better times:

> For I am about to create new heavens and a new earth; the former things shall not be remembered or come to mind. But be glad and rejoice forever in what I am creating; for I am about to create Jerusalem as a joy, and its people as a delight. . . . They shall not labor in vain, or bear children for calamity; for they shall be offspring blessed by the Lord—and their descendants as well. . . . The wolf and the lamb shall feed together. (Isaiah 65:17–25)

Some four or five hundred years later, people could well wonder what happened to these confident predictions. Where was this transformed world they had been led to believe would come? Where was the peace with "wolf and lamb feeding together"? Where were the promised blessings that Third Isaiah had so eloquently envisioned? What had gone wrong? The times were not as promised. There were still Jews dispersed in other lands, probably in many more places in the first century B.C. than at the time of the Babylonian Exile—not just in Babylonia but also in Turkey, Greece, Italy, Spain, the northern shores of Africa, and Egypt. They had been lured there by jobs, trade, and diplomatic ties. The wealth of nations had not flowed into Jerusalem. More to the point, the world had not seen the glory of God. In Hellenistic times, with its array of religious choices, the world seemed farther away than ever in acknowledging the supremacy of the one God. Political independence did not exist, and Jewish religious institutions were carefully monitored by the occupying foreign forces.

Something clearly had gone wrong. To what could Second and Third Isaiah be referring? Did they have in mind the time immediately following the Babylonian Exile? Or, as these detectives from the first century B.C. suspected, could these writings be referring to later times? This insight provided a startling clue.

CLUES FROM DEUTERONOMY

More scriptures had to be searched. Some found enlightening passages toward the end of Deuteronomy. Here Moses urged the people of Israel to remain faithful to the covenant by following the Torah, not only those present at his time of speaking but also "those who are not here with us today" (Deuteronomy 29:15), that is, those who will come in the future and who are similarly bound by the agreement. He warned the people that if they failed to follow the laws, dire consequences would come upon them. He cautioned them against heeding what he called "a root spouting poisonous and bitter growth . . . who think we are safe even though we go our own stubborn ways" (Deuteronomy 29:18–19). Whatever he meant by this "bitter root," Moses' point was clear. An ignorant attitude that condoned laxness in Torah observance would only bring about calamity, devastation, and afflictions. Abandoning the covenant was not a solution, he cautioned.

Reading back into this text, some saw in the terrible events of the second and first centuries B.C. the consequences of this bitter root. Leaders of society had led them astray, bringing about the loss of political sovereignty and the threat of cultural assimilation. These leaders were the bitter root Moses had spoken of. For these dissidents, the threats of Hellenization imperiled their very existence and their future as inhabitants of a re-created world. The cozy compromising policy of the Sadducees was not the right tactic, they thought. Nor were the sound teachings of the Pharisees the only effective strategy for shielding people from the consequences of their own folly. They found comfort in Moses' words, which assured them that "the secret things belong to the Lord our God, but the revealed things belong to us and to our children forever, to observe all the words of this law" (Deuteronomy 29:29).

Maybe the Babylonian Exile had not truly ended, even though biblical historians today consider the exile to have ended after Cyrus the Great assumed the throne, allowing minorities to return, some people in the second and first centuries B.C. wondered if this really was the case. The signs were not really there: universal return of the exiles, the exalted international status for Israel, and worldwide acknowledgment of the God of Israel. None of these events had occurred. So maybe, they thought, the exile was ongoing.

These texts raised exciting new possibilities for these biblical detectives. Maybe they were referring to future events. Could they, in fact, be referring to the times in which they lived? Were they themselves living in the end-times?

What is to be made about Deuteronomy's references to "secret" and "revealed" things? Where were these to be found? What "revealed things"? What was God's timetable for human history?

CLUES FROM ZECHARIAH

Further clues could be found toward the end of the Book of Zechariah. We don't know much about this visionary, but the latter chapters of the book that bears his name appear to come from Hellenistic times. Whoever he was, his views became tremendously influential as he staked out the end-time scenario. In a series of powerful pronouncements in chapters 12, 13, and 14, his voice thunders about what will happen "on that day" (Zechariah 12:3, 4, 6, 8, 9, 13).[4] Over and over he repeats that phrase, referring to that tremendous earth-shaking time when God will truly make good on his promises to Israel and bring about a dramatically changed world. Zechariah envisaged warfare that would eventually culminate in triumph for the forces of righteousness. Nations will come against Jerusalem: "On that day I will make Jerusalem a heavy stone for all the peoples . . . And all the nations of the earth shall come together against it" (Zechariah 12:3). These nations will ultimately be destroyed, but not without significant cost in Jewish lives. Through this process, Jerusalem will be cleansed. Then the Lord God himself will appear on the Mount of Olives, just east of Jerusalem across the Kidron Valley from Temple Mount: "On that day, his feet [God's] shall stand on the Mount of Olives . . . and [it] shall be split in two from east to west by a very wide valley" (Zechariah 14:4). Fresh water will flow out of Jerusalem toward the East down to the shores of the Dead Sea and to the West, out toward the Mediterranean. All the mountains will be flattened except for the two hills on which Jerusalem is built.

Other major changes will occur. Jews from the Diaspora—from Egypt, Lebanon, Babylonia, and from around the Mediterranean Basin—will return. Zechariah confidently predicted that when this happens—"on that day"—human history will culminate in the universal worship of the one God: "the Lord will become king over all the earth; on that day the Lord will be one and his name one" (Zechariah 14:9). Survivors of the nations of the world, he asserted, will trek annually up to Jerusalem, "to worship the King, the Lord of hosts, and to keep the festival of Booths" (Zechariah 14:16). The festival of Booths refers to Succoth. It commemorates the wanderings of the Israelites in the desert after the escape from Egypt, a time when they were vulnerable to forces of nature as well as hostile tribes. In essence, it celebrates God's protection against overwhelming odds, and this theme ties in with Zechariah's depiction of the gratitude of the people for divine deliverance "on that day."

Zechariah's powerful vision established the main parameters of Israel's eschatological or end-time vision. As he presented the scenario, there were three phases to the time of the end. This established the agenda for divine intervention. First of all, there had to be a period of extraordinary evil—enormous pain and suffering with massive bloodshed and political turmoil. It would have to be a time when things had become so dreadful that there was absolutely no alternative other than God intervening directly in world history. After this, in the second phase, God would act decisively to bring about a dramatic transformation of the world. In Zechariah's vision, there was no provision for a Messiah: God himself would act directly, with evil defeated and swept away from earth. Finally, a new regime would emerge: the righteous would be rewarded, evildoers punished, and the righteous dead restored to life. This final "just desserts" phase would represent the high point of human history, a whole new chapter in our development. The glorious outcome would be that humanity would live in universal peace under one God, with Jerusalem and its Temple preeminent. This threefold end-time model surfaces time and time again as people in many generations—both ancient and modern—look for insider information.

So *when* will all this come about? Certainly for some living in Israel during Hellenistic times, it would appear as if the nations of the world had come to Jerusalem. Moreover, there had been significant bloodshed, persecutions, sexual immorality, and loose observances of the Torah. Clearly these were enormously evil days. Surely these signs pointed to the time of "the end," some speculated, along with imminent world transformation.

CLUES FROM THE BOOK OF 1 ENOCH

An influential writing that lies outside the canon of the Hebrew Bible or Old Testament was *1 Enoch*. Again, like Zechariah, we know nothing about the author of this influential work. Dating from sometime in the second century B.C., after Antiochus Epiphanes' persecutions, Book II of this work looks forward to the appearance of a "congregation of the righteous" (*1 Enoch* 38:1).[5] This was an important sign, for the appearance of this unique community would trigger significant world events.

As Enoch saw it, this will be a great time for the righteous. They will triumph over the wicked and be rewarded with eternal life. The righteous dead will be resurrected. The wicked will be punished, forfeiting eternal life. So justice will be done. More than that, Israel will become the preeminent state, with Jerusalem the predominant city. God will be worshipped by all humanity. This is the redemption long awaited. Enoch's vision was consistent with that expressed by Zechariah and reinforced the expectation that God was about to intervene.

HOPES AND DREAMS

For some outside mainstream Judaism, the appeal of having access to secret information was vital. In the first century B.C., members of the Dead Sea Scroll community, for instance, thought that they, and they alone, possessed precisely this. Their Teacher of Righteousness, they contended, possessed true insight into the times. He alone knew God's clock. Of that they were confident as the members of this reclusive society went about their daily routine of work, study, and prayer. In the midst of uncertainty and great temptations, these people knew what would happen. Their insider perspective on the scriptures gave them the clue, and this provided them with a firm anchor for daily living.

Interpreting some of the psalms from the Dead Sea Scroll community as autobiographical, Michael O. Wise points out that the Teacher of Righteousness claimed to understand the dynamics of world history.[6] This inspired leader knew that the time when God would establish his sovereign rule over all humanity was at hand. In one hymn, the Teacher of Righteousness talked about his role as a "banner" to the righteous, a seer who could discern "marvellous mysteries." In the *Community Rule*, the inspired leader of the movement sang a song that affirmed,

> *My eyes have gazed on that which is eternal*
> *On wisdom concealed from men,*
> *On knowledge and wise design*
> *(hidden) from the sons of men.*[7]

He was surrounded by enemies who wanted to kill him, because he upheld the covenant. He criticized the Pharisees for leading the people astray, saying that they speak "smooth things" to the people. Jesus, too, in time would also criticize the Pharisees for their convenient interpretations of the law, making exceptions where none should exist. The Teacher of Righteousness had nothing but contempt for them: as he says, he will have "no pity on those who depart from the way."

A number of groups within Israel found comfort in this eschatological vision, holding out hope that the world would soon be a dramatically different place. They shared a common dream. Hellenization would disappear. The wicked would be gone and everyone would worship the one God in peace. Most importantly, they, the righteous ones, would live eternally. Such was the vision of the members of the Dead Sea Scroll community. Several fragments from the Dead Sea Scrolls make clear that they thought they owned the key to understanding history. These writings refer to knowing "the secret of the way things are" (4Q417 Fragment 2 + 4Q418, column 1). This secret refers to the time when evil will vanish and the righteous will be established forever, when those who are truly righteous will inherit eternal joy without end.[8]

But there were others as well who reveled in this great end-time dream. This included devout Jews unaligned with any faction who delved into this underground literature, savoring its insights. Zealots shared these expectations, and for them, insights had to give way to actions, to force God's hand in getting rid of the Roman colonizers. Others who entertained the end-time dream included John the Baptist, Jesus, Jesus' brother James, as well as the members of the early Jesus Movement in Jerusalem. For all these people, the reign of God was just around the corner. What's more, many confidently expected they would live to see it all happen.

There was a catch, however. For most groups, everything depended on keeping the law. That explains why the members of the Dead Sea Scroll sect left Jerusalem and relocated to the Judean wilderness, down by the shores of the Dead Sea. They went there partly to escape the contamination of Hellenization in Jerusalem so that they could keep all of the law all of the time. They also went out into the wilderness, in fulfillment of the command through Isaiah "in the wilderness prepare the way of the Lord, make straight in the desert a highway for our God" (Isaiah 40:3). This highway they interpreted as the study of the Torah.[9]

I think, too, that they went out to the shores of the Dead Sea in literal fulfillment of Zechariah's prophecy that "on that day," the Mount of Olives will be split in two and water will flow from Jerusalem toward the West and East. The hills of Judea are best imagined as a sheet of corrugated cardboard. The two hills on which Jerusalem sits are the highest points, with other rolling mountains tapering off as one descends eastward into the Jordan Valley. If the Mount of Olives were to split in half and water were to flow out of Jerusalem, then going east, this river would cascade down the slopes toward the shores of the Dead Sea hundreds of feet below sea level. This would have the effect of creating a new Garden of Eden. Perhaps the members of the Dead Sea Scroll community thought that they had snagged the best address outside Jerusalem in the world to come.

One law was of overriding importance. Quoting the prophet Malachi (Malachi 1:10), the *Damascus Document* of the Dead Sea Scroll community urged members not to "enter the Temple to light his altar in vain."[10] Better to have no sacrifices than ones that were improperly offered. Because members of this community had a solar calendar, unlike the Sadducees who followed a lunar one, every sacrifice in the Temple in Jerusalem was being offered improperly. *Nothing* was being done right. Of special importance in this connection were the observances of Yom Kippur, the solemn Day of Atonement, when collectively the sins of Israel against God would be forgiven by him. With this festival celebrated on the wrong day (as the members of the Dead Sea Scroll movement maintained, due to the wrong calendar the Sadducees followed), the whole community was mired in sin, to its utter detriment. Hence they charged members to "take care to act according to the exact interpretation of the Law during the age of wickedness."[11]

So, this truly was "the age of wickedness." That was how these people viewed the world in which they lived. And that triggered fantastic expectations. From selected passages in their ancient writings, they knew what was about to happen. The pressing question, however, was when. When would these events take place? Zechariah had simply said "on that day." Enoch looked for a "congregation of the righteous" to appear. The Dead Sea Scroll community, perceiving themselves to be in the vanguard of history, thought that world transformation was just around the corner. Jesus said "soon." Everybody wanted a timetable.

Strict Torah observance mattered. Nothing less than the end of Hellenization and experiencing world transformation was at stake. Nothing could be of greater consequence.

THE ROAD MAP TO VICTORY

How would these times come about? Zechariah thought that God himself would intervene in human history to create world transformation. Enoch attributed change partially to a heavenly being he called "the Lord of the Spirits" (*1 Enoch* 38:4; 39:7–10). Others thought that a human leader would emerge, a Messiah, who would play a role in God's liberating people both politically and religiously. The Dead Sea Scroll community looked either for one leader or possibly two Messiahs—one priestly and one military—who would work with God in bringing about the new world order. Still others thought that angels rather than a Messiah would be involved in leading the transition team.

The Jewish belief in a Messiah grows out of this vision of what will happen when God establishes his rule over all humanity. The focus, however, is on *what* will happen during this great new era in human history, not on the instrument by which it would be achieved. This means that hope for a Messiah represents a marginal issue for Judaism. The concept of the Messiah is clearly subordinate to eschatology, that is, to *what* will transpire at the end-time when God will intervene in human history to re-create the world. The *what* was the important component of the expectation, not *who* would bring it about or *how* it would occur. Whether by God acting alone, through the agency of one or more Messiahs or with the assistance of angels, these devout Jews expected world transformation within their lifetime. Nothing less.

There is perhaps no clearer exposition of the Jewish idea of the Messiah than in the work from the first century B.C., the *Psalms of Solomon*. This document is not the Book of Psalms found within the Bible, but a separate and later writing. Written sometime after the Roman invasion of Israel in 63 B.C., this moving document takes us through an eyewitness account of the dreadful happenings that occurred in Jerusalem. Terrible events—that, you will recall, triggered the first phase of the end-time scenario. The awful events of the Roman conquest stirred up bitter remembrances of the great persecutions of Antiochus Epiphanes a hundred years earlier. The Romans had broken down the walls of Jerusalem with a battering ram. They had invaded the Temple, arrogantly trampling upon sacred ground. They did "in Jerusalem all the things that gentiles do for their gods in their cities" (*Psalms of Solomon* 17:14). Even worse, some Jerusalemites followed their example and desecrated the Temple. Some people became enslaved, and everywhere sexual immorality was evident as young Jewish women cavorted with Roman troops. Rape, prostitution, looting, stealing food, begging, famine—disruption to the social fabric was the norm. Obviously these were evil times. Having documented that these are the worst of times, we know where the story is headed.

In a time such as this, the writer of the *Psalms of Solomon* went on to say, echoing Zechariah and *1 Enoch* before him, surely God can be relied on to act. His vision was that the Lord Messiah will appear and become the Davidic king over Israel. He will assist God in purging Jerusalem of Gentiles. The world will be rid of unrighteous rulers, thus ending the problem of Hellenization. The righteous who have persevered will be vindicated. They will live to see God worshipped in a place high above the earth, and nations will flock to Jerusalem to see God's glory. This represents a familiar refrain for those who know the end-time clues from *1 Enoch*, Zechariah, and Isaiah.

What a Messiah must accomplish is formidable. He must help overthrow foreign authority, establish an independent Jewish state, be the Davidic king and, with God's help, usher in an era of universal peace, establishing the universal rule of God, the Kingdom of God. During this time, the wicked will be eradicated and the righteous will be rewarded. The righteous dead will suddenly reappear. The world will experience a peace never before realized, and all humanity will acknowledge and worship the one true God. This was the messianic dream of ancient Israel, and it had fantastic appeal. It represented a way out of truly dreadful times, bringing an end to all the social pressures of Hellenization and giving people a reason to hope . . . and be righteous.

In Jewish terms, a Messiah is a leader anointed by God to act as an agent or political catalyst, to assist in bringing about God's rule. Most messianic expectations were that the Messiah would be human: he would be born and he would die.[12] He would not have a special birth,[13] and, while a righteous individual, he would not be a divine being. He would have to be a political leader, as a descendant of David, who would help establish the supremacy of Israel. God would work through him in bringing about this wonderful new era in human history. The world would be a dramatically different place as a result of his efforts. Anyone living at the time would be able to detect tremendous changes in the political and religious structures of the world after the Messiah appeared.

The devout people who knew in their hearts that they held the key to world history were uncompromising radicals. They saw the world simplistically, in clear black-and-white terms: the righteous versus the unrighteous, saints versus sinners, good people versus evildoers, true followers of Judaism versus Hellenizers. The growth of a "dualistic" mind-set was significant, for it pitted one segment of the Jewish community against all others. If you are not seriously for the covenant, or understand it differently, then you are its enemy. From this perspective, there was no room for compromise in confronting the perils of Hellenization.

It is a familiar battle, one that we see in our day as people within Judaism, Christianity, Islam, and other world religions become threatened by secularity, modernity, and religious pluralism. For Jews, it can mean shunning the world and becoming holed up in the minutiae of *halakhah*, that is, interpretations of Jewish law. For Christians, it usually takes the form of biblical literalism and shouting proof texts at nonbelievers without taking into account the social, historical, and literary contexts of biblical writings. For Islam, it expresses itself through a fundamentalist and militant rejection of all that is modern. The root of the crisis is the same, however: an inability to combine one's religious outlook with modern beliefs and practices in a pluralistic society. This was the plight of many in the first centuries B.C. and A.D. who could not tolerate a multicultural, religiously diverse society.

The spirituality of these ancient and modern groups is absolutist, that is, they hold firmly to the view that there is one and only one correct religion. Furthermore, these dogmatists maintain, there is one and only one correct interpretation of that religion—theirs. Such a spirituality has the effect of locking people into the prison of their own perspective, impervious to the views of others and preventing growth by savoring alternative ideas. The claim to a monopoly on religious truth constitutes an effective defensive position, however, setting up a shield against argument and discussion. But it also impairs the person holding such a view. It shuts down the ability to consider competing claims to religious insight and destiny, hampering a person's intellectual and spiritual growth.

Tremendous dreams and deeply felt hopes were attached to those who shared the vision of a radically transformed world—all the nameless devout Jewish people who produced these mysterious writings, members of the Dead Sea Scroll community, Zealots, and the Jesus Movement in Jerusalem. So while the Sadducees were plying their trade with the Romans at their side and the Pharisees were running schools, others were busily preparing for nothing less than total world transformation. They knew they were right and that secularism, pluralism, multiculturalism, and alternative religious expressions were wrong. For them, the approaches of the Sadducees and Pharisees were far too accommodating. Accurate Torah interpretation was a matter of ultimate concern. For these true believers, absolutely *everything* depended on it.

So, for these cult members, God had a plan for Israel and for all humanity. He had conveyed this through the prophets—Moses, Isaiah, Zechariah, and

Enoch, among others. It was there for all to see, and they had uncovered it. Maybe, some likely thought, there was a conspiracy. Perhaps the leaders of Jewish society, the Sadducees and the Pharisees, were engaged in a cover-up. Very likely they knew the times—that it was the age of wickedness—but were just not prepared to share this insight with the rest of their society. More likely, the Sadducees and Pharisees just didn't pay attention to these end-time speculations, which, admittedly, were couched in extremely vague language: "an age of wickedness," "on that day," "a community of righteousness," a new world coming "soon." If only someone would rise to the fore, to herald God's Kingdom, they must have dared to dream. Someone who could make these endtime visions more specific and real to people living in the age of wickedness.

But where could such a champion be found?

5

THE CHALLENGE OF JESUS

Where was the end-time champion to be found? One who'd encourage the people to live up to a higher standard of conduct in preparation for the wonderful new environment God had planned for people?

For many, Jesus was just that champion. He *challenged* and he *promised*.

He challenged his followers to observe Torah, strictly. This may come as a surprise, for Christians today do not observe Torah. Yet, like the prophets and all Jewish leaders before him, Jesus did exactly that. He taught, debated, and practiced Torah. His earliest followers, under the leadership of his brother, James, also observed the law as Jesus himself had done. This meant keeping the Sabbath, observing the dietary laws, practicing circumcision, honoring the Ten Commandments, and all the other requirements of the law. In light of well-founded fears over Hellenistic assimilation and annihilation, no responsible Jewish leader of the time would have dared suggest abandoning the Torah. That would have been a suicidal message for any Jewish community and that was not Jesus' position.

His challenge was supported by a promise. Jesus regaled his audiences throughout the Galilee with amazing parables that assured them that dramatic changes were on the way. These stories drew people into a marvelous world in an enchanting way, inviting them to consider the tremendous possibilities of a new social order that he claimed was dawning on the world stage, the Kingdom of God. This was the moment when God would make good on his promises to the Jewish people and establish God's sovereign rule over all the earth. Jesus thought it would occur within his lifetime and that he would have an important role in bringing it about. That powerful vision galvanized his followers, and it tapped deep into the underground dreams for a Messiah who would come to assist God in bringing about a transformed earth. This confirmed what the secret biblical detectives had known all along: that the times were historic. The age of wickedness was about to be replaced by something truly spectacular.

Through persuasive parables, Jesus presented the Kingdom message—what it would be like and who would be included—and this raised enormous expectations that the end of Hellenization was near. Gone would be the Romans, the hated colonizers and occupiers of the land. Soon there would be God's rule over the entire earth. This was a sentiment shared by other Jewish factions of the time: the Dead Sea Scroll community, the Pharisees, the Zealots, and the nameless underground groups looking for signs of the times. Jesus' message resonated with all the Jewish groups of his time—everyone, that is, except for the Sadducees who favored the status quo and its easy accommodation with the Romans. It is therefore not surprising that later on in Jesus' life he was condemned to death by a Sadducean high priest and his unruly crowd of supporters.

In setting forth his message, we need to recognize that Jesus himself wrote nothing during his ministry in the 20s. He probably didn't because he expected God's Kingdom to materialize on earth within his lifetime. Consequently, there was no need for him to write down his thoughts. His task was to proclaim the Kingdom and get the people ready for a wonderful new future. As well, the earliest Christian writings—the letters of Paul—tell us very little about the life and teachings of Jesus. Paul only mentioned that Jesus was born, that he was Jewish, and that he died—all very frustrating when we want details. His interests clearly lay elsewhere, as we will discover. In addition, there are no accounts contemporary with Jesus' mission during the 20s. The gospels did not appear until long after the death of Jesus and Paul. Mark, the earliest gospel, is dated by scholars to have been written about the time of the destruction of the Temple, that is, around A.D. 70. The others are even later: Matthew from the 80s, John, the 90s. Luke's gospel is dated anywhere from the 90s through to the 120s.[1] In other words, our "records" date some forty to ninety years after Jesus' life and death—two, three, and four generations later. Nor do we know who wrote these gospels, two, three, and four generations after Jesus. Later tradition only attributes these to a "Mark," a "Matthew," a "Luke," and a "John." But those traditions are no more reliable than those that attribute other gospels to a "Thomas," a "Mary," a "Philip," a "James," or "the Savior."

Moreover, as we might expect, concerns and issues in the late first century helped to shape their narratives, and so their account of Jesus' words and activities are filtered through their individual perspectives and the needs of their respective audiences. Matthew, for instance, is writing for a predominately Jewish group; Luke is writing for Gentiles. That helps to shape what they write. Matthew is writing in part to position the religion of Rabbi Jesus as an alternative to mainstream Judaism. Luke, on the other hand, is striving to present the new religion as one fit for the Roman world.

Writing down these various accounts was likely sparked by several factors. The death of Jesus' earliest followers—James, Paul, and Peter, and undoubtedly many others during the 60s—made preserving the teachings of Jesus all the more urgent. No longer could these be confined to oral transmission. Written records were required. Moreover, the tremendous upheaval in Judea with the destruction of Jerusalem and the Temple in A.D. 70 raised fears about the survival of Judaism and its religious offshoots. Would the new movement itself survive the Roman onslaught? Just as the members of the Dead Sea Scroll community relegated their writings to jars in the Judean desert to await friendlier times, so also the followers of Jesus committed their oral traditions to written scrolls. They, too, could not be sure of their future in such uncertain times.

As well, it should be admitted, there was growing disenchantment within the movement caused by "the delay." This is getting ahead of our story somewhat, but it needs to be recognized here that the Kingdom did not materialize as Jesus promised. Some followers, a few years after Jesus' death, began to grow tired, waiting for the Kingdom. Where on earth was it? they rightfully asked. Jesus had promised it in his lifetime. Paul, moreover, had urged people not to marry—or if they did, not to have sex—on the grounds that the time of the end was too close to permit that kind of behavior. But even more importantly, the decisive victory by the Romans over the Jewish people raised doubts that a wonderful new era of world peace was at hand. By 70, the Kingdom of God vision seemed to be an empty promise.

Whatever the complex set of catalysts for writing down the life and teachings of Jesus, we now have four gospels included in the canon of the New Testament, as well as many more that weren't chosen for inclusion.

MATTHEW'S JESUS

We will follow the portrait presented primarily in the Gospel of Matthew, with some side references to the other gospels.[2] There are two very good reasons for favoring this representation of Jesus. First of all, in the Sermon on the Mount, Matthew preserved teachings of Jesus shared by the earliest form of Christianity, the Jesus Movement in Jerusalem.[3] The views presented in this gospel correspond to how this early community understood him. This group included his brother, James, and this should make us sit up and take notice. If anyone would have been in a position to know what the authentic Jesus said, it would likely have been his brother. So Matthew is a good place to start since this writing reflects a view of Jesus that was widely shared by his earliest followers.

Second, the Gospel of Matthew placed Jesus centrally within the political and theological debates of his time. In this document, for instance, we see the Jewishness of Jesus coming through in discussions with other Jewish leaders of the time on such questions as keeping the Sabbath and following the Torah. Situating Jesus within the context of his own time, now better understood by our having the Dead Sea Scrolls at our disposal, represents a sound move. That way, his outlook, challenges, and expectations can be placed in their proper context.

By using Matthew's gospel, we can also focus on Jesus' parables. Here we will see Jesus' social message shining through, attacking society and proposing a radical alternative—what he called the Kingdom of God. Along with strict Torah observance, this represented Jesus' provocative response to Hellenization. The Kingdom proclamation attracted massive attention—from ordinary people weary of occupation, and also from the authorities who were threatened by this new political possibility.

So what is Matthew's "take" on Jesus in the 80s, some fifty years or so after his death?

JESUS AS A YOUTH

According to the Gospel of Matthew (Matthew 2:1), Jesus was born in Bethlehem in Judea sometime toward the end of Herod the Great's reign.[4] Since Herod died in 4 B.C., Jesus was likely born around 5 or 6 B.C. In time, his parents relocated to Nazareth in the Galilee. He would not have recognized his name as "Jesus," which is Greek. Nobody ever called him that. His name was "Yeshua" or "Yehoshua," that is, "Joshua" in English. He had four brothers: James ("Ya'akov," Jacob in English), Joseph or Joses, Simon, and Judas, and at least two sisters who are not named (Matthew 13:55). His parents—Mary ("Miriam") and Joseph ("Yosef")—were observant Jews. He exercised a ministry during the 20s and was put to death around 30. He was Jewish.

Whatever the precise circumstances surrounding his birth, he was born of a Jewish mother in Bethlehem only a few miles south of Jerusalem. In friendlier times than now, it was an easy walk from Jerusalem to Bethlehem. Today from some modern high-rise hotels in this ancient city, we can look south from Jerusalem and see the hills of Bethlehem in the distance. It's that close. Matthew indicated that shortly after the birth of Jesus, the family fled into Egypt to avoid the wrath of Herod the Great. This, however, seems to be an artificial device so as to allow Jesus' family eventually to return from Egypt. Thus Matthew could feel comfortable applying Hosea's saying to Jesus: "Out of Egypt have I called my son" (Matthew 2:15 quoting Hosea 11:1). The prophet Hosea clearly meant Israel as God's son, referring to the Exodus of the

Israelites out of Egypt, but here Matthew applied it directly to Jesus. Even today, taking Matthew's account literally, some Coptic Christian churches in Egypt have been named to mark significant milestones in this very young infant life of Jesus.

Writing early in the second century and likely without knowing the Gospel of Matthew, Luke recorded a very different tradition. Shortly after the birth of Jesus, his family returned to Jerusalem, directly into the heart of the lion's lair—the exact opposite of what Matthew would have us accept. As required by Jewish law, he was circumcised on the eighth day (Luke 2:21). Also, in accordance with Torah obligations, his mother, Mary, underwent a purification ritual in a *mikvah* or "ritual bath" in Jerusalem and participated in the redemption of the firstborn ceremony there:

> *When the time came for their purification according to the law of Moses, they brought him up to Jerusalem to present him to the Lord (as it is written in the law of the Lord, "Every firstborn male shall be designated as holy to the Lord"), and they offered a sacrifice according to what is stated in the law of the Lord, "a pair of turtledoves or two young pigeons." (Luke 2:22–23)*

Just in passing we should note that the gospels are inconsistent. We cannot, for instance, reconcile both Matthew's and Luke's accounts of what happened immediately after the birth of Jesus. We cannot have Jesus' family both going to Jerusalem, to Herod's stronghold, while simultaneously fleeing into Egypt away from Herod's influence. Siding with Luke on this matter, most scholars today interpret Matthew's flight into Egypt either as symbolic or highly artificial.

JESUS AND JOHN THE BAPTIST

We know very little of Jesus' youth and teenage years. We do not know, for instance, where he studied, with whom, what languages other than Aramaic he may have known (both Hebrew and Greek are possibilities), who his friends were, how he interacted with his brothers and sisters, how he got along with his mother and father, what relatives he had other than his cousin, John the Baptist (or "Baptizer" as some call him, so as to avoid picturing John as "a Baptist" in contemporary denominational terms). How did he support himself, his studies or his travels growing up? Did he visit Sepphoris, that fabulous Hellenized city situated high on a hill only a few miles from Nazareth? Did he or his father perhaps work there, helping to construct this magnificent new city that only today is being unearthed? Why did he start his ministry? And what was the relationship between Jesus' movement and that of John the Baptist? We cannot now reconstruct his day-to-day life, but we can imagine a combination of work and study, synagogue attendance, conversation, and good family times centered on the weekly Sabbath meal and the annual major Jewish festivals.

Certainly he knew the scriptures, especially the books of Deuteronomy and Isaiah, which he quoted extensively. Both support his understanding of Torah and the hope for a better world where God reigns supreme. He shared with his cousin, John the Baptist, a political message. John himself was an interesting character, being a Nazirite (Luke 1:15), that is, a Torah-observant Jew who had taken a special vow of "separation" from ordinary society for a spiritual purpose. A Nazirite was dedicated to the service of God, abstained from wine, did not shave, and avoided contact with the dead (Numbers 6:1–21). Other Nazirites included two great heroes of the Old Testament, Samson and Samuel. Interestingly enough, Jesus' brother, James, was also a Nazirite.

John was a rough fellow and must have presented a strange, charismatic figure to the people of his era. Clothed in a camel's hair garment with a leather belt, he operated by the shores of the Jordan River, baptizing people there. He ate a strange diet: locusts and honey. According to Josephus, John's water ritual was a sign of repentance—a change of heart—a rededication to the covenant with God as expressed in the Torah. That is probably why he undertook Nazirite vows, to embark on a special mission to recall the Jewish people back to the demands of Torah. This commitment or renewal he dramatized and symbolized through a purification ritual. A *rededication to Torah* was John's strategy for dealing with Hellenization, and he seems to have been immensely popular, attracting a huge following. Both the gospels and Josephus attest to this. It was his political views, however, criticizing Herod's multiple marriages, especially a marriage to a niece, that seem to have landed him in hot water—and ultimately got him killed. John's ritual was not unusual. The members of the Dead Sea Scroll community immersed themselves periodically in a mikvah, as a symbol of cleansing. Similarly, others in a state of impurity—women after childbirth as well as pilgrims going up to the Temple—would immerse themselves completely in water.

What were Jesus' connections to John the Baptist? Did they share a common political vision of the Kingdom of God? Did they work together? We know that several of Jesus' earliest disciples had originally been members of John's group, so there were those links—Peter and his brother Andrew being two. We hear of Jesus baptizing, not in the Galilee where we would expect, but farther south, in Judea, around the hills of Jerusalem. In this connection, James Tabor draws attention to a neglected passage in the Gospel of John:

> "*After this, Jesus and his disciples went* into the Judean countryside, *and he spent some time there with them and* baptized. *John also was baptizing at Aenon near Salim.* . . ." (John (3:22,23; emphasis added).

Jesus baptizing is unusual and does not fit with the usual picture of Jesus. But here he is, at the start of his ministry, engaging in the same occupation as John the Baptist. Did Jesus and John then share a baptism mission?[5] And how did Jesus react to the death of his cousin, John?

The gospels appear to be divided in their impressions of whether Jesus was himself baptized by John. Theological subtleties lurk here, and the gospels rewrite the story to accommodate later concerns. The sequence is truly amazing. The earliest story is straightforward: according to Mark, Jesus was baptized by John. That's a straightforward account—no issues and no perceived problems. Matthew, however, writing a decade or so after Mark and using Mark's gospel as a basis for his, sensed a difficulty. John's baptism was for the forgiveness of sins. If Jesus were baptized by John, this would imply that, like other human beings, Jesus was a sinful being. So in rewriting what Mark had recorded, Matthew portrayed John as reluctant to baptize Jesus. He did so, eventually, but only because Jesus insisted.

The two later gospels try to skirt the issue entirely. Luke, for instance, depicted Jesus being baptized, but omitted reference to John as the agent. We are left wondering, in his account, just what happened. Did Jesus just immerse himself in the Jordan River? So Luke sidestepped the issue completely. The most radical solution is found in the Gospel of John. While outlining the baptizing activities of John the Baptist, this gospel avoids mentioning if Jesus was himself baptized at all. Clearly, later gospel writers were intent on preserving a unique status for Jesus as being without sin. Growing beliefs about the nature of Jesus dictate the story.

Later Christians also interpreted John as the expected Elijah figure who would return just prior to the "great and terrible day of the Lord" (Malachi 4:5). But we should be cautious in how we visualize such an interpretation. John was thoroughly Jewish, not a "pre-Christian," and the mission he undertook was conducted in accordance with the Judaism of his era. Just prior to this phrase about the day of the Lord, the prophet Malachi had urged his hearers to "remember the teaching of my servant Moses, the statutes and ordinances that I commanded him at Horeb [Sinai] for all Israel" (Malachi 4:4). These two passages in the prophet Malachi tie together Torah observance and preparation for the Kingdom: they are inseparable. Both John and Jesus shared a common religious task: to urge people to observe Torah and to return to the full demands of the covenant with God before that great and terrible day arrives. This demonstrates that both John the Baptist and Jesus shared that great end-time dream of Judaism. Sensing that the "day of the Lord" was at hand, they urgently sought to prepare people for this great event in which they'd participate. Those people alive at the time in the mid to late 20s were living through historic times. The world would never be the same—soon.

Whatever the connections were between Jesus and his cousin John the Baptist, early Christians were frustrated by the lack of information about Jesus prior to his ministry in the late 20s. This led to some interesting fabrications on their part. The midsecond century writing, the *Infancy Gospel of Thomas,* for instance, had Jesus at age five molding twelve clay birds on the Sabbath and bringing them to life.[6] Rather alarmingly, he was reported to have killed several children who interfered with his own play. He exhibited disrespect for his teachers and showed off from time to time. Occasionally he used his unusual talents positively, to perform several healing miracles, rescuing his brother James, for instance, from certain death due to a snakebite. He even helped his father, Joseph, lengthen a piece of wood that he had inaccurately cut when making a bed for an important client. Such stories have little evidentiary worth, except to disclose the mind-set and interests of some early Christians who regarded these stories as appropriate of Jesus. Why they would have chosen to depict the young Jesus as out of control and destructive has baffled scholars for centuries.

Every year, Jesus' parents went to Jerusalem from the Galilee for Passover, not an insignificant trip in the first century A.D., and one that demonstrated strong commitment to Torah observances (Luke 2:41). Likely it was a three-day trip, each way, from Nazareth up north in the Galilee to Jerusalem. During one of these visits, when Jesus was twelve, he spent a number of days in the Temple, studying with Torah experts who expressed astonishment at his depth of knowledge. While the bar mitzvah celebration is a more recent development within Judaism, the incident in the Temple when Jesus was in his thirteenth year bears some resemblances to taking on the adult obligations of Torah personally. Not only did he engage leading scholars in the Temple in a discussion of Torah, but he also seems to have been responsible for his own welfare and didn't leave Jerusalem when his family left. In fact, after several days, they backtracked to locate him among the long line of pilgrims trudging back along the valley road to the Galilee. They were clearly annoyed at his insensitivity. Where were you? they rightfully asked. Instead of submitting to their rebuke, however, he arrogantly responded that they should know that he had his own matters to look after. Sounds like a typical teenager comment.

How long this tradition of going up to Jerusalem lasted within his family is not recorded. His final trip up to Jerusalem, shortly before his death, was to celebrate Passover. Obviously this festival represented an important family and personal tradition that would not be missed.

JESUS' MISSION

In the late 20s, Jesus emerges as a Jewish teacher in Galilee, the hilly northern region of Israel. Leaving his native Nazareth, he moved north and east, setting up a headquarters at the top end of the Sea of Galilee. The place was Capernaum or, in Hebrew, *Kfar Nahum,* the village of Nahum. Nahum was one of the prophets in the Old Testament. With its spectacular views of the magnificent

oval Sea of Galilee to the south and the mountainous Golan Heights to the
east, Capernaum formed a convenient base of operations from which Jesus
could venture out to speak with people throughout the region. His choice of
headquarters may also have been symbolic. Seven centuries earlier, Nahum had
proclaimed that Assyrian power was about to be swept away. God would enter
the human arena to do away with the notorious cruelty and immorality of the
Assyrians. While Nahum was said to have hailed from the town of Elkosh, a
village bearing the prophet's own name might have seemed to Jesus a fitting
place to launch his message that Roman rule was about to end and that God's
sovereignty would soon be established over all the earth.[7]

From the vantage point of an impressive fourth-century white synagogue,
we can today look down on to the pavement of an earlier first-century black
basalt synagogue that Jesus may have frequented with his followers at Capernaum. There he may have studied and commented on Torah. It was in Capernaum, too, that Jesus gathered together a core group of twelve main followers.
These were named by Matthew as follows: Simon Peter; Simon Peter's brother
Andrew; James and John, the sons of Zebedee; Philip; Bartholomew; Thomas;
Matthew; James; Thaddaeus (Judas); Simon; and Judas Iscariot (Matthew
10:2–4). The "James, Judas [not Judas Iscariot] and Simon" mentioned here
may, in fact, have been three of his brothers.[8] Many of his disciples came from
the immediate region.

There were others associated with Jesus' entourage, women as well as men.
Mary Magdalene, for instance, hailed from the nearby town of Magdala only a
short distance to the west, well within a day's journey by foot. From time to
time we hear of many more followers than just the twelve disciples. At one
point, we learn that he sent out seventy emissaries on an urgent mission. Who
they were and whether they were part of some permanent infrastructure is not
known.

Together with this core group of twelve individuals, he embarked on missions throughout the Galilee. This was no easy endeavor. Thirteen people had
to be provided for on a daily basis—food, shelter, and clothing. How did these
individuals get along? Did they have squabbles? Who did the shopping? Who
cooked? What did they eat? Did they live together, as a commune, or did they
live separately in the same village, congregating from time to time? Did they
work, or were they like some contemporary ultraorthodox Jews who devote
their lives to study and prayer while others do the work and raise the money?
How did they decide where to go? Did they have access to the ancient
writings—scrolls of the Torah, the Prophets and the Writings? If so, who provided these? How were they studied? We don't know the answer to these
lifestyle questions. Some of the disciples appear to have been married, and perhaps they had children to look after.[9]

More importantly, who funded the movement? Thirteen people moving about through Galilee, perhaps over a three-year period, represented a major financial undertaking. This mission cost a lot of money: food, shelter, and transportation were just some of the expense categories.

In a little observed passage in Luke,[10] we find the following:

> *The twelve were with him, as well as some women who had been cured of evil*
> *spirits and infirmities: Mary, called Magdalene, from whom seven demons had*
> *gone out, and Joanna, the wife of Herod's steward Chuza, and Susanna, and*
> *many others, who provided for them out of their resources.* (Luke 8:1–3)

So there we have the answer: wealthy women were the financiers. They underwrote the movement, chiefly Mary Magdalene, Joanna (who had strong political connections), and Susanna, among "many others." But how did they do that? What sources of revenue did they have? Who was Mary Magdalene, and how did she come to have such funds?[11] Unfortunately the records are silent on these matters.

Jesus observed the Sabbath and the annual round of Jewish festivals, including Succoth and Passover. He went into synagogues, participated in the services there, and taught. This is just what we'd expect a Jewish rabbi to do. His "last supper" occurred just before Passover, either the first evening of Passover or the night before. This was held at the home of an unnamed follower in Jerusalem, with his inner circle of followers gathered around the table. We are familiar with this scene from Da Vinci's famous painting *The Last Supper*, but this portrait is very misleading. It shows only thirteen people present, Jesus and the twelve disciples. Undoubtedly there were many more people present at this festive meal than just Jesus and the twelve. Who cooked? Who prepared the traditional fare? Certainly his host was present and his family. Mary Magdalene was undoubtedly there. Probably also his mother. Likely his brothers. The wives of his married disciples. Undoubtedly some youngsters. And probably many more besides. If it did take place during Passover, it would have been a crowded, noisy affair, with conversation, laughter, storytelling, anecdotes, lots of good food and relaxation—not the sedate, highly structured pose that Da Vinci painted.

Jesus never converted to another religion. Nor did he start one. If he were to return, he'd probably be amazed—perhaps bewildered or possibly even angry—at what has been created in his name.

JESUS' DEATH

Toward the end of his life, this inspiring teacher traveled up to Jerusalem. There he was betrayed by one of his followers, Judas Iscariot, who turned him over to the Romans. Why he did so is a matter for speculation.[12] Perhaps Judas was a Zealot who had become disillusioned with Jesus' lack of proactivity in overthrowing Roman rule by violent means. Now that they were in Jerusalem, Judas probably reasoned, why hadn't Jesus started his divinely sanctioned campaign? What was the delay? Why were the Romans still in charge? Perhaps he wanted to force Jesus' hand, to prompt him to act immediately. Or maybe he felt let down by someone who seemed to him to be all talk and no action. Perhaps that is why Judas handed him over to the Roman authorities. Or as the recently discovered *Gospel of Judas* suggests, perhaps Jesus himself invited Judas to turn him in—which would have probably also been an attempt to hasten the advent of the promised Kingdom that his imprisonment might precipitate.

We don't know Judas's motivation, but whatever it was, Jesus was quickly condemned to death. He was executed by crucifixion in Jerusalem around 30 or slightly later by the Romans and mocked for being "the King of the Jews" (Matthew 27:37). The charges were political: Jesus was condemned for being a claimant to the throne of David. The Romans clearly recognized the enormous political thrust of his message. *They* saw the explosive implications of what he said.

His brother, James, carried on the family leadership as head of the Jesus Movement until he was killed in 62. After him, Jesus' cousin,[13] Simeon, became bishop or head of the movement in Jerusalem. He survived until the early years of the second century when the emperor Trajan had him crucified.[14]

JESUS AS A JEW

So, what was so Jewish about Jesus? Well, everything.

We really need to pause for a moment and ponder what this means. What does it mean to visualize Jesus as "really" Jewish? Too often we pay only lip service to this fact and perhaps see him only through the eyes of some particular Christian denomination, imagining him in our minds as a Catholic priest, Baptist preacher, or Methodist minister. We should perhaps picture him growing up as having a close-knit family, stopping work on the day of rest, welcoming the Sabbath through the Friday evening meal that his mother and sisters likely prepared. Good food, song, prayer on Friday evening led by his father as they followed the time-honored traditions of their ancestors, along with every other household in Nazareth. We would see him going to synagogue and participating annually in the great Jewish festivals such as Passover and Succoth. He would have read from the ancient Hebrew texts, worn a tallit (prayer shawl) when praying, strapped on tefillin (arm- and headbands), and had a mezuzah on the doorpost of his house.

We need to see him later on as a rabbi working with devoted students, considering scriptural passages and studying their meaning. In contemporary terms, we should visualize him as much closer to an Orthodox rabbi than a Christian priest or minister.

JESUS' INTERPRETATION OF TORAH

We have seen that Hellenization challenged the fundamentals of Jewish practice, and that various groups defined themselves in relationship to Torah observance. The Essenes, or Dead Sea Scroll community, were stricter in keeping the law than the Pharisees and certainly the Sadducees. Torah—then and now—was the bulwark against assimilation.

In Matthew, the picture is clear: Jesus practiced and taught strict Torah observance and challenged his followers to do the same. Since most Christians today reject Torah, this crucial aspect of his teaching is completely obscured in Christianity's liturgy, writings, and sermons. Christians today register complete surprise—and shock—that at least this gospel portrays Jesus as *thoroughly* Jewish, including what was most central to Jewish life: following the law. Jews have a very different reaction. They express amazement. Here is a Jewish teacher, responsible for Christianity, which does not follow the law, teaching Torah observance. They ask, What went wrong? How could this happen? All very good questions. What, indeed, "went wrong"?

According to the Sermon on the Mount, Jesus encouraged his followers not only to observe Torah, but to do so even more strictly than did the Pharisees. That begins to sound suspiciously like the stance of the Essenes, who denounced the Pharisees for being too soft in their interpretation of the law. But, according to Matthew, Jesus took his view of Torah in a different direction. Let's see how Matthew describes Jesus' stance.

For Matthew, Jesus was the new Moses. He stood on the mountain, interpreting the Torah of God. Like the historical Moses on Mount Sinai bringing the tablets of the law down to the people some thirteen centuries earlier, Jesus brought a new understanding of Torah to the people. Nothing Jesus said did away with the necessity for keeping the law. Rather the reverse was true: "Do not think that I have come to abolish the law or the prophets; I have come not to abolish but to fulfill. For truly I tell you, until heaven and earth pass away, not one letter, not one stroke of a letter, will pass from the law until all is accomplished" (Matthew 5:17–18). This passage is fundamental, for here Jesus acknowledged the binding authority of Torah regulations. It cannot easily be dismissed. Not one stroke of a letter of Torah was to be abolished until "all is accomplished." In this he was consistent with Jewish tradition and the entire Old Testament.

Did Jesus actually stand on a mountain in the Galilee and preach this sermon? Some contemporary American Evangelicals think so and are building a "theme park" in northern Israel near the Sea of Galilee on a hill selected as "the mount." Or was this an image constructed by the writer of the Gospel of Matthew to fit his message that Jesus fulfilled Old Testament prophecy? Scholars usually prefer the latter approach, as stage directions fitting Matthew's agenda of showing the importance of Jesus as an interpreter of Torah, like a Moses. For Matthew, however, Jesus was more important than Moses: he was an active interpreter of the law, not just its passive recipient, as Moses had been.

In case we missed the point, Jesus drove home the real importance of this message. Those who break the commandments or teach others to do so, he said, "will be called least in the kingdom of heaven" (Matthew 5:19). In Matthew's day, only the Christ Movement stemming from Paul's teachings advocated abandoning Torah observance. Matthew's Jesus may be designed, in part, to correct Paul's position. Matthew is counteracting what he would have considered Paul's false teachings, which were gaining in circulation and popularity by the 80's when he was inscribing his own scroll.

In fact, the point for Matthew's Jesus was not to replace Torah but to *enhance* its observance, to abide by its provisions even more scrupulously than did the adherents of other parties within Judaism: "Unless your righteousness exceeds that of the scribes and Pharisees, you will never enter the kingdom of heaven" (Matthew 5:20). Thus Jesus was portrayed by Matthew as teaching "the higher righteousness," or super-Torah-observance.

What is this "higher righteousness"?

In the Sermon on the Mount, Jesus extended the parameters of the law, and he gave various examples. His move was to *stretch* the law, to cover underlying attitudes, not just behavior. This did not, of course, do away with the need for right action. It just made the obligation even harder to follow. Jesus' position was consistent with the outlook of the Book of Deuteronomy— Torah observance included choices, actions, and attitudes—but his halakhah or Torah interpretation was even more rigorous.[15]

One of the important commandments was "not to murder." Jesus stretched this law to embrace not only the act of murdering someone, but also not being angry at other human beings (Matthew 5:22). Overt action is extended to an underlying attitude that could give way to hostile behavior. This in no way replaced the injunction not to murder—Torah still applies—but now it included not being angry at people. Thus Torah was not diminished or abolished. It was, in fact, augmented.

The way of higher righteousness was more demanding that just doing what the law required. The law now covered circumstances not entirely envisaged in the original commandment. Thus "do not murder" was extended to "don't even be angry," because the latter could lead to the former. Even insults were ruled out since these could incite murder. All these prohibitions encouraged a Torah-observant lifestyle, avoiding attitudes and conditions that would place one in danger of violating the law.

Matthew's Jesus was consistent with Pharisaic practice, that of "building a fence" or "hedge" around the law. If the commandment was not to murder, then, Jesus says, do not even be angry. That extension to underlying attitude has the effect of creating a buffer zone. Avoiding anger represents a good first step in avoiding behavior likely to lead to murder.

Similarly, Jesus enhanced the commandment "not to engage in adultery" to include mental attitudes: do not lust after other people (Matthew 5:28). According to Jesus, the mere act of thinking about or imagining adultery was as much a violation of the commandment as the action of actually committing adultery. This is a much tougher requirement. The point Jesus made is that one kind of activity (thinking about adultery) could lead to another activity (committing adultery). And so, again, a fence is erected around the biblical injunction.

Another commandment was "not to swear falsely," in other words, to tell the truth when we speak. Jesus extended this requirement by prohibiting the uttering of any oaths (Matthew 5:33–37). A simple yes or no should suffice. So Jesus would not countenance swearing "on the Bible" or "on your mother's life" or saying "cross your heart and hope to die." A simple declaration should be adequate.

Regulations in Deuteronomy required that the husband give his divorced wife "a certificate of divorce" (Deuteronomy 24:1–4). The matter of marital breakup had been debated in the generation before Jesus. The issue had to do with the circumstances under which divorce was permissible. Shortly before Jesus, Hillel had adopted a lenient approach, saying that a man might divorce his wife for any reason, even if she had spoiled his dinner. For Hillel, divorce was terribly simple. The opposing School of Shammai, however, adopted a stricter interpretation, saying that divorce was not permissible unless there was some "indecency" on the part of the spouse—perhaps unfaithfulness or some other marital impropriety.

Jesus adopted a strict line of interpretation, comparable to Shammai's. Divorce was only permitted in the case of a wife being unchaste. But he then added an important zinger: there was to be no remarriage for a divorced female (Matthew 5:31, 32). Again, the interpretive direction was one of much greater rigor—stricter, as it turns out, than either Shammai or the more liberal Hillel.

Nothing, though, was said about the male and his behavior.

One often-quoted law from the Torah is "eye for eye, tooth for tooth" (Exodus 21:24). This has frequently been misinterpreted as a cry for revenge, although it really states a principle of equitable justice. "Eye" is a metaphor for any kind of injury. The point of this catchy saying is that the penalty for a crime should not exceed the damage caused, so no "going overboard" when it comes to setting punishments. Do not, for instance, exact "two eyes" when only "one eye" has been damaged.

Jesus suggested, instead, that those who commit evil should not be resisted (Matthew 5:38–42). This is tantamount to affirming not even one eye in exchange for an eye, a very difficult commandment to follow. In its most literal form, it could mean lying down in the face of evil or oppression, even in self-defense—extreme passivity in the face of moral evil. In its original context with Romans occupying the land of Israel, it could be interpreted as simply letting them rule and not resisting them with military force. This saying would also have caused considerable consternation among a segment of his closest followers who looked to him to overthrow the Romans and establish the Jewish state and the Kingdom of God.

Jesus went on to observe that some people have said, "you shall love your neighbor and hate your enemy."[16] He rejected the second half of this phrase, maintaining, instead, that enemies should be loved and people should pray for those who persecute them. This may have been one of Jesus' most difficult sayings for the people of his time, for "neighbor" included the Romans. How then were the hated occupiers to be overthrown? How does this relate to Jesus' message about the coming Kingdom of God that would soon replace the *Pax Romana* (the Roman Peace)?

JESUS AND THE SABBATH

Jesus participated in the great Jewish debates of his time—how to keep Torah faithfully—and he commented on Sabbath observances, healings, and work. What was meant, for instance, by "not to do any work" (Exodus 20:10) was an open question at the time. All Jewish groups agreed that the Sabbath should be observed and sanctified. The Torah required this. The law in the Book of Exodus linked remembrance of the Sabbath to the very structure of creation, citing as the reason for its observance God's resting after the work of creation (Exodus 20:8–11). By sanctifying the Sabbath, then, humans share in a process honored by God: creative work, then rest.

Deuteronomy provides a different rationale from that given in the Book of Exodus, linking the observance of the Sabbath not to creation but to the experience of freedom from enslavement in Egypt (Deuteronomy 5:12–15). So, in this version, the Sabbath commemorates divine redemption, coming out of a life of hard toil and oppression into one of liberation. Still other passages remind the Israelites to keep the Sabbath "as a perpetual covenant" and as a "sign forever between me and the people of Israel" (Exodus 31:16, 17).

So it is clear that the Sabbath is to be observed. That is the objective: it represents a joyous celebration of time, a gift from God, a time marking one day a week as special. The crucial question, however, was *how* to honor the Sabbath day. What strategies existed for achieving this unique objective?

The written text of the Bible does not explicitly indicate how this special day is to be sanctified by not working. There were clues, however, and Jewish leaders began to notice the specific word used for *work* and its associated contexts within the writings of the Books of the Law (or the five Books of the Torah).

WORKING ON THE SABBATH

It should be noted that "work prohibited on the Sabbath" (in Hebrew, *melakhah*) does not describe the same set of activities as that covered by the English word *work*. For us, work suggests physical effort, exertion, or the kind of activities we engage in at our place of employment. That's not what is meant by *work* in this context.

In time, Judaism came to embrace thirty-nine categories of work forbidden on the Sabbath (Mishnah, Shabbat 7:2). These categories of work come from an interpretation of Exodus 31:1–17 and Exodus 35:1–39:43. The rabbis noticed that the word for "work prohibited on the Sabbath" (melakhah) was the same word for *work* in the building of the Tabernacle. Moreover, the injunction not to do work on the Sabbath immediately preceded this passage about the kinds of activities involved in building the Tabernacle. These two clues provided the basis for understanding what "work prohibited on the Sabbath" meant. Louis Jacobs notes,

> Important though the building of the Tabernacle was, the Sabbath was even more important. It follows, declare the Rabbis, that every activity required for the erection of the Tabernacle constitutes "work" and is forbidden on the Sabbath. On the basis of this, the Rabbis speak of thirty-nine main categories of work—those that were for the purpose of erecting the Tabernacle, and many others resembling them and derived from them.[17]

These include such activities as sowing, plowing, reaping, grinding, baking, shearing or washing wool, spinning, weaving, tying, tearing, writing, lighting a fire, using a tool such as a hammer, or transporting goods from one place to another (e.g., from one's house to the outside), and so on, including all their modern equivalents. Thus, driving an automobile on the Sabbath would be ruled out as "lighting a fire." Similarly, making notes with a pen or pencil, compozing e-mails, or working on a computer document would be subsumed under "writing."

The type of work in question is *creative* activity, that is, producing, making, manipulating nature, or changing creation. God rested from this kind of work, and humans are instructed to share in this rest. It is not work requiring physical exertion per se. Rather it is any creative activity that changes the status quo. As a result, such activities as cooking, preparing food, washing clothes, making home repairs, writing, working on the computer, starting a fire, fishing, buying, and selling are prohibited. The focus is on accepting the world as it is, without engaging in activities that would change it on that day. This frees up the person to do other kinds of activities, such as reading, contemplating, socializing, enjoying a previously prepared meal, and so on, without having to do or make things.

The extent to which these categories were formally recognized in Jesus' time is uncertain, but certainly Judaism was headed in the direction of clarifying what was prohibited. Since keeping the Sabbath was an important commandment—it was, after all, included as one of the Ten Commandments—explaining what could or could not be done was imperative. It would be chaotic to leave it up to everybody's imagination. Some interpretive rules had to be given. We know how one group interpreted the command to keep the Sabbath holy. This was the Dead Sea Scroll community. Their interpretive rules, or halakhah, for the Sabbath included refraining from idle words, loans, business matters, talking about work, walking more than a thousand cubits from the town, eating unprepared food, taking items in or out of a house, lifting an animal out of a pit, spending the Sabbath near Gentiles, or carrying children.[18] We do not know how the leaders of this community arrived at this list, but they remarkably anticipated many of the thirty-nine categories found in the Mishnah.[19]

In all likelihood, most people interpreted "work forbidden on the Sabbath" at the time of Jesus as at least including not using money, cooking, traveling or engaging in commercial activities in general. They would have observed it as a day of rest, eating previously prepared food, going to synagogue, talking, socializing with family and friends, and refraining from physical labor.

EATING ON THE SABBATH

In Jewish law, only food that has been prepared ahead of time may be consumed on the Sabbath: no cooking, cutting up of meat or vegetables, grinding grain, or lighting fires. Jesus dealt with the question of work on the Sabbath in the following passage. Note what it says and what it does not say:

At that time Jesus went through the grainfields on the Sabbath; his disciples were hungry, and they began to pluck heads of grain and to eat. When the Pharisees saw it, they said to him "Look, your disciples are doing what is not lawful to do on the Sabbath." He said to them, "Have you not read what David did when he and his companions were hungry? He entered the house of God and ate the bread of the Presence, which it was not lawful for him or his companions to eat, but only for the priests." (Matthew 12:1–4)

The issue has to do with Sabbath observance, specifically working by harvesting food. As customary, Jesus did not answer the question directly. Rather his response was circuitous.

There is much that is missing from this incident. For one thing, Jesus chose not to deal with the issue of theft—plucking and eating "heads of grain" from a farmer's field. Did his disciples pay for it? If they hadn't, then there was a violation of the commandment not to steal. If they had paid for it, then the disciples would have run afoul of another Sabbath requirement, not to engage in commercial transactions on this day. The use of money would constitute a violation of work prohibited on the Sabbath.

Rather Jesus focused on the issue of his disciples harvesting and eating food they had not prepared ahead of time. The disciples were hungry and no one had prepared the Sabbath meal ahead of time. In dealing with this issue, Jesus cited the example of King David a thousand years earlier. David had eaten bread offered to God at the shrine at Nob, which only the priests could eat. However, David's situation reflected extreme and exceptional circumstances: he and his followers were "on the run" (see 1 Samuel 21:1–6). So Jesus' answer to the question of whether one could break the Sabbath by harvesting and eating food one has not prepared ahead of time was, "yes, *in extreme circumstances.*" It does not follow from this exceptionally rare situation—once in a thousand years—that the Sabbath ought generally to be disregarded.

There is much more missing from the incident. The passage does not indicate how Jesus' rationale applied to the specific case. That is, it does not tell us the specific "extreme circumstances" that would have permitted his followers to raid the farmer's field on the Sabbath. Why did they require food desperately? Were they, like David, fleeing for their lives? Why had they not prepared for the Sabbath ahead of time? What made this incident "exceptional"?

Regardless of the answers to these important questions, the teaching was clear: the Sabbath was to be observed and remembered. Only in exceptional circumstances could it be broken. This is certainly not an endorsement of the view that the Sabbath should be disregarded completely. This important boundary marker between Jew and non-Jew in Hellenistic times was maintained by Jesus.

HEALING ON THE SABBATH

In another instance, while in a synagogue, Jesus healed on the Sabbath and was questioned about this:

> *He left that place and entered their synagogue; a man was there with a withered hand, and they asked him, "Is it lawful to cure on the Sabbath?" so that they might accuse him. He said to them, "Suppose one of you has only one sheep and it falls into a pit on the Sabbath; will you not lay hold of it and lift it out? How much more valuable is a human being than a sheep! So it is lawful to do good on the Sabbath."* (Matthew 12:9–12)

Again there is a lot missing from this account and again the answer seems disconnected from the question. The passage, for example, does not indicate how the analogy of a sheep falling into a pit fits the example of healing a person with a withered hand. A sheep falling into a pit represents suffering and a possible life-threatening situation. Without quick action, the sheep would suffer and likely die. In these extreme and exceptional life-threatening circumstances, it was agreed that Sabbath requirements could be set aside to come to the assistance of people or animals in serious trouble.[20] The situation of the man with a withered hand, however, would seem not to fit the example. Presumably his healing could wait one day. This might explain why Jesus' opponents wished to accuse him. If it had been a clear-cut life-threatening case, they would have had no grounds for criticism.

So while the principle of exceptional circumstances did not fit the specific situation of a person with a withered hand, it did indicate that there were situations requiring forbidden work on the Sabbath. In this, Jesus agreed with other Jewish leaders of his time (and subsequently) that life-threatening situations require appropriate action. So, to the question, could one heal a person on the Sabbath? Jesus' answer was "yes . . . if life is jeopardized." In neither instance, however, were Sabbath laws set aside. The general injunction not to do work forbidden on the Sabbath was interpreted compassionately in such a way as to allow for exceptional circumstances.

THE FOUNDATIONAL PRINCIPLES OF TORAH

A Pharisaic lawyer encountered Jesus and posed the question, "Teacher, which commandment in the law is greatest?" (Matthew 22:36). In reply, Jesus quoted Deuteronomy 6:4–5, the Shema: "Hear, O Israel: the Lord is our God, the Lord alone. You shall love the Lord your God with all your heart, and with all your soul and with all your might". This was immediately paired with Leviticus 18:19, "you shall love your neighbor as yourself." The Gospel of Matthew omitted the lawyer's response, but we find that the earlier Gospel of Mark has provided the balance of this exchange. The lawyer agreed with Jesus, adding that this summary of Torah was more important than the laws pertaining to offerings and sacrifices in the Temple. Jesus complimented him, adding that he was "not far from the kingdom of God" (Mark 12:28–34). If these commandments were "the greatest," then it is not surprising that they were more important than the laws regarding Temple sacrifices and offerings. This did not mean, however, that one should set aside Temple rituals while that establishment was still in existence.

Jesus' position on this topic is virtually identical to that of the Pharisaic leader Hillel, who lived in Jerusalem just prior to the time of Jesus. As we have seen, Hillel reduced the foundational principle to one: "that which is hateful to you, do not do to your neighbor" (Babylonian Talmud, Shabbat 31a). Neither Jesus nor Hillel would ever have dreamt that these statements would or could be used to set aside Torah. In Hillel's case, he prevented this perverse interpretation by urging his questioner to go and study Torah.

These were foundational principles for Torah observance providing for obligations toward God as well as toward other human beings. Citing "the greatest" commandment did not mean that it was "the only" commandment. Derivative laws were not to be set aside or ignored. So Torah remained intact, and, at least as Matthew conveyed the message of Jesus, this represented Jesus' central teaching.

John the Baptist appears to have held a similar position. Josephus wrote that John the Baptist urged his fellow Jews "to exercise virtue." By this, Josephus indicated, John the Baptist meant right behavior toward one another as well as piety toward God. While expressed in philosophical language, this dual emphasis is similar to Hillel's and Jesus' summaries of the law. John encouraged people to undergo "baptism" for purification as an outward manifestation that the person had already been cleansed by right attitudes and right actions.[21] For John, the Torah was the path of right behavior. His response to the threat of Hellenization was to challenge people to rededicate themselves to the law, of which baptism was the symbol. His actions were political as well as religious, for his approach was uncompromisingly set against Hellenization with its easy accommodation toward a common Mediterranean culture. John the Baptist refused to remove the boundary markers.

John's territory included places only a few miles away from Qumran, the headquarters of the Essenes, or Dead Sea Scroll Community. Was there contact between these two movements not too far distant from one another? Again, there is only speculation in regards to this intriguing question. While both the Essenes and John the Baptist focused on Torah observance, clearly there were differences. John's movement was a popular one, reaching out to ordinary people in an attempt to reorient them toward God and the covenant. The Dead Sea Scroll community was reclusive.

Higher righteousness was Jesus' contribution to the application of Torah, extending actions to include behavior in a way that is more explicit—and more extensive—than the Book of Deuteronomy. That book placed choice, obligations, and attitude within the parameters of Torah. There was no suggestion that Jesus attempted to do away with or replace Torah by anything else. That would have created an immense outcry—from other Jewish leaders, from his family, and from his cousin John the Baptist. There was no evidence that anything of the sort ever occurred. In the context of the time, it would have been regarded as a major shift toward assimilation into Hellenistic culture, a policy that would have reminded everyone of the policies of Antiochus Epiphanes. That clearly was not Jesus' teaching or practice. If it had been, his mission would probably not have lasted as long as it did, and we would not know of him today. His execution by the Romans, moreover, had nothing to do with his teachings in regard to Torah observance. Their interests were purely political: was he or was he not a claimant to the Jewish throne?

So, what happened? Why did later Christianity depart from what Jesus clearly taught? For the answer to that question, we will need to investigate, in a later chapter, Paul's position and its overwhelming impact.

THE CHALLENGE

Jesus' challenge to his audience was straightforward. Be better than the Pharisees, the teachers of Torah. Outdo them in righteousness. Live the covenant with God to the fullest, following the law carefully, paying attention not only to the required conduct but also to the corresponding right attitude. That was an exceptionally demanding requirement. He dared his followers to set the standard.

Jesus' message reinforced the teachings of Deuteronomy. His merit was that he reminded people in highly dramatic terms just what this meant. Did people sit up and take notice? Did they—the crowds and his disciples—mend their ways and achieve this level of perfection? Unfortunately we do not know, either with Jesus or John the Baptist, what their efforts really amounted to with the masses of people who encountered these two remarkable individuals. We just know that the message was popular and that it was well received.

Jesus was one of the ancient world's greatest motivational speakers. Like many who hear such engaging figures, the message can be quickly forgotten. It is difficult to sustain enthusiasm for the life-changing insights we hear in the course of a presentation, however inspiring.

But there was more to the teachings of Jesus. Not only did he insist on a higher standard of conduct, but he also *promised* them something of tremendous value—something that would shake the very foundations of their lives and give them something to look forward to, eagerly. What was that wonderful promise that motivated his audience to live up to his daring challenge?

6

THE PROMISES OF JESUS

A better world coming soon—that's what Jesus proclaimed. It was a radical message that resonated and attracted huge attention. The greatest time in human history—that's the vision that drew the crowds, generated buzz, and ultimately got him killed. And it was about to happen. It would be the end of everything that plagued the Jewish people—Hellenization, the Roman way of life, and their subjugation by occupying armies and transplanted cities. Soon Israel would be an independent state, revered by the world. God would bring about a whole new era in human history—a time of universal peace for all humanity. It would be nothing less than a newly minted earth and an entirely different political system. Best of all, they'd live to see it materialize right before their eyes.

THE KINGDOM OF GOD

This was not a new dream—Isaiah, Zechariah, and Enoch had paved the way—but Jesus had the knack of making it sound enticing and wonderfully close. But his was not the only vision of a better world on the horizon.

The Romans, too, had their ideas of what constituted a better world. They thought they had already shared it with the world through the Pax Romana, their greatest gift to civilization. Dating from 27 B.C. when the Roman emperor Caesar Augustus quelled all opposition to his rule, the Pax Romana spanned an entire empire around the Mediterranean at peace with itself. Rome prided itself on providing the centralized leadership required to give a turbulent society the gift of stability. The vision was a secure, calm world, offering economic development and a network of communications that facilitated trade and fostered travel throughout the empire. It was an arrangement that valued order and stability, backed by Roman law, administration, and military might.

The Pax Romana also created the climate for a greater harmonization of local cultures into one large common culture, ideally sharing the same Roman values, beliefs, and aspirations. The exercise of virtue, piety toward the gods, a noble life, individual dignity, and physical and intellectual prowess were all prized Roman values. For the first time ever, people could be citizens of the world, sharing in the triumphs and glory of stable Roman rule. They expected local peoples would wholeheartedly embrace the Roman vision. True, there was colonization, occupation, and the omnipresence of foreign beliefs and practices. But to the Romans, this seemed a minor price to pay for the glories of their cultured civilization. Only a barbarian would not want to be part of this better world.

Jesus and many Jews of the time were hardly likely to share this vision. The Romans were, after all, an occupying force. The Jews chafed under Roman rule and longed for the time when God would make good on his eventual plans for all humanity. Jewish society found in Jesus just such a promiser. And what a promise he made—the greatest event in human history for a weary and angry people.

Jesus' vision of a better world was encapsulated in his remarkable parables.[1] These stories dramatized in story form his view of the coming Kingdom of God. This political reality, he maintained, was just around the corner and would result in a vastly different world than the one created by the Pax Romana. He seems to have thought that the Kingdom would come within his own lifetime, and he promised his followers that they'd live to see that great day (Matthew 16:28). In fact, as Mark portrayed it, Jesus came on the scene announcing, "The time is fulfilled, and the kingdom of God has come near; repent, and believe the good news" (Mark 1:15). That got everybody's attention.

It was like taking the Doomsday Clock and setting the hand at ten seconds to midnight. Zero hour was approaching. Countdown Rome.

Jesus undoubtedly thought that he would have a role in helping to bring about this new state of affairs. He certainly was its proclaimer, announcing this fantastically better world and enticing people to prepare for its marvelous possibilities. The Kingdom of God would develop rapidly, Jesus said. From small beginnings it would mushroom dramatically into a wonderful new era in human history. Those who care about others, who are compassionate, who forgive others, and who do God's will—they are the ones who will be part of the Kingdom of God. It will be a time when God will reign supreme and the righteous will be vindicated. All the foreign occupiers of the land will simply vanish, along with all the unrighteous.

Was Jesus just a promiser and proclaimer? Or was he more than that? His followers certainly thought so. They claimed that he was the longed-for Messiah, the catalyst for world transformation. Whether he personally thought of himself in this instrumental role is an open question. Clearly he thought of himself as living in a pivotal era when tremendous world-shaking events would take place. What was about to happen was the focus of his preaching. Jesus' vision of a new world order capitalized on the powerful underground dream for the end-times. Recall the earlier discussion of Second and Third Isaiah, Zechariah, *1 Enoch*, the *Psalms of Solomon,* and the Dead Sea Scrolls. The writers of these documents anticipated a climactic period in human history when God would set things right. When Jesus announced, "the time is fulfilled. The Kingdom of God has come near," he was tapping into the potent end-time dream of ancient Israel that was never far below the surface of public consciousness. He fully expected all the ancient prophecies about the wonderful—but dreadful—time of global transformation to bubble up into his hearers' minds.

As we have seen, Zechariah had laid out the three-stage road map for God's victory: first evil times; then dramatic world transformation; and finally, the period of just desserts. By saying that "the time is now," Jesus unleashed fantastic expectations. His audience knew exactly what he was talking about. They recognized the agenda, and what they wanted were the crucial details— when and how would this take place? Who would be part of this new Kingdom—specifically, would *they*? What were the membership requirements? Jesus' message resonated with people who shared this great end-time dream of Israel. Obviously these were evil times—that part of Zechariah's model had been realized. Now people expected world transformation with the reward of the righteous to ensue—both the righteous living at the time of world change as well as the resurrection of all the righteous who had died. What a great reward—the time of just desserts had arrived, when God would be seen truly as a supreme God of justice and righteousness.

Jesus' audience also would have read into his Kingdom pronouncements an assurance that they'd live forever—provided they met the requirements of righteousness. That, too, was God's promise. Moreover, the unrighteous, the hated Roman colonizers, would be gone forever within just a short while.

Such thoughts were exceptionally dangerous. Jesus' vision represented nothing less than the greatest coup d'état of all time: the collapse of all world governments. Jesus must have hoped that he would have sufficient time to inform people before the Romans—and their spies, the Sadducees—heard of this gigantic plot. In fact, he must have sensed that time was not on his side, for at one point in his ministry, he sent out a massive and urgent mission to reach everyone within Galilee and Judea. Seventy of his followers were sent out in a hurry to all towns and villages, to announce to them that "the Kingdom of

God has come near to you" (Luke 10:9). Note, in passing, that Jesus' ability to win over seventy followers, train them in his message, and send them forth as representatives of his ministry represented a huge undertaking for the times. This was a major communications initiative to inform people urgently of the current political situation and to warn people that redemption was at hand. We also do not know what became of these seventy, whether they remained part of his permanent entourage or not.

THE PARABLES

Jesus' parables take us into the heart of his Kingdom of God message. Different ones focus on various aspects of the Kingdom, and no one parable contains the full story.

Some parables forecast amazing growth. Such well-known images as the sower (Matthew 13:3–8, 18–23) and the mustard seed (Matthew 13:31, 32) highlight the exponential development of the Kingdom. The parable of the Sower was presented as a straightforward allegory. A sower went out to plant seed. Some seeds fell on the path or on rocky ground and failed to take root. Some fell among thorns where the stronger weeds crowded out the good seed. Many seeds fell on good soil and they thrived, growing as much as "a hundredfold"—an incredible yield.

The story was easy to decode. Some people fail entirely to respond to the message of the Kingdom (the seed that fell on the path or poor soil). Others become enthusiastic about its prospects initially, but then their interest withers as they become preoccupied by other matters (like the seeds crowded out by the thorns). For others, however, the message takes root and fantastic growth occurs—those are the seeds that have landed on good soil. This parable served a number of purposes. It encouraged people, telling them that the Kingdom message would spread with lightning speed, at least among those who are receptive. It's also a call to action: Don't be left behind. Prepare now. Let the message "take root."

The "taking root" is important, for parables were designed to tease and prod us. Like Jesus' earliest audience, we, too, begin to ask questions of these stories. What is the message that is to take root? Who are those who fail to respond? What is "growth"? Is it individual personal growth? Or is it collective growth, the total number of people within the movement? If it is the former, what are we to do? How do we personally become transformed, turning metaphorically from a seed into a blossoming plant?

By asking these questions, we become actively engaged in the task of thinking through the Kingdom message. Jesus probably intended these stories as challenges to conventional thinking and imagination. Those questions formed part of what is involved in preparing for the Kingdom, opening minds to new possibilities. Our mental dialogue with Jesus demonstrates that we are ready to become participants in this new reality that's about to materialize.

Other parables were sheer public relations. Echoing Hillel before him, Jesus contended that the Kingdom of God should be of the highest value, our greatest priority. Short parables such as the Hidden Treasure (Matthew 13:44) and the Pearl of Great Value (Matthew 13:45, 46) made the point succinctly. Again we are motivated to ask questions. So what is it, this coming Kingdom? Why should it be our highest good? Why should we seek it? Expect it? Look for it? Prepare for it? How would this affect our daily lives? Does this require abandoning our responsibilities, giving up our families or our livelihood? Our interest is aroused, and Jesus' teaching method encourages us to immerse ourselves in questions such as these. We sit up and take notice.

Dealing with another provocative topic, Jesus addressed the *process* whereby the Kingdom would come to be. The Weeds in the Wheat parable (Matthew 13:24–30), for instance, presented the Kingdom as having three phases. First there is the sowing, the early stages of the Kingdom. Then a period of growth occurs. During this stage, the righteous and the unrighteous—that is, the wheat and the weeds—coexist. Finally there will be the harvest, or judgment, when the weeds will be discarded and the wheat saved. This parable raises some interesting interpretive questions. For one thing, what does it mean to be righteous? How do we become "wheat" and not "weed"? But also—and frustratingly—no schedule is given. When will the harvest occur? What must we do in order to be saved?

Moreover, did Jesus envisage himself living only in stage one, at the time of sowing or announcing? That is, was his role simply to start the Kingdom? How long would the second phase last, the time of growth where good and evil coexist? Days? Weeks? Months? Did Jesus imagine that he would be around when harvest time would take place, at the culmination of history when world transformation will occur? It would appear that Jesus thought that "harvest time" would happen very soon. That was his motivation for sending the seventy on an important "wake-up call" to all Israel, to let everyone in on the secret. He saw this as sending his "staff" out into the harvest, surely a tip-off that he thought the time of the end was exceptionally close at hand.

An even more radical question may occur to us at this point. Did Jesus envisage that he would have a role at the end-time? Was he just the messenger of the Kingdom? Or was he something more—perhaps the hoped-for catalyst of world transformation, that is, the Messiah? Was he, in fact, "the king"?

So what's the timetable? we ask. Jesus and his early followers thought that the time span was exceedingly short—months or a few years at best—not decades or longer. Jesus' message is a call to preparation. But how should we prepare? What is required of us? So the big question on everyone's mind concerned who would be part of this coming Kingdom. What's required for membership? That's the crucial question. How does the Kingdom relate *to me*?

Consistent with his teaching on Torah, Jesus emphasized two key aspects in preparing for the Kingdom. *Right action* is fundamental. The parable of the Talents (Matthew 25:14–30), for instance, compared the Kingdom of God to a person who gave his servants some money. One received five coins; another, two coins; and a third person, only one coin. The gracious benefactor then went away for a while. Upon his return he inquired what each had done with the money they had been entrusted with. The servants who had received five coins and two coins doubled their investment. They were praised for their actions. The servant who had received only one coin hoarded it and did nothing with it. He was severely chastised for being lazy and sent away. If "coins" indicate inner resources and talents, then this parable emphasizes the importance of making the most of what we have, building creatively and imaginatively upon personal strengths and abilities. It also involves an element of risk—venturing forward, becoming involved, and taking a chance on living life fully, not sitting back passively waiting for God to act. Utilizing what God has given us is one requirement for membership in the Kingdom of God.

A *right attitude* is also important. In the parable of the Lost Sheep (Matthew 18:10–44), Jesus stressed caring for the welfare of others. The Kingdom of God was compared to one who left the ninety-nine obedient sheep and actively searched for the one lost sheep. That's the sort of person who'd be ideally suited to the Kingdom. While the story could be interpreted as involving a person who neglects his primary responsibility, the emphasis is not on this, but on that individual's going out and looking for that which is missing. In modern terms, noticing, caring, and acting are chief personal hallmarks for inclusion in the Kingdom.

Forgiving others is also an essential characteristic of those worthy of the Kingdom. The parable of the Unforgiving Slave (Matthew 18:21–35) related the story of a servant whose debt was forgiven by his master but who, in turn, failed to forgive a fellow servant his debt. The unforgiving servant was condemned. As with other parables, this one indicates that membership in the Kingdom demands that we *act*—in this instance, by forgiving others.

Now we are beginning to build a profile of the Kingdom of God. We must focus on it as our highest priority, be prepared for its coming by forgiving, using our own inner resources and actively caring about others. *Attitude* plus *action*: both are required. This profile is reinforced in the parable of the Great Judgment (Matthew 25:31–46). This story imagined the end-time when the Kingdom culminates in God's rule. It is set at the harvest time when all the nations of the world will be judged. Some are saved; others are not. The difference is vital. Those who are deemed righteous are those who have recognized other people's needs and who have responded to them—providing food to the hungry and drink to the thirsty; giving clothes to the naked; welcoming strangers; helping to care for the sick; and visiting prisoners. These specific examples show us that those who actively respond to the needs of others are the righteous. They are the ones who will be part of God's Kingdom and they will have eternal life. Those who fail to respond in this manner face eternal punishment and banishment from God's Kingdom. In this vision, personal piety and passive submission are of little value. The Kingdom involves risk taking, engaging in constructive action, and having the personal courage to become involved, perhaps even making a wrong judgment call as one tries to respond positively to the needs of others. That's what truly matters.

As with other parables, this one, too, challenges our expectations. *Doing* is the basis for salvation and membership in God's Kingdom. Not faith in Christ. Not baptism in the name of the Trinity. Not assent to creeds about Jesus. Kingdom membership and living require action. That is an interesting perspective. It is consistent with Jewish belief. It raises eyebrows, however, when compared with later Christianity, because it runs counter to what is conventionally expected. How did the message of Jesus get so turned around? That's the interesting story that will be probed shortly.

How would his audiences have reacted to this parable when Jesus uttered it in the late 20s? Did his initial hearers sustain the excitement that world transformation was about to take place? And did they really expect it to occur within their lifetimes, or were they skeptical, adopting a wait-and-see attitude? How aware were they of all the specifics of end-time promises—the eradication of the wicked, the rewarding of the righteous, the resurrection of the righteous dead, a Davidic king on the throne of Israel, and universal peace? Did they really think that a political alternative to the Pax Romana was actually on their horizon?

Even more radically: Did Jesus' message have any impact at all—did they shape up and respond positively by demonstrating greater concern for others and actually making a difference? Did they actually think Jesus would become the Davidic king on the throne in Jerusalem?

More to the point, did Jesus?

We can ask the same questions of a different audience, some fifty years after the death of Jesus when the Gospel of Matthew was being written. How did these later hearers of this parable react? Would they have asked different questions? Would they, for instance, have wondered more about the timetable? Would they have demanded to know when "the harvest" would occur? Would they have pestered their leaders with the question, Where is this promised Kingdom? How long do we have to wait? Will it really happen in our lifetimes? This last is especially poignant given that it did not happen in the lifetime of the initial hearers of the parable. Or, with the all-too-obvious delay of the promised Kingdom, had disillusionment started to set in?

JESUS VERSUS HELLENIZATION

The challenge of Torah plus the promise of the Kingdom: that was Jesus' twofold strategy for dealing with Hellenization, and they dovetail. His message of strict Torah observance was similar to but more rigorous than the Pharisees on one side but less demanding than the interpretation of Torah provided by the Dead Sea Scroll community on the other. He occupied the middle ground, but, nonetheless, it posed a significant challenge. He also promised people their redemption with the dawning of the longed-for Kingdom of God. The righteous—the living and the dead—would be saved within the new world God was about to create. They would live eternally.

The Kingdom made demands. It wasn't for free. Nor did it just rely on faith. Actions expressive of caring, compassion, and forgiveness were mandatory for those seeking membership in this new world order. The linkage of *Torah* with *Kingdom*—the challenge and the promise—is not usually noticed. The message of the Kingdom of God and strict Torah observance come together in several New Testament passages. One such exchange occurs in the Gospel of Luke. A lawyer comes to Jesus asking, "What must I do to inherit eternal life?" (Luke 10:25). Jesus, quoting Deuteronomy, answers this question with the Shema: "Hear O Israel, the Lord is one. And you shall love the Lord your God with all your heart, soul, strength and mind." And he couples it with another commandment from the Book of Leviticus: "love your neighbor as yourself." He ends by telling the lawyer to do this and assures him that he will have life eternal. That's the Torah challenge part of Jesus' answer.

The exchange continues with the lawyer asking a follow-up question: "And who is my neighbor?" It is in this context that Jesus sets forth his famous parable of the Good Samaritan (Luke 10:29–37). The story concerns a mugging on the Jerusalem-to-Jericho road. The person lay beaten and was bypassed by two Jewish religious figures. Then someone from outside the victim's immediate culture, a Samaritan, happened to come by, stopped, looked after him, and took him to an inn where his wounds were attended to. At the end of the story, Jesus asks, Who of the three was a neighbor to the person mugged? Obviously, it was the Samaritan. Jesus then urges the lawyer to show mercy on others just as the Samaritan had done on the unfortunate victim. Here we have the Kingdom message, that compassion and going out of our way to help other people is required.

So here the two central themes to Jesus' teaching come together, linking the summary of the Torah with the parable of the Good Samaritan. To the lawyer's question about what he had to do to inherit eternal life, Jesus makes clear that it includes both observance of Torah plus acting in a way consistent with the Kingdom message.

Another central passage reinforces this point. The Lord's Prayer, after the sanctification of God's name, makes praying for the Kingdom the first petition: "Thy kingdom come." It is then immediately coupled with another petition that asks that God's will be done, on earth, as it is in heaven. The Lord's Prayer (Matthew 6:9–13), is situated in the context of the Sermon on the Mount (Matthew 5–7), right in the heart of Jesus' insistence on full Torah observance. The will of God is Torah observance. That's what the Lord's Prayer means . . . and demands. Preparing for the Kingdom requires doing the will of God, which focuses upon the requirements of the law.

Jesus' dual message was powerful. Prepare for the Kingdom by following Torah in the enhanced way that Jesus has promoted. Expect the Kingdom soon. You'll be a part of it. This position was politically subversive, for it contained strong anti-Roman elements within its popular appeal. It pitted the Jewish expectation of the end-time, as construed by Jesus, against the massive might of the Roman Empire with its much touted Pax Romana. Secured by Roman government, laws, and military force, the Pax Romana fostered peace, trade, and cultural exchanges in a way the world had not before known. It was the height of modern thinking for the times. For the Romans and those who bought into their culture, things could not get much better than they currently were experiencing—free trade throughout the empire, a system of laws, an organized society, and relative peace. For many, the world was as good as it was going to get.

And yet, for many Jews, this was not their perception. For those who reveled in the underground end-time literature, these were the *worst* of times—not the best—and the "age of wickedness" was the catalyst for end-time expectations. Jesus' message resonated with this anticipation as well as with the resentment against the occupying troops with their foreign ways and different cultural mores. By preaching the Kingdom of God, Jesus set his face firmly against the Romans. Jesus' preaching was a courageous act of political defiance, for he was attacking a key benefit of Hellenization—the Pax Romana—and taking on the world's mightiest power of the time. No wonder he couched his message in parables. Safety demanded it.

Tremendous dreams and hopes were attached to those who shared the vision of a changed environment. Such dreams were dangerous, and the Sadducees and Romans quickly caught on. Executing Jesus as "King of the Jews," *they* clearly saw the direction of his message and, for them, it was subversive. This was especially the case during the last week of his life when he appeared in Jerusalem just before Passover. He made a symbolic entrance into the old city on a donkey and was heralded by the crowds who had thronged into the city for the festival. That was a powerful political statement, for the prophet Zechariah had envisaged the king entering the city riding on a donkey (Zechariah 9:9). It signified that Jesus was claiming the throne of David. He symbolically attacked Temple practices by overturning the booths of the currency converters. This, too, was high drama—political theater—and leaders attuned to keeping the peace clearly recognized its import and were not amused. It is no wonder that within a few days of these controversial actions, Jesus was dead. Jesus was expressly declaring himself a claimant to the Jewish throne—the successor of David—with all the Messianic overtones this generated in the popular imagination.

So Jesus' dual strategy for dealing with Hellenization was revolutionary. He reinforced the necessity of following the law. He coupled it with persuasive and dramatic portrayals of what the Kingdom of God would be like. And he promised that it would soon take shape upon earth. That earthly nature of the Kingdom was clearly indicated in the Lord's Prayer. It is not a spiritual kingdom. Nor is it one that is located in a supernatural place to which the soul travels upon death. Jesus' message was firmly rooted in the traditional Jewish expectations of the time: world transformation. Here was exactly the champion those end-time devotees had sought. His genius was to have dramatized the concept in a way that none of the prophets, the Dead Sea Scroll community, or the author of the *Psalms of Solomon* ever managed to do. In essence, he made the Kingdom seem real and attainable. He touched multitudes with his message. Such a message struck at the foundations of the Roman world. It was clearly subversive and threatening to the ruling authorities, the Romans and their compliant Jewish allies, the Sadducees.

But he died before the Kingdom materialized.

7

JESUS' EARLIEST FOLLOWERS: THE JESUS MOVEMENT

However unfamiliar it may be to many readers, Jesus' two-pronged approach to Hellenization is what the Gospel of Matthew presents. Modern Christians are not Torah-observant and haven't been for centuries. But the evidence is overwhelming. Jesus was an orthodox Jew who taught and practiced Torah. Why later Christians moved away from this position is something that will be considered in due course. Moreover, the Kingdom Jesus promised didn't arrive as expected. That, too, created problems for later Christians as they struggled to match reality with expectations.

Aside from Matthew's sketch of Jesus, there is further corroborating evidence for the pro-Torah stance of Jesus. It's to be found in the beliefs of his immediate followers who also combined the challenge of Torah with the promise of the Kingdom. The Jesus Movement was a Torah-observant group, ensconced within Judaism as one more form of this religion alongside such other Jewish factions as the Sadducees, Pharisees, Essenes, and Zealots. These people were Jews, operating well within the Jewish orbit and accepted by other Jews as Jews. That did change over time, but, at the outset, this was how they were regarded.

JAMES

Following Jesus' death, the leader of the Jesus Movement was Jesus' brother, James. This group expected that Jesus would return quickly to establish the Kingdom of God as an alternative to Roman rule. That absolutely had to happen, for Jesus' death before the arrival of the Kingdom represented a huge setback.

Jesus' desperate cry upon the cross, "My God, My God, why have you forsaken me?" (Mathew 27:46) could easily be construed as his recognition, close to death, that the Kingdom was not going to materialize as he had promised.

But his earliest followers entertained that great end-time hope. They thought that Jesus would return to finish what he had announced. Soon. Then and only then would he truly be the Messiah. Jesus would become the Davidic king with Israel freed from the shackles of Roman authority. Moreover, it would become a beacon for all humanity and God would be worshipped in holiness by all. That's what Zechariah had said would happen on that day when God will establish his sovereign rule: "And the Lord will become king over all the earth; on that day, the Lord will be one and his name one" (Zechariah 14:9). In the meantime, James functioned as the prince regent, waiting for the king to return and the Roman Empire to fade away.

James was the undisputed leader of the Jesus Movement, from the early 30s through to his murder some thirty years later in 62. Others present with him in Jerusalem included Jesus' immediate family—Mary, his mother; his brothers; Mary Magdalene; and the disciples. These loyal individuals, headed by James, were a royal court in waiting. They were the heart of the movement and its undisputed leaders. They knew the historical Jesus, were aware of what he taught and practiced, and were with him when he died. Recognizing what he stood for, they constituted the solid nucleus of the movement. These were leaders with credibility. Some contended they witnessed his resurrection. And so the members of the Jesus Movement waited. They stoked the Kingdom message, followed Jewish law rigorously, and kept alive the hope that the world would soon be transformed dramatically.

According to the Book of Acts, James was an orthodox Jew who looked upon Jesus as a teacher and Messiah claimant. The *political* nature of the Jesus Movement he led was reflected in a very important question the risen Jesus was asked by the disciples in Jerusalem: "Lord, is this the time when you will restore the Kingdom to Israel?" (Acts 1:6). The question drips with political overtones. It was tantamount to asking, Is this the time when you will act as the Messiah, to establish the independence of Israel, assume the throne of David, and help God bring about the promised Kingdom? In other words, when would Rome be overthrown? The risen Jesus deflected the question, saying that only God knew the agenda.

The members of the Jesus Movement followed the Torah as interpreted by Jesus. They observed the Sabbath, kosher laws, the great festivals of Judaism; they practiced circumcision and kept all the other commandments required of faithful Jews everywhere. They certainly did not think of Jesus as having walked away from Torah. Nor did they think of Jesus as having established a new movement or church. They went to the Temple frequently, participating in its rituals. There was no question in their minds that the Jewish priesthood and the Temple were legitimate. Legends grew up about the devotion of James, so much so that he eventually became known as James the Righteous, an epithet given only to those who followed Torah strictly.

Christian tradition places the Jesus Movement on the western ridge of Jerusalem. Today we can visit "the upper room" at a location above what is alleged to be the tomb of King David. How far back this tradition of the location of the upper room goes is not known, but the remains of an ancient synagogue have been discovered on this site at its lowest levels, below the upper room and the tomb of David. Whether these early followers of Jesus were actually situated here on the western ridge or elsewhere in Jerusalem—or whether that upper room was *the* upper room of the Last Supper—it would have been only a short walk to Temple Mount, where they could have participated in the prayers and sacrifices.

Along the way, they would have bumped into Sadducean priests coming and going, fulfilling their functions, Roman soldiers keeping peace, Pharisees and their *yeshivas,* or schools, and perhaps an Essene or two who had strayed from their quarter of the city. Tourists would have flocked through on their way to the broad pavement stones that took them up into the Temple precincts. These stones still stand there on the south side of Temple Mount, and we can walk where Jesus and James once strode up to the Temple. On the Sabbath, they would have heard the trumpeter standing on the high southwest corner of Temple Mount call out the times for keeping the day of rest. They would have honored that call, refraining from work prohibited on the Sabbath. The great festivals of Succoth, Shavuot, and Passover would come and go, and these devout Jews were part of the annual cycle of Jewish prayer and worship. Rooted within the diverse family of first-century Judaism, the Jesus Movement was not a separate religion. It jostled with the other ways of being Jewish for recognition and membership.

Picture the early followers of Jesus, not in our terms as Christians today, but as Orthodox Jews carrying out their Jewish beliefs and practices under the inspiration of their rabbi, Jesus. We need to visualize them as having long hair and wearing the prayer shawl—the tallit—as they prayed. They stopped working at sundown on Friday evening. They welcomed and observed the Sabbath, sharing in its festive meal, likely all together, singing, rejoicing, and resting from labor.

James, in fact, was a Nazirite or "super Jew," like his cousin John the Baptist. As we said, a Nazirite was a Torah-observant Jew who had taken a special vow of dedication to God. Their rabbi was Jesus, and it was his interpretation of Torah that commanded their allegiance. But they hoped for more: surely he would fulfill the role of the Messiah, returning to usher in this great end-time when he would become king of Israel and they, the royal family. Their vision of what Jesus taught and practiced dovetails with Matthew's image of Jesus as proclaiming both Torah observance and the Kingdom message.

As James, so Jesus. The best indicator of what Jesus of the 20s actually taught is likely to be James, his brother. James knew the man and what he stood for. He knew Jesus taught and practiced Torah, as they did. In addition to what the Gospel of Matthew depicts in passages like the Sermon on the Mount, the example of James is the best clue we have today concerning the beliefs and practices of the Jesus of history.

James was murdered in 62, and Josephus provides us with some of the details. An interim high priest (a Sadducee) had him killed. Josephus also notes that the Pharisees lamented the slaughter of this righteous leader and had tried to come to his rescue, but not in time. The early church historian Eusebius tells us that the surviving blood relatives of Jesus, his apostles, and other followers gathered together sometime after the capture of Jerusalem in 70 to determine who would succeed James as leader of the movement. Simeon, Jesus' cousin, was unanimously selected. He was the son of Cleophas, the brother of Joseph, Jesus' father.[1]

These were very difficult times for Jews in Israel. The Temple had been destroyed and Jerusalem lay in ruins. Its priesthood—the Sadducees—had been virtually wiped out. The Essenes had been decimated at Qumran in 68 by Roman troops heading up to Jerusalem. The Zealots would meet their fate a few years later, in 73 or 74, high atop the fortress of Masada. Members of the Jesus Movement also must have experienced tremendous upheaval. The Romans hunted down all those of royal blood—all those who could claim lineage from the family of David. This quest was carried out during the reign of Emperor Domitian (81–96) who issued orders that the descendants of David be slain. The emperors understood very clearly the political threat. Another ancient church historian quoted by Eusebius, Hegesippus, noted that at this time there were grandchildren of Judas, one of Jesus' brothers, still alive. Domitian interrogated them, but, upon learning that they were poor farmers and that the Kingdom in question would only come at the end of the world, he dismissed them as simpletons. Clearly they posed no threat to the peace and stability of the Roman Empire. Hegesippus went on to note that they were still alive by the time of the emperor Trajan (98–117). During Trajan's reign, however, Simeon, Jesus' cousin and the second bishop of Jerusalem, was tortured and finally crucified. He was alleged to have been 120 years old at the time.[2]

This ended control of the Jesus Movement by blood relatives of Jesus. Eusebius named thirteen subsequent bishops of Jerusalem, noting that they were all Jews: Justus, Zacceus, Tobias, Benjamin, John, Matthew, Philip, Seneca, Justus, Levi, Ephres, Joseph, and Judas.[3]

BIRTH OF RABBINIC JUDAISM

During this time, Judaism was itself evolving, even though Christians today tend to think of Judaism as the religion of the Old Testament, forgetting that it, too, has been transformed. Its history has not been static. It sometimes comes as a remarkable surprise to Christians that the Judaism of today, while having continuity with biblical religion, has also changed dramatically. After A.D. 70, this was a dire necessity. The Romans had destroyed the Temple, the focal point of Jewish life for hundreds of years. Jerusalem lay in ruins. Social life in Israel was disrupted. The priesthood represented by the Sadducees had been decimated. Other than the Jesus Movement, only the Pharisees survived.

70 represents a key turning point. It was the catalyst for change—for everyone. The Pharisaic sages, the rabbis, took Judaism in one direction. They did what had to be done, that is, reconstruct Judaism along lines that did not involve the Temple. Hence we get the development of modern Judaism, built along communal participation in the synagogue and in the family rituals that keep alive the ancient practices prescribed by the Torah. Judaism moved on with its development while various forms of early Christianity forged their own separate identities. Henceforth Judaism would be led by rabbis and their remarkable debates and decisions would, in time, enter into literature through the Mishnah and the Talmud.[4]

At the same time, the Jesus Movement in Jerusalem pulled in another direction, trying to maintain close ties with mainstream Judaism but, in time, evolving its own distinctive infrastructure. Certainly at the outset they would have considered themselves Jewish, but that probably changed over time as the two religions diverged. Paul's Christ Movement veered in yet a third direction. Its innovative message and few demands appealed to people around the Mediterranean, and it experienced tremendous growth. While Paul was ethnically Jewish, in light of his critique of Judaism, it is highly unlikely that he considered himself Jewish by the time he was writing his letters in the 50s and early 60s.

THE EBIONITES

Somewhat later, in the second through fourth centuries, Jesus' followers who sought to retain Torah observance were referred to by their opponents as the Ebionites (the Poor) or as the Nazarenes.[5] They were likely successors to the original Jesus Movement led by James and the other disciples of Jesus.

It is a remarkable irony of history that their beliefs are not well known today, and they differ markedly from the tradition of contemporary Christianity, which derives from Paul. In the fourth century, Eusebius even referred to these original followers of Jesus as heretics (*Ecclasiastical History*, Book 3, Chapter 27)—well, heretics as far as the religion of Paul was concerned. The Ebionites followed the Torah, as required of all Jews. In obeying Torah, they undoubtedly felt they were observing the religion taught and practiced by Jesus. They were distinguished from other forms of Judaism by their attachment to the teachings and example of their rabbi, Jesus. But whatever that meant, it did not mean the abandonment of the ancient covenant expressed through the Torah.

Believing Jesus to be the promised Messiah, they waited for him to come to restore Israel to prominence and bring about the long-awaited end-time. We do not know how they handled the problem of "the delay," how their leaders responded to questions from their followers of why the promised Kingdom had not yet materialized on earth.

They held that Jesus, like all who are holy and righteous, was resurrected. Unlike Paul's Christ Movement did, they seem not to have attached any significance to his death and resurrection. He was not a savior. It was not as if people could now participate in Jesus' death and resurrection and so be saved. Identifying with Jesus' resurrection was not their view of salvation.

Presumably they held to traditional Jewish views of resurrection and redemption. This concept projected that at the end-time, when the Kingdom would come upon earth, the righteous dead would be resurrected. They would then join the righteous people who were alive when that great event happens. In the meantime, the dead were dead, awaiting God's judgment at the end of history. Jesus' resurrection, however, was proof that resurrection does occur and that the end-time must soon be approaching.

Jesus was fully human, they thought, born in the usual way, having Mary as his mother and Joseph as his father. Their preferred gospel text was the Gospel of Matthew, written in Aramaic but without the virgin birth story, unlike our version of this gospel, which, like Luke, includes a virgin birth narrative. In fact, they did not accept the virgin birth story at all since this mythology does not find its roots in Jewish thinking. So, unlike later Christians, they did not see Jesus as a divine being. Nor did they think that Jesus "preexisted" his human form in any fashion. That is, he was not God incarnate. He was not "a Christ" or a "Son of God" in any sense other than in the way we might be said to be children of God when we address him as "Our Father" in prayer. He was, like you and me, human in all respects, feeling our pain, joy, sorrow, and gladness. He became God's chosen Messiah because God judged him more righteous than any other person.

The emphasis on the full humanity of Jesus, to the exclusion of any aspect of divinity, set apart the Ebionites from other forms of Christianity in the second through fourth centuries. There were other pictures of Jesus emerging in other communities. Some viewed Jesus as solely divine, only appearing to be human. Other groups, however, holding that Jesus was both divine and human, tried valiantly to reconcile two aspects of Jesus in one nature. These proponents searched for philosophical terminology that would enable them to say how Jesus combined in one person two aspects, divinity and humanity. For the Ebionite community, however, Jesus had only one nature: fully human. That simplified matters, for it avoided all the intricate Trinitarian formulas that were being bandied about in the third and fourth centuries, and all the cantankerous disputes associated with pinning down the correct way of speaking of the person of Jesus.

The Ebionites possessed gospels other than their version of the Gospel of Matthew. We now unfortunately only have brief portions of their *Gospel of the Nazareans,* the *Gospel of the Ebionites,* and the *Gospel According to the Hebrews.*[6] They did not accept the writings of Paul, nor did they recognize the Gospel of Luke or the Book of Acts. All these writings, in their judgment, represented false teachings. We do not know what else they may have accepted as authoritative. Certainly they used the Septuagint, since they honored and followed the Old Testament. But what other documents they may have included in a growing canon of Ebionite writings we simply don't know.

Later Ebionite writings that have survived include the *Homilies of Clement* and the *Letter of Peter to James* and its *Reception.*[7] These last two works make it clear that the Ebionites were strongly opposed to the teachings of Paul and his followers. In their view, Paul was simply a false teacher. The *Letter of Peter to James* and its *Reception* by James, for instance, maintained that the true authentic teachings and practices of Jesus would only be conveyed through those who were circumcised, that is, through the true successors of Jesus. The real truth had been hidden away from Paul and his followers, who denied the validity of Torah observance. According to Ebionite sources, Peter even referred to Paul as "the man who is my enemy" (*Letter of Peter to James* 2:3). While we are accustomed to viewing Paul as a trusted teacher, that was not how he was regarded by many during the first three centuries after Jesus' death.

A FORGOTTEN PERSPECTIVE

The Jesus Movement functioned well within the parameters of the Judaisms of the times. In outward practices, the members of the Jesus Movement did not differ from other Jewish groups of the time such as Sadducees, Pharisees, Essenes, or Zealots. Like most other Jewish groups, they had an anti-Roman, anti-Hellenistic stance. This political conviction would land them in trouble time and time again with the puppets of Roman authorities, the Sadducees and the high priests who were willing to make compromises with Hellenization. Jesus Movement members revered their rabbi as an inspired teacher who was resurrected and who would return, they hoped, to fulfill messianic expectations. This was not just a pious religious belief: it was fundamentally *political*. They expected Jesus to return to act as a catalyst in overthrowing Roman authority with its Pax Romana, thus ending Hellenization once and for all. He would help establish an independent Jewish state under himself as the Davidic king, ushering in an era of universal peace. This would reflect the sovereign rule of God, which Jesus had announced was imminent.

Belief in a Messiah was certainly not out of bounds for a Jewish sect. The Essenes—the Dead Sea Scroll community—openly looked for two Messiahs, one political and one religious, and other groups were receptive to the view that one day, a messianic leader would come to bring about a changed world. Nor was an anti-Roman stance unusual. The Essenes, Zealots, and Pharisees all expressed this view. Only the Jesus Movement, however, had a king and a royal court-in-waiting. This political orientation had considerable popular appeal. It envisaged the day when the dreaded Romans would be gone, with their alien customs, temples, philosophies, and practices. The land would revert back to the true observers of Judaism. But the big payoff was this: the righteous who had kept the law against tremendous odds in a multicultural world would be rewarded. Finally there would be tangible proof that Torah observance made a difference.

So far as other groups of Jews were concerned, the conviction by the Jesus Movement sect that Jesus was the Messiah who would return to accomplish these political objectives was just one of their idiosyncrasies. Only the Sadducees with their pro-Roman stance would have been threatened—but no more so by the Jesus Movement than by the Pharisaic, Essene, or Zealot factions. They, too, were anti-Roman.

Along with the Gospel of Matthew, the beliefs and practices of the Jesus Movement and its successor, the Ebionites, demonstrate the uniqueness of Jesus' powerful challenge and promise—Torah and the Kingdom message—linked together inseparably. That's what he preached and that is how his closest followers understood him, including family members. In a way that no other individual of his time managed to achieve, he dredged up end-time expectations and made them appear real, giving people hope and providing an alternative to the Pax Romana. He was an exceptional teacher, a gifted human being, a possible Messiah, and an inspiring leader who attracted a substantial following.

That was how he was profiled by his friends, family, and followers. But that is not the image of Jesus that would pass down into history. Things quickly changed.

8

WHAT HAPPENED TO JESUS?

Jesus—Jewish. Torah-observant. Fully human. No virgin birth. A revered teacher-rabbi. Herald of the long-awaited Kingdom of God. Resurrected. A potential Messiah, who was expected to return promptly to fulfill traditional messianic expectations. That was the portrait of Jesus among his earliest followers and his family. Their beliefs and practices are somewhat unfamiliar to most people today. Some may even ask, you mean Jesus had a brother? In fact, several brothers and at least two sisters? How come we haven't heard about them?

Like Jesus himself, his earliest followers in Jerusalem were Jewish and Torah-observant. They waited patiently for Jesus to return to carry out his dream of a Kingdom of God on earth in contrast to rule by Rome. That was the political hope they cherished as they went about their daily lives. Christian doctrine today, however, is characterized by beliefs of a very different nature. This includes a special, virgin birth. It also abounds with various titles ascribed to Jesus: Son of God, Christ, Lord, Savior, Redeemer. The Gospel of John calls him the Logos (the Word) that became flesh. He became viewed as a preexistent being who took on human form, combining elements both of divinity as well as humanity. For many, he was God incarnate, the second person of the Trinity. These are all reflective of the cult of personality that surrounded Jesus after his death. These beliefs originated from the Christ Movement led by Paul.

The image of Jesus changed dramatically over the course of just over one hundred years. Jesus became seen as a divine being holding cosmic importance. Along with that development went another: a repudiation of his Jewish heritage. Torah observance was swept away and with it, the Sabbath, Passover, the dietary laws, circumcision, and the whole code of Jewish ethics. Gone, too, were the major festivals. Over time, Christianity separated from Judaism and created its own separate infrastructure with a hierarchy and buildings of its own. No longer did it worship in the Temple or in Jewish synagogues. Its distinctive liturgical cycle of Advent-Christmas-Epiphany-Lent-Easter-Pentecost came, in time, to replace the time-honored Jewish calendar. Sunday eventually replaced the Jewish Sabbath as the day of rest—but not as strictly observed as the Jewish Sabbath, at least not in modern times. The new religion ceased being in any sense Jewish and came to acquire its own unique character, separate and distinctive. How that detachment took place is an interesting story and it can be documented, virtually decade by decade, from writings that have survived. Without giving too much away prematurely, the separation story has to do with the new movement's rejection of Torah observance and the promotion of Jesus as in some sense divine. Either view would have served to cast the movement out of the Jewish family.

The image of Jesus changed radically, while his roots within Judaism were forgotten. By the midsecond century, Christian leaders were touting Jesus as an incarnate savior who redeemed humanity by his death and resurrection. *Who* he was thought to be came to obscure *what* he had taught and practiced. This represents a remarkable shift in emphasis—away from the religion *of* Jesus and toward a religion *about* Christ.

A CHANGED FOCUS

The transformation is absolutely dramatic. By the late second century, Christians had composed the basis of the Apostles' Creed.[1]

> I believe in God, the Father almighty,
>   creator of heaven and earth.
> I believe in Jesus Christ, God's only Son, our Lord.
>   He was conceived by the power of the Holy Spirit,
>   and born of the Virgin Mary.
>   He suffered under Pontius Pilate,
>   was crucified, died, and was buried.
>   He descended to the dead.
>   On the third day he rose again.
>   He ascended into heaven,
>   and is seated at the right hand of the Father.
>   He will come again to judge the living and the dead.
> I believe in the Holy Spirit,
>   the holy catholic church,
>   the communion of saints,

the forgiveness of sins,
the resurrection of the body,
and the life everlasting. Amen. [2]

Even for denominations that do not recite this creed, this flagship statement of faith puts Jesus into the conceptual context most Christians today know and recognize. But we need to pause to consider what this creed says—and, perhaps more importantly, what it omits.

What it sets forth is impressive. Jesus is now linked to God the Father and to the Holy Spirit in keeping with the developing doctrine of the Trinity, that Jesus is fully human and fully divine. It positions Jesus Christ as "God's only Son." It references his virgin birth and attributes paternity to the activity of God's Holy Spirit. It skips over his life and moves very quickly to his death, his resurrection, and his status today, in heaven with God. It proclaims that he will return to judge all humanity. It ends with an affirmation of the church as the community of the saints and professes belief in forgiveness, resurrection, and eternal life. This is the image of Jesus shared by Christians today and it is a more recognizable form of the religion than its earliest expression.

In terms of setting forth who Jesus is claimed to be, the Apostles' Creed was truly a breakthrough document.

But let's consider what this statement of faith fails to say. What it ignores is substantial, and this is usually not recognized. Where, for instance, are the central teachings of Jesus? Where are the references to the teachings of the parables, that powerful Kingdom of God message? Where is there mention of the long-anticipated Kingdom of God, that political reality expected to replace the Pax Romana? What about the Sermon on the Mount, with its reinterpretation of Torah requirements? What happened to Jesus' demand that his followers practice a pattern of righteousness stricter than that observed by the Pharisees? Where is the cut-and-thrust vitality of Jesus' message, that radical challenge to the world power of his time with all its startling impact, enhanced expectations, and newsworthy implications? Moreover, where is its daring subversiveness? Everything Jesus taught in his parables or in the Sermon on the Mount is bypassed.

Why didn't the creed say something along these lines?

We revere our teacher, Jesus, who taught us to make the Kingdom of God our highest priority and to prepare for its manifestation on earth, through deeds of compassion and caring backed by an inner spirit of generosity and forgiveness.

We follow the example of Jesus who taught us to be sensitive to the needs of others and to respond appropriately.

We believe in the teachings of Jesus who challenged us to live the life of Torah to its fullest, to embrace correct attitudes as well as right behavior.

We acknowledge with gratitude the Jesus who gave us the hope that God's rule would eventually be sovereign over all the earth and that the righteous will truly inherit the earth.

We have confidence in God, creator of the universe, who alone can redeem and who, forgiving us our failings, will resurrect us from the dead into life eternal.

Why none of this? There's a lot missing from the Apostles' Creed—*all* of Jesus' teachings, in fact. This is truly astounding.

A CHANGED IMAGE

Moreover, what happened to the image of Jesus? How did a human, Jewish rabbi, a messianic claimant, suddenly become a divine being robbed of his historical context and Jewish identity? He is now "God's only Son," linked to God the Father Almighty and to the Holy Spirit. What are the connections between these aspects of divinity? Clearly the creed wants to affirm that Jesus was a preexistent supernatural being who became incarnate in human form. It commits us, moreover, to one mode of incarnation, taking the virgin birth literally as biology, as a divine being impregnating a young Jewish woman.

What has happened to Jesus? Why this dramatic makeover? How could this have happened? Who was responsible?

Instead of right actions arising out of a right attitude as one would expect from a Jewish teacher, the mandate now centers on *correct belief* in the person of Jesus: who he was. From *orthopraxy*—or right action—typical of Judaism, we have been catapulted into *orthodoxy*—right belief—which came to characterize Christianity. A seismic shift in perspective has taken place. The creed's exclusive focus is on the messenger, not the message.

There are no overt references to anything Jewish about Jesus. That is eliminated. The creed also effectively abandons the claim that Jesus was the Jewish Messiah—there is no talk of his fulfilling a political role, his claim to the throne of Israel, assisting God in the task of world transformation, or any such requirement that a Jewish Messiah must fulfill. Remarkably, nothing at all is said of Jesus' messianic status. The whole political thrust of Jesus' mission is ignored. It is replaced by a cosmic one—Jesus in relation to God the Father and the Holy Spirit.[3] That's a very different picture.

There is minimal linkage between this Jesus, the Christ of faith, and the actual historical human Jesus who lived and taught in the 20s. Only the references to Pontius Pilate and Jesus' mother, Mary, anchor him within time and therefore in history. The Apostles' Creed, we find, dehistoricizes the portrait of Jesus, shearing him from his Jewish context and stripping him of his humanity. He is now a supernatural being engaged on a rescue mission, someone who swooped down from heaven to take loyal followers with him back there. We would not think of him as human, debating the Torah, encouraging strict adherence to its requirements, honoring the Sabbath, sharing bread and wine with his followers, engaging in the festivals, planning and plotting his next moves, and delighting audiences with his amazing parables about the coming Kingdom. All of this is lost.

By the time of the Apostles' Creed, Jesus and his message had become overtaken by a cult of personality, a development foreign to Jewish ways of thinking. For all the impressiveness and importance of Abraham, Moses, Samuel, David, Solomon, or Ezra—or any of the prophets for that matter—no hero worship grew up around any of these worthy and righteous individuals. To a large extent this haloing of Jesus drowns out the vibrancy of his message—so much so that we have trouble even today seeing him as human or even identifying his message.

So the human teacher and Messiah claimant became elevated quickly into a Christ and then into a God. All this occurred suddenly, within just over a century of his death. How did a God come to replace a thoroughly human, Jewish Jesus?

JESUS NOW DIVINE

The strength of the image of Jesus as divine is extremely powerful, then and now. The controversy over Dan Brown's popular book and film, *The Da Vinci Code*, attests to the overwhelming power of this perspective.[4] Part of the appeal of this work lies in its sense of adventure. The clandestine Opus Dei and the secretive Priory of Sion all play a role. There's a hidden truth that is being ruthlessly suppressed. The provocative feature of Dan Brown's book, however, lies elsewhere than in this supposed secret. It resides in his portrait of an all-too-human Jesus that challenges our ingrained image of Jesus as divine. Building upon the views of Michael Baigent, Dan Brown puts forward the view that Jesus was married to Mary Magdalene, that they were intimate and had children.[5]

The affront to Christian sensibilities lies in the picture of Jesus being married, having sexual intercourse, and being a family man. Official Christian doctrine maintains that Jesus, the second person of the Trinity, was fully divine. It also contends that he was fully human. To think otherwise is heretical. So, on the face of it, thinking of Jesus as having a companion and partner in life should not upset anyone. But this is not how Christians of most denominations picture Jesus in their thoughts. A sexual Jesus, married with kids, shatters the usual preconceptions of divinity. There was, in fact, a cover-up, but it was much more powerful than the thesis *The Da Vinci Code* presents.

So how did we get from the Jewish man Jesus who taught a political message to the divine being who became incarnate through a virgin birth, a supernatural God-man, dying and rising again to achieve salvation for all humanity? This is one of the greatest mysteries of the New Testament and early Christianity: how a Gentile God came to replace a Jewish Jesus.

For the answer to this question, we turn to Paul and his vastly different Christ Movement.

9

THE TROUBLE WITH PAUL

Nothing in the early Jesus Movement prepares us for Paul. Written in the mid 50s, Paul's Letter to the Galatians was a "bombshell" document. While intended to settle a dispute within one of the communities he founded, its impact has extended far beyond the mere arbitration of a local and temporary dispute. It laid out the main tenets of Paul's radical Christ Movement, which is considerably different from both Judaism and the earlier Jesus Movement centered in Jerusalem. Galatians remains one of the most influential documents ever written within Christianity, for its views represent the underpinnings of a new religion.

PAUL'S LIFE

So who was Paul? What do we reliably know of his career and message? Probably born in the first few years A.D., Paul grew up in the Jewish Diaspora. Paul himself does not indicate where he was born. The later Book of Acts claims that it was in the city of Tarsus located in what is modern-day southeastern Turkey. Paul was a Hellenized Jew, living and working in the Greek language. Somehow his family had achieved prominence and even acquired Roman citizenship in the process. How Jewish was he? Did he come from a Torah-observant home? As an adult, did he follow the law? Did he know Hebrew, the language of the ancient scrolls? Did he understand Aramaic, the language of Jesus and his disciples? What was his education like? We do not know the answers to these questions. We can surmise, however, that like all Jews living in the Diaspora, he would undoubtedly have shared at least some beliefs and values with his non-Jewish counterparts. This would have included some knowledge of Greek drama and philosophy as well as familiarity with the beliefs and practices of the Roman mystery religions, whose temples were everywhere.

At some point, he moved to the center of Jewish life, Jerusalem. A few decades before Paul arrived there, Herod the Great had built up this city as a showcase center with its vastly extended Temple Mount area, huge retaining walls, majestic entrances that paid careful attention to crowd control, and, of course, the magnificently restored Temple itself that shone like the sun. That towering edifice formed the heart and soul of Jewish life. It was the nation's hub of culture and commerce, encompassing far more than a place of worship. Jerusalem itself supported tourism from all over the Roman Empire, especially on the three pilgrimage festivals when devout Jews would "come up" to Jerusalem from the Galilee and from all around the Mediterranean. Larger than the Acropolis in Athens, Temple Mount in Jerusalem had also become a must-see destination for wealthy first-century Romans who could afford to tour. The sight of the Temple would have impressed Paul as he first arrived.

The Temple was also the center of government, with its judges, law courts, scribes, and the archives. The Sanhedrin met on Temple Mount, the Jewish high council composed of Sadducees and Pharisees who helped guide the nation's affairs. All this was presided over by Roman troops stationed not too far off in the distance to handle any disturbance that might occur. For the most part, however, there was relative peace between the Jews and the Romans in the first few decades of the first century.

Paul talks about his past in several of his writings. In his Letter to the Galatians, he indicates that he underwent a dramatic mystical experience of "the Christ," perhaps, as the Book of Acts says, on his way to Damascus (Acts 9:3; 22:6; 26:12). He doesn't tell us much about this life-changing experience. Later accounts in the Book of Acts will depict it dramatically: a bolt of light from heaven, a voice confronting him about his persecution of people in the Jesus Movement, and temporary blindness.[1] Paul himself did not provide these details. Instead he chose to emphasize that he did not discuss his experience with anyone. Rather than returning to Jerusalem, he headed off "to Arabia" for a period of time.

At that time, "Arabia" was different from what we know today as Saudi Arabia. It encompassed Damascus in modern-day Syria, parts of western Jordan along the Jordan River, and much of the Arabian Peninsula. Arabia also included the fabulous Nabatean city of Petra, whose beautiful buildings were carved into the face of mountains. These remain impressive today, providing the breathtaking background for parts of the 1980s movie *Raiders of the Lost Ark*. The nearby endless red sands of Wadi Rum that look like the red rock area of Sedona, Arizona, form the impressive backdrop to the film *Lawrence of Arabia*.

The Nabateans were the wealthy traders of the Roman world, controlling the lucrative trade routes between the Mediterranean and the Indian Ocean. Goods would be unloaded from ships in Gaza and taken by camel across southern Israel, where today tourists can trek along the old Nabatean "spice route." The caravans then headed toward Petra in modern-day Jordan. Petra was the center of the trade, the world's first megawarehouse for raw and manufactured goods traveling between Roman cities and other cultures. Spices, woven cloth, exotic animals, pottery, and jewelry all passed along this route, as well as people unfortunate enough to have been captured in the high-profit slave trade. From Petra, the bundles were transported by camels across the Arabian Peninsula into Yemen, where they were loaded onto ships bound for India, the east coast of Africa, and probably even more distant lands. Where Paul went in Arabia, or why he went, we do not know.

It is significant, however, that Paul never met the Jesus of history, that charismatic rabbi who gathered disciples around himself and taught and practiced Judaism during the 20s. By his own admission, he never conferred with Jesus' successors, the senior members of the Jesus Movement in Jerusalem, until at least three years after his dramatic experience, and even then only briefly. Paul remained curiously detached from those who knew what Jesus stood for and represented. In his writings, he constantly positioned his Christ Movement as separate and distinct from the Jesus Movement. This is considerably different from the picture the Book of Acts will paint some fifty or so years later. This latter work tried to fuse the two movements together, but it is likely this is more revisionist history than actual fact in the midfirst century.

During the late 40s, 50s, and early 60s, Paul traveled throughout the Diaspora—what we know of as Turkey, Greece, and Italy—formed congregations, taught, and wrote letters. We are fortunate to have his letters, for they give us firsthand insight into his thinking. His message emphasized freedom from the Jewish law. Moreover, he urged believers to undergo the same kind of mystical experience of "the Christ" that he himself had had years before on his journey to Damascus. Much of Paul's thought paralleled that of the Roman mystery religions familiar from his youth growing up in the Diaspora. The belief structure is the same in both religions. Both portray a dying-rising savior God-human who comes to rescue humanity from its plight. Paul's views would have shocked anyone who was Jewish: his was a thoroughly Hellenized religion. Any member of the Pharisaic movement, for instance, or, for that matter, anyone in the Jesus Movement in Jerusalem would have seen this non-Torah-observant movement focused on a dying-rising savior figure as a separate religion from Judaism. They would have regarded these views as utter nonsense and blasphemy, to be avoided at any cost. This view was, in their opinion, just as wrong as the religions of Mithras, Isis, or Dionysus with their savior figures.

Paul did manage to shock people. He was a feisty, fiery teacher who had tremendous success with Gentiles in the Jewish Diaspora. He typically went into Jewish synagogues where he was invited to speak. His message resonated with one particular constituency found within Hellenistic synagogues, the "God-fearers." We don't normally think of non-Jews frequenting Jewish synagogues on a regular basis, but that was an important phenomenon of the Roman world.[2] The God-fearers were Gentiles who liked the ethics and monotheistic beliefs of Judaism. They valued its antiquity. They found that these writings, discussions, and intellectual debates represented a sober contrast to the enthusiastic and orgiastic celebrations of the Roman mystery religions. They did not want, however, to convert to Judaism, being content to be associated on the periphery of Judaism. The God-fearers attended the services, participated in the discussions, supported it financially, and shared in the study of the sacred texts . . . but they were not converts and not Jewish.

There was one major barrier to conversion to Judaism and that was adult male circumcision. All forms of Judaism required circumcision as a sign of fidelity to the covenant with God. This applied equally to all expressions of Judaism, whether the Jesus Movement, Pharisees, Zealots, Sadducees, or Essenes. It was a nonnegotiable requirement of Torah, going back to the time of Abraham, likely some eighteen hundred years earlier.

There were other requirements, too, but these would have presented less of an impediment. There was immersion in a ritual bath, a mikvah, a ceremony that Christians would later come to call baptism. That experience was rooted in Judaism. Then, too, there were the obligations of the Jewish law, the 613 commandments observed by all Jews everywhere including not only Sabbath observance and high ethical demands but also dietary laws, festivals, and male circumcision. The Torah was a prescription for a lifestyle and demanded commitment to all facets of life.

The practical problems this raised for the observant Jew in the Diaspora were enormous. Keeping the Sabbath as a day of rest from creative activity was only one problem, for not everybody within the ancient Roman world took Friday night through to Saturday evening off. Most likely, however, the dietary laws posed even larger problems. In Judaism, the dietary laws reflect the view that eating is a spiritual act and has to be treated as such. Meat had to be slaughtered in the appropriate manner, in the Temple, by experts who knew how to minimize suffering to the animal and drain off as much blood as possible.

Eating meat, for instance, would have been problematic for Jews in the Diaspora. As in all ancient societies, meat was only available through the temples, as a sacrifice. There were no convenience or grocery stores around the corner selling meat. If someone wanted a meat meal, they would have to take an animal to a temple to be sacrificed. The problem for Jews living in the Diaspora was that the only nearby shrines were those dedicated to Roman, Persian, or

Egyptian gods, notably to Dionysus, Mithras, and Isis, among a host of other lesser-known divine beings. Eating meat from these sources would involve these deities in the dinner, and this would be idolatrous. In practice, therefore, most observant Jews in the Diaspora would have been vegetarian.

So God-fearers remained on the margins of Jewish society—admirers of the religion, but remaining as Gentiles.

No Torah observance did away with the necessity for adult male circumcision. This subtext underlay the enormous attractiveness of Paul's message, and he appealed to it time and time again. Paul was obsessed with the foreskin, its removal being symbolic for him of all that Torah observance demanded. He called his opponents members "of the circumcision faction" (Galatians 2:12). He hoped that they would all drop the knife and castrate themselves (Galatians 5:12). Judaism demanded circumcision; Paul's movement removed the requirement.

Paul's dispensing with Torah obligations represented a major religious breakthrough, something new on the horizon of the first century A.D. It offered enormous advantages: an expanded dietary menu, for one thing, and a welcoming stance for the God-fearers who no longer had to become Jewish to gain access to the promised Kingdom. It had major disadvantages as well. Paul's views created massive dissension. Not everyone was in agreement, certainly not the members of the Jesus Movement who considered Paul's position anathema.

PAUL'S NEW RELIGION

Paul's Christ Movement differed considerably in origin, beliefs, and practices from the Jesus Movement and from other Judaisms of the time. It owed its *origin*, for instance, not to the historical Jesus who was a teacher and Messiah claimant, but to Paul's personal experience of the mystical Christ. Paul himself rarely referred to the teachings of the Jesus of history. That just wasn't his focus. This differs significantly from the Jesus Movement, that group of observant Jews in Jerusalem who were faithful to the teachings and practices of the historical Jesus, their rabbi. Under the leadership of James, Peter, and John, these individuals knew the Jesus of the 20s, walked with him, saw him killed, and understood what he represented.

Paul's *beliefs* were also distinctive, conceiving of Christ as a savior, not the political Messiah come to reestablish the David throne and do away with Hellenization. Not for Paul was the Kingdom of God message with its subversive anti-Roman slant. His *practices*, moreover, differed fundamentally, denying the legitimacy of keeping the law. So Paul's movement bypassed both Jesus' challenge of Torah and promise of the Kingdom—the two pillars of Jesus' thought and his bulwark against Hellenization.

Moreover, according to the later Book of Acts, Paul got into confrontations with "the Jews" everywhere, in Damascus, in Jerusalem, and in the Diaspora, in a way that members of the Jesus Movement did not. Things Paul said and did aroused tremendous anger wherever he went. Historians, clergy, and biblical scholars have for centuries failed to realize the radical nature of Paul's message and why it engendered such hostility. There are a number of reasons for this.

For one thing, we automatically link Paul's teachings with those of the Jesus Movement, although, in fact, they were drastically different. The Jesus Movement was part of Judaism; Paul's enterprise was not. The Jesus Movement was Torah-observant; Paul's wasn't. The Jesus Movement was led by people who knew the historical Jesus; Paul's movement wasn't. Jesus and his early followers were anti-Roman and anti-Hellenistic; Paul's movement wasn't.

Joining the two movements together was not something that happened at the time of Paul. In his letters, Paul was extremely insistent that he had only minimal contact with the leaders of the Jesus Movement. He was very clear that *his* movement was separate and different. The synthesis was only created some forty to sixty years after the death of Paul and James, by the author of the Book of Acts. Acts' splicing together the two movements—Paul's Christ Movement with James's Jesus Movement—was so successful, however, that we now tend to think of Paul's Movement as just another form of the early Christianity. It wasn't. It was a brand-new religion entirely. The Christ and Jesus Movements are in fact, *different* religions, not rival interpretations of the same religion.

Another reason why we miss the radical nature of Paul's message has to do with the order in which documents are listed in today's New Testament. When we open up this section of the Bible, we first encounter the four canonical gospels presented in the following order: Matthew, Mark, Luke, and John. These tell the story of Jesus' sayings and doings, each one from a somewhat different perspective. Then we come across a history book, the Book of Acts, which is really a continuation of Luke's Gospel. Only after five books into the New Testament do we finally arrive at Paul's writings. The order in which all these documents are presented is strategic. By placing Paul's letters after the first five books of the New Testament, including the four gospels, the impression is created that, of course, people in Paul's time knew all that information about the sayings and doings of the historical Jesus. That was not the case, however. In the 50s, the gospels had yet to be produced. All of Paul's letters had been written, and Paul had died, before the first gospel was written.

We often assume that the writings in the New Testament are arranged chronologically. They aren't. The gospels are not presented in the order in which they were likely written. Modern scholars would list the gospels in the following order: Mark first (70s), then Matthew (80s). The last two would be John (90s) and Luke (90s–125). Paul's letters are not arranged chronologically either, being presented in our Bibles in descending order of length, from longest to shortest.

So, in reading Paul today, we should bear in mind that the first recipients of his letters did not have any gospel documents in front of them. We do not know what people understood of the traditions reflected in these later gospel writings. They would only likely know what Jesus taught, observed, and did from what they had been told by their leaders. We have no way of knowing how much—or how little—this was.

Judging from his letters, Paul would have conveyed very little about the historical Jesus. He rarely quoted him and seldom referred to his teachings. He typically did not use Jesus as an authority to back up his preaching. Surprisingly, he seemed totally indifferent to the Jesus of history. Unlike contemporary Christian preachers who often appeal to the words of Jesus to support a point of view in the course of giving a sermon, Paul didn't do so. Paul usually appealed to his mystical experience and to "the Christ" who spoke through him.

The issue Paul addressed in his famous Letter to the Galatians concerns the relationship of his religion to Torah. His arguments are radical as he tries to sweep away Torah observance, by everyone, everywhere—all Jews everywhere, including members of the Jesus Movement. Paul envisaged a religion that was devoid of Torah, based not on the teachings and practices of the historical Jesus but rather on insights he gleaned from the mystical Christ. This had massive repercussions. Paul's teachings wrecked havoc in Jewish and Jesus Movement communities around the eastern Mediterranean. They recognized the radical import of his message and they reacted swiftly, reporting his views promptly to James in Jerusalem. Paul's views also quickly resulted in the formation of a new religion, one that, by removing all the Jewish boundary markers, made it fundamentally Hellenistic in nature. This was not, in any sense, a continuation of Judaism—not a "reform" Judaism, nor a "Judaism light." It really wasn't a Judaism at all. Nor was it an extension of the religion founded by Jesus. It was radically different from both. Paul accomplished by argument what Antiochus Epiphanes had tried to achieve by force: a religion detached from Torah, assimilated into common Hellenistic culture.

It's time now to look at Paul's arguments for getting rid of Torah observance. We will see how truly flimsy some of them were. Others were far-reaching, for the considerations Paul advanced apply equally to Jews as to Gentiles. This has not always been fully appreciated. The rumors that swirled around Paul and were reported to James in Jerusalem were, in fact, very well founded. Paul was actually teaching the abandonment of the traditions of Torah and, in so doing, was laying the groundwork for the creation of an entirely new religion. Along the way, we will also note the most important consideration he might have used—but couldn't.

THE BATTLEGROUND: LETTER TO
THE GALATIANS

The circumstances that prompted Paul to write the Letter to the Galatians were straightforward. Paul had made many converts to the Christ Movement in the area of Galatia, now part of midcentral Turkey. They were from a Gentile background, most likely God-fearers from local synagogues. While Paul was away from this region, he learned that rival teachers had come into this part of the world, telling his Gentile converts that they needed to observe the law. Paul did not identify who these individuals were. He did not say that they were emissaries from James in Jerusalem. Nor did he identify them as members of the Jesus Movement.[3]

Paul used very strong language to denounce these other leaders: they were presenting a "different gospel" (Galatians 1:6). They were "confusing you" (Galatians 1:7). He ascribed a negative motivation to them—they wanted "to pervert the gospel of Christ." (Galatians 1:7). He cursed them (Galatians 1:9) and then crudely added, "I wish those who unsettle you would castrate themselves" (Galatians 5:12). Moreover they had been "bewitching" these new members within Galatia (Galatians 3:1). Rather than engaging in dialogue with their understanding of the movement's tenets, he simply rejected and vilified them.

The immediate issue faced by Paul was this: should Gentile converts to his Christ Movement be made to follow the entire Jewish law, including circumcision? That is, expressed in modern terms, must they become Jewish in order to become Christian? Certainly the Jesus Movement would have demanded that. For them, to become a member of their movement, Gentiles would have had to convert to Judaism. The Jesus Movement was, after all, a form of Judaism. In this it was no different from other Jewish movements of the time. The Pharisees agreed. For them, Gentiles who wished to become members of their group had to undergo the conversion process.

Paul was clear that his opponents insisted that Gentiles had to follow Torah to be part of the new movement. He appears to have understood his opponents to be claiming much more, however—that Torah observance was necessary *for salvation*. This interpretation goes far beyond typical Jewish teaching. From the standpoint of Judaism, the righteous of all religious traditions may be saved, that is, they would have a share in the world to come when God transforms the earth and establishes his Kingdom. The only requirement for righteous Gentiles was that they observe what became known as the Seven Noahide Laws binding on all humanity.[4] These laws derive from the covenant between God and Noah, who represented all humanity after the flood. These laws include abstaining from: food sacrificed to idols, illicit sexuality, eating meat from animals that have not been properly killed, and murder. They also include not stealing or cursing God as well as the injunction to be just. Noahide Laws prescribe basic human behavior and morality, what is expected of all humans, whatever their culture and whatever their religion. Unlike the requirement for Jews, there is absolutely no need for Gentiles to observe all 613 laws of Torah to achieve salvation. So Paul may be overstating his opponents' case. All they may have been claiming is what all Jews of the time would have insisted upon: if you wish to become Jewish, you have to convert. And that applied to the Jesus Movement as much as to the Pharisees.

It is interesting to note what Paul did *not* do in forming his response to the members of the movement in Galatia. Paul did not say, for instance, that "it's all a misunderstanding." If the account of his career in the Book of Acts were correct, then Paul could have clarified the situation easily and simply. He could have pointed out that the whole issue rested upon a mistake. This is getting somewhat ahead of our story, for we have yet to evaluate the Book of Acts as a source of information about Paul. For our purposes here, however, we need to note that Acts mentions that an important conference had been held in Jerusalem. This would have occurred in the late 40s, a few years prior to the Letter to the Galatians. There it was decided, according to Acts, that Gentiles who wished to be part of the new movement would be required only to observe the Seven Noahide Laws, whereas Jews are required to observe the whole Torah.

Paul, writing to the Galatians a few years later in the 50s, could easily have appealed to this authoritative decision—if it had occurred at all. As we shall see, there is good reason to believe that this conference never happened and that it formed part of Luke's agenda in writing the Book of Acts to graft Paul's Christ Movement on to the earlier Jesus Movement. For the moment, let us note that Paul seems to know nothing about any such decisive decision. If he had, he could have told his rival teachers upfront that he was simply honoring the decision coming from none other than James, the authoritative head of the Jesus Movement. That would have silenced them.

Instead, Paul threw a very angry fit. He launched a detailed attack upon Torah observance while defending his own credentials. In so doing, he did not argue that whereas Jewish members were obliged to continue to keep Torah, Gentiles were not. His point was much more radical: *no one* should observe Torah. It is wrong to heed the requirements of Torah. Observing Torah reveals a fundamental misunderstanding. These are strong contentions.

Paul's arguments against Torah observance are stated in rather terse terms in the third chapter of Galatians. Later commentators might very well wish that Paul had taken the time to spell out his arguments in detail. They were written in a "heated moment" and a lot of ideas are jumbled together. Paul himself would probably be surprised that some two thousand years later, people are still discussing his ideas. Had he known that, he might have taken time to step back from his anger, clarifying key points in his highly contentious diatribe.

ABRAHAM'S FAITH

Paul started off by appealing to the example of Abraham, an ancient patriarch who probably lived some eighteen hundred years prior to the time of Paul. Abraham had been a nomad, living in what is modern-day Iraq. Called by God, he left his ancient roots behind and emigrated northwest, up the Euphrates River to Haran. There he received a remarkable promise that if he were to go to the land God would show him, he would possess this land and become a great nation. Moreover, through Abraham, "all the families of the earth" would be eventually blessed (Genesis 12:1–3). So Abraham went. Along the way, God makes a formal agreement with him. In one version of the covenant (Genesis 15), Abraham is told that he shall have descendants as numerous as the stars in the sky, a promise he is skeptical of at the time since he was well on in years without any children. He is also told that God would give his descendants the land of Canaan (Israel). In another version of the agreement (Genesis 17), God made "an everlasting covenant" with Abraham. He was to be the ancestor of a multitude of nations. He and his offspring would be granted the land of Canaan (Israel) as "a perpetual holding." The sign of this covenant was circumcision. Abraham is told that this is to be kept throughout the generations as an everlasting covenant. On either version of the covenant, Abraham clearly is a person promised an exciting future: land, many children, and a role as a blessing to all the families of the earth.

Let's see what use Paul makes of Abraham. In Galatians, he noted that Abraham believed in God and that he was deemed righteous as a result (Galatians 3:6, referring to Genesis 15:6). So, he concluded, those who believe in Christ are the real descendants of Abraham. They share in the promises God made to him, that through him, all the nations of the world will be blessed. So Paul's argument reaches way back into Jewish history. Abraham was judged to be righteous because of faith or trust in God, not by observing Torah. The Torah came later, given through Moses some five hundred years or so after the time of Abraham. This represents an important detail in Paul's argument. While dates vary, most scholars date Moses to around 1280 B.C. or possibly somewhat earlier.[5] The Torah was given to the people of Israel on Mount Sinai during the Exodus from Egypt. Wandering for forty years in the wilderness, they finally entered the Promised Land, Canaan (Israel). Meanwhile, they had formed a nation, with a constitution, the Torah, which provided a framework for religious and civil life. So, by the time of Paul, Torah had been around for some thirteen hundred years. It was the permanent backbone of Judaism.

Paul jumped back to the example of Abraham and his faith, ignoring all of Jewish history between Moses and his own era. In effect, Paul leapfrogged over a span of some thirteen centuries back to the one figure in Jewish history he thought would clinch his case. The whole course of history from Moses to himself was to be set aside, nullified, and discarded. By going back to the example of Abraham, Paul thought that he could demonstrate that belief was sufficient for righteousness, not works of the law. Consequently, he argued, members of his Christ Movement should focus their efforts on belief in Christ, not observing Torah.

It is not known, of course, how his initial readers or listeners in Galatia interpreted his missive. It would have been instructive to learn what these other leaders would have made of his remarks. There are major flaws in his argument, as any astute reader in Galatia or these critics of Paul would have noticed. Paul's argument made an all-too-easy transference from belief or trust in God (as Abraham did) to belief in Christ. Rival teachers might very well have asked, What justifies this leap, from God to Christ?

Moreover, they would have charged, who had the authority to unilaterally change the terms of the contract? The covenant, after all, was a contract, a mutual agreement, made by two parties. In the case of the Torah, the "signatories" were God and the people of Israel. It was a document that was ratified. Could such an agreement be set aside by an outside third party, whether Paul or Christ? They weren't, after all, the parties to this agreement. Moreover, could it be nullified without the consent of both parties, the signatories to the agreement? Why was Paul, an outsider, tampering with the deal? What status did he have in interfering with contract law? Questions like these may have occurred to Paul's rival teachers as they grappled with the implications of his position. They might very well have suspected that Paul was setting up a covert comparison between Christ and God. They would have sensed that Paul's way of putting the matter came very close to contending that Christ was divine. After all, if God gave the Torah, then surely only God could take it away. So what was Paul claiming about the status of the Christ? they might very well have inquired. Was he, in some sense, claiming Christ was God?

Moreover, Paul's argument ignored the whole development of biblical thought up until his time, which included the centrality of Torah observance, at least for Jews. One cannot read *any* work of the Old Testament without being struck by this fact. It consistently hammers away at the need for members of the covenant to keep the law, faithfully. As we have seen, this means keeping *all* of the law *all* of the time, not some of the law some of the time. For biblical writers, much was at stake in this. Without fidelity to the law, the community would forfeit the land of Israel, and individuals would lose blessings such as long life and good health. How did Paul think he could pass over everything in the Bible from Genesis chapter 25, which concludes the saga of Abraham, to the time when he produced his own letter? This cuts out the rest of the Torah, all of the Prophets and the Writings. It skips over the Book of Exodus, which talks about the giving of the Torah on Mount Sinai, the whole history of occupying the land of Israel, all of the deep insights of the prophets, the Psalms, the Book of Job, and all of Judaism after the Babylonian Exile. What could justify this gigantic leap across history? It reduces Paul's entire bible to just fifteen chapters, from Genesis 11 to 25. That's all that would be relevant if one were to take Paul at his word. Paul's position was tremendously destructive, and it was perceived that way by his critics.

Anyone familiar with the story of Abraham would immediately have recognized that Paul appealed very selectively to the text of Genesis. Had he cited the covenant with Abraham outlined in Genesis 17, mentioned on page 118, rather than Genesis 15, he would have arrived at a very different conclusion. That formulation of the covenant agreement promised Abraham that he would be the ancestor of many nations. The details of this agreement, however, included observance of an "everlasting covenant" (Genesis 17:7) of which the rite of circumcision was an integral part. In fact, in this passage, male circumcision is spoken of as a practice throughout the generations. It requires every male to be circumcised as symbolic of the human portion of the contract with God. This gives a very different impression of Abraham than does the selective reading from Genesis 15.

TORAH OBSERVERS ARE "UNDER A CURSE"

This represents a very strange part of Paul's argument, and it raises more questions than it solves. Paul's intent was clear: he tried to show that the law cannot bring about divine acceptance, because anyone who follows it is "under a curse." In making this claim, Paul appealed to a variety of Old Testament texts. Each reference, however, distorts the clear sense of these writings. They are piled one on top of another, like a stack of cards on the theme of curses. Readers who are not careful to look at the original texts and their contexts may be taken in. If you look carefully, the whole house of cards collapses.

In Galatians 3:10, he quoted, for instance, from a curse made originally in Deuteronomy 27:26. This passage cursed everyone who fails to keep all the requirements of Torah. So people who murder, cheat, or steal or who fail to observe the Sabbath, male circumcision, or Passover would be said to be "under the curse of God." That's consistent with Old Testament teaching. The problem, however, is this: Paul quoted the passage correctly, but it makes *the opposite point* to the one he wishes to affirm. Paul wanted to claim that anyone who follows the law is cursed. That's consistent with his objective to reject Torah. The passage in question, however, curses those who do *not* keep the law. In other words, *Deuteronomy curses the very position Paul is advocating.* Clearly the Bible does not endorse Paul's position but its exact opposite. Anyone trained in Pharisaic schools would have known this, and Paul's misuse of a fundamental scripture belies the claim that others would later make on his behalf that he had studied with the most famous of Pharisaic leaders of the time, Gamaliel. Likely he had no such education.

Paul then proceeded to quote from the Hebrew prophet Habakkuk, to the effect that the righteous shall live by faith (Galatians 3:11). This would appear to support Paul's position, that only faith in Christ counts, not doing the works of the law. Paul's point here, however, fares no better than the first one. He distorted the meaning of Habakkuk's message. Some six hundred years earlier than Paul, Habakkuk had tried to rally his fellow Jews. He wrote just as the Babylonians were about to invade Judea and Jerusalem. He knew the horrors that attended warfare: destruction, death, exile, rape, looting, and devastation. He urged them to hold fast to their traditional teachings, to be faithful to the teachings and practices of the law. He did so because that is the covenant with God. God will keep Israel safe and secure in the land of Israel provided they honor the covenant through the keeping of the law.

Habakkuk saw "the wicked" surrounding "the righteous." "The wicked" would have consisted of not only the invading Babylonians, but also fellow Jewish citizens of Jerusalem who failed to follow the Torah. "The righteous," conversely, were those who did follow the law. He predicted the temporary triumph of the wicked but also envisaged their eventual downfall. God's word is sure. Habakkuk urged the Judeans to stand firm, to resist the temptation to abandon Torah observance in light of an imminent invasion by a vastly superior force. So, yes, the righteous will live, by being faithful to the law. The emphasis on "faith" is not having beliefs about a religious figure but on being faith*ful* to the law. Paul's argument is way off the mark. He has completely misrepresented the meaning of the passage and substituted a different meaning for what the original text means by "faith." Paul's opponents would have undoubtedly been able to point out this flaw quickly.

Undeterred, Paul went on to quote from Leviticus 18:5 that whoever does the works of the law will live by them (Galatians 3:12). The point of Leviticus, and the Books of the Torah generally, was that Torah observance produces life. The Torah itself is sometimes referred to as "the tree of life" (Proverbs 3:18). The law itself rests on a covenant or agreement made between God and Israel: Torah represents the responsibilities of the Jewish people. The terms of the covenant rely on Jewish faith that God will honor his part of the agreement if they honor theirs.

Paul continued on with the theme of curses. He contended that Christ saves humanity from the curse of the law by becoming himself a curse. As we have seen, the curse of the law applies only to those who do not keep the law. But let's move on to what Paul said about Christ becoming "a curse for us" and so removing the curse of the law. Here Paul quoted Deuteronomy 21:22, 23. This passage mandates that if someone is convicted of a capital crime and is executed by being hanged upon a tree, his corpse cannot remain there overnight. The Torah requirement is to bury an executed criminal the same day as he is killed. It represents an act of compassion, so that the executed criminal is not left to rot on the tree for days on end, a spectacle for other people to see and a source of food for scavenger birds. The passage says that anyone who is hanged on a tree is under a divine curse, that is, disgraced.

This text would only apply to Jesus if Paul thought that Christ was guilty of an exceptionally serious crime, so severe that it would place him under "God's curse" as a disgraced criminal. Accusing Christ of committing such a heinous crime that would merit this ignominious death sentence was probably not what Paul intended. There is no suggestion in Paul that Jesus deserved his death, let alone that he committed a capital offense.

So far, Paul has only succeeded in misapplying texts that fail to support the point he wished to make, that Torah observers are somehow "under a curse." But there is more, and this takes us into the heart of Paul's radical message.

BYPASSING JUDAISM

Paul's next contention was that there is a direct connection between Abraham and the Christ. In advancing this line of thought, Paul relied on a semantic twist, interpreting a collective noun for a singular one. He noted that the promises to Abraham in Genesis were to his "offspring," not "offsprings" (Genesis 12:7; Genesis 22:17, 18). So the link between Abraham and the Gentiles, he said, was to one individual, Christ, not to a collective or a group such as Jews generally. Why he made this quick identification of "offspring" with "Christ" is not clear.

The strength of Paul's argument lies in the collective use of the word "offspring." A natural reading would be that Gentiles are eventually to be blessed from the offspring of Abraham, that is, from his descendants, the Jewish people. Judaism envisaged that when God transforms the world to correspond to his will, Judaism would be shared with all the families of the earth and the one God would be worshipped by all humanity, living in peace and harmony with one another. In other words, the promises to Abraham will come about at the end-time. Gentiles would then be blessed through the offspring of Abraham, the Jewish people. This is the most plausible reading of the passage in Genesis.

The word "offspring" is a collective noun. In fact, the original context makes this clear. Genesis 22:17 depicts God as indicating to Abraham that his offspring will be as numerous as the stars in the sky and sand on the seashore. In interpreting this collective noun as referring to a specific individual, Paul was offering us an extremely narrow and forced interpretation of the text.

In leaping back from Christ to the example of Abraham, Paul attempted to bypass hundreds of years of Jewish history. He was distancing the Christ Movement from anything that is Jewish. So he rewrote history. Having made the move from Christ back to Abraham, skipping over the whole time of Torah, Paul had to answer the question that any Jewish person of the time, including members of the Jesus Movement, would have raised: If what you're saying is correct, Paul, why then did God give Torah? Why was it necessary?

Paul's answer was as straightforward as it was radical. He contended that the time of Torah was over. He said that "before faith came" (Galatians 3:23), we were under the law. He likened this to a prison experience, being confined and restricted in our movements. In effect, the Torah functioned as a disciplinary measure, to curb our behavior "until Christ came" (Galatians 3:24). Henceforth, he contended, we are all made righteous not by Torah, but by faith. He confidently asserted that we are all one in Christ Jesus. In one grand often-quoted sweeping statement, he claimed that distinctions such as gender, ethnicity, and status no longer have any relevance.

Here Paul has developed his own theology of history, and it's a powerful one. There are three phases to history, says Paul. First there was the time of faith: from Abraham to Moses. Next there was the period of Torah: from Moses to Christ. Finally there has appeared another time of faith—faith in Christ—the period of human history from Christ onward. Now that Christ has come, Paul said, there is simply no need to observe Torah. This "Torah bypass" position of Paul has far-reaching consequences. If Paul were right that the time of Torah is over, then this argument would apply not only to Gentiles but also to Jews generally, including all the members of the Jesus Movement.

This argument would have caused deep concern among members of the Jesus Movement who, quite correctly, would have interpreted Paul as teaching the abolition of Torah observance for *anyone,* whether a member of his own movement, the Jesus Movement, or any form of Judaism. Years later, the Book of Acts would record how rumors reached James in Jerusalem to the effect that Paul was teaching that the laws of Moses were no longer applicable (Acts 21:20, 21). Those reports were correct.

An argument abolishing Torah observance for all time requires much greater justification. Paul presented no biblical or other justification for contending that the time of Torah observance was over: he simply asserted that it was. Why the appearance of the Christ rules out Torah was never made clear. There was no appeal at all to what the Jesus of history said or did. There was no mention of any prophet. There was no reference to any saying of Jesus. It just rested on Paul's saying that it was so. There was nothing in prior Jewish tradition to lead anyone to suppose that Torah was temporary. To say that the argument is "flimsy" is to be kind: it is simply expedient and self-serving. It's an attempt to change the terms of the contract unilaterally, by an outside party. Paul's saying that the Jewish charter agreement with God has been terminated is analogous to some outside party, say the United Nations or the French Parliament, declaring the U.S. Constitution null and void. Just not credible.

It is abundantly clear, then, that Paul did not link his Christ Movement to Judaism as it was known and practiced in his day. He did attempt to relate it, however, to an ancient Jewish patriarch, Abraham, who lived centuries before Moses. Why he felt compelled to link his movement at all to Jewish sources, especially when he wished to deny the validity of Torah observance, is a mystery. What was his motivation? Did he, perhaps, wish to create a sense of antiquity for his Christ Movement, a prized value in Roman eyes? The Roman mind-set detested novelty, valuing ancient Greek, Egyptian, and Persian philosophies and ideas. Without an ancient pedigree, a religion would have minimal appeal. Moreover, the religions that competed with Paul's movement—the cults of Dionysus, Isis, and Mithras—all had impressive ancient roots that helped attract members. So perhaps the example of Abraham, an ancient Jewish hero, would have served his need to position his movement as the outcome of a lengthy and honorable heritage.

Was he also driven by practical considerations? Probably the best way to reach his target audience, the God-fearers, was through the synagogue. And the way into the synagogue was through appeal to Jewish roots. In this case, appealing to Abraham would have been an effective ruse to get into the one distribution network that would help him succeed with his enterprise. Unlike the run-of-the-mill Gentile audience, God-fearers would likely have been familiar with the figure of Abraham from readings from the Jewish scrolls. Thus God-fearers would have been impressed with Paul and pleased that they could inherit the promises to Abraham without having to undergo the onerous conversion process to Judaism. Here they could have all Judaism's benefits, with none of the responsibility. Perhaps Paul found in Abraham just the linchpin he needed to detach the God-fearers from the synagogue and recruit them for his own enterprise.

Later on in Galatians, Paul continued his bypassing of Judaism. In a provocative passage, he claimed that Christians are descended from Abraham via Sarah, the free woman. Jews, however, as those who keep the law, were, he said, descended from Abraham via Hagar, the slave woman. This would have the effect of robbing Judaism of its heritage. It simply makes no sense biblically. Jewish descent is via Isaac and Sarah. It also robs Arabs of their heritage through Ishmael, but that's another story.

This genealogy was completely wild. It is hard to imagine someone trained in Pharisaic Judaism, as Acts would have it, making this argument. It does demonstrate, however, the lengths to which Paul was prepared to go to deny Judaism its heritage and its validity. If the time of Torah is truly over, then Judaism as a religion serves no purpose.

WHAT PAUL COULDN'T SAY

The one really good argument that Paul could not use is this: he could have appealed to the practice and teachings of Jesus, to the effect that he did not advocate Torah observance. That would have been a legitimate appeal to authority—see what Jesus said and did. Paul could then have concluded that Torah observance should not be obligatory for any member of the Christ Movement.

This one argument would have clinched the case. He could not make this argument, however. As we have seen, the historical Jesus taught and practiced Torah observance. So, too, did his earliest followers in Jerusalem. So Paul couldn't say that Jesus agreed with him. He didn't. Paul's position was at odds with what Jesus himself practiced. Moreover, what the historical Jesus did and said did not seem to matter to Paul: he focused on what the Christ figure told him and on his death and resurrection. This demonstrates clearly how much at odds Paul's religion was with that of Jesus. His was not a continuation or reinterpretation of the religion Jesus started and did not find its point of origin in what Jesus said or did.

WHAT CREDIBILITY DID PAUL HAVE?

Paul would have had no credibility with members of the Jesus Movement in Jerusalem or any other Jewish faction of the time. They would have found his ideas totally repugnant both because he rejected Torah observance and also substituted a Roman savior Christ figure for that of a Jewish teacher and Messiah claimant. His was a Hellenistic religion, with very little—if any—Jewish content. Anyone with a Jewish background would have read his position as a capitulation to the assimilationist forces of Hellenization. Pharisees, Sadducees, Essenes, Zealots, and Jesus Movement members alike would have not only rejected but also despised his views.

Did Paul have any credibility with his rivals in Galatia? Would they have been impressed by his inaccurate biblical quotations and sketchy arguments? Would they have just walked away from Torah observance? Unfortunately we don't know their response, but judging from parts of the Jesus Movement who caught wind of Paul's position, they likely went on the attack.

It is undeniable that Paul's position had massive appeal, but at what cost? As Mason and Robinson point out, "Evidently Paul has been accused of perverting the (originally Jewish) gospel, by omitting the demands of the Jewish covenant, in order to please men."[6] Paul's abolition of Torah did create a religion that was easier to follow than one that insisted on Torah observance. No wonder Paul was accused of developing positions to please people. Paul persistently had to answer the charge that he was "a liar."[7]

In defense of his credibility, Paul maintained that he had his message "through a revelation of Jesus Christ" (Galatians 1:12). Through this transforming experience, Paul claimed to have had a privileged revelation from "the Christ." The impact of that voice or vision changed his orientation in life, and out of this grew the Christ Movement.

Paul also claimed to have received his message from this experience, not from the historical Jesus or from the leaders of the Jesus Movement: "For I want you to know, brothers and sisters, that the gospel that was proclaimed by me is not of human origin; for I did not receive it from a human source, nor was I taught it, but I received it through a revelation of Jesus Christ" (Galatians 1:11, 12). There was nothing within the various accounts of his experience that would lead us to predict that he would eventually advance positions that would run counter to Judaism and the Jesus Movement. And yet he did. Whatever this experience was, it was not a "conversion" experience from one form of Judaism to another such as the Jesus Movement. This life-changing event was a conversion *out of* Judaism *into* something else—something entirely different.

Paul was killed not long after James, in the early to mid 60s, likely in Rome under Nero's reign, confident that his new religion was gaining momentum. What Paul created was enormously successful: the religious dynamic he set in motion ultimately resulted in what eventually became Christianity.

RIVAL RELIGIONS: THE JESUS AND CHRIST MOVEMENTS

As we have seen, Paul's views were vastly different from those of the Jesus Movement and from Jesus himself. They rested on Paul's mystical experience: everything flowed from that deep spiritual connection made between the Christ and Paul. Through this ongoing relationship, Paul received information that differed from the original followers of Jesus and from what the Jesus of history taught and practiced. It was a separate revelation. From this movement, and from his experience, however, emerged subsequent Christianity. It is not often noted the extent to which the foundations of Christianity depend crucially on Paul's personal experience. That vision defined the central character of Paul's message, the shape of his movement, and subsequent Christianity.

The contrast between the two rival movements is stark, differing in terms of origins, practices, and beliefs, as we have seen. More than that, the focal point of the two movements differed. The Jesus Movement represented the religion *of* Jesus. The Christ Movement, however, was a religion *about* the Christ. These were two separate religions.

Two traditions were born in the early decades of the first century A.D. One tradition goes from Jesus, through the Jesus Movement under James, into the Ebionites as they were later called. We have carefully profiled this movement and its subsequent history will be traced later on. The other tradition stems from Paul through the Christ Movement and then on into modern Christianity. Scholars such as Bart Ehrman refer to the Christ Movement as it moved out into the wider arena of the Roman Empire in the second through fourth centuries as Proto-Orthodoxy.[8] We will use this convenient phrase rather than the more cumbersome "what eventually became Christianity." The Proto-Orthodox represents the faction that, in time, became the dominant expression of the new faith. This tradition won out over every other form of early Christianity, the Ebionites and Gnostics included. Leading figures of early Christianity such as Ignatius of Antioch, Justin Martyr, Irenaeus, Tertullian, and Augustine were all Proto-Orthodox writers.

The Proto-Orthodox did not know that they were Proto-Orthodox; that is, they were not aware, of course, that they represented the group that was destined to become Christianity. During the period of intense rivalry within the early church—the second through fourth centuries—everyone proclaimed their movement to be the true faith and denounced others. Why the Proto-Orthodox eventually won out is a complex story that Bart Ehrman traces through several chapters of his *Lost Christianities*.[9] They include such reasons as having a superior infrastructure—a worldwide network of bishops in communication with one another—as well as a vast writing apparatus that undertook the task of producing gospels, theological and philosophical treatises, legends, romances, letters, and attacks upon every conceivable heretical position. They were driven to succeed, answering every objection and battering down every perceived heresy in a way that their rivals did not. In modern terms, they controlled the airwaves, winning what Ehrman terms "the battle over texts."[10]

But there were other factors at work as well. The shape of Paul's new religion offered immense advantages over that of the Jesus Movement. It was simpler to join. It encouraged faith in a religious figure who bore strong similarities to other saviors who were well known throughout the ancient Mediterranean world. That made it much easier than having to back up through the history of Israel to explain the necessity for a political Messiah. It offered immediate rewards: eternal life through faith in Christ. It opened up food choices, with dietary restrictions abandoned. It was easier—much easier—to follow, with none of the laws of Torah constantly on the minds of its members. In fact, like most Hellenistic religions, it made few demands on its members. Furthermore, it radically reduced the need to read and understand what we call the Old Testament since its central message, that of Torah observance, had been shattered. God-fearers no longer had to attend synagogue services. The welcome mat was out for them in the new Christ Movement, which greeted them without making them second-class members. No more were they appendages to Judaism but full-fledged members of the new movement. And it was inclusive. Everyone was welcomed on the same terms. Paul unleashed a powerful new religious dynamic within the world of his time. It was appealing and inviting.

That is not to say that Paul's movement was not without its problems. It faced strenuous opposition. Paul was constantly attacked. Virtually every one of Paul's letters addresses issues raised by various kinds of opponents, most of them coming from Jewish or Jesus Movement teachers. We tend to ignore the anger that Paul's views stirred up wherever he went, but his catalogue of opposition is immense. The earliest letter of Paul (and, thus, the earliest Christian writing we possess), 1 Thessalonians, for instance, talked about being treated shamefully at Philippi and that he faced great opposition in Thessalonica. Somewhat later, in 1 Corinthians, he mentioned several rival factions at work within that congregation, one led by Apollos and another by no less a personage than Peter. In Philippians he criticized opposition leaders who, he maintained, preached out of envy or rivalry. There, too, he attacked those who practice circumcision—that is, every form of Judaism, including the Jesus Movement people—as "dogs" and "evil-workers" (Philippians 3:2). In 2 Corinthians, he denounced Judaism as a "ministry of death" (2 Corinthians 3:7) and advanced the view that whenever Torah is read by Jewish people, a veil clouds their understanding. He battled against what he sarcastically called "the super apostles," (2 Corinthians 11:7) probably referring to the original followers of Jesus, and brands them as "false apostles," "deceitful workers," and agents of Satan.

In addition to being confronted with immense opposition, Paul's religion faced other significant challenges. He had to contend with a number of major ethical questions. Letters such as 1 Corinthians testify to this, where family, sexual, and social matters dominate the discussion. Even at the end of Galatians, he cautioned his hearers that freedom from the law does not mean anarchy. In the process of abandoning Torah, however, he could not refer to these ready-made ethical principles to resolve the contentious matters that had surfaced. In practice he tended to answer these issues on a rather ad hoc, piecemeal basis.

In addition, Paul had to face problems about which we hear very little. What replaced the Sabbath? Did his members take a day off work? If so, when? How did his new converts get along with their old Jewish friends and acquaintances in the synagogues they had recently left? How much social interaction was possible between them and observant Jews? How much bitterness was present? Did Paul's pragmatic instructions that it makes no difference what one eats, including meat from temples dedicated to idols, really persuade his membership to engage in this practice? And, apart from having faith in the Christ and waiting for his return, what else did his membership have to believe?

Moreover, without the distinctiveness of Torah, what distinguished Paul's followers from those of the mystery religions of the time? It would appear that only the name of the dying-rising savior divine-human differs—Christ for Mithras or Dionysus, for instance.

On the other side of the fence were the members of the Jesus Movement. They were shocked by Paul's teachings; they opposed him vigorously and were probably dismayed by his success. They viewed him as a false teacher, someone who had developed a thoroughly Hellenized religion. They thought of themselves as the true successors of Jesus, following in his footsteps and continuing his practices. Ironically, however, this did not seem to count as Paul's religion swept through the Mediterranean. The Jesus Movement had little in common with its rival. There could have been little interaction between Paul's group and the Jesus Movement. Everything was different: the holidays, the food they ate, the beliefs they entertained, and the practices they considered important. Outsiders, however, Jews and Gentiles alike, might make the mistake of supposing that they were similar, sharing as they did some common terminology including mention of Jesus, whom Paul typically called the Christ. No wonder outsiders were confused.

In time, Paul's Christ Movement and its successors, the Proto-Orthodox, won out over all the alternatives. It's difficult to date the birth of Christianity as a church, but I would date it to the fourth century. It was during this century that the Proto-Orthodox faction became favored by Constantine and subsequently decreed the official religion of the Roman Empire under Emperor Theodosius in 380. This imperial backing allowed this dominant group to do away with all their rivals, their rivals' leadership, and their rivals' writings—the Ebionites, Gnostics, as well as many other forms of Christianity that had emerged by this time.

The Proto-Orthodox succeeded for many reasons, some of which we have cited—imperial backing, the shape of the religion created by Paul, strong episcopal leadership, and a network of communications. In modern business terms, they occupied an enviable and strategic position. They had the *product,* a flexible, welcoming, easy-to-follow religion. They had the *distribution network,* bishops scattered around the Mediterranean in constant communication with one another. They controlled the *communication* process, producing endless writings that supported their own position while responding to every criticism in a way that the Ebionite and Gnostic Christians failed to do. They wrote gospels, letters, romances, fictitious histories, attacks on heretics, and defenses of the faith. They advanced an effective *public relations* campaign, contending that their bishops were descended from the original disciples of Jesus. They also had the *branding*—a modern Roman religion with some links to an ancient and respectable Jewish ancestry.

But there was another important factor at work. None of this would have happened without the Book of Acts, which glued the Christ Movement on to the Jesus Movement—at least on paper. That, of course, never happened in reality. The Jesus and Christ Movements were *parallel* movements, at odds with each other. But Acts tries to tell us otherwise.

10

THE BIG SWITCH:
CHRIST FOR JESUS

It used to be so simple. The history of Christian origins was straightforward. Two thousand years ago, so the story goes, Jesus preached, gathered together disciples, and eventually founded a church. Jesus himself was betrayed by one of his own, Judas. He was tried, convicted, and crucified. Astonishingly, he was resurrected from the dead, and many witnesses claimed to have seen this surprising event. His followers—the apostles—responded and began to spread the word about Jesus, initially in Jerusalem and surrounding areas. In time, Paul became part of the movement, proclaiming that through Jesus' death and resurrection, all could be saved in Christ. This message resounded throughout the Roman world, and the movement attracted many Gentile members, flourishing well beyond anyone's expectations.

THE CONVENTIONAL MODEL OF
CHRISTIAN ORIGINS

According to what I'll call the Conventional Model of Christian Origins, that's how the early church developed. It's a straightforward chronological model: from Jesus to church to Paul to phenomenal success. This is the impression that the remarkable Book of Acts created some forty or so years after the death of Paul and James. Written in the late first or early second century by the same author who wrote the Gospel of Luke, the Book of Acts described how the early Christian movement became multinational.[1] After the crucifixion and resurrection of Jesus, under the vigorous impetus of Paul, this new religious enterprise moved out of Jerusalem into other countries—into modern-day Lebanon, Syria, Turkey, Greece, Croatia, Cyprus, and Italy. Acts portrayed Christianity as friendly to Roman values, positioning it so effectively that ultimately it would become the official religion of the Mediterranean world. That outcome, of course, would require some three hundred years. There were many organizational as well as theological details to work out—especially articulating the precise nature of the relationship between Jesus and God, as well as the human and divine natures within the person of Jesus. More than any other work in the New Testament, however, Acts provided the link between Jesus and a church growing exponentially under the genius of Paul's leadership.

The arrangement of the books of the New Testament supports this Conventional Model of Christian Origins. As we have noted, the documents in the New Testament are not presented in the order in which they were written. We first encounter the four gospels, which present the mission and message of Jesus, even though all four were written after Paul's death in the early 60s. This upfront placement conveys the false impression that *everyone* knew of Jesus' life, teachings, practices, and doings. Then we come to Acts, the fifth book in the New Testament, which focuses on the thirty years after Jesus' death. It shows how the message spread throughout the Roman Empire, and it ends with Paul in the capital city itself, Rome. Only after these five books do we come across Paul's letters, even though they represent the earliest Christian writings. Chronologically they should appear first in the New Testament.

This strategic ordering of the documents, with the *later* gospels and Acts coming before the *earlier* letters of Paul, creates a very important effect. It cradles Paul within the setting of Jesus' message and early church expansion. We see easily and quickly how he fits into the overall picture and how his efforts contribute to astounding success in terms of Gentile converts. Within this framework, it does not readily occur to us to raise critical questions concerning the actual linkage between Paul and Jesus.

It's a brilliant arrangement that dovetails with Acts' account of how early Christianity developed. The order of the New Testament documents and the alleged history presented in the Book of Acts conspire to give us the impression that the religion was transmitted from Jesus through Paul to us today. This became the dominant model of early Christian origins. It is commonly taught, and it has entered the popular imagination as the model of Christian origins.

But what if history didn't unfold this way?

The neat and tidy Conventional Model has undergone intense scrutiny as we come to know more about Christian origins thanks to the discovery of the Dead Sea Scrolls and the Gnostic writings.[2] Both sets of documents have made us much more aware of the diversity of Judaisms and Christianities that existed in the first century A.D. The Conventional Model now seems a faulty version of history, and a newer model of Christian origins is emerging.

For one thing, Jesus didn't establish a church: he *announced* the Kingdom of God as a radical alternative to the Pax Romana. As scholars probed these far-from-simple stories, the Kingdom of God began to look less and less like a structured church with leadership, sacred texts, places of meeting, and rituals. The parables emphasized right behavior—being prepared for the coming Kingdom, acting in a kind and compassionate manner, seeking out the alienated and welcoming them into family, and valuing membership in the Kingdom above all else. So the claim that Jesus had come to found a church now appears somewhat questionable.

Nor did the parables focus on Jesus himself, other than as teacher, preacher, and teller of stories. That is, they did not erect an elaborate belief system about Jesus as a condition of membership in the Kingdom. The parables of Jesus do not reinforce the need for such beliefs as his preexistence, special virgin birth, divinity, role as crucified Christ, or savior of all humanity. This highly elaborate ideological superstructure is missing from the parables of the Kingdom. Instead, Jesus is the intriguing teller of tales, proclaiming a Kingdom of God that would occur soon, sweeping away Roman rule with its Hellenizing tendencies.

In fact, the parables talked a lot more about what the hearer had to *do* to be a member of the Kingdom of God than what was to be believed. We have seen how the parable of the Talents focused on the need for making the most of what one has been given. The parable of the Great Judgment showed that those who are redeemed are those who have provided food, drink, or clothing to others or who have welcomed strangers, treated the sick, or visited those in prison. Right actions are what counts in the Kingdom, not right beliefs.

So the institution of a structured church and complex belief systems about the person of Jesus are not vindicated by a critical study of the parables.[3] Consequently this aspect of the Conventional Model has been thrown into question: What if Jesus did not come to establish a "church"? How did we get from Jesus of the 20s to what we have today: Catholic, Orthodox, Anglican, Protestant, Evangelical, Coptic, Armenian, and many other forms of Christianity?

Moreover, the Conventional Model ignores the significant role of James and his leadership in Jerusalem from the 30s to the early 60s. Why was he so overshadowed by Paul? We didn't hear much about James ten or twenty years ago. Why has his story only now resurfaced?

PARALLEL MOVEMENTS

Let's back up for a moment, examine the situation in the 60s, and then see how the Book of Acts created an influential model for understanding early Christian origins.

As we discussed in the last chapter, there were two rival and parallel movements in the 60s: the Jesus Movement in Israel, and the Christ Movement in the Diaspora.[4] They were not the same religion: one came from Jesus; the other came from from Paul. One was within Judaism; the other was not. One focused on the teachings of Jesus; the other focused on the figure of Christ.

We need to visualize these two movements like two rival baseball teams. The Los Angeles Angels and the Texas Rangers have different histories and ownership. They are different businesses, competing with each other. They share many things, however—an intense interest in the sport and business of baseball; a need to generate income; a striving for personal fitness and stamina on the part of the players; and a strong desire on the part of the organization to create revenue for players, owners, and shareholders. Nonetheless, while they have much in common, they remain competitors.

The Christ and Jesus Movements were like that—*competing* religions. They not only jostled with each other for members, they themselves also had different competitors. The Jesus Movement, for instance, had to vie with other forms of Judaism in Israel. This was not the competitive forum for the Christ Movement, however, which had a different sphere of operation. The Christ Movement strove for converts against Roman mystery religions while competing with Diaspora Judaism for the God-fearer segment of its congregations.

Moreover, as we have seen, there were significant differences between these two groups in terms of origins, beliefs, and practices. Not surprisingly, however, some of Paul's terminology overlaps that of the Jesus Movement. He makes only a few references just to "Jesus." Mostly he combines "Jesus" with titles such as "Christ" or "Lord" or both. So we have "Christ" or "Christ Jesus" or "Lord Jesus Christ." We should not be misled by this wording into supposing that Paul has in mind the Jesus of the 20s who taught in the Galilee. Paul's primary focus was on what the mystical Christ of experience had conveyed to and through him. That represented a distinctive source of information: direct encounter with the Christ. He received and conveyed a message *no one* in the Jesus Movement had ever heard or expressed. As a result, his beliefs differed as did his practices. Paul was at pains to emphasize how separate his movement was from the Jesus Movement. We should take him at his word. Most importantly, the two movements were not "branch operations" of one common enterprise.

We are familiar with other competing religions that have similar terminology. Judaism and Christianity today provide one example, with overlapping terminology in terms of covenant, Bible, Messiah, redemption, prophets, and so on. Yet Judaism and Christianity have separate places of worship, cherish different preferred writings, and maintain their own leadership.

Similarly, Islam has links to both Judaism and Christianity. Moses and Jesus, for example, are both revered prophets within the religion of Islam. Jews and

Christians, as "People of the Book," occupy a privileged position within its theology, and Abraham represents the common ancestor of all three monotheistic religions. Islam's permissible foods, Halal dietary observances, are similar to some of the biblical kosher laws of Judaism. Islam, too, is an uncompromising monotheistic religion, as is Judaism. Islam, however, grew out of a separate revelation to Mohammed in the seventh century A.D. Mohammed heard things that the leaders of Christianity and Judaism did not hear. Islam developed its own literature, centers of study, places of worship, and clergy. So while Islam shares a significant overlap with its predecessors, it remains a separate religion, fiercely competing for members—especially with Christianity—in many places throughout the world.

Another example can be found within the American religious scene in the relationship between Mormonism and Christianity. The Mormons or Latter-day Saints had a separate revelation, which serves to distinguish this movement from Christianity. Mormonism emerged out of a distinctive religious vision to Joseph Smith, Jr. and the golden plates he discovered that provided the basis for the Book of Mormon. To some degree, Mormon terminology overlaps with that of Protestant, Catholic, and Orthodox Christianity. Because of their separate revelation, however, Mormons have heard things that Christian leaders have not. As a result, their beliefs and practices differ.

So it is not surprising that both the Jesus and Christ Movements shared overlapping terminology, and that it would have been confusing to outsiders. Each, however, maintained a separate infrastructure, leadership, and collection of favored writings. Moreover, by the midfirst century, these two religions faced vastly different problems. These are important to understanding the dynamics between the two rival movements.

Israel was in turmoil in the 60s, and this crippled the Jesus Movement. A ferocious conflict raged from 66 through to 73 or 74, being both a civil war as well as a war against Rome. Josephus told the painful story in *The Jewish War,* probably written shortly after the war, in the mid 70s. He rebuked the divisions that existed within Jewish society of the time and accused his countrymen of the same barbarism and butchery toward one another as the Romans exemplified toward them.[5] He estimated that close to one hundred thousand were taken captive and over a million killed throughout the war. Not all the casualties were inflicted by the Romans. Many occurred through Jewish infighting as the different factions battled one another. It was a civil war as much as it was a war against the foreign occupiers.

During this conflict, the Jewish revolt in the Galilee was brutally suppressed by Roman legions. From there Roman troops swooped down the Jordan River valley, destroying Qumran, the headquarters of the Dead Sea Scroll community in 68. In Jerusalem, the revolt had driven out the occupying Roman garrison early in the conflict and lawless bands of thugs, Zealots, and many other factions patrolled the city, looting the Temple and its treasury and putting to death anyone suspected of harboring moderate sentiments. Just prior to 70, Roman troops, bent on revenge against the rebels, encircled Jerusalem. They crucified everyone—women and children as well as men—who tried to escape the city. The hills around Jerusalem were littered with grim reminders of this ruthless suppression. Finally, in 70, the city of Jerusalem itself was destroyed, along with the Temple. Even today, one can enter "Burnt House" in the Old City of Jerusalem and see evidence of this massive destruction. Belonging to a priestly family, this house has been excavated several stories below the current level of Jerusalem. Finds include a spear and the arm bone of a woman who was likely hiding from the occupying Romans. It is an eerie reminder of that awful time in Jewish history. Masada, the last stronghold of the Zealots, towering over the Dead Sea, was captured in the early 70s. There, Josephus tells us, the Roman legions surrounded the mesa-shaped fortress and built a causeway from the floor of the valley to the top of the mountain. He also reports that, sensing that the end was near, almost a thousand Zealot inhabitants of Masada preferred to commit suicide than surrender their freedom to Rome. That was the end of Jewish resistance toward Rome for decades.[6]

Shortly before this conflict, James, the brother of Jesus, was killed, in 62. Along with the immense disruption due to the siege of Jerusalem, its capture, and its destruction by the Romans, the execution of its bishop severely incapacitated the leadership of the Jesus Movement. While threatened from without by the rival Christ Movement gaining momentum in the Diaspora, it was hobbled at a crucial time in its history. One ancient church source indicates that the fledgling community escaped to Pella to the north and east, just below the Sea of Galilee in modern-day Jordan. Even if this tradition is correct, they appear to have returned to Jerusalem sometime later to elect Simeon as James's successor as bishop of that city. Clearly the Jesus Movement suffered immensely during the violence of the 60s and was in decline. It was not in a position to exert its leadership.

By way of contrast, Paul's Christ Movement caught on and spread rapidly. Capturing the God-fearer segment from synagogues was a highly successful maneuver. These spiritual seekers responded eagerly to Paul's message that they could have all the benefits of Judaism without any of its obligations. It was an incredibly good deal. Paul succeeded wildly beyond anyone's imagination.

WHAT ACTS PROPOSES

So, in the 60s, there were a variety of religious choices: the Jesus Movement, other forms of Judaism, the Christ Movement, and various mystery religions.

They saw themselves as distinctive. Yet we conflate the Christ and Jesus Movements. Conventionally we think of Paul as coming from Jesus. Some go so far as to put Paul on a pedestal, as the major leader within early Christianity, so much so that it becomes difficult to see James and his movement underneath what we might dub "the prism of Paul."

So how did this come about? How did we gain the perception that the tradition flowed from Jesus through Paul into modern Christianity, to the virtual exclusion of James and his movement? Much of the obscurity of James and the Jesus Movement has to do with the model of Christian origins created by the Book of Acts in the early second century. It is this account that underlies the Conventional Model of Christian Origins we have inherited today. Simply put, the Book of Acts fuses together—at least on paper—two different religions into one common enterprise. In spite of being parallel, rival religions, Acts hooks the Christ Movement on to the Jesus Movement. It was a bold and radical invention.

The grafting had an important effect: it submerged the Jesus Movement under the Christ Movement. It used the Jesus Movement to gain legitimacy, as we shall see, but it smothered its contribution and perspective so effectively that we have a difficult time today seeing it and James at all. It's buried under the weight of Paul. Thus Acts' narrative shapes our visualization of early Christian roots. Because of the power of this model, we read back through the history of these times as if the Pauline Christ Movement went back to Jesus and not just to Paul himself.

Acts' Model of Christian Origins proposes that we envisage early Christian history as follows. While Judaism was forging Rabbinic Judaism under the leadership of the Pharisees, simultaneously there were two early Christian movements. Each originated from Jesus. One movement was led by James, the other, by Paul. Acts also presents the view that mutual understanding existed between these two groups. By virtue of a decision by James at a Jerusalem conference, it was decreed that each movement, as part of one common enterprise, would focus on two jurisdictions. Paul and his group would constitute a mission to the Gentiles. James and his followers would address a Jewish constituency. That's the author of Acts' reconstruction of earlier history, some fifty to sixty years prior to his time of writing.

That's *what* Acts proposed. It linked the Christ Movement to the Jesus Movement, and, through it, back to Jesus and biblical Judaism. Henceforth members of the Christ Movement could claim legitimacy. They had a mandate from a personage no less in stature than James, the head of the Jesus Movement, for what they were saying and doing. This is, however, fiction. It was designed to serve a particular need that had surfaced at the time Acts was written. Acts invented information about Paul and the Jerusalem leadership. By comparing what Acts said about Paul with what Paul said about himself, we can unravel the confusion. We can detect the creative hand of Acts in shaping his narrative.

THE JESUS COVER-UP MODEL OF
CHRISTIAN ORIGINS

Contrary to the Book of Acts, the Jesus Cover-Up Model of Christian Origins contends that we need to visualize Paul's Christ Movement and James's Jesus Movement as two different religions having separate origins. They were linked retroactively by the author of the Book of Acts, years after Paul and James died. It is not as if they both had a common origin in Jesus and then subsequently diverged. Rather they had separate origins and were then converged by Acts. Acts would like us to accept the view that two rival and parallel religions actually had a common origin. The author wants us to visualize the relationship between the Christ and Jesus Movements as similar to that which exists between Protestantism and Catholicism, or Catholicism and Orthodoxy. Each had common ancestry but eventually parted ways. That's how the author of Acts sees the relationship, as two fronts to one united religion.

In fact, what Acts achieved was far more ambitious and innovative. In linking the Christ Movement to the Jesus Movement, what the writer of Acts has succeeded in doing is fusing together two separate religions. It's as if he blended together two different movements—say, in contemporary terms, something like Islam and Christianity—in spite of their having different origins, beliefs, and practices. That's the truly radical nature of Acts' proposal. It joined together independent, separate movements into one united whole.

Let's see the evidence for this. *How* did Acts create this synthesis?

ACTS' CREATIVE HISTORY

The highly influential Book of Acts claims to trace the early development of the Christian movement. Its structure is straightforward. It focuses initially on the work of the leaders in Jerusalem—James, Peter, John and, some others. Then it switches to Paul, describing his "conversion" and outlining his career. This includes reports on his meetings with Jerusalem leaders as well as a summary of his various missionary trips throughout the Diaspora. It concludes with Paul's eventual preaching in Rome in the early 60s. It would be very helpful if we could use the information presented in Acts to supplement Paul's own account of his career and message. Some have gone this route.[7]

However, upon examination we find that Acts distorted what we know of Paul from Paul himself.[8] It was not that the author of Acts just added detail: he *contradicted* what Paul himself clearly said. This represents a fictitious Paul, and that subterfuge provides the tip-off that there is a hidden agenda at work in Acts. It represents nothing less than a reinterpretation of the movement prior to his times. Let us trace how the author of Acts reworked the origins of Paul's movement and attempted to legitimize Paul's distinctive teachings and practices. It's a tremendous tour de force. The effect of Acts' endeavors was to put forward the illusion that Paul's movement arose out of the religion originating with Jesus, when it clearly hadn't. Why Acts concocted this connection we'll explore in a subsequent section.

Acts created the linkage using three main strategies.

First of all, Acts radically reined in Paul's independence. This writing provided marvelously creative details about Paul's mystical experience on the road to Damascus. Acts tells us that immediately after this remarkable event, Paul went into the house of Ananias, a member of the Jesus Movement living there. Ananias healed and baptized him (Acts 9:10–19). Paul then preached in the synagogues in Damascus, arousing the anger of "the Jews," and he narrowly escaped when "his disciples" caught wind of a plot on his life.

Some details here should set off alarm bells in the mind of a wary reader. Were there already members of the Jesus Movement so far from Jerusalem? Also, how was it that Paul already had disciples—where did they come from? Did Paul already have "a movement"? Moreover, would any member of the Jesus Movement have referred to the worshippers in synagogues as "the Jews"—as "other"—or was this a reflection of a much later stance, when the Christian community was separating from Judaism? A lot of things do not ring true in this account.

After this, Acts says, Paul went up to Jerusalem where Barnabas introduced him to "the apostles" (Acts 9:27). He moved about freely in Jerusalem, getting into a serious debate with "Hellenists"—that is, Greek-speaking Jews—who attempted to kill him. He was then rescued, taken down to the port city of Caesarea and packed off to his hometown of Tarsus. Why Paul aroused such anger is not made clear, especially when members of the Jesus Movement appear to have lived in harmony with other Jewish factions (except for the Sadducees). This represents an important clue that others recognized that Paul's teachings differed from those of the Jesus Movement.

If we take Acts' account as accurate, Paul immediately aligned himself with the Jesus Movement. In quick order he was baptized, preached in an antagonistic manner, escaped with the help of his disciples, and headed up to Jerusalem.

That's not what Paul said happened, however. In his Letter to the Galatians, Paul stressed that after his remarkable experience, he "did not confer with any human being" (Galatians 1:16). There was no mention of an Ananias or other members of the Jesus Movement resident in Damascus. He made no mention of having his own disciples. Nor did he say that he preached in Jewish synagogues in Damascus. Moreover, Paul emphasized that he did not go up to Jerusalem to confer with leaders of the Jesus Movement. He said, instead, that he immediately went away "into Arabia" (Galatians 1:17), returning after a while to Damascus. Why he did so, or where he went in Arabia, we do not know. Legend associates him with the fabulous city of Petra, the headquarters of the wealthy Nabatean traders.

Then, three years later, Paul did go to Jerusalem for fifteen days, to visit Cephas (Peter) and James, but no others. After that, he went into the regions of Syria and Cilicia, and we know nothing of this venture. For a recent high-profile "convert," as Acts makes him out to be, this does not represent much contact with the Jerusalem leadership. Fourteen years later he mentions another visit to Jerusalem, along with Barnabas and Titus.[9]

Acts attributed the trouble Paul experienced in Damascus to a political issue, namely the animosity of "the Jews" of Damascus who wanted Paul arrested. This writing noted that Paul—at his own request—had originally been sent to Damascus by the pro-Roman high priest in Jerusalem to arrest certain of its citizens. This is an odd detail, for the high priest in Jerusalem would have had no authority over Jews living outside his jurisdiction. Moreover, the non-Roman Nabatean government authorities would not have taken kindly to this intrusion into their domestic affairs. These were not Roman subjects Paul was after, but citizens of Arabia, of which Damascus was a part. If Acts is to be believed, Paul was a bounty hunter—engaged in some unsavory scheme to abduct foreign nationals, to bring them forcibly to religious authorities in another country. Just not ethical or plausible.

Nor is it clear why the high priest would want to abduct those "who belonged to the Way" (Acts 9:2). Or even why he would have agreed with Paul's request to undertake this mission in the first place. The only issue between the Sadducean high priest and the Jesus Movement had to do with belief in resurrection. That was no different, however, than the issue between the Sadducees and the Pharisees. If the high priest wished to stamp out those who believed in resurrection, he did not need to concentrate all his efforts on one tiny sect so far from its center in a different political jurisdiction. He could have tackled a larger faction, the Pharisees, right on his doorstep in Jerusalem and elsewhere throughout the land. Or he could have picked on the Essenes. Or, for that matter, he could have harassed the members of the Jesus Movement resident in Jerusalem, within blocks from the Temple and the high priest's own residence. Why send Paul on a wild goose chase to hunt down a minuscule minority outside his religious and political jurisdiction?

Once again, the details provided by Acts simply do not ring true.

Paul himself located his mystical experience in Damascus but did not explain the reason for this journey. He was more concerned to emphasize that through this experience "God was pleased to reveal his son in [to] me, so that I might proclaim him among the Gentiles" (Galatians 1:15–16).

So we have two differing and contradictory perspectives: Paul's and Acts'. The differences are dramatic. Paul distanced himself from the Jesus Movement leaders. Acts put him squarely in their midst soon after his experience near Damascus. Moreover, Paul emphasized that the message he preached came directly from the mystical Christ who he believed was revealed "in" him (Galatians 1:16), not through any human agency. That was very important to Paul—the immediacy of his knowledge of the Christ. Unlike what Paul said he did following his experience, the Book of Acts has him trotting up to Jerusalem immediately. Finally, Acts wanted to create the impression of a linkage right from the get-go. The only trouble is, Paul himself says it didn't happen that way at all.

Acts is clearly inventing history in order to create the desired association. But there is more revisionist history in the making, as we shall shortly discover.

Second, Acts invented the Jerusalem Conference to legitimize Paul's distinctive teachings and practices. The writer of Acts had a problem. After linking Paul to the Jesus Movement immediately after his Damascus experience, he now had to account for Paul's distinctive teachings and practices with respect to Torah observance. He would have known how contentious and infuriating these were to leaders like James and others within the inner circle in Jerusalem. His issue was how to link a non-Torah-observant movement with one that was. That synthesis would be no mean feat; passions ran high over Torah obligations since so much was at stake. Acts' solution was truly ingenious: it created authorization for Paul's position.

As Paul tells it, there was no significant relationship between his movement and that of the Jesus group in Jerusalem. Some fourteen or seventeen years after his dramatic mystical experience, Paul says that he visited the leaders of the Jesus Movement. They conferred "behind closed doors," sharing their respective messages. The upshot of these conversations was a handshake and an agreement to operate in two different jurisdictions—his, among Gentiles; theirs, among Jews. They represented two different operations. They requested that Paul "remember the poor" (Galatians 2:10). For Paul, that constituted the only linkage: to take up collections to help those less fortunate financially. It is not as if there is one common movement under one leader, with two prongs—one to the Jews and one to the Gentiles. So, as Paul described the situation, he was not "under" anyone, least of all James in Jerusalem.

The picture in Acts 15, however, is vastly different. In this account, when Paul goes to Jerusalem, it is apparent that many members of the Jesus Movement there were insistent that the Torah be observed, even for Gentile members (Acts 15:1). Paul, it seems, was widely believed—correctly, as it turns out—to be teaching otherwise, that Torah observance was not required. What he said could easily be interpreted as applying to everyone, Jew or Gentile. In Acts' account, Paul was hauled before James and the leaders in Jerusalem. This is the scene that represents the famous Jerusalem Conference. Paul was "on the carpet" for his views. Peter was there, too, and he spoke. James, however, decided the issue, proposing a dual structure for the movement (Acts 15:13–21). According to the account in Acts, James decreed that Jewish members of the Jesus movement would continue to obey all the rules and laws of Torah. On the other hand, Gentile members of the movement would have a lesser obligation. They would be required to observe only the Seven Noahide Laws incumbent on all humanity, not the full Torah required of Jewish members.

These requirements represented much stronger obligations than simply "remembering the poor," as Paul would have it. The key point to notice, however, is that the device of the Jerusalem Conference bound the Christ Movement to the Jesus Movement as an integral part of a larger mission. It was this conference that created the impression that both movements worked harmoniously, hand in hand, each with the other, but having separate jurisdictions.

A common enterprise with a two-prong mission: that's the image Acts painted for us. Stemming from Jesus, we have James and Paul, each with their respective mandate—one to the Jews and one to the Gentiles. The big news, however, was that it generated legitimacy for the Christ Movement, being supported and authorized by no less a person than James and the leadership in Jerusalem. This is the model Acts would have us accept, with all the differences between the Jesus and Christ Movements glossed over. This act of historical revisionism fashioned the picture we tend to use today.

This account of Christian origins achieved several important strategic objectives. For one thing, it made it appear that Paul's Christ Movement was part of the movement that originated with Jesus. As we shall see, this lineage was very important to the author of Acts. It also positioned Paul's movement as an integral part of a larger enterprise, setting up a common infrastructure. More importantly, it had James validating and legitimizing Paul's teachings and practices with respect to not observing Torah. Here was the smoking gun—the Jerusalem Conference was exactly what Acts needed to tie Paul into the Jesus Movement.

It is tempting to say that, for once, Acts got it right and that Paul minimized the story. The incident placed Paul in an unfavorable light, unlike most of Acts, and that might argue for its authenticity. Moreover the position on the part of James, if reported correctly, was consistent with the attitude of other Jewish leaders of the time. The Pharisees, for instance, would have held that Gentiles do not have to take on the full responsibility of Torah observance to be regarded as righteous or to achieve salvation. For them, following the Seven Noahide Laws was sufficient. They would not, of course, be Jews: they'd remain

Gentiles. If, for some reason, they wished to be converted to Judaism, they could do so through male circumcision and immersion as well as agreeing to follow the law. But there was no necessity linked to salvation to do so. There was no question that the righteous of all the nations, who observe the Noahide laws faithfully, would have a share in the world to come. Redemption was not the issue at all. Thus the position of James would have been consistent with that of other Jewish leaders of the time, especially the views of the Pharisees. So perhaps Acts told the story correctly.

But that's not the case. History didn't unfold the way Acts told us it did. Let's see why not.

ACTS GOT IT WRONG

There are significant problems with Acts' version of history and its decisive Jerusalem Conference decree. Simply put, no one seems to know anything about it at all. That is truly amazing and it provides the all-important clue that it never even happened. It was Acts' creative genius that invented this fiction. The Jerusalem Conference—if it were held at all—would have dated from the late 40s.[10] Paul's Letter to the Galatians was later, from the mid 50s.[11] As we have seen in an earlier chapter, Paul had to deal with the issue of Torah observance. Other teachers had come into Paul's part of the world, telling Paul's Gentile converts in Galatia that they needed to observe the law.[12] They may have been members of the Jesus Movement who shared the belief that Gentiles who wish to become part of the new movement within Judaism must observe Torah.

If an authoritative decision had been rendered by James only a few years earlier exempting Gentile converts from this requirement, then it is absolutely astonishing that Paul's rival leaders did not know of it. Nor is it clear why they would be stepping into his jurisdiction—the mission to the Gentiles. Clearly whoever was disturbing the community in Galatia was completely unaware of this decree of James, the undisputed leader of the movement. They clearly thought that any new member must become Jewish first, observing all the requirements of Torah. That, of course, was simply waving a red flag in front of Paul. It was a position, however, espoused by the Jesus Movement.

When Paul responded to these opposing teachers, it is surprising that Paul did not seem to know of this Jerusalem Conference decree either. He did not refer to James's authoritative pronouncement, which supposedly came only a few years earlier. That would have nipped the issue in the bud and settled the matter decisively. The Letter to the Galatians could have been considerably shorter: Paul could have referred them to the judgment of James. But he didn't. Instead he resorted to convoluted arguments, misquoting and misapplying scripture in the process. A polite "remember James's decree" would have sufficed and settled the matter.

It is as if the major decision of the supreme pontiff of the movement had come and gone without anyone knowing anything about it.

It probably never happened. The idea of a Jerusalem conference, presided over by the wise James, rendering decisions about Gentiles and Torah observance seems to have been a fantasy invented by the author of Acts. It represented a very important and imaginative move on the part of the author of the Book of Acts to graft Paul's radical Christ Movement on to the original Jesus Movement. Without it, nothing would stick the one to the other. The Jerusalem Conference is the sole support giving legitimacy to the teachings and practices of the Christ Movement. If it never happened, then Acts' synthesis crumbles to pieces.

PAUL'S JEWISHNESS

There's a third point of contrast between Acts and Paul himself. Acts exaggerated Paul's Jewishness. Paul himself dismissed his Jewishness, and he denounced those who would uphold Torah requirements for Gentile members of the movement. He contended that they are perverting the message, spreading confusion, and that they are cursed. He satirically hoped that those who circumcise would suffer an accident and castrate themselves (Galatians 5:12). He said that those who follow the law have fallen away from grace (Galatians 5:4). He counted his former life in Judaism as "rubbish" (Philippians 3:8). He did not give any credence to the position that there might be another legitimate understanding of the new movement. In particular, he provided no support to those in the Jesus Movement who saw matters differently. He never acted as if there existed an alternate version of his gospel, namely, the Jesus Movement. For Paul, there was only one way of understanding the message: his way. He was absolutely consistent on this. There was one and only one correct way of understanding his religion. Every other religion, including Judaism, was simply wrong.

It would be difficult to imagine that, at the end of his life, Paul thought of himself as in any way Jewish. His teachings and practices were anything but. Not only his denial of Torah but also his portrait of the Christ would have been at odds with all forms of Judaism. This contrasts with James, who undoubtedly lived and died as a Jew, so much so that latter generations referred to him as James ha-Zaddik (James the Righteous).

Acts, however, enhanced Paul's Jewishness. Paul, it claimed, had been brought up in Jerusalem as a student of Gamaliel, the leading Pharisaic teacher of his time, and strictly educated in Torah. Paul himself was much more modest, just noting in passing that he was a Pharisee (Philippians 3:5). He never claimed more than that, even when his credentials were on the line and he needed all the support he could muster. By claiming to have been a Pharisee, Paul may have meant only that of all the Jewish movements of the time, he sympathized with them the most, at least at one stage of his life. It did not imply formal training.

Many members of the Jesus Movement came out of the Pharisaic party within Judaism without arousing any antagonism from other Pharisees (Acts 15:5). The great Pharisaic leader Gamaliel defended members of the Jesus Movement when Peter was brought before the Sanhedrin (Acts 5:34–39). Josephus noted that a group of "reasonable" or "equitable" people, most likely the Pharisees, took great offense when the Sadducean high priest had James killed.[13]

Acts stretches believability to the absolute limit when it presented Paul defending himself before Roman authorities by saying "I worship the God of our ancestors, believing everything laid down according to the law or written in the prophets" (Acts 24:14). That is hard to picture from someone who penned the vicious anti-Torah Letter to the Galatians. At best, Paul is lying. More realistically, the author of Acts, many years later, inserted words into Paul's mouth—words the Paul of history could never have uttered with a straight face.

Acts' insistence on Paul's Jewishness is highly overblown, and Paul's self-assessment is much more accurate. He had a Jewish background and came to lead a movement that was anything but. He was a Jewish dropout.

ACTS' REVISIONIST HISTORY

What can we conclude from all this? Simply that the Book of Acts invented history. We know that the Book of Acts represents an unreliable source for information about Paul. Acts contradicts what we know of Paul from his own writings. Acts' Paul is a later creation that serves the author of Acts' purposes well. It is not, however, a reflection of the historical Paul. It is, rather, the Paul the author of Acts needed to invent to support the linkage between the two movements. We should look to Paul's own writings if we wish to grasp the Paul of history. Paul took every opportunity to separate his movement, his message, and his career from that of the Jesus Movement. Paths did cross, and when they did, as with an incident with a member of the Jesus Movement, Peter, Paul pressed his religious commitments. There was no indication from Paul that there existed another perspective or that another arm of the movement might have differing practices.

What we know of Paul, then, is from Paul himself, and his "authentic Paul" is vastly different from Acts' "revisionist Paul." Therefore, we cannot use the Book of Acts to supplement Paul's own account of his career and message. We simply have no way of knowing what additional information is fictional and what is historically accurate.

Most importantly, we cannot use Acts to say with confidence that the Christ and Jesus Movements simply represent two differing views of one common enterprise. Because Acts creates a different Paul than the real one revealed in his letters, we know that Acts has a hidden agenda—and we can now recognize what that is. The author of Acts is at pains to demonstrate that both Paul's movement and James's were part and parcel of one religious impetus stemming from Jesus himself.

WHY THE LINKAGE?

In both his gospel and the Book of Acts, Luke was writing for a Roman audience, trying to impress upon them that the movement was a religion fit for the Roman Empire. But he had a problem. This was a new religion on the scene, bereft of noble ancestry. But noble ancestry is precisely what the religion needed if it were to succeed on the Roman stage. In linking the Gentile Christ Movement through the Jesus Movement back to Jesus and biblical Judaism, he was creating an impeccable heritage for this new religion. It had the virtue of antiquity, a prized Roman virtue. With this historical legitimacy, the author of the Book of Acts positioned the new religion as one that possessed an impressive pedigree, going back into the history of Israel, back to David, Moses, Abraham—even back to the first human, Adam.

He was also grounding the Christ of Paul in an actual historical being, Jesus, through the Jesus Movement. In reading Paul's letters, it is surprising how little is made of anything that comes from the Jesus of history. There is not much in Paul's writing that would give us grounds for thinking that Jesus had anything important to say. As we have noted, Paul disclosed only that Jesus was born, was Jewish, and died. Moreover, he did not ground his own message in the teachings, observances, or sayings that come from the religion of Jesus. There are no parables, no Lord's Prayer, or no Sermon on the Mount. There is nothing that would reflect the relationship one would expect from a disciple of a rabbi. There is just what Paul says he got mystically from the Christ whom he claims reveals himself in him. Devoid of linkage to the Jesus Movement and to Judaism generally, Paul's Christ Movement would have appeared suspiciously like a Hellenistic mystery religion—and this may be an impression Luke was attempting to avoid.

Acts' great achievement was this: it created a highly influential model for understanding Christian origins. We have seen how it accomplished this—by asserting Paul's close contact with the Jesus Movement immediately after his remarkable Damascus experience, by glossing over key differences in belief, by legitimizing his position on non Torah observance through the Jerusalem Conference, and by enhancing his Jewishness. The author of Acts wanted us to visualize a common connection, and that is tremendously important for him. We see only the common connection. That's what we are intended to see. We're supposed to imagine that from ancient roots in Judaism, the religion of Jesus and that led by James validated and authorized Paul's Christ Movement and the growth of the church. We—and the Romans before us—are supposed to appreciate the wonderful ancestry of this religion. That is what Acts had to create if the new religion were to gain a sympathetic hearing around the Roman Empire. Acts' synthesis was tremendously successful. The leaders of the Christ Movement and Proto-Orthodoxy could all stand up and take pride in its ancestral roots (all the while, of course, rejecting its main tenets). Romans, not knowing the history, would be impressed with such an ancient movement that had entered their world. It was also successful in that this account shapes our perceptions and authorizes us to see the New Testament through the eyes of Paul.

But historical reality was different.

SO WHAT REALLY HAPPENED?

The fusion Acts created is suspect. Acts distorted known information and grafted one movement onto another, without regard for strong differences in origin, beliefs, and practices. The Jesus Movement people remained unconvinced. They continued their separate observances, undeterred by the growing popularity of the Christ cult. They did not accept the amalgamation. We should not imagine that, as a result of Acts, there suddenly appeared joint congregations, common celebrations, socializing, and intermarriage, or a unified administrative center. They retained separate infrastructures—congregations of the Christ Movement versus assemblies of the Jesus Movement—each operating independently. The linkage was simply on paper, for the benefit of the Christ Movement members who could now regale Romans with stories of an ancient heritage and authoritative mandate.

Instead of Acts' model, a newer understanding of Christian origins is developing. The Jesus Cover-Up Thesis advances the view that there were four *separate, parallel* religions that sprang up in the first-century Middle East. Two stemmed from biblical Judaism. These included Rabbinic Judaism, led by the Pharisees and the sages who after 70 had to reconstruct Judaism. The other child of biblical Judaism was the Jesus Movement, inspired by its Jewish teacher

Jesus, Torah-observant and messianic in nature. There were, however, two other religions that did not derive from biblical Judaism. One was the Gnostic Movement with its emphasis on "the living Jesus" who provided a saving knowledge to humans trapped in this dreadful world. The other one was Paul's Christ Movement, which, from its inception, constituted a religion outside Judaism.

So, according to the Jesus Cover-Up Thesis, we have four independent religions, each operating separately, competing with one another, and acting as rivals. In particular, the Christ Movement was never linked with the Jesus Movement, as Acts would have it. Two of these four religions eventually disappeared: the Jesus and the Gnostic movements. But two did succeed. Rabbinic Judaism became modern Judaism, and Paul's Christ Movement evolved into Christianity.

By contrast, Acts converged two separate religions and fused them into one common enterprise, at least on paper. Acts' synthesis was a literary creation, not a description of sociological reality. Two religions, each having separate origins, beliefs, and practices, were deliberately linked by the author of Acts for Roman consumption, but, "on the ground," they remained separate. Looking back, we can recognize how effective Acts' Model of Christian Origins was. We live with the legacy of this model today without realizing that Acts merged two disparate movements. The beliefs and practices of the Jesus Movement became obscured by Acts' creative history, for it privileged Paul's view as the dominant one through which to view early Christian origins. The teachings of Paul about the Christ became fused with memories of James and the Jesus Movement, but the latter were well hidden.

This was the place where the Christ of Paul's personal experience became substituted for the Jesus of history: the Christ for Jesus, beliefs about the Christ for the teachings of Jesus, the religion of Paul for that of Jesus. Acts gave validity to Paul's inspiration and to the figure around whom he had built his death and resurrection theology. All this was accomplished allegedly with the consent of Jesus' earliest followers.

This synthesis also allowed later Christians to supplement Paul's letters with various gospels that were being written by the Christifying segment of the early church. These include gospels like Luke and John. The latter makes strong claims about the person of Jesus—all the "I am" statements are typically found in this gospel: "I am the Good Shepherd," "I am the Way, the Truth and the Life," and so forth. We should not imagine that gospels represent independent sources. They are the creations of actual communities. Just as the Christ Movement created their own, the Gnostic and Jesus Movements fashioned theirs.

Thus there was not one common body of literature on which to draw or one neutral set of texts that could be used to judge what was authentic Christianity. The Jesus Movement people and Ebionites used a version of the Gospel of Matthew. But they shunned the virgin birth story and rejected Paul's letters and such Christified gospels as Luke and John. Similarly, the Gnostics preferred their own materials, including the *Gospel of Thomas,* the *Gospel of Mary,* the *Gospel of the Savior,* the *Apocryphon of John,* and many other writings now known to us from the scrolls discovered some sixty years ago.

The gospel writings did not create the church. Rather these influential documents are the church's creation—and not the church as a whole but only one faction within the early Christian clustering of communities. The present New Testament reflects the writings preferred by the Proto-Orthodox, the heirs of Paul's Christ Movement. It excludes the literature emanating from other groups, the Gnostics or the Ebionites, for instance. So the New Testament does not represent an unbiased or neutral collection of early Christian writings. We have a circular loop: the Proto-Orthodox producing and authenticating its writings; these writings, in turn, validating the Proto-Orthodox.

PAULINITY

What we have in Christianity today is Paulinity. It is the religion envisaged and vigorously promoted by Paul and given a respectable history by the Book of Acts. It is a Hellenized religion about a Gentile Christ, a cosmic redeemer, and it is through that perspective that the later gospels are read. It is not the religion of the Jewish Jesus, the Messiah claimant and proclaimer of a Kingdom of God. That religion—the religion of the Jesus Movement and the Ebionites—eventually died out.

┌─────┐
│ 11 │
└─────┘

THE JESUS MOVEMENT
FADES AWAY

Where was the outcry? The outrage? The barrage of letters and writings from the Jesus Movement? Its legitimacy and credibility had been expropriated by the exceptionally clever Book of Acts to bolster the credentials of the rapidly expanding Christ Movement. The latter was boldly sketched as a natural outgrowth of the former, with everyone in harmonious agreement. It was as if there had been a seamless transition from Jesus to Paul and everybody was in on the plan.

They weren't. When they came across the Book of Acts, they would likely have been apoplectic. "We never agreed to any of this," they probably said. Or, "James would never have approved of Paul's position." They certainly didn't. They acted as though they knew nothing of a Jerusalem conference setting up a dual mission. They shadowed Paul's mission, opposing him at every turn. They rejected his writings . . . and the Book of Acts as well. They despised his teachings and labeled him a "false teacher" for centuries. Bitter sentiments about Paul continued to bubble up in the Ebionite writings that have survived.

We have glimpses of warnings from the Jesus Movement just before the Book of Acts was written. Some of its leaders sensed that a major threat was brewing. They wrote to fend off incursions into their ranks, but they may have vastly underestimated the strength and persuasiveness of the Christ Movement. We find these warnings in several late-first-century writings—the Gospel of Matthew, the Letter of James, and the *Didache*. These important documents show us that leaders of the Jesus Movement knew something was afoot and that erroneous teachings and practices were being promulgated throughout the Diaspora. All these originated with Paul.

THE GOSPEL OF MATTHEW

In the 80s, a few years after the death of Paul but before the Book of Acts was written, the author of the Gospel of Matthew condemned Paul's central teaching, and, interestingly, he did so through the words of Jesus. In the Sermon on the Mount, for instance, we find the following passage attributed to Jesus:

> *Do not think that I have come to abolish the law or the prophets . . . For truly I tell you, until heaven and earth pass away, not one letter, not one stroke of a letter, will pass from the law until all is accomplished. Therefore, whoever breaks one of the least of these commandments, and teaches others to do the same, will be called least in the kingdom of heaven.* (Matthew 5:17–19)

This is a crucial passage for understanding Matthew's Jesus. As the new Moses, Jesus did not believe in the abolition of Torah. This passage is aimed squarely at the heart of Paul's teaching, which had denied the validity of Jewish law. It is also very easy to see Paul and his followers in the last phrase "whoever breaks one of the least of these commandments, and teachers others to do the same, will be called least in the kingdom of heaven." Paul's Christ Movement was the only religion on the horizon teaching that people should not observe the law.

Matthew sent a stern warning to those who would find Paul's position attractive: Jesus would not have agreed with you. He made clear to his followers that Paul's religion was not for them. Steer clear of these people was his advice. Their message violates the religion of Jesus. Abandonment of Torah was not consistent with the religion taught and practiced by Jesus. Matthew's Jesus was even more stringent than the Pharisees and required his followers to live up to the challenge of the higher righteousness. That's a far cry from what Paul demanded of his followers, in his new religion.

It is ironic that this anti-Paul gospel was ever preserved, let alone included in our New Testament. It ran completely counter to Paul and his teachings. Most likely, Jesus' teachings from the Sermon on the Mount were simply ignored, while the anti-Pharisaic statements in Matthew's Gospel were highly regarded by the Christ Movement and the Proto-Orthodox. We'll examine Matthew's attack on the Pharisees later, but his bitter denunciations of these leaders of Judaism would have appealed to the Proto-Orthodox, providing them with yet more ammunition in distinguishing their movement from that of Rabbinic Judaism.

THE LETTER OF JAMES

The Letter of James reads like a rambling sermon and is addressed from a "James" who is described as "a servant of God and of the Lord Jesus Christ" (James 1:1). This has traditionally been identified as James, the brother of Jesus, the head of the Jesus Movement. It is unclear, however, if this document was written by James himself prior to his death in 62 or by a devoted follower a few decades later who attributed the letter to him. Whatever its authorship, it reflects the views of the Jesus Movement at a crucial time in its history, the late first century. For convenience' sake, we'll refer to this writing as "James."

Much was on the line when James was written. The Christ Movement was gaining momentum, spurred on by huge growth in the Diaspora as Gentiles flocked to its welcoming message. No longer could the Jesus Movement rest on its laurels, smugly content that it was the legitimate expression of the faith, the true successor to Jesus. It was under serious attack, and this was definitely not the time for complacency. The Letter of James was intended as a heartfelt warning to communities in the Diaspora (James 1:1). Someone in a leadership position within the Jesus Movement made a desperate bid to try to stem the tide of history, to fend off encroachments by a much larger rival religion in areas of Jewish life outside Israel. Much like Paul Revere hoping to awaken fellow citizens with the cry "the British are coming," this author sought to rouse members of the Jesus Movement to action. It was a stirring call to arms: The Christ Movement is coming your way very soon. The threat was real.

James focused on "trials" within the "synagogue" (James 2:2)—yes, that's the word used in this writing. While we do not associate "synagogues" with Christianity today, it was natural at the time for members of the Jesus Movement to be worshipping in synagogues. One of the trials concerned deceptions. There were deceivers, this writer observed, who were going about propagating the idea that faith, and faith alone, sufficed for true religion. For James, this religious proposition was false. In his judgment, a faith-only religion amounted to absolutely nothing. Like his initial readers, we recognize immediately whom James has in mind. His attack zeroed in on one of the main props of Paul's preaching, his sharp contrast between faith and works. Paul had confidently proclaimed that religion should focus on "faith in Jesus Christ" (Galatians 2:16), not on the works of the law. That all-too-easy view was deceptive, asserted James. It allowed people to fool themselves into thinking they really had an effective religion. Whatever faith a person has should be exemplified in action. Otherwise, how could we possibly tell if a person "has faith"? For James, faith-only people fail to make a difference. Their religion is futile and, even worse, perhaps illusory.

James put forward a series of examples designed to demonstrate the absurdity of rooting a religion just in faith. Some, said James, boast that they love their neighbor as themselves (James 2:8). Then they go out and discriminate against people and treat them poorly. They might, for instance, cozy up to the rich and ignore the poor within the synagogue, treating people unequally and shamefully. Clearly their faith means nothing in practice, for their actions are not congruent with what they say they profess. Such faith is a sham.

Others might take pride in having faith but then fail to do any good deeds. James mocked those, for instance, who would unfeelingly tell the naked and hungry "go in peace" (James 2:16) but not lift a finger to help meet their material needs—food, clothing, shelter, and the like. Faith can amount to nothing more than empty sentiments, as this example illustrates, making no difference at all in people's lives. Such talk is cheap, but, worse than that, it can be tremendously cruel and highly insensitive. True religion requires effort, action, and results, not just pious rhetoric.

James went on the attack, challenging his opponents. "Show me," he said, "your faith apart from your works, and I by my works will show you my faith" (James 2:18). If religion makes no difference in behavior, what good is it? It amounts to nothing. Even more significantly, without good works, how can one tell a person who has faith from one who does not?

The message was clear. Paul's quick dismissal of the merits and worth of "good works" was far too simplistic. It was not good enough just "to have faith." In stressing the importance of behavior, James operated out of Jewish modes of thought. Following the law required decision, action, and a willing disposition. Deuteronomy had made that clear. So had Jesus.

What is faith? James would have regarded it from a Jewish perspective. This would not have consisted of beliefs about the Christ or a warm mental or emotional attitude. Rather faith requires being *faithful* to the law. The differences are profound. Paul's view positioned faith as an interior experience, something experienced by a person and confined to that individual. It's something a person feels, perhaps profoundly. But there it ends. The other perspective—James's—regards it as something interior *and* exterior. Being faithful requires that personal convictions and loyalties manifest themselves in everyday living, in social and interpersonal contexts, in the decisions we make on a daily basis concerning how to treat other people. On Paul's view, faith could be bottled up inside the person without ever coming out. On James's view, that could never happen. That wouldn't be what is meant by being faithful.

Like Paul before him, James appealed to the example of Abraham. He may have had the passage from the Letter to the Galatians in front of him where Paul argued that Abraham was the model of faith and thus the exemplar for Christians. James, however, cited another event in the life of Abraham: the near sacrifice of Isaac. Abraham did not just have faith in God: here he actually took steps to carry out the sacrifice. He might have gone through with it had not an animal fortuitously appeared just in the nick of time. James drew the obvious conclusion from this example. Just having faith is insufficient: it needs to be expressed through action. Consequently, a person is not justified simply by belief but by doing the works of the law.

He drove the point home and stated as a fundamental religious principle the exact opposite of what Paul had preached:

> *You see that faith was active along with his works and faith was brought to completion by the works. Thus the scripture was fulfilled that says, "Abraham believed God and it was reckoned to him as righteousness," and he was called the friend of God.* **You see that a person is justified by works and not by faith alone.** (James 2:22–24; emphasis added)

Salvation or "justification" comes through righteous actions, not just by having faith. So the battle lines were clearly drawn between Paul and James.

James pressed his point even further. The danger of a faith-only religion was that it might result in nothing. It might give the believer a nice warm personal feeling but nothing more. True religion had to matter. It had to be open to the needs of others, caring and compassionate, just as the parables of Jesus had taught. He gave specific illustrations of religion at work—caring for orphans and widows, for instance; responding to the material needs of others; being hesitant to speak, slow to anger, and quick to listen. These were the hallmarks of a person who was truly faithful and who manifested his commitment in action. This religion was not just a personal, inner experience. It was much more than that. All James's examples relate to social situations, how we get along with other people and how we respond to their needs and sensitivities. As with Jesus, religion that mattered was religion that demanded personal performance. Religion requires doing, not just boasting that one has faith.

The Letter of James represented an important attempt at consciousness-raising. It was prompted by the perception that Pauline deceptions were beginning to affect the well-being of members within the synagogue at large, perhaps confusing them with his siren call to a simpler, less demanding path. Paul and his followers must have caused sufficient "trouble" within the synagogues in the Diaspora to have provoked this warning.

This letter placed Paul in the category of "deceiver." We tend not to think of him this way. But the Jesus Movement and Ebionites were very clear: Paul was pulling the wool over people's eyes and spreading a false message. No wonder in his letters he persistently had to answer the charge that he was deceiving people. Many of his generation just didn't find his message authentic.

James also tackled the topic of angry verbal assaults, and here he tried to calm things down. Members of the Jesus and Christ Movements were likely violently denouncing each other, rejecting each other's religion with nasty insults.

They had a lot to fight over. Concerned about inflammatory speech, James issued a dire warning about the perils of "the tongue," urging members not to speak evil against one another: "the tongue is a fire" (James 3:6). Here James echoed some of the warnings of the Dead Sea Scroll society whose leaders had counseled verbal restraint for members living in close proximity to each other within the community of righteousness. Angry words said in the heat of argument are immensely destructive, hurting and damaging relationships, often making forgiveness difficult or impossible. Rather than boasting about their accomplishments, James observed, people should demonstrate understanding and gentleness in their actions. Again, following the teachings of Jesus, James focused on right behavior, how people should treat one another.

It is very likely that James had one particular point of view in mind when he cautioned members of the community at large to watch what they say. People, he said, should not speak of the law as if it were evil (James 4:11). Again, like his original readers, we immediately recognize whom James has in mind. Only Paul had spoken in this fashion, repudiating the law, saying that those who practice it have forfeited grace and salvation and have failed to understand the significance of Christ. Paul's followers may have gone much further than their leader's harsh condemnation, perhaps personally ridiculing family members, friends, or neighbors who still observed the Sabbath, circumcision, the dietary laws, or the Jewish festivals.

James noted that people who revile the law are not themselves advocates or practitioners of Torah. That's an obvious point, to be sure, but then he injected an interesting twist. When people denounce Torah, he observed, they place themselves over it as its superiors. They presume to act as judges of Torah, thinking that they themselves are above God's law. They arrogantly act as an elite group who suppose they are not bound by it. For James, this haughty outlook displayed a defective spiritual attitude.

Because of its content, the Letter of James wasn't a popular writing, at least not among Gentile Christians. It definitely didn't convey the message they wanted to hear. It was shunned, just as the members of the Jesus Movement were. Two centuries later, Eusebius spoke of the Letter of James as one of the "disputed writings" (*Ecclesiastical History*, Book 3, Chapter 25, Section 3), not high on the list for inclusion in the New Testament. Eventually, though, it was included, although it has always sat tucked at the back of the book, vastly overshadowed by the more popular and more numerous writings of Paul. At the Reformation, Martin Luther, a devoted follower of Paul's perspective, proposed that it be dropped from the Protestant New Testament, referring to it in his *Preface to the New Testament* as an "epistle of straw." It wasn't. Simply put, the Letter of James represented an important and insightful warning that went unheeded. It stands as a monumental challenge to the simplistic views of Paul. But it was clearly "off strategy" for the evolving Christ Movement and its successors, the Proto-Orthodox.

SETTING BOUNDARIES

What was it like, being a member of the Jesus Movement in the late first century, faced with an evolving Judaism on the one side and the growing Christ Movement on the other? How did the Jesus Movement worship? Interpret Torah? What were their relationships with other Jews? To what extent were they aware of the momentous decisions coming out of Yavneh where the sages were beginning the arduous task of reconstructing Judaism after the destruction of the Temple? In fact, did they have any input into their deliberations? Did mainstream Judaism confuse them with the radically different Christ Movement? They were, of course, acutely aware of the differences, but did the rest of Judaism understand the nuances? Did they suffer guilt by association with this other movement, perhaps because of overlapping terminology? On the personal level, did they eat or intermarry with other Jewish families? Likely they were shunned by mainstream Judaism.

Even more radically, did followers of the Jesus Movement socialize with members of the Christ Movement? How could they? That would likely have been much harder to do than with Jews, with whom they had much in common. The Jesus and Christ Movements represented separate religious organizations, using different meeting places, much like Anglicans and Baptists today. But they were even further apart from each other than these two contemporary expressions of Christianity. Anglicans and Baptists can and do socialize, but how much social interaction there was between these two ancient communities is unknown. Presumably because of differing practices, contact would have been minimal. Sharing meals would have been difficult because of food and purity concerns. Intermarriage would have been impossible. They would also have not shared the same festivals. The texts they read differed. Their theologies were not congruent. Their views of Jesus' birth, the relative merit of his teachings over doctrines about his person, the meaning of redemption, the significance of his death, the basis for ethics and Torah as the path of righteousness—all these drove powerful wedges between the two communities. In practice, Ebionites and Proto-Orthodox probably stayed in their own sectors with little crossing over.

THE DIDACHE

An intriguing document that we call the *Didache* or the *Teaching of the Twelve Apostles* sheds light on some of these questions.[1] We don't know who wrote it—clearly the twelve apostles didn't. Whoever he was, the author set forth brief instructions, as a guide to the maturing Jesus Movement. The writing was known to us through quotations from ancient writers, but the full text was considered lost. In 1883, however, a copy of this writing surfaced, and it created a huge stir at the time. It opens up for us—as no other writing does—the thinking and practices of one segment of early Christianity in the late first century.

Like the *Community Rule* of the Dead Sea Scroll community, this manual of discipline is devoted to a number of practical topics. Its author focuses initially on a summary of Christian teachings organized into a twofold path: the way of life and the way of death. The way of life builds on Jesus' summary of the law—to love God and to do nothing to a fellow human being that one would not want done to oneself. In contrast, the way of death emanates from those who do not know God. The author painted a vivid picture of the wicked. He imagined them lying awake at night, plotting evil deeds and strategizing how to take advantage of others. The writing then moves to brief instructions concerning how to baptize, fast, and pray. A longer section takes us through the special weekly communal meal, the Eucharist or thanksgiving celebration; we'll consider this shortly. Jumping around from topic to topic, the document gives us a short homily on leadership qualifications. The bishops and deacons must be carefully selected. Here personal character is all-important: they should be humble and not greedy for wealth. Presumably being righteous is taken for granted. A final section focuses on the end-time. Keep yourselves ready, is the message, for we can never be sure when the Lord will return.

It's a brief but important document. It establishes boundaries, giving us valuable insight into how this group viewed its relationship to Judaism and the Christ Movement. We see, for instance, a growing divergence from the rest of the Jewish community. Members are to pray the Lord's Prayer three times a day—not the Jewish prayers such as the Shema or Amidah (the Shemoneh Esrei), although these are not specifically precluded.[2] They are also to fast on Wednesdays and Fridays—unlike their Jewish counterparts, who are said to abstain from food on Mondays and Thursdays. They should keep the dietary laws—"as far as you are able" says the author of the *Didache* (*Didache 6*)—a rather curious way of putting the requirement. In particular, members must avoid idolatry, that is, participating in the worship of idols by eating food offered to these deities. In practice, this may have required them to be vegetarian.

Like the Gospel of Matthew from the same era, the *Didache* reinforced the need to create a fence around the law. Some extensions to the law are similar to the ones Matthew cited. Do not be angry or overly zealous, the *Didache* asserted, because this might lead to murder. Do not be lecherous, for that can lead to sexual immorality. The *Didache* also provides examples not found in Matthew. Do not practice divination or sorcery or astrology, the *Didache* says, since this is conducive to idolatry. Similarly, do not be a liar, for that can lead to stealing. Or do not be a complainer or evil-minded, since this can quickly turn into blasphemy against God. Because of the similarities, biblical scholars believe that the author of the *Didache* either knew the Gospel of Matthew or else tapped into a common tradition that underlay both.

Like Matthew's community, we see in the *Didache* a messianic Jewish group becoming somewhat removed from the larger community. It was still, however, Jewish. If we were to ask a member of this community what religion they practiced, they would have said something like, "Judaism, following Jesus." The document makes no claim that Jesus is anything other than human and so there is no whiff of deification. Jesus is simply the expected Messiah for whom the community waits patiently. Similarly, too, Torah observance, as interpreted by Jesus, is mandatory.

THE EBIONITE COMMUNAL MEAL

The *Didache* takes us into the heart of one of the Ebionites' major ceremonies, and here we are afforded a rare treat, a glimpse into how this ritual was really conducted. This was an actual meal, and the appropriate blessings are indicated. These are especially intriguing for they differ markedly from Paul's account of the Eucharist and from later Christian tradition, which built on Paul's version.

Just before the communal meal, everyone joins in a prayer of confession— a recital of "unlawful deeds," as the *Didache* puts it—so that everyone approaches the celebration with a pure heart (*Didache* 14:1). We should imagine a group of devoted followers of the Jesus Movement, gathered together, sharing their shortcomings and looking forward to participating in the feast to come. Extended family members would be present, several generations, and children as well. Unlike present-day sedate church services, it was a noisy, boisterous scene, with people gathered around tables, some seated, some serving, and others chasing after kids. There would be wine and bread on the table, all specially prepared and ready for the special event. Other prepared foods would be ready to be served at the appointed time. Perhaps it was a potluck dinner, with each family bringing something to share. Everyone would be happy and looking forward to the highlight of the week. Conversation and singing would all play a role in this joyous celebration.

The meal starts with a blessing over the cup of wine:

> *We give thanks to thee, our Father, for the holy Vine of thy servant David, which thou has made known to us through thy servant Jesus* (*Didache* 9).

We notice that, unlike contemporary Christian practice, this dinner starts with the cup of wine rather than the bread. This corresponds to Jewish Sabbath evening rituals with its blessing of the children, blessing over the wine (Kiddush), washing of hands, and then blessing over the bread—the cup first, then the bread. It also reflects the same practice at Qumran among the Dead Sea Scroll community. There, one scroll envisaged a special celebration when the Messiah appears. Gathering around a common table, that end-time community would celebrate the meal. First the priest would bless the wine; then the Messiah of Israel would say the blessing over the bread.[3] So the order of the blessings at Qumran is clear: first wine, then bread. The same practice is evident here. It is authentically Jewish.

Surprisingly, we notice that this dinner has nothing to do with Jesus' death and resurrection. It was not a commemoration of that event. For the Jesus Movement and the Ebionites, no particular significance was attached to Jesus' death and resurrection. He died and was resurrected, like all righteous people will be. They did not look upon him, as Paul's followers did, as a savior. More dramatically, we are startled to notice that the blessing has nothing to do with "drinking his blood." That really leaps out at anyone familiar with the traditional wording in the Mass—or Communion, Eucharist, Divine Liturgy, or Lord's Supper, as it is variously called in different Christian denominations today.

The *Didache*'s blessing is somewhat akin to the traditional Jewish blessing over wine: "Blessed are you, O Lord our God, King of the Universe, Creator of the fruit of the vine." The Jewish prayer thanks God for creating wine. In this adaptation of the standard Jewish prayer, however, the *Didache*'s blessing thanks God for having created a metaphorical vine, that is, the community itself, as the vine of David made known through Jesus, God's servant.

Next comes the breaking of bread with its blessing:

We give thanks to thee, our Father, for the life and knowledge thou hast made known to us through thy servant Jesus (Didache 9).

The traditional Jewish prayer over bread, "Blessed are you, O Lord our God, King of the Universe, who brings forth bread from the earth," becomes interpreted metaphorically as bread that sustains life spiritually. Bread symbolizes the life and knowledge that come from Jesus. The blessing in the *Didache* continues,

As this broken bread, once dispersed over the hills, was brought together and became one loaf, so may thy Church be brought together from the ends of the earth into thy kingdom (Didache 9).

So the bread also symbolizes the community, brought together from many parts of the world.

The meal then follows. It would have complied with the biblical dietary laws, so no pork, ham, bacon, shellfish, or meat sacrificed at pagan temples would have been served. Everything would have been biblically kosher.

When the meal is finished, before cleaning up and returning to their homes, there are further blessings, thanking God not only for material goods but also for "spiritual meat and drink, together with life eternal, through thy Servant" (Didache 10). The liturgy concludes with a prayer for the community as a whole, to deliver it from evil, perfect it, and gather it into the Kingdom God has prepared. At the end, everyone says, in Aramaic, "Maranatha. Amen," that is, "Come, O Lord. Amen," a prayer for the Lord's speedy return to establish the promised Kingdom. There are some similarities in this concluding prayer after dinner to the Birkat Ha-Mazon, the Jewish grace after meals. This prayer thanks God for providing food for the whole world, for giving the covenant and the land of Israel. Like the Didache's grace after the meal, it, too, looks forward to the time of redemption.

Clearly Jewish models furnished the basis for the blessings in this festive, ceremonial meal in which everyone participated. Its focus was on celebrating the life of the community, giving thanks to God for having brought them together, and praying for continued protection. It provided a time for socializing, for conversation, an opportunity to catch up with one another and hearing everyone's news. It would have been a time of joy as families came together to celebrate and rejoice. It was probably the high point of the week, an important time marked by a special celebration, a period set aside for different purposes than the everyday, mundane round of chores. It was, in contemporary terms, a typical Jewish Sabbath dinner.

PAUL'S EUCHARIST

As we step back from this community's ceremony of the Eucharist, we may be struck by what it does not correspond to. It differed substantially from Paul's version of the Lord's Supper (1 Corinthians 11:23–26), and the contrasts are overwhelming. The order differed, for one thing. For Paul, the sequence was first the bread, and then the wine—just the reverse of the Didache's pattern and common Jewish practice. But that is the least of the differences. What is most remarkable is the significance of Paul's ceremony. This is a ceremony of ritual participation of the worshipper into the death and resurrection of the divine-human. It is a totally different experience. The bread becomes Jesus' body. The cup represents the new covenant in his blood. For Paul, the meaning of the ritual consists in proclaiming Jesus' death until his return. It's a way of becoming part of that event, with all its powerful implications: the hope of resurrection and eternal life.

Its overwhelming importance is underscored by Paul's condemnation of those who participate in this ceremony unworthily: they are "answerable for the body and blood of Jesus." The Gospel of Mark in the 70s shared this view, explicitly equating the bread with Jesus' body and the cup of wine with his blood (Mark 14:22–24). The Gospel of John, which does not place Jesus' words at a Last Supper, had Jesus say, "Those who eat my flesh and drink my blood have eternal life. . . . Those who eat my flesh and drink my blood abide in me, and I in them" (John 6:54–56).

Contrast this with the *Didache*'s version celebrating the life and vitality of a community awaiting redemption. That was a characteristically Jewish meal with the prayers adapted to the needs of that particular group. The elements of bread and wine were interpreted metaphorically, to honor the role of their teacher in giving life and knowledge. They were not mystical or magical symbols, that is, they did not involve eating or participating in the body or blood of Jesus. Moreover, the ceremony in the *Didache* did not commemorate or memorialize Jesus' sacrifice, his death or resurrection. In fact, nowhere did it reference these events at all. It was a Sabbath celebration—either at its onset or at its conclusion—in which the whole community joined in. It wasn't a sacrificial ceremony. It just wasn't that kind of meal. It celebrated life, not death.

As a thanksgiving meal, the *Didache*'s prayers ring truer as a celebration stemming from a Jewish Jesus than the alternate version that originated with Paul in the Diaspora. Hyam Maccoby, for instance, has pointed out a number of powerful objections to Paul's version of the ceremony.[4] For one thing, it is exceptionally difficult to imagine the injunction to drink blood arising in a Jewish context. The whole idea would have been absolutely abhorrent. The Torah provided stern prohibitions against the consumption of blood (Leviticus 7:26). In addition, the laws pertaining to the ritual slaughter of animals required the draining of all blood from the meat so that none of it is ingested. Equating wine with blood and encouraging adherents to consume this just doesn't sound right in a Jewish context. It would be like having Jesus say that it's okay to eat pork. Just not credible.

The ceremony that Paul described and that Mark related, Maccoby contends, finds its natural home in a Hellenistic mystery religion environment. It was in that context—not a Jewish one—that participating in the body and blood of the divine-human made sense. These rites allowed the participant to become one with the savior, sharing in his power to save. Others have noted this, too, including Freke and Gandy, who have observed the following:

> By partaking of the bread and wine offered by Jesus, his disciples symbolically eat his body and drink his blood, so communing with the Christ. The idea of

> *divine communion through eating the god is a rite so ancient that it is found in the Egyptian Book of the Dead. . . . Such a "holy communion" was also practiced in the Mysteries, as a means of becoming one with Osiris-Dionysus.*[5]

Paul's ceremony represents a true communion, a participation of the individual in the death and resurrection of Jesus.

Paul's ritual, moreover, shifts the focus away from Jesus as Messiah to Christ as God:

> *The Eucharist signifies the mystical incorporation of the initiate into the godhead by eating the body and drinking the blood of Christ. Such a ceremony implies the deification of Jesus and is quite impossible to reconcile with a view of Jesus as merely a Messiah in the Jewish sense.*[6]

The Messiah was a political and religious figure in Jewish thought, expected to bring about world transformation. Paul's version of the Eucharist, however, lifted the meal into an entirely new dimension, a cosmic one—Christ as the savior of humanity, the liberator from sin, and the means of achieving eternal life. This contrasts strikingly with the *Didache*'s understanding of the meal as a celebration of the community enriched by the life and teachings of Jesus, eagerly awaiting his return to establish the promised Kingdom.

Finally, it is also difficult to contemplate human—or a God-human—sacrifice within a Jewish context. Yet this is what Paul's version of the Eucharist seems to imply. It involves participating in Christ's death and resurrection, seen as an atonement to God for sin and thereby achieving eternal life through his sacrifice. Paul made his objective clear when he wrote, "I want to know Christ and the power of his resurrection and the sharing of his sufferings by becoming like him in his death, if somehow I may attain the resurrection from the dead" (Philippians 3: 10–11). The significance of Christ's death was that of a sacrificial offering made on behalf of all people: "they are now justified by his grace as a gift, through the redemption that is in Christ Jesus, who God put forward as a sacrifice of atonement by his blood, effective through faith" (Romans 3: 24–25).

To the extent that Paul envisaged Christ as a human figure, this concept of atonement involved human sacrifice. Maccoby writes, "The implication of the Eucharist that salvation is to be obtained through Jesus' death and the shedding of his blood is thus a radical departure from Judaism and a return to pagan concepts of atonement."[7] Judaism rejected human sacrifice in any context, redemption included, as the example of the near sacrifice of Isaac by Abraham makes clear. A human sacrifice for sin, as Paul described it, makes no sense in a Jewish context.

AN INCREASINGLY MARGINALIZED COMMUNITY

The dire warnings of Matthew and James went unheeded. The Christ Movement grew exponentially. Acts had created an impressive lineage for the Christ Movement, giving it credibility and authority by linking it to the Jesus Movement and back through Jesus to biblical Judaism. Without probing the details of this saga, Gentile readers accepted this version of history, and it entered into the mythology and arsenal of Proto-Orthodoxy as it expanded around the Mediterranean.

Things were not so optimistic in the Jesus Movement camp, however. The view from the Jesus Movement in the late first and early second centuries would have been extremely unsettling. It was evident that it was in considerable difficulty. Its Jerusalem leadership had been severely crippled by troubles in Judea in the mid 60s and early 70s with infighting and the war against the common enemy, Rome. There had been an interregnum between the time its leader, James, was killed in 62 and his successor as bishop was named sometime after 70. And it would be faced with another disastrous Jewish struggle against Rome in the mid 130s.

The Christ Movement was most likely expanding throughout Israel and into the Jewish Diaspora, into what is modern-day Lebanon, Syria, Iraq, and Turkey. Paul referred to rival teachers that he met on his journeys through synagogues of the Diaspora and, most likely these came from the Jesus Movement. Like Paul, they were "on the move," and they seem to have trailed him wherever he went. They, too, headed into the Diaspora, searching for converts to this form of Judaism. Growth, however, was modest, for this group targeted primarily Jews, who did not flock to affiliate themselves with this new movement. Potential Gentile converts were deterred from the rigors of conversion, including male circumcision. The response from Jews toward the Jesus Movement was probably far less than expected.

Some of the parables of Jesus reflect conditions later than the time of his mission in the 20s. The parable of the Great Banquet (Luke 14:15–24), for instance, suggested that the Kingdom should be given to those ready to receive its message—that is, Gentiles—not necessarily to those for whom it was primarily intended—the Jewish people. This message reflects disappointment in Luke's time, some seventy or more years after the mission of Jesus, with the failure of Jews from other factions to embrace the newcomer.

There were other disappointments as well. Messianic expectations remained unfulfilled some fifty or more years after Jesus' death. The throne of Israel was unoccupied. After the two defeats of the Jewish people by the power of the Roman legions, an independent Jewish state headed by a descendant of

David seemed a very remote possibility. Hellenization was still in sway, with strong cultural pressures to assimilate to Roman philosophy, religion, and values. The imminent replacement of Roman rule by the Kingdom of God could hardly be imagined. From time to time, Roman emperors—Domitian and Trajan, among others—hunted down regal claimants to the Jewish throne. The sustainability of any messianic sect without its promises coming true has always been a problem, and the Jesus Movement was no different.

The destruction of Jerusalem and the Temple in 70 also had an impact on the Jesus Movement, as it did on Judaism in general. The focal point of Jewish worship with its elaborate infrastructure had been decimated, and the possibility loomed that the religion of Judaism could disappear now that its defining anchor had been destroyed. It was entirely possible that Jews throughout Israel and the Diaspora would simply be absorbed into other religions. Theological questions percolated as well. Why had this happened? Why had God allowed his holy Temple to be destroyed? Why were the Romans prospering when God's people were decimated? The book of *4 Ezra,* written around 100 by a Jewish author, raised these very questions. Like the earlier Book of Job, *4 Ezra* concluded that the ways of God were inscrutable. This writer looked forward to a day when God would act to intervene, to set things right upon earth, but that seemed now a long way off.[8]

Other than the members of the Jesus Movement, the only surviving group within Judaism was the Pharisees. Sometime after 70, under the leadership of Rabbi Yochanan ben Zakkai, rabbis gathered together at Yavneh (Jamnia) to begin the process of salvaging the religion. The decisions they and their successors made saved the day. Lee Levine notes that under ben Zakkai's successor, Gamaliel II, decisions were made with respect to daily prayer, the contents of the Hebrew Bible, the codification of Jewish law, and the development of holidays.[9] The positions the sages at Yavneh and their successors developed were recorded in the Mishnah and Talmud. These provided the basis for Rabbinic Judaism. The religion became centered in the home and in the synagogue instead of the Temple. Prayer was substituted for sacrifice. The leaders were lay leaders—teachers, rabbis—instead of priests. It was a monumental transformation of a religion made under extreme duress.

The same problem existed for members of the Jesus Movement. They, too, had lost the focal point of their worship, the Temple. How should they regroup and reorganize after this major debacle? What kind of infrastructure should they have? How should they worship . . . and where? There are many things about the Jesus Movement that we simply don't know. We are not privy to their internal deliberations as they sought to revamp the movement after the destruction of the Temple. How did they relate to synagogue services? Had they already started to worship in their own "synagogues"? Was their voice heard within mainstream Jewish circles? How centralized was the Jesus Movement?

Was it one cohesive movement or did it proliferate? How were its missions planned? How extensive were these? Moreover, how did they see themselves alongside an evolving Judaism?

And what was to be made of that promised Kingdom? Where was it? These were poignant questions especially when the Temple, Jerusalem, and the Jewish state had been devastated in the debacle of 70. When that Kingdom failed to materialize quickly—as decade after decade dragged on—how did they explain to their followers "the delay"? How did they hold on to their membership? We simply don't know.

The Jerusalem community survived the death of its leader, James, brother of Jesus. But, so far as we can tell, it never produced a champion of the stature of Paul. No one rose to carry the day, to defend its entirely plausible claim that it and it alone was the legitimate successor to the religion of Jesus. That voice was just not heard.

Torah-observant Jesus followers—the Ebionites—were found even as late as the time of Eusebius in the early fourth century. Ehrman writes of them:

> The Ebionites were a group of Jewish Christians located in different regions of the Mediterranean from at least the second to the fourth centuries. What distinguished this group of Christians from many others was their attempt to combine Jewish views and lifestyles with the belief that Jesus was the Messiah.[10]

There are some surviving Ebionite writings, including the *Letter of Peter to James*, its *Reception* by James, and *the Homilies of Clement*. [11] These probably date from the third century, perhaps using materials that are older. These writings present alleged sayings and doings of various early-church leaders. They are works of historical fiction, however, although their initial Ebionite readers may not have thought of them that way, any more than the initial audience of the Book of Acts recognized that it was historical fiction. Historical fiction was well known within early Christianity and made for popular reading. The *Acts of Paul* and the *Acts of Thecla* provide other illustrations of this genre.[12] Such fictitious works are useful not as providing a history of the times they purport to depict but in allowing us to gauge opinions at the time when they were composed. Thus these surviving Ebionite writings give us a window into the Ebionites' thinking as of the third century.

What do they tell us? The *Letter of Peter to James* focused on the need to preserve authentic teaching. In this document, Peter is depicted as writing to James. He says he wants to ensure that the books containing his sermons will be conveyed only to individuals whom James deems reliable. He was anxious that "some from among the Gentiles have rejected my lawful preaching and have preferred a lawless and absurd doctrine of the man who is my enemy."[13] That "enemy" preaching a "lawless" doctrine is Paul, and Peter does not want his own teachings to fall into the wrong hands. Bear in mind that this is not history but historical fiction. It's someone living in the third century defending views of that time, imagining that two centuries earlier, Peter had written to James with regard to his sermons. The correspondence continues. Its *Reception* or receipt of the letter by James makes it clear that James will pass on Peter's teachings only to "circumcised" persons, that is, to Ebionites, not to members of the rival Proto-Orthodox faction, the successors to Paul. This exchange portrays the Ebionites as alone possessing the true faith descended from the apostles.

Peter, in the *Letter of Peter to James,* also makes the point that some people have distorted his words. They have advanced the view that Peter himself advocated the abandonment of the law. Not so, says Peter. This passage has in mind a story about Peter created by the Book of Acts. There Peter has a vision of a large sheet descending from the sky, containing in it all kinds of animals, reptiles, and birds. Peter hears a voice instructing him to eat. He refuses to do so, on the grounds that this would violate the traditional laws of kashrut. He hears the voice a second time, saying "What God has made clean, you must not call profane" (Acts 10:15). As Acts interprets this remarkable dream, Peter is persuaded to set aside the dietary laws of Judaism, thus reinforcing the views of Paul who had likewise rejected Torah.

Peter's trancelike experience in Acts sounds suspiciously similar to the mystical encounter with the Christ that Acts describes concerning Paul. The *Letter of Peter to James,* however, contests this version of events. Peter said nothing of the sort ever happened. The author of this Ebionite document wrote,

> For to do such a thing means to act contrary to the law of God which was made known by Moses and was confirmed by our Lord in its everlasting continuance. For he said, "The heaven and the earth will pass away, but one jot or one tittle shall not pass away from the law." (Letter of James to Peter 1:5)[14]

Here Peter is shown quoting the famous passage from Matthew's Sermon on the Mount that Torah observance is mandatory for all of Jesus' followers.

What we have here constitutes important evidence that the Ebionites disputed the historical truth of the Book of Acts. According to this source, Acts has completely falsified the position of Peter. It would seem that the author of Acts was not interested in either the historical Paul or, it now seems, the Peter of history. It, like the *Acts of Thecla,* was historical fiction. This represents the clearest evidence we have today of how some Christians reacted to the linkage Acts created. Their Peter did not correspond to Acts' Peter. They believed that Acts invented history to suit the purposes of the Christ Movement, specifically, to have the early leaders endorse non Torah observance.

In time, members of the Jesus Movement and its successors found themselves in a difficult position, caught between a rock and a hard place. They were squeezed, on the one hand, by the growing popularity of the Christ Movement. On the other hand, they were being shunned by an evolving Judaism. Increasingly they became isolated from both communities. We do not know when they ceased to exist. Perhaps, some speculate, they were absorbed into Islam, which shares some of their views of Jesus—as human, teacher, and prophet.

12

PAUL THE RADICAL

As we have already noted, by the second century there were four major parallel religions that had come out of the Middle East: Rabbinic Judaism, the Jesus Movement (Ebionites), the Gnostic Movement, and the Christ Movement (Proto-Orthodoxy). The latter movement *never* existed within Judaism because right from the outset it promoted non-Jewish beliefs and practices. It paralleled Judaism and the Jesus Movement. Christianity as we know it today grew out of Paul and his Christ Movement during the second through fourth centuries. It fought hard against its rivals—Ebionites, Gnostics, and, in time, Marcionites, Arians, Nestorians, Monophysites, and probably dozens of other sects and movements. During this period, no one tradition was "right" and the others "heretical." They all attracted members, promoted themselves as the authentic expression of the faith, and considered others to be disseminators of falsehoods. These centuries must have been exceptionally confusing for ordinary people trying to make sense out of radically conflicting claims.

By the late fourth century, Proto-Orthodoxy had won the day. Constantine favored this form of Christianity, and Theodosius proclaimed it the official imperial religion of the Roman Empire in 380. Moreover, it was a fourth-century Proto-Orthodox bishop, Athanasius of Alexandria in Egypt, who promulgated a list which became the authoritative canon of scripture. Paul's writings were prominently included, as was the Book of Acts, which glorified the work of Paul. No Gnostic or specific Ebionite documents were included, although the Gospel of Matthew and the Letter of James were, standing in stark contrast to Paul's position, silent reminders that not everyone had come onboard. It was during the fourth century, then, that the Christian "church" was born. By then it possessed one creed, one recognized hierarchy, and one set of canonical writings paralleling those of the Old Testament. There was, finally, one church backed by the power of one state. Proto-Orthodoxy had achieved what no other Christian faction had come close to accomplishing.

One curious feature of Proto-Orthodox writings was their persistent preoccupation with Judaism. Bitterness, anger, vilification, demonization—these ugly traits tainted the relationship between Proto-Orthodox Christianity and Judaism. Every aspect of Jewish identity, culture, and religion was systematically assaulted, rejected, and devalued during the decades between Paul and such figures as Justin Martyr and Marcion some ninety years later. This sustained attack can be traced, decade by decade, on the basis of surviving documents that showcase pivotal moments in the discussion.

A bigger problem is this: Why would Proto-Orthodoxy even bother with such a campaign of vilification? Why did it not simply ignore Judaism? Why did it feel it had to attack *everything* Jewish? What stood behind this unrelenting preoccupation? Why was it so obviously defensive . . . and threatened by Judaism?

Flashes of anger hit us from time to time as we read the New Testament. The Gospel of Matthew, for instance, lashed out at the Pharisees. But the angriest document by far was Paul's Letter to the Galatians. He was absolutely livid. He berated his readers for having been "bewitched" by other teachers (Galatians 3:1). Whoever these were, Paul sensed that they had seduced his flock, and he rose on his haunches to protect what he felt was rightfully his. He angrily criticized his readers for listening—apparently receptively—to their message. Writing in an abrupt, curt fashion, he set the record straight in no uncertain terms.

The hostility we encounter in Paul and Matthew sounds very much like the fearful anger expressed by some of the Hebrew prophets. Centuries before, Amos had denounced a segment of his society for adopting Canaanite beliefs and practices—polytheism, Canaanite worship, and sexual practices—along with a general failure to observe the covenant with God. His anger was fueled by fear, a deeply rooted anxiety that the community would increasingly abandon the covenant and consequently experience God's rejection. His fears were well grounded. The religion of the Canaanites seduced many a young Israelite—so much so that the Bible indicates that both the Northern and the Southern Kingdoms fell to foreign powers as a result of this turning away from the covenant.

Does the anger we find in some early Christian texts also betray fear—a deep concern that members of the new movement would continue or even adopt Jewish beliefs and practices? Why was there this underlying anxiety? Weren't Paul's arguments convincing? Did some members of this new movement feel the constant "tug" of the ancient scriptures that emphasized the importance of Torah? Did they, perhaps, share Matthew's convictions that Jesus

himself taught and observed Torah? Why did they require such strong direc-
tives from their leaders to abandon things Jewish? Did they, in fact, relinquish
all things Jewish?

Proto-Orthodoxy made it very clear—right from the outset—that theirs
was not a Jewish movement in any sense. Their stance was venomous, fueled
by rage and bent on seeing only the worst within this ancient and competing
religion. These attitudes originated in the earliest days of the Christ Movement and continued long after Proto-Orthodoxy became the official Christian
religion of the Roman Empire. Paul's rejection of Torah is the right place to
start, for he set in motion the anti-Jewish dynamic that reverberated for centuries.

PAUL'S RADICALISM

What are we to make of Paul?

A Torah-free, Christ-centered movement was not at all what Jesus envisaged when he announced the Kingdom of God in his parables. Nor did it
agree with what Matthew had Jesus preach in the Sermon on the Mount.
From its inception, Paul's religion represented a radical alternative to the one
that Jesus proclaimed and his brother maintained. We tend not to see the radical nature of Paul's thought, since our perceptions of the New Testament are
often shaped by the power of Paul's thought.

Paul's position enjoyed enormous appeal, and its many advantages over its
rivals need to be acknowledged. For one thing, it was a much easier religion to
follow than that of either Jesus or James. Obedience to a complex code of behavior was not required, and a whole series of don'ts and do's did not plague
the minds of his members. Minimal necessity to refer to the Old Testament
also vastly reduced the amount of background information needed to function
knowledgeably within the movement. It also held out the welcome mat to
Gentiles, without any strings attached, providing an easy entry into the movement. The convenience of a Torah-free religion allowed Paul's sect to spread
rapidly among Gentiles, who probably had little in-depth exposure to Judaism.
It offered salvation, assurances that its members were the offspring of Abraham,
part of an ancient heritage favored by God, all without Torah obligations—
and, best of all, no circumcision. Clearly this constituted a winning formula.

But many of Paul's contemporaries found what he said absolutely shock-
ing. We need only to review the mind-set of his peers to understand why this
was the case. Two centuries prior to Paul, Antiochus Epiphanes had forcefully
tried to "do in" Judaism. That had sent shivers down the spines of Jewish leaders, who proposed different strategies for dealing with the threat of Hellenization. All these involved Torah. When Paul came on to the scene proclaiming a

Torah-free religion, however, it exposed old wounds, reminding people of what Antiochus had tried to. They recognized what Paul was up to. Here was another figure trying to do away with Judaism, this time by persuasion. No wonder Paul experienced opposition wherever he went: he was perceived as undermining Judaism and hastening assimilation into Hellenistic culture. Paul's religion unleashed a host of radical questions.

NO ROOM FOR JUDAISM?

Paul's innovative theology of history sidelined Judaism and appropriated for the new Christ Movement the promises made to Judaism. It was, after all, through Judaism in the messianic era that the promises of blessings to the Gentiles would be conveyed. No longer was that going to be the case. Paul divided history into three segments: from Abraham to Moses, from Moses to Christ, and then from Christ onward. He admitted that Torah had legitimacy, but only for a specific period in history. Its limited role was that of a teacher, providing moral guidelines and prescribing right behavior. Now, Paul contended, the time of maturity had emerged when true religion was to be rooted in faith in Christ. There was no room for a religion that continued to focus on Torah.

Paul's intent was clearly to cut out Judaism. The promises to Abraham would come about, he maintained, not through the Torah-observant approach of Judaism but through his new movement whose members have faith in Christ. Members of his Christ Movement might not be Jews, but they were, he said, "children of Abraham," and therefore entitled to all the promises God made to their ancient patriarch.

Paul's theology of history, therefore, served to dismiss Judaism. By contending that the period in history had ended when the law was legitimate, he left no room for Judaism as the continuing religion of Torah. Its validity, whether biblical or rabbinic, was destroyed. This view has had enormous consequences in subsequent history. It represents the origin of the audacious claim that Christianity has "superseded" or "replaced" Judaism as the religion of Abraham, a position that allowed Judaism no room in the new Christian era.

Supersessionism has the effect of declaring that Judaism is no longer a valid religion and possesses no legitimacy, and that the Jewish people no longer have a covenant with God. They have ceased to be the people of God or even "a" people of God. There is, on this view, one and only one covenant, namely, that between God and the church. Therefore there is no reason to follow Jewish law—or, for that matter, to be Jewish. Supersessionism takes away the right to be Jewish in a Christian era, depriving the religion and the people a right to exist. While many modern Christian denominations have attempted to denounce supersessionism in official documents, this powerful position has been evident in Christian writings over the centuries, with exceptionally serious consequences for Jewish communities in the midst of Christian culture.[1] All this was created through a few words, dashed off in the heat of controversy, and yet with horrendous impact throughout subsequent history.

DOES THE OLD TESTAMENT HAVE ANY VALUE?

Of what use, then, was the Hebrew Bible or Old Testament? This question would surely have surfaced early on as a result of Paul's rewriting Israel's history. If the religion from Moses to Christ was now null and void, having served its temporary historic purpose, what was to be made of the Books of the Torah, the Prophets and the Writings? How should one understand such leaders as Moses, Amos, Hosea, Josiah, Isaiah, and Ezra? All these figures emphasized the covenant between God and the Jewish people. The importance of Torah shouts from every page of the Hebrew Bible. It is inescapable.

The implications of Paul's thought were not lost on his audience. In time, they began to ask questions as issues pertaining to the shape and content of the Christian canon become debated. Should *any* of the books of what now is called comprises the Christian Old Testament be included? If so, what was the rationale? If the law of Torah was not binding on Christians, why retain, read, and refer to texts that clearly made its observance their focal point?

It would be interesting to envisage a conversation in which Paul is confronted by such figures from the Bible as Moses or Amos. What would these towering defenders of the covenant say to him? What would Paul and the author of the Gospel of Matthew have in common? What would he and the Teacher of Righteousness at Qumran have discussed? What would James the brother of Jesus have said to him?

More radically, how would the discussion go between Jesus and Paul?

IS REVELATION TRUSTWORTHY?

Religious believers usually wish to view their sacred texts as embodying ideas that emanate from God, however the process of transmission is conceived—whether through an immediate direct revelation or through a gradual historical process of insight. Jewish believers were no exception. Then and now they believe that their scriptures contain the will of God for themselves. It outlines a path to be followed, promises redemption, and paints a picture of a great destiny that awaits all humanity in a transformed world. What, then, is to be made of that view, if the Old Testament is to be set aside?

By dismissing the validity of Torah, Paul's views questioned the trustworthiness of revelation. The covenant was envisaged by Jews as one in perpetuity—"to a thousand generations" (Deuteronomy 7:9).[2] Paul presented a new perspective, however, that it was only meant to serve for a period of time. That's very convenient for his point of view, but it gave rise to profoundly troublesome questions. How do we reconcile the view that God at one point enacted a covenant in perpetuity with Paul's view that this no longer applies? Does this change our understanding of the nature of deity? Is God a deity who changes his mind?

Moreover, if God can cancel one contract, why not another? What assurances are there that God will honor *any* agreement with humanity? Trust, reliability, and the integrity of deity are fundamentally at stake.

WHAT DOES DOING AWAY WITH TORAH MEAN?

We have explored how Paul dismissed Torah observance in his Letter to the Galatians. His arguments centered on three main considerations. He appealed selectively to Abraham as an exemplar of faith. He developed a unique theology of history no one else had ever advanced. And, contrary to scripture, he claimed that all who follow the law were "under a curse." Paul did not dare, of course, to claim that Jesus himself supported these radical views, nor did he appeal to a decision of the so-called Jerusalem Conference. Those who heard him were well aware that what he was saying applied as much to Jews as to Gentiles. Even the Book of Acts recorded rumors to this effect (Acts 21:17–22).[3] This message was very much part of Paul's enormous appeal. It had all the benefits of Judaism without any of its obligations.

Paul's dismissal of Torah was far-reaching. As he correctly pointed out, anyone who was circumcised was obligated to follow the entire Torah (Galatians 5:3). There is no disagreement there. The law is not just one item. It constituted a whole package: the Ten Commandments, the dietary laws, keeping the Sabbath, observing festivals like Passover, circumcision, wearing reminders of the central passages of the Torah, having a mezuzah on doors, and so on. Paul was opposed to *all* of these: his objection was to Torah itself, not simply one aspect of Torah. Paul is not correctly interpreted as focusing just on ritual or dietary laws or festivals. It is not as if Paul made an exemption for part of the law, say, the Ten Commandments. Nor did he present Torah observance as an option, as if we could choose to keep the law or not, depending on our personal preferences. He was also not saying that whereas Gentiles must not obey Torah, Jews could and should.

He referred to Torah observance as "slavery" (Galatians 4:25). In even stronger language, Paul asserted that Torah observance was emphatically not a matter of choice. It had, in fact, dire consequences for achieving salvation.

Those who observe Torah have cut themselves off from Christ and lapsed from grace (Galatians 5:4). For Paul, Torah observance and being a member of the Christ Movement were incompatible. "No one," Paul decreed, "will be justified by the works of the law" (Galatians 2:16). Once again, we see the broad implications of Paul's position—he writes "no one." He was not just advocating that only Gentile members should refrain from keeping Torah. His edict applied across the board, to all human beings, Jews included. He believed that he had found a superior way.

In rejecting Torah observance for all, Paul clearly set his movement apart from Judaism and the Jesus Movement. His religion was defined, in part, by what it was not: it was not Jewish. That set off a powerful dynamic of competition, to win over Gentiles, God-fearers, and Hellenized Jews, and to convince them that there existed a religious option that did not involve Torah. Creating a Torah-free religion was a brilliant maneuver. But what was its impact on his new followers? Did they have to change their lifestyle? Gentiles who were God-fearers might miss Sabbath observances, but, since they had not been obligated to follow Torah, the impact might have been minimal, even less for Gentiles who had had no connection with the Jewish synagogue at all. Those impacted the most would have been Jewish converts to the new movement. Just because Paul said that the time of Torah was over didn't mean that they suddenly dropped Sabbath and Passover observances and started violating dietary laws. Setting aside the entire biblical tradition and its thirteen-hundred-year-old covenant could not be so easily accomplished for this segment of Paul's flock.

What holidays and festivals did Paul's group observe? Doing away with Torah removed the "rhythm" to Jewish living—not just the weekly routine of Sabbath observance as a special day of rest and contemplation, but also the yearly cycle of special events recalling significant experiences in the Old Testament. Unlike Jesus, his family, and his followers, we do not see Paul preparing for Passover. That time-honored festival commemorating the liberation from slavery in Egypt was not to be observed. Nor was Succoth, the Festival of Booths, to be remembered—celebrating the circumstances under which the Israelites lived in the desert after the Exodus. Shavuot, the great festival celebrating the giving of the Torah, was abolished. Thus Paul's members would be under no obligation to even consider making the annual pilgrimage up to Jerusalem. No Hanukkah, that wonderful magical festival that trumpeted the preservation of Jewish identity in the midst of hostile Gentile forces. The entire Jewish calendar was just swept away . . . with nothing to replace it. All those great festivals, with opportunities to pass on to children the traditions of the ancestors, were bypassed.

By rejecting Torah, did Paul's members cease work on the Sabbath? Or did they fall into line with their contemporaries and work as they worked?

Gone, too, was the Jewish lifestyle expressed through dietary laws. This pattern sanctified the act of eating, giving it an ethical dimension. According to Torah, people are called upon to make choices regarding what they eat and how they eat, turning this basic necessity of living into a religious act. Associated laws also helped ensure a humane killing of animals. These were not just boundary markers—although they were that—but, more importantly, they reflected what the Jewish people considered to be the divinely mandated pattern of holy living. Paul's view opened up a whole new dietary spectrum including not only shellfish, but also meat from any source, including meat butchered at local temples, which were associated with the worship of idols.

Amazingly, Paul indicated that there was no problem eating food, specifically meat, sacrificed in temples devoted to pagan deities. His reasoning was that since idols do not exist, then one was "no worse off if we do not eat, and no better off if we do" (1 Corinthians 8:8). Clearly Paul lacked awareness that there had (supposedly) been a Jerusalem conference that expressly prohibited Gentiles, like Jews, from eating food sacrificed to idols. This constitutes yet more evidence that such a conference never occurred. If it had, then Paul was in clear violation of its terms.

Doing away with Torah observance immediately raised issues with which Paul had to struggle for most of his life. For generations, Torah had grounded ethics in Jewish life. They were debated, interpreted, and followed. But with Torah gone, what would provide the basis for ethics? What behavior would be consistent with Paul's message? Removing Torah, for instance, immediately eliminated the Ten Commandments. These foundational laws included injunctions to uphold monotheism, not to succumb to idolatry, to honor parents, to remember the Sabbath, not to murder, not to steal, not to be envious, and so on.

So, too, went the whole fabric of ethics: the treatment of spouses, strangers, animals; marriage and divorce laws; laws pertaining to sexual relations; the judicial system and the means for resolving disputes; and laws relating to property rights. Everything. The whole Torah package meant for regulating communal life disappeared. That was a major loss, in one fell swoop. What did Paul think would replace these principles? Conventional Roman wisdom? Popular mores? Common sense?

Paul must have been aware that he had a huge problem on his hands. In his Letter to the Galatians, after tossing out Torah, he immediately cautioned his readers that being called to freedom was no excuse for "self-indulgence" (Galatians 5:13). He urged his followers to live by the Spirit, not the desires of the flesh, noting that "if you are led by the Spirit, you are not subject to the law" (Galatians 5:18). This latter point, incidentally, again reinforces the view that Paul intended his sweeping generalizations to apply to all humans.

He then contrasted the fruits of the Spirit with those of the flesh. These fruits of the Spirit included "love, joy, peace, patience, kindness, generosity, faithfulness, gentleness and self-control" (Galatians 5:22). These are all wonderful qualities but very difficult to translate into a practical and actionable system of ethics. Throughout all his letters, Paul had to put out ethical fires. Most of his letter we call 1 Corinthians concerns how to behave when one is living a life that is Torah-free. The issues he had to respond to were major: divisions within the community, dissensions over leadership, handling lawsuits, directions regarding marriage, sexual improprieties, and eating food sacrificed to idols. His followers appear not to know what was expected of them by way of appropriate behavior. That is not at all surprising. Evidently living in the Spirit fails to provide actionable guidelines.

The potential danger of a Torah-free religion was that it lacked clear moral guidelines for members. Paul constantly found himself having to respond to urgent crises, one at a time. Without having at his disposal a set of overarching ethical principles to guide decision making, and being unable to appeal to the authority of the Old Testament, Paul personally acted as the arbiter of correct behavior, often appealing just to his own personal preferences. For example, to the question, Should one get married? he replied, no, the unmarried and widows should remain as they were, as he was, that is, stay single or widowed. Only if they could not practice "self-control" should they contemplate marriage (1 Corinthians 7:8–9). Not surprisingly, this is not a passage quoted in Christian marriage services, which are hard pressed to find *any* New Testament justification for marriage at all.

Nor did Paul appeal to the words of the historical Jesus for his ethical pronouncements. He—and he alone—decided what "living in the Spirit" meant. Occasionally he appealed to "the Lord," but this more likely referred to insights he had received from the Christ of experience than the Jesus of history. Over time, Proto-Orthodoxy did develop ethical principles to replace Torah. These were based on Jesus' twofold summary of the law—love of God and love of neighbor—as well as the Ten Commandments, which crept back into Christian thinking, although the injunction to remember the Sabbath became reinterpreted and eventually transferred to Sunday.

WAS CHRIST JEWISH?

By focusing on the Christ, Paul stripped Jesus of his Jewish identity. If we search all of Paul's writings for references to the historical Jesus, we come up with very little. Only a few historical details surface: that Jesus was born of a woman (Galatians 4:4); that he was Jewish (Galatians 4:4); and that he died (for example, 1 Corinthians 15:3). He dwelt on Jesus' death, contending that God raised Jesus from the dead (Galatians 1:1) and interpreting this resurrection along the lines of the savior mythology of Roman mystery religions.

Looking through the letters of Paul, we find that he rarely quoted the Jesus of history. He never cited his example. Some matters he said he received from "the Lord." These included the sayings pertaining to the Last Supper. But even where he could usefully have cited the words of Jesus, he doesn't. Paul's verdict of no divorce at all (1 Corinthians 7:10–11), for example, was stricter than the position of Jesus presented in Matthew (Matthew 19:9), which allowed for divorce in specific circumstances.

In reading Paul, we have no sense that the Christ was *really* Jewish. There were no references to Jesus' insistence on the higher righteousness. How could there be when Paul denied the validity of Torah? Nor did Paul mention the parables of Jesus, with the possible exception of one single phrase, that the Kingdom of God would come "like a thief in the night" (1 Thessalonians 5:2; compare Matthew 24:43). What happened to Jesus' anti-Roman political vision, that radical alternative to the Pax Romana? Did Paul share these anti-Roman sentiments?

There is also no evidence from Paul that he practiced Judaism or thought of himself as Jewish in any sense. In Galatians, he noted that earlier in his life he had progressed in Judaism far more than many of his contemporaries, being enthusiastic for the traditions of the elders (Galatians 2:14). The later Book of Acts depicted Paul studying Judaism in Jerusalem with one of the leading Pharisaic teachers of the time, Gamaliel (Acts 22:3), but this may simply represent an attempt to enhance Paul's credentials. Either way, Paul dismissed his Jewish education as "rubbish" (Philippians 3:8).

In removing the Jewishness of Jesus, it was not as if he were attempting to somehow universalize him, moving him beyond ethnicity, perhaps in an attempt to portray him as a model for all humanity. Paul just wasn't interested in the Jesus of history.

WHAT'S A MESSIAH?

Stripping the Christ of his Jewishness had another crucial implication for Paul's understanding of Jesus' identity. It altered the meaning of Jesus as the political Messiah, the Jewish leader expected to return to drive out the Romans and bring about a transformed landscape—the Kingdom of God instead of the Pax Romana. Early on in his career, Paul expected Jesus to return soon: "the appointed time has grown short," and "the present form of this world is passing away"(1 Corinthians 7:29, 31). As time progressed, however, Jesus did not return. The world looked very much the same after Jesus as before. This was an absolutely devastating turn of events, and it represented a very major problem for Christian theology, then and now. If Jesus truly were the Messiah, how was it that the world after him looked very much like the world before him? A Messiah *must* bring about a dramatic change in world politics. News-paper headlines have to shout: "Evil destroyed. Governments fall. Peace reigns. A successor of David sits on the throne of Israel." That's what a real Messiah *has* to do.

Clearly Paul had to shift emphasis. Without world transformation, Jesus re-mained a Messiah-in-waiting. Paul probably saw the problem. What did Jesus-as-Messiah mean if the world had not been radically transformed? One option was to continue to wait. If so, for how long? For decades? centuries? millennia? Waiting is one perennial solution. The ancient Jesus Movement waited. So, too, do some contemporary Christian groups. Waiting is a position promoted, for instance, by some modern-day mass media evangelists heralding the end-time, still expected "soon." This is often tied in to signs that the waiting period is vir-tually over—establishment of Israel, the ingathering of the Jews from around the world coupled with an expected gigantic military battle in the Middle East.

Another alternative, however, was to abandon the claim and look else-where for a Messiah. This happened later on when another Messiah claimant appeared, namely, Bar Kokhba, during the Second Jewish Revolt against Rome in the mid 130s. But he failed to drive the Romans out and so never became a Messiah.

But there was a third innovative solution that occurred to some. Why not spiritualize the concept? Redefine the expectation? Paul chose this route, preparing the way for spiritualizing the concept of the Messiah. As we have noted, he focused on the Christ figure, not the Jesus of history. *Christ* is the Greek form for the Hebrew for "anointed one," the root meaning of *Messiah*. That is fine, but there is more to the story than just that. By putting the word into Greek, Paul bounced the concept out of its original Jewish context into a Roman one. This had two significant consequences.

First, it removed its political overtones. In its original context, Israel's Mes-siah was a *political* reformer. He'd play a prominent role in bringing about the independence and sovereignty of Israel. In the context of Paul's time, this would mean eliminating the Romans. There would be other consequences, to be sure, a transformed world in which the righteous are rewarded for their heroic efforts, the wicked eliminated, and the messianic era of universal peace established. Paul's view, however, was decidedly apolitical. It had nothing to do with replacing Romans or establishing an independent Jewish state.

Furthermore, Paul's Christ image was that of a dying-rising savior God-human, the one with whom the individual believer becomes identified and through whom the believer becomes saved. Many passages in Paul's letters demonstrated the intimate relationship Paul claimed a believer can have with Christ: "I have been crucified with Christ; and it is no longer I who live, but it is Christ who lives in me. And the life I now live in the flesh I live by faith in the Son of God who loved me and gave himself for me" (Galatians 2:20).

The Christ assumed a cosmic dimension. This was expressed in Paul's letters in several ways. In his Letter to the Philippians, Paul wrote the following of the Christ, a preexistent divine being, who became incarnate and who died and was raised again:

> *Let the same mind be in you that was in Christ Jesus, who though he was in the form of God did not regard equality with God as something to be exploited, but emptied himself, taking the form of a slave, being born in human likeness. And being found in human form, he humbled himself and became obedient to the point of death—even death on a cross.* (Philippians 2:5–8)

Plus, in Romans 8:3, Paul talks about how God sent "his own Son in the likeness of sinful flesh."

In 1 Corinthians, Paul waxed eloquently about how all will be redeemed in Christ who has defeated all enemies, including death (1 Corinthians 15:21–26). Believers, through identification with the Christ, will inherit eternal life. In so doing, Paul changed the concept of the Messiah. It was no longer that of a political leader who acts as a catalyst in bringing about world transformation. It was now that of a dying and rising savior sallying forth to do universal battle with all the forces of evil, including the power of death. The idea has been fundamentally altered.

Tom Harpur notes the larger dimension of the Christ figure in Paul's thought:

> *Since Paul was, above all things, a communicator par excellence, he spoke to the people of his time in the mystical language they understood—the vernacular of the Mystery Religions. . . . All his language about being "in Christ" or having "Christ in you" reflects the current Hellenic theosophy and philosophy. It is really Orphic-Platonic-Mystery cultism, almost pure Hindu or Vedic yoga mysticism, with no immediate reference to the Gospel life of Jesus at all.*[4]

The similarities were immediately apparent to opponents of the Christian religion as it came into prominence on the Roman stage, so much so that early apologists such as Justin Martyr and Origen had difficulty explaining the uniqueness of Paul's vision. For some critics, Christianity was another of the old familiar mystery religion cults dressed up in a new name.

For Paul, the Christ was a preexistent being, "in the form of God," who "emptied himself," taking on "the form of a slave, being born in human likeness" (Philippians 2:6, 7). He talked about "gaining Christ" and how faith in Christ—not the Torah—created righteousness (Philippians 3:8–9). He wanted to "know Christ and the power of his resurrection," sharing in his sufferings and death and participating in his resurrection, making him one of his own. In

1 Corinthians, Paul discussed the resurrection: "all will be made alive in Christ" (1 Corinthians 15:24). Christ represented a major cosmic power. He will hand over the Kingdom to God the Father after he has destroyed "every ruler and every authority and power" (1 Corinthians 15:24), including, finally, death itself. Christ, then, is the transformative power available to all who have faith in him. The focus of the Christ is upon rescuing humanity, offering eternal life to all who participate in his life—in his body and blood. More than human, Paul's Christ is a divine being who existed prior to and after his earthly span of life.

In short, Paul's view of the Christ removed the Jewish concept of the Messiah from its Jewish matrix and plunked it into a Gentile one. It had the advantage of being much easier to explain. For his Gentile audience, this different concept of the Messiah would not require Paul to conduct ancient history lessons before talking about the Christ. That is, with his view of the Christ, he would not have had to take potential converts through the history of Israel to explain why a Messiah was needed and what was expected. He would not, for instance, have had to explain the significance of having a descendant of David on the throne of Israel. His was an easier sell.

Politically, too, Paul would have had a less difficult time. He would not have had to confront the position that, in accordance with Jewish expectations for messianic times, Jerusalem and Israel would become the preeminent centers of world power and Gentiles would flock there to worship God. Gentiles living in Greece and Galatia, with loyalties to their own jurisdictions, might find that political view somewhat of a stretch.

GOING FORWARD: IMPLICATIONS FOR JUDAISM

Paul detached his new religion from Judaism. But it was not enough for the Christ Movement to win out over the rival Jesus Movement. It needed also to undermine Judaism itself, to erase, if it could, any vestige of that ancient religion. And so the attacks began. Paul led the way, with his rejection of Torah and his introduction of the dying-rising Christ figure, the savior. The communities that arose in the Mediterranean in the wake of Paul were increasingly communities of the Christ, emphasizing belief over behavior. While the daily lives of the people in these communities generally reflected the customs and practices of the greater world around them, their spiritual focus was entirely different. They focused on the Christ and sought to become one with his death and resurrection, mingling with his blood and body through the rite of Communion. This set them apart from their neighbors and brought them into conflict with the local agents of the emperor, whom they refused to worship.

Some paid with their lives. For them, there was only one divinity: the Christ, the incarnate son of God.

As the community of the Christ grew in number and influence, it would find ways to address various smaller rivals. This included the Torah-observant Ebionites as well as the Gnostic Christians, who believed their spiritual insight and understanding to be more intense than that of the more powerful mainstream Christ movement. But Proto-Orthodoxy's first priority was to purge their movement of Jewish practice and influence, and to denounce the validity of Jewish faith and tradition.

The assault had begun and would last for centuries. And it would quickly become personal.

13

DEMONIZING JEWISH LEADERSHIP AND THE JEWISH PEOPLE

On the shores of the eastern Mediterranean lies the city of Antakya—Antioch in ancient times. Located in modern southeastern Turkey just where it curves down the coast toward Syria, this city was once the third largest city in the Roman Empire. Peter passed this way. So, too, did Paul and Barnabas, who spent a year here in what was then a thriving metropolis. Paul noted that it was in Antioch that he engaged in a dispute with Peter concerning dietary laws. From this city Paul set forth on several of his missionary journeys. Here, too, the followers of Christ were first called Christians (Acts 11:25–27).

THE GOSPEL OF MATTHEW

It was probably in Antioch—or at least within the Roman province of Syria—that the document we call the Gospel of Matthew was composed, some fifty or so years after the death of Jesus and two decades after the death of Paul. An intriguing writing, Matthew is simultaneously the most "pro-Jewish" gospel we have, as well as the most "anti-Jewish" one. The former aspect was evident in Matthew's portrayal of Jesus as the new Moses, standing on the mountain, teaching his followers the higher righteousness and promoting strict Torah observance. That message targeted Paul and the growing influence of his Torah-free message. The anti-Jewish side, however, comes out in his sustained attack on the Jewish leaders of his time, the Pharisaic sages who had survived the disaster of 70. This attack was partly personal, as he raked them over the coals for their behavior. But it was much more than that.

We don't know who the author of the Gospel of Matthew was or if he knew the Jesus of history personally. It's an anonymous document and only later tradition attributes it to a "Matthew." We can imagine this writer, hard at work, using several prior documents—well before the age of computers, which would have made editing easier. He had the Gospel of Mark in front of him, for instance, a work that had been written only a few years before. Matthew quoted Mark extensively, changed details here and there, omitted some sayings and added others. Like many other gospel writers, he did not treat this text as "sacred scripture" that could not be altered.[1]

In addition to Mark, Matthew also used another source, as did Luke later on, one that scholars refer to as Q. He also had his own information found in no other writing.[2] We do not know if this derived from firsthand knowledge of what Jesus said and did. Perhaps it came from others who had heard Jesus. Or it might have come from oral tradition, that is, from someone who had heard someone who had heard Jesus. Much of his unique material is to be found in the Sermon on the Mount.

Matthew clearly knew the Gospel of Mark, but yet he wrote another one. That's a significant undertaking. Why *another* gospel? This intriguing question is rarely asked. Why do we need more than one gospel? What prompted Matthew, and later on, John and Luke, to write their accounts? What motivated others whose works are not included in the New Testament also to write theirs—gospels attributed to Thomas, Mary, Peter, Philip, or even Judas? If we already had Mark, why did we need another document? What was Matthew's motive in writing? Did he perhaps think there was something wrong with Mark? Was his objective to "correct" Mark, to give a more authentic portrait of Jesus, as he saw him? Or was his intent even more radical, to bury the gospel of Mark and to replace it with his own?

Turn these questions around. Since we have a "rewritten" Mark in Matthew, why keep Mark around at all? Was it like a "first draft" of a gospel? Why was Mark even retained by early Christianity and not discarded? After all, at least 90 percent of Mark is preserved in Matthew.

How did Matthew think of himself? Anthony J. Saldarini cautions us not to think of him as someone who has broken from Judaism and who is criticizing his former religion.[3] Unlike Paul, Matthew was not a convert to something else. His writing represented an *internal* debate, Saldarini contends, but given the vehemence with which he denounced the primary Jewish leaders, his community represents somewhat of a fringe group. Matthew's community had only recently separated from the synagogue, likely after a bitter fight with its leaders over the future direction of Judaism. Should it be along the new lines the rabbis at Yavneh were beginning to suggest as they revamped Judaism after the destruction of the Temple? Or should Judaism, Matthew dared to assert, be reconstructed along the lines suggested by Rabbi Jesus? It was an audacious position, nothing less than a fresh perspective on Judaism in light of post-70 reality. In the heat of the moment, ripe from rejection by the Pharisaic leaders of the local congregation, Matthew addressed his gospel *to them*, to these local leaders as well as to the Pharisaic community at large. He tried to persuade them of the truth of his minority position.[4]

He was, of course, also writing for his own group of dissident Jews, anxious to hold on to them and to give them ammunition with which to counter the barrage they likely faced from former friends and, possibly, family members. The community was divided, and good people were caught on both sides of the divide.

Matthew's people were a dissident, disaffected lot, thrown out of the main sanctuary. They were on their own and undoubtedly embittered by rejection. He and his followers continued to think of themselves as Jews, but their allegiance had shifted to Jesus as their rabbi and promised Messiah. Matthew was uncertain what to say about Jewish leaders who were very likely former friends and associates. On the one hand, he was exceptionally bitter. The wounds of confrontation, after all, were still fresh. On the other, he openly acknowledged their legitimate authority and the correctness of their teachings. When we set Matthew's community in the context of his times, we see a fledgling group, still claiming to be Jewish, but not part of the mainstream synagogue.

Whether this writing ever reached the sages busily reconstructing Judaism at Yavneh farther south along the eastern Mediterranean coast or remained a purely local dispute in Antioch is unknown. Nor do we know if the Pharisees whom he vilified ever read this attack. What they would have made of it, had they heard it, is also not clear. Matthew's proposal made no impact on Judaism as it developed along rabbinic lines, but it probably did encourage his band of followers.

DEMONIZING JEWISH LEADERSHIP

So, when it was composed, the Gospel of Matthew represented a dissident Jewish document—not an external critique. Probably still reeling from recent hostile dealings with local leaders, Matthew cast strong accusations against Judaism's leaders of the time, the Pharisees. He possessed a powerful weapon. He attacked them through the words of Jesus, by developing scenarios where Jesus confronted the Pharisees. We do not know, of course, whether these vignettes actually originated with the historical Jesus or whether this was just Matthew speaking through the words of Jesus. It is apparent, however, why Matthew would pick out the Pharisees for engagement with the historical Jesus. They were, after all, the Jewish leaders of Matthew's own time, and they were the ones involved in reconstructing the religion. It would have made no sense for

Matthew to portray Jesus disputing theology with representatives of the Zealot, Essene, or Sadducean factions. They no longer existed as recognizable groups within post-70 Jewish society, and his readers would probably not have known much about them.

Matthew's agenda with the Pharisees was twofold. He stressed the need for members of his own community to uphold Torah observance in an even stricter sense than they affirmed. That constituted major one-upmanship. He also tried to position his movement as a viable alternative to mainstream Judaism. Perhaps he naively thought he could persuade the Pharisees to adopt his point of view, but his harsh language seems to belie this. The nasty tone of his denunciation—which he placed in the mouth of Jesus—did not lend itself to dialogue or good intercommunity relationships. It is unlikely that he expected the Pharisees to respond.

The Gospel of Matthew sheds light on one first-century community on the shores of the eastern Mediterranean. It's a valuable window into their beliefs and provides a snapshot of a new group in the process of social formation. They are only a stone's throw away from Judaism. Matthew's gospel, however, raises some intriguing questions to which we do not know the answers. As we have seen, Matthew's teaching, with respect to the higher righteousness, reflected the earlier position of James and the Jesus Movement. But did Matthew's criticisms of the Pharisees also represent the position of the Jesus Movement in the 80s? Had they, too, like Matthew's group, become antagonistic toward these leaders? How far removed had they become from mainstream Judaism?

Elaine Pagels places Matthew's attack in perspective:

Matthew, proclaiming the message of Jesus the Messiah c.80 C.E., found himself in competition primarily with those Pharisaic teachers and rabbis, who were successfully establishing themselves throughout the Jewish world as authoritative interpreters of the Torah. The Pharisees wanted to place the Torah at the center of Jewish life as a replacement for the ruined Temple. Their aim was to teach a practical interpretation of Jewish law that would preserve Jewish groups throughout the world as a separate and holy people. Matthew saw the Pharisees as the chief rivals to his own teachings about Jesus.[5]

The issue for Jewish thought in the 80s and 90s changed to questions concerning the Temple, the Torah, and Jewish life. What, for instance, should replace the Temple now that it had been destroyed? Should it be family and synagogue, focusing on reading the law and prayer? That was the stance of the rabbis. But there were other suggestions as well. Perhaps it should be oriented around Jesus' interpretation of the law. This was Matthew's contribution as he attempted to think through the ramifications of his rabbi's perspective. For all the antagonism expressed by Matthew toward the Pharisees, there still remained substantial common ground. Both groups agreed on the necessity for keeping the law, and in this they were closer than Matthew would have been to Paul's Christ Movement. Matthew and the Pharisees parted company on how the law should be interpreted—but they may not have been all that far apart at the time.

In fact, the degree of commonality goes far deeper. In a remarkable passage, Matthew's Jesus agreed that the Pharisees exercised legitimate leadership and teaching authority: "The scribes and Pharisees sit on Moses' seat; therefore, do whatever they teach you and follow it; but do not do as they do, for they do not practice what they teach" (Matthew 23:2–3). Whatever the "seat of Moses" was, it would have been a symbol of authority. Matthew did not question their right to sit there, as authoritative leaders of the community. Even in Matthew's angriest moments, he acknowledged that the Pharisees constituted the true leaders of Judaism. In fact, Matthew's position was far more reaching than that. Amazingly, Matthew had *Jesus* acknowledging the legitimacy of Pharisaic leadership. That is truly astounding given subsequent history.

But there's even more. Matthew's Jesus told his followers to "do whatever they [the Pharisees] teach you." Here Jesus recognized the validity of Pharisaic teachings. Surely this is one of the most overlooked passages in all of the New Testament, and it is powerful in its implications. A close bond exists between the teachings of Jesus and that of the Pharisees. For all their disagreements, their central teachings concur. The communities are also close—Matthew's own community and the synagogue group from which they had sprung. True, they had their disputes, but they were still part of the same religion. That wasn't the issue. On the other hand, what a huge chasm existed between Matthew's Jesus and Paul. What a remarkable contrast. Paul could never have uttered the words that Jesus was alleged to have said. He would have choked on them.

For all his support of the Pharisees, Matthew's Jesus also hurled seven vicious woes or curses at them. These reek of utter condemnation. Jesus' followers, Matthew said, should observe Pharisaic teachings but not their practices. They are called "blind guides" (Matthew 23:16) and "hypocrites" (Matthew 23:13).

One criticism seems to be that the Pharisees failed to practice what they taught. But what does this mean? In what way did their actions fail to conform to their teachings? It is unfortunate that Matthew's Jesus provided no examples to help us understand this searing indictment. Were there huge infractions, like stealing when they preached not stealing? Breaking the Sabbath when they taught strict Sabbath observance? Bearing false witness against other people? Being mean to people, perhaps even to the point of evicting them from synagogue fellowship? Or were the deeds relatively trivial? Some examples of how their behavior deviated from their teachings would have lent credibility to the attack.

Another criticism focused on their desire to be recognized by others. According to Matthew's Jesus, they wanted their deeds to be seen by others, preferring places of honor in public, sitting in the best seats in the synagogue and demanding respect. The desire for recognition on the part of the Pharisaic survivors may have been a natural consequence of the post-70 reality. Authority was the issue. Who would speak for Judaism now that there were no high priests, priests, or political leader? As teachers and as the only faction that survived (other than the Jesus Movement), they exerted their rights to provide leadership at this extremely crucial time in Jewish history. It is to be expected that they would seek to occupy positions of authority within the synagogue and to use these as a base for disseminating their reinterpretations. Is Matthew's gospel taking us inside synagogue politics of the late first century?

These accusations of usurping authority probably relate more to Matthew's own time than to Jesus'. The indictment about occupying leadership positions may very well have reflected "sour grapes" on Matthew's part. He had just lost a major power struggle within the synagogue. He had run afoul of the Pharisaic leaders in his community, and that hurt and rejection still smarted. His people probably rallied around him, cheering him on as he engaged in his denunciations of their former spiritual leaders. They must really have liked what he said, and they could picture in their own minds these rabbis sitting smugly at the head of the congregation. Matthew pulled them down a peg and they probably loved it.

Good rhetoric. The reality, however, was different. The rabbis were still there; Matthew and his entourage weren't. The rabbis were still in authority; Matthew wasn't. They were "in"; he and his community were "out."

A fussy point then emerges having to do with religious attire. Matthew's Jesus complained that the Pharisees were ostentatious in their observance of the Torah. They made "their phylacteries broad and their fringes long" (Matthew 23:5). This refers to the Jewish practice of wearing tefillin (straps and boxes containing scriptural passages on the forehead and arm of men) and a tallit or prayer shawl when praying. Note that neither Matthew nor Jesus objected to their wearing these badges of Jewish observance. They were, after all, commanded in the Torah. Right after the Shema—that the Lord is one and that people should love the Lord with all their heart, soul, and might—Deuteronomy said that the people should "Bind them as a sign on your hand, fix them as an emblem on your forehead" (Deuteronomy 6:8). Thus the phylacteries or tefillin reminded people of the central teachings of Torah. Matthew's objection was to the size of these devices, not their use. It is likely that Matthew and his group also wore tefillin and a tallit when praying, as probably did Jesus, James, and their followers. At best, this is a criticism of fashion.

The concern with minutiae of the law rather than with "justice and mercy and faith" (Matthew 23:23) constituted yet another accusation. Tithing and purity laws are mentioned, and these were certainly under discussion in Jewish circles in the first century A.D. The Dead Sea Scroll society tackled some of these issues, for instance, being concerned with the purity of utensils and liquids. These were thorny questions at the time, for Hellenization had brought these to the fore. How were the utensils made, for instance? By whom? Did this include non-Jews as well as Jews? If so, was the manufacturing process "secure," that is, were there assurances that the items had been produced without any contact with forbidden foods, either directly or indirectly through the hands of foreign workers? How were the utensils cleansed? How secure was this process in avoiding contamination with forbidden foods? So every step of the manufacturing, distribution, and cleansing process had to be carefully examined in light of ancient prohibitions concerning forbidden foods and the new modern environment in which foreigners might very well have produced and handled these commonplace household items in bringing these to market. These were important issues if Torah was to be observed faithfully.

But what is Matthew's evidence—or Jesus'—for the charge that the Pharisees were ignoring the more important aspects of Torah? What did Matthew have in mind? Again, unfortunately, the charges were very general and vague. Matthew's credibility would have been enhanced if he cited specific behaviors. The thrust of Matthew's unsubstantiated accusations was clear, however. In his judgment, their religious priorities were skewed.

The curses conclude with a strong denunciation. According to Matthew, Jesus cursed them, saying, "You snakes, you brood of vipers. How can you escape from being sentenced to hell?" (Matthew 23:33). Commenting on this passage, Elaine Pagels observes:

> Philosophers did not engage, as Matthew does here, in demonic vilification of their opponents. Within the ancient world, so far as I know, it is only Essenes and Christians who actually escalate conflict with their opponents to the level of cosmic war.[6]

Rather than engaging in debate, Matthew demonized his opponents. Through the words of Jesus, it was an exceptionally strong personal attack that positioned them as evil.

Matthew's assault on the Pharisees was itself inconsistent, if not hypocritical. The curses against the Pharisees were laced with anger, and these sentiments Matthew attributed to the historical Jesus. This was the same person who is portrayed earlier in Matthew's writing as having preached the higher righteousness, extending the commandment "do not murder" to include "do not give way to anger." Matthew—or Jesus—seems to have forgotten this injunction in his raging attack on the Pharisees.

The attack itself also unfairly stereotyped the Pharisees. It represented a sweeping blanket condemnation covering all of them, with no exceptions. This simplistic approach just labeled "the other" as evil and demonic, just because they were "other." We know of many exemplary sages, not only from rabbinical literature but also from the Book of Acts. This latter work mentions that some Pharisees had aligned themselves with the Jesus Movement, that one of their prominent leaders defended the movement from persecution by the Sadducees, and that they were probably the group of "reasonable" people who protested the unjust killing of James. This is hardly the picture presented in Matthew. It raises the question whether these are Matthew's own words rather than those of Jesus.

Curiously inconsistent. That's a legitimate impression of Matthew. We are told that Jesus approved the leadership of the Pharisees and their teachings. On the other hand, they are condemned as villains. Only the latter part seems to have been heard within Proto-Orthodoxy as it evolved over the second through fourth centuries. The good things that Jesus said about Pharisaic leaders were swamped by utter invective.

ATTACK ON ORAL LAW

The Pharisees held that Torah consisted of two parts: a written law found within the biblical text, and an oral law that reflects the process of deciding what the written law means and how it applies to specific situations. This tradition, the Pharisees contended, provided the key for understanding scripture. It represented a powerful interpretive device, for with it, the Pharisees could claim that they, and only they, possessed the correct basis for understanding scripture. We observed earlier how oral law functioned with respect to interpreting the commandment to honor the Sabbath day and keep it holy, and the kind of creative work it forbade. Oral law constituted a powerful weapon, and, in the hands of the Pharisaic sages using it to reconstitute Judaism, it was a significant threat to the emerging early Christian community with its methods of interpretation.

Not surprisingly, we find that Matthew's Jesus rejected oral law. Matthew had to have Jesus say this, and, again, this rejection probably relates more to Matthew's own day, with its problems, than the time of Jesus fifty years earlier. If Jesus were to act as the new interpreter of Torah, as Matthew was proposing, then it couldn't be left in the hands of oral law and its practitioners. Let's see how Matthew made this work, for the reasoning in the following passage is somewhat convoluted. A bit of background is necessary: oral law was sometimes referred to as "the tradition of the elders." We'll see that terminology used in the quotation below.

The scenario is this: Pharisees had come to Jesus with a question: "Why do your disciples break the tradition of elders? For they do not wash their hands before they eat" (Matthew 15: 1–2). The issue has to do with purity regulations and holiness, not sanitary practice. Following oral law tradition, the Pharisees washed their hands prior to eating, just in case they had come into contact with anything impure. Oddly enough, Jesus' followers didn't wash their hands before eating. We don't know why their practice deviated.

One approach would have been for Jesus to agree with the Pharisees and to move quickly to amend the lax practices of his followers. Instead, Jesus launched into a tirade. He didn't address the immediate issue—namely, washing hands prior to eating. Instead he focused on the overall approach the Pharisees adopted toward scripture. He accused them of making exceptions, specifically to the commandment to honor thy father and mother. The Pharisees, Jesus contended, using their oral law principle, outlined circumstances in which it might be considered right to "weasel out" of obligations toward parents. For example, they might give donations to the Temple instead of helping to support their aged or infirm parents. That way, they might escape their obligations to honor their parents (one of the Ten Commandments) by giving their wealth to the Temple (also a righteous act). Jesus' general point was this: the Pharisees use oral law to make exceptions. That, incidentally, provides evidence that the Pharisees interpreted Torah leniently. Some of these interpretations allowed people to escape their legitimate obligations. That's fine, so far as it goes, but Jesus does not return to the question at hand. How does accusing the Pharisees of making exceptions clarify the issue under discussion? What is it about washing hands that constituted an exception? An exception to what? We are left dangling.

The issue appears to be that of impure hands defiling food entering the mouth. Although we are given few details, this might very well have been the Pharisees' concern. This has nothing to do with modern concerns over viruses and bacteria. Unclean hands that had come into contact with, say, a dead body—not a rare possibility in ancient villages and towns—would defile food brought to the mouth in the act of eating. Jesus, however, disagreed. His point was that unclean hands do not necessarily render pure food impure:—"it is not what goes into the mouth that defiles a person, but it is what comes out of the mouth that defiles" (Matthew 15:11). His emphasis is placed on what one says, not how one eats. But that was all. He was not advocating total abandonment of the dietary laws. He was just affirming that we should not wash our hands prior to eating because, for him, what we say is more important than how we consume food. There is something of a false dilemma here, as perhaps the

Pharisees, had they been given the opportunity to respond, might have pointed out. Could we not, for instance, both wash our hands prior to eating and also pay attention to what we say? The Dead Sea Scroll community had already made this point. They urged scrupulous hand washing prior to eating along with injunctions to be guarded in what they said as part of a larger community of righteousness. Dietary laws and considerate speech are not mutually exclusive.

Purity laws were very much debated among Jewish movements in the first century A.D. by Pharisees, Sadducees, and Essenes. And with good reason. These concerns were prompted by the practical implications of Hellenization and the presence of foreigners in their midst, with their different dietary and lifestyle habits. Jesus seems to have these debates in mind as thinkers of the time struggled to make sense of biblical injunctions. The Pharisees are portrayed as having settled these matters, in keeping with oral tradition. Jesus seems to be putting forward a different approach to interpretation. According to him, not washing the hands will not render impure the food that enters the body, even if the hands themselves might be ritually impure through prior contact with anything that might defile them.

Regardless of the merits of this particular case—the purity implications of not washing hands prior to eating—the major point was that Jesus' response was regarded by Matthew as setting aside the whole oral law interpretation of scripture. Instead of oral law being the way the written law should be interpreted, Matthew suggested that Jesus himself should be the interpreter of scripture and arbiter of sound practice. For Matthew, Jesus, the new Moses, represented the alternative to oral law tradition.

This critique of oral law had far-reaching consequences. One effect was that it freed up Christians from taking seriously Jewish leaders who used this interpretive principle. Biblical interpretation for the new community, henceforth, would proceed along very different lines. While both might make reference to the same set of texts—the Hebrew Bible, or Old Testament—the meaning attributed to these writings would differ because of the varying perspectives of the interpreter. Each community would come in time to filter these ancient writings differently.

RIDICULING JUDAISM

An example of the contemptuous attitude adopted by early Christian authors is to be found in the *Epistle to Diognetus*, a work of absolute propaganda that dates from sometime in the second century.[7] This writer dismissed paganism and then moved to what he called the "follies of Judaism." He ridiculed both paganism and Judaism for thinking that the creator of heaven and earth required sacrifices: "One party, it seems, makes its offerings to creatures which cannot partake of the gifts [paganism], and the other [Judaism] to One who needs none of them" (*Epistle to Diognetus* 3). This established the arrogant tone of his writing, which was well circulated among Gentile communities.

The author then dismissed Jewish practices: "As for their scrupulousness about meats, and their superstitions about the Sabbath, and their much-vaunted circumcision, and their pretentious festivals and new-moon-observances—all of these are too nonsensical to be worth discussing" (*Epistle to Diognetus* 4). Hence ridicule and sarcasm substituted for argument and biblical interpretation. There was no attempt here to examine passages from the Old Testament that supported these practices or to understand the underlying issues. Presumably the writer of the *Epistle to Diognetus* would also have considered much of the Old Testament "nonsensical," since many of those writings addressed these matters.

For the writer of this letter, it was "impious" to suppose that some things that God has created are commendable but that others are useless. So, for him, there was no point to prohibitions against eating pork or shellfish. Gone were all the dietary laws. It was "profanity" to think that God would object to a good deed being done on a Sabbath day even if it meant engaging in creative work to do so. So there are to be no Sabbath observances and no pretense at honoring the Ten Commandments, one of which enjoins keeping the Sabbath. For this writer, a day of rest did not preclude righteous actions. And it should be "laughed out of court" that circumcision provides any basis for having some special claim on God's love. So the covenant with Abraham was airily dismissed. Curiously, the letter criticized observances of festivals as the product of "a deranged intellect" (*Epistle to Diognetus* 4)—but it is difficult to imagine what he could have found wrong with the observances of Passover, Succoth, and Shavuot. What was wrong with honoring historical experiences of the community?

We see in the *Epistle to Diognetus* what the Proto-Orthodox were thinking and saying in the second century. This shows us how far they had come from Paul's Letter to the Galatians. Everything Jewish was being swept aside, not by argument, however faulty, but by arrogant contempt. Gone was any respect for the tradition of oral law, and, with it, regard for its practitioners, the rabbis. No pretense at serious intellectual engagement. None whatsoever.

BLAMING THE JEWISH PEOPLE

While affirming Jesus' support for Pharisaic teachings but rejecting the rabbis' leadership and oral law interpretive principle, Matthew had one more nasty salvo up his sleeve. It was one of the most powerful condemnations ever issued;

its impact throughout history has been overwhelmingly negative. It's one of the foundations of Christian anti-Semitism, and it is rooted in one of the most important New Testament writings.

Jesus was brought to trial before Pilate, the Roman procurator. After having interrogated him, asking him if he was the King of the Jews, Pilate took him outside, to the "crowd." He asked them if they wanted him to release Jesus Barabbas or Jesus who was called the Messiah. The crowd—under the control of the chief priests (Sadducees)—screamed that they wanted a prisoner, Jesus Barabbas, released and that Jesus of Nazareth should be crucified. Seeing that a riot was about to ensue, Pilate washed his hands before the crowd and proclaimed that he was innocent of the blood of this man. Matthew then added one of the most influential statements of all time: "Then the people as a whole answered, 'His blood be on us and on our children!'" (Matthew 27:25).

This is the nucleus of the charge that the Jews were responsible for the death of Jesus, not the Romans. "The Jews killed Jesus" is a phrase that has been uttered by Christians throughout the ages, authorizing some of the most horrendous pogroms and massacres as an integral part of ongoing anti-Semitism. It's a phrase that has been responsible for countless Jewish deaths over the centuries up to the present time.

It is important for us to realize, however, that the people in question constituted only an exceptionally minute fraction of Jewish inhabitants of Jerusalem in A.D. 30, a mob whipped into a frenzy by leaders who wanted Jesus killed. They were agitators assembled by the Sadducees, not ordinary citizens of Jerusalem, or a cross-section of Jewish people of the time.

Jesus was then executed by Roman authority, the cohort of soldiers mocking him as King of the Jews and placing over his head on the cross "This is Jesus, the King of the Jews" (Matthew 27:37). The charge was political; the trial was political; and the crucifixion was political. The fear itself was political, that Jesus would lead an insurrection against Roman power, to help bring about the independent Jewish state as required by a Messiah. While the Zealots and Essenes would support that, the Sadducees, in cahoots with the Roman occupiers, would not. And they controlled the Temple. Matthew's focus should rightfully have been on blaming the Romans and their puppets, the Sadducees.

Instead, Matthew blamed the mob who demanded the release of Barabbas instead of Jesus and placed upon them the culpability for his death, not only for their generation but for all ensuing generations. This misplaced blame—one single sentence—has caused enormous pain, suffering, and death for many subsequent generations of Jewish people. That passage, as traditionally interpreted, stands as a monument to hatred and causes enormous pain for Jews who hear it read or proclaimed, on the radio, on television, or in popular films over and over again each year during Easter. While contemporary Christians do not read this text as blaming Jews in perpetuity for the death of Jesus, many early and medieval Christians did, ignoring the plain sense of the passage that this was a small group of Jews, a riotous crowd, stirred up by the Sadducees.

For all its emphasis on Torah observance, higher righteousness, the marvelous beatitudes, and the whole Sermon on the Mount, there is a very dark side to the Gospel of Matthew. Perhaps too much of its message reflected the author's undistilled anger and hostility, still fresh from an internal synagogue confrontation. Its negativity packed an exceptionally powerful punch. Its message was clear to his contemporaries. Do not listen to those Pharisaic leaders who were busily reconstructing Judaism. Do not accept their oral law approach to Torah. Do not listen to them. Put the blame for Jesus' death on the Jewish people. These were truly deadly words and the Gospel of Matthew has been one of the most influential writings of all time. It was widely circulated. The pro-Jewish elements were certainly overlooked—the higher righteousness, Jesus' affirming Pharisaic teachings—in favor of its anti-Jewish stance, demonizing Jewish leadership and blaming the Jewish people for the death of Jesus.

It's a vindictive writing. Matthew certainly got even with those who had thrown him out of the synagogue.

But these attacks were only the beginning. Much more lay in store for the Jewish community.

14

CONFISCATING
JUDAISM'S HERITAGE

"I will make of you a great nation . . . and in you all the families of the earth shall be blessed" (Genesis 12:2,3). That was the ancient promise to Abraham for his descendants. "A light to the nations" (Isaiah 42:6) was how Isaiah pictured the new Israel on its return from the Babylonian Exile. People would flock to Jerusalem and look up to Israel as a beacon of hope and inspiration. Israel would be the servant of God. End-time prophets extended the vision to encompass all humanity. Assisted by the Messiah, God would create a transformed world, with Israel restored to prominence, ushering in an unparalleled rule of righteousness. That was the Jewish dream and hope for all mankind. It was upbeat and optimistic and it propped up Israel's sense of mission on the world stage.

The destruction of the Temple dashed many of these Jewish hopes for humanity. Attention turned to questions concerning how to understand God's sovereign rule in a world where evil seemed to predominate. How could such a massive devastation fit into God's plan as expounded by the prophets and writers of the Old Testament? Why, they asked, had the Hellenistic Romans succeeded? When would the land of Israel again be restored to the Jewish people? How long would this new exile last? Exile—that is the way they saw the cataclysm of 70 and its later one, in 135, under the failed revolt of Bar Kokhba. It was the start of a whole new exile that would last far longer than anyone at the time could have imagined—until 1948.

But Judaism faced other issues as well. Early in the second century, leaders of the emerging Proto-Orthodox faction denounced many elements of the historic Jewish religious heritage. They warned their members, for instance, not to participate in Jewish worship—the Friday evening and Saturday morning

Sabbath observances and the annual cycle of Jewish festivals. Temple observances had passed into the church, some said, and Jewish Sabbath observances simply had to go. Others expropriated the Jewish religious heritage, claiming that it belonged solely to Christianity. This took several forms. Some claimed that Judaism never had a covenant with God at all, and that only Christians had a deal with God. Others accused Jewish leaders of failing to understand their own sacred writings. Even more radically, some suggested that the writings of the Hebrew Bible weren't meant for them at all, only for Christians. No covenant; no Bible; no understanding—everything of value was confiscated and relocated within the domain of Christianity.

Theft of a legacy—that was what some early Proto-Orthodox leaders attempted, asserting that only their movement possessed what had formerly belonged to the Jewish people. In fact, some arrogantly argued, the Jewish people did not even constitute the true Israel. That resided in the church, not the synagogue. Christians were the true Israelites. If successful, this "heritage grab" would have deprived Judaism of its identity, its historic mission, and its fundamental self-understanding. Here's how this confiscation took place.

IGNATIUS OF ANTIOCH

Around 115, some thirty or so years after the author of the Gospel of Matthew, another leader appeared in Antioch. This was Ignatius, the powerful bishop of Antioch. A colorful and influential figure, Ignatius had a strong personality that shines through in his writings some nineteen centuries later. He comes across as a stalwart, robust individual, the model bishop very much convinced of his own authority and unassailable role in the church. He entertained absolutely no doubts about the correctness of his views.

During the latter years of the Roman emperor Trajan (98–117), Ignatius was condemned to death, convicted for being a Christian. We do not know the circumstances of his arrest, nor his life history up until this time. Was he old enough to have known whoever wrote the Gospel of Matthew? How did he become bishop? What were the issues faced by his congregation in Antioch? Was there one community or several? What was their relationship to the synagogue that had caused Matthew's group so much distress earlier on? Was Ignatius's congregation a continuation of that fledgling community? And what relation did these groups bear to the community Paul encountered when he was in Antioch? These questions tantalize us. Presumably, because of Antioch's importance as a major city—the third largest in the empire at the time—the Romans were making an example of Ignatius. Undoubtedly one of the issues Ignatius had faced in Antioch concerned the locus of authority within the local congregation. Who made decisions when issues arose? Over and over again, Ignatius defended the view that the bishop is ultimately in charge.

Ignatius's teachings tied in with a growing attempt to define the parameters of Proto-Orthodoxy. While there were many models of ministry within the first century, early on in the second century the idea of an "apostolic succession" arose. According to this view, the only authentic leaders were those who could trace their origins back to one of the original apostles. Thus pedigrees of legitimacy were created. We saw the careful naming of James's Jewish successors as bishops of Jerusalem preserved by Eusebius. He also took great pains to point out other successions, for example, that within Rome. Linus succeeded Paul and Peter in Rome.[1] We also learn from him that Ignatius was the second bishop of Antioch, succeeding Evodius. Eusebius went on to name the following seventeen bishops of this illustrious city. The doctrine of apostolic succession excluded leaders who could not trace their descent back to the apostles. Thus self-proclaimed preachers or self-appointed itinerant missionaries chosen by "the Spirit" would forfeit legitimacy, not being from the lineage of correct teachers and pastors.

By upholding the value of episcopacy, Ignatius was one of the earliest proponents of what became one of the most impressive management systems ever created. It was so successful that many attribute the eventual success of Proto-Orthodoxy over all its rivals to the effective infrastructure it created and the worldwide network of communication it established. We can see in Ignatius's writings his sincere attempt to work with other bishops, to reinforce their position within their congregations, and to help preserve the unity of the church. He wrote to Polycarp, for instance. He was the bishop of the church at Smyrna (modern-day Izmir in Turkey), urging him to make unity within the church his priority. Later on, Polycarp himself would write to the "colony of God's Church at Philippi," (Preface, *The Epistle of Polycarp to the Philippians*), encouraging them in their beliefs. For Ignatius, that centralized structure—one bishop locally who keeps in communication with a network of faithful like-minded bishops globally—would result in one unified teaching, one church. This single-minded faith was Ignatius's vision, and it was a powerful one.

Even today, apostolic succession plays a role in modern Christianity, with traditional churches such as the Orthodox, Roman Catholic, and Anglican communities carefully safeguarding the lineage of their leaders. Thus Pope Benedict XVI is the 263rd successor to Peter. The present Anglican archbishop of Canterbury, Rowan Williams, stands in succession from Augustine of Canterbury in 597, and, through him, back to the apostles.

When we first meet him, Ignatius was being transported to Rome, for execution. Surprisingly, we find him expressing great happiness about this turn of events. He was not at all bitter and in fact welcomed the prospect of death and being united with Christ. With gruesome relish, he depicted himself being ground up by the teeth of wild beasts in the Coliseum in Rome. In his estimation, the Romans were about to do him an immense favor. They had given him the means to participate in the suffering and death of Christ. As he was moved from Antioch across the landmass of Turkey to the shores of the Aegean Sea to catch a ship bound for Rome, he used the opportunity to write seven letters to various congregations. Composed around the same time as the Gospel of Luke and the Book of Acts, these letters reveal a community developing its own infrastructure and hierarchy. Unlike Matthew sitting on the periphery of Judaism, Ignatius's writings disclose how separate from Judaism and the synagogue the community within Antioch—and elsewhere—had become within just a few decades. We see Ignatius eager for martyrdom, refusing help from church leaders along the way. He fervently desired to experience what he called "the passion of my God" (*Epistle to the Romans* 6).

THE ROLE OF THE BISHOP

One letter was sent to a Christian group located in Magnesia, near Ephesus, on the west coast of modern-day Turkey. This writing addressed a growing factionalism with the community. Ignatius stoutly defended the role of the bishop as the focal point of authority within the congregation. There is an established hierarchy—God and Christ; then the bishop; and finally, the laity. The hierarchy deserved to be obeyed, just as Jesus' followers were obedient to him and he himself, to God: "In the same way as the Lord was wholly one with the Father, and never acted independently of Him, either in person or through the Apostles, so you yourselves must never act independently of your bishop and clergy." (*Epistle to the Magnesians* 7).[2] Eucharists and baptisms, for example, were never to be celebrated apart from the bishop or those whom he has authorized. From this warning we might infer that roving preachers and pastors were conducting their own ceremonies independently of central authority.

Clearly there were divisions and differing opinions about what the movement should believe and practice. Without mentioning from whom these other views stemmed, Ignatius cautioned his readers not to follow their own private judgments about these matters. He urged them to be of one mind and have one hope. Curiously, he advised them that there should be only one worship service that everyone attends—no multiple services or deviant sectarian practices: "On no account persuade yourselves that it is right and proper to follow your own private judgment; have a single service of prayer which everybody attends." (*Epistle to the Magnesians* 7).

REJECTION OF JEWISH PRACTICES

Ignatius's insight was that the church was the new Temple. He saw the church—a separate gathering from the synagogue—as the only place in which Christian worship could legitimately occur. Ignatius would not have issued this caution unless some members of the community in Magnesia were worshipping in several places. They may, for instance, have participated in the Sabbath services in the synagogue first and then met for the specifically Christian service Saturday evening after sundown or the following morning. This pattern of devotion reflected one practice within early Christianity and it presupposed the legitimacy of synagogue worship. That cozy outlook in no way represented Ignatius's position, however. For him, there was one and only one place of true worship. As bishop, he was thoroughly determined to abolish any easy accommodation with what he undoubtedly thought were outmoded or deviant practices:

> *Never allow yourself to be led astray by false teachings and antiquated and useless fables. Nothing of any use can be got from them. If we are still living in the practice of Judaism, it is an admission that we have failed to receive the gift of grace . . . . We have seen how former adherents of the ancient customs have since attained to a new hope; so that they have given up keeping the Sabbath, and now order their lives by the Lord's Day instead. (Epistle to the Magnesians 8)*

So the ruling is unambiguous: no Christian participation in Jewish Sabbath services. Continuing such practices revealed, Ignatius said—echoing Paul before him—a failure to have received "the gift of grace." In fact, it appears, Ignatius banned participation in *all* Jewish practices. As he wrote in the passage just quoted, they reflect "false teachings" and "useless fables." Undoubtedly some early followers of Christ were rightfully confused. Scripture clearly indicated the necessity to keep Torah requirements. Remembering the Sabbath to keep it holy was, after all, enshrined as one of the Ten Commandments. To the extent that they were familiar with the writings of the Hebrew Bible, members of his congregation may have raised thorny questions concerning the relationship of Torah observance to the beliefs of the new community. Ignatius was clear, however: no Jewish practices. How this affected Ignatius's hearers is not known. It may have driven families apart, for likely there were relatives both within Judaism and without in the emerging Proto-Orthodox community. Familial disruption and the demise of shared experiences and ancient common practices might have been the price tag for Ignatius's unrelenting quest for unity. Ignatius's warnings probably did not deter everyone from practices mandated by scripture, for, centuries later, we still hear bishops urging Christians to drop Jewish worship. John Chrysostom, for instance, the fourth-century bishop of Antioch and, later, of Constantinople, preached eight sermons against Christians observing the Sabbath as well as Jewish fasts and festivals.

Interestingly, in the passage just quoted, Ignatius did not make the argument that the Lord's Day was the Sabbath transferred to a new day. That would have preserved the mandate to observe the Sabbath. He simply said, give up the Sabbath with no attempt to preserve the intent of this component of the Ten Commandments. Clearly, honoring the Decalogue was not part of Ignatius's teaching.

Ignatius has also given us one of the first clear-cut indications of how separate the two religions—Judaism and Proto-Orthodoxy—had become. In the following passage, he drew a sharp contrast: "To profess Jesus Christ while continuing to follow Jewish customs is an absurdity. The Christian Faith does not look to Judaism, but Judaism looks to Christianity" (*Epistle to the Magnesians* 10).[3] It was abundantly evident to Ignatius that Christianity had completely replaced Judaism and that it should look to the new movement as its fulfillment. There was nothing of value left in Judaism for Christianity to embrace.

THE EPISTLE OF BARNABAS

Sometime in the early second century, a work we refer to as the *Epistle of Barnabas* was widely circulated.[4] It is attributed to Barnabas, a traveling companion of Paul, but its author is not identified within the text. Like many ancient writings, its author is anonymous. Some early Christian communities apparently considered this work authoritative, but it was not included in Athanasius's fourth-century list of canonical New Testament writings. It's a relatively short work, some twenty-one chapters in length, and it's motivated in part by end-time concerns. It concluded with the assurance that the Lord is "at hand" (*Epistle of Barnabas* 21) and with the advice that his readers should prepare themselves for the coming new age.

Like Ignatius, the author of this document made it clear that he regarded the new movement as distinct from Judaism. In differentiating the two, he made provocative—even outrageous—claims. As Bart D. Ehrman observes, "For this author, the Jewish Scriptures can be understood only in light of Christ; for him, the Old Testament is a Christian, not a Jewish, book."[5] Carrying Paul's delegitimizing of Judaism to a greater extreme, the *Epistle of Barnabas* asserted that Jews do not have a covenant with God and that they fail even to understand their own writings. The unspoken conclusion of his position was evident: Judaism had no mission, mandate, or writings.

The *Epistle of Barnabas* was written during a time of crisis, but that we one cannot now determine. The author mentioned mysteriously that "these are evil days" (*Epistle of Barnabas* 2), but that could apply to many periods of history. He referred obliquely to three rulers being simultaneously humbled (*Epistle of Barnabas* 4:5), but these men cannot now be identified. He knew that the Temple itself had been destroyed, and he referred to a brief period when hopes were momentarily raised that the Temple might be rebuilt. But these were dashed after the decisive Second Jewish Revolt Against Rome in the 130s. The best we can date this letter is sometime after 70 and before 135.

NO JEWISH COVENANT

Immediately after warning his readers about "the crisis," he cautioned them about thinking that "the covenant is both theirs and ours" (*Epistle of Barnabas* 4:6), that is, imagining that both Christians and Jews share the same covenant with God. Those who kept both the Sabbath as well as the Lord's Day and who continued to observe Torah might hold this view, that there is one common covenant shared by both communities. For them, Christianity represented an "add-on" to Judaism, not a replacement. That view threatened many early Proto-Orthodox leaders bent on establishing their authority which they would not share with any rabbi. It also violated their understanding of the faith received from Paul. They would have none of it.

As far as the author of this letter was concerned, however, there was one and only one covenant, namely, the one between God and Christians. It is not as if there were an "old" covenant and now a "new" one that replaced it. Nor are there two separate and parallel covenants, each one having its own legitimacy and both being still in force—an ancient one with the Jewish people still applicable to them and a newer one with Christians. Rather, there is just one covenant, and that is the one between God and the Christians. So there is no Jewish covenant, not now, and, it appears, not ever.

This writer advanced an innovative argument. The Jewish people, he said, immediately forfeited the covenant shortly after Moses received it. This was a much stronger claim than Paul had put forward in Galatians. For the *Epistle of Barnabas*, a time of Torah *never* existed. It was null and void right from the start. This represents a startling claim, given the amount of space devoted to the provisions of the Torah in the first five books of the Bible.

Quoting Exodus 31:18, this author contended that Moses received the covenant from the Lord, "stone tablets written with the finger of the Lord's own hand" (*Epistle of Barnabas* 7). However, Barnabas said, the Jewish community immediately lost it. As Moses descended from the mountain, he encountered the Israelites worshipping an idol, the golden calf. He took the two tablets and smashed them on the ground. Barnabas said that this action makes the situation clear: the smashing of the tablets meant the termination of the covenant. Thus he concluded that the Jewish people had no covenantal relationship with God. Never did. They forfeited it almost as soon as it was delivered.

This line of interpretation ignores the continuation of the story in Exodus in which the covenant was reinstated by God with the Jewish people. Moses was instructed to take two new tablets of stone. God said, "I will write on the tablets the words that were on the former tablets, which you broke" (Exodus 34:1). Barnabas also makes nonsense of such writings as Deuteronomy, which noted carefully how the covenant was ratified (see Deuteronomy 26). Prophets such as Amos, Hosea, Isaiah, Jeremiah, and Ezekiel would be rendered unintelligible on this view. They, after all, used the covenant as a basis for understanding contemporary events and for recalling people to the observance of Torah. Quite frankly, the argument would have convinced no one familiar with biblical texts.

But that's not all.

JEWISH MISUNDERSTANDING OF SCRIPTURE

The *Epistle of Barnabas* claimed that the Jewish dietary laws have been misunderstood by Jews as literal commandments. Rather they should be understood allegorically. For example, the commandment "do not eat pig meat" really meant that we should not associate with piggish people, the danger being that these traits would somehow stick to us. The injunction "not to eat birds of prey" indicated that we are not to congregate with people who do not know how to prepare their own food but who seize food belonging to others. Building upon the idea that rabbits multiply profusely, the dietary law "do not eat hare" really meant do not engage in perverse sexual activities. He also said that the commandment "do not eat the lamprey eel, the octopus or the cuttlefish"[6] required us not to be like people who are cursed and who hover in the mud.

The basis for this interpretation lies in his insistence that Moses was speaking spiritually. Barnabas contended that "an evil angel" (*Epistle of Barnabas* 9) had misled the Jewish people into thinking that the Torah was to be interpreted literally. The idea that dietary laws were an integral part of an overall holy lifestyle was not within the purview of the writer of this treatise. And where did he find this convenient "evil angel"? The whole thousand-year history interpreting and practicing the dietary laws as if they had to do with actual food was just dismissed. It's sheer propaganda, weakly defended.

Similarly, circumcision was not a physical matter. It was not a sign of anything, Barnabas maintained, since it was not a unique practice. Syrians and Egyptians, he noted, followed this custom as well. Abraham was the first Israelite to circumcise and to see this act in relation to a covenant with God.

However, this does not provide a justification for perpetuating the custom as a physical act. Abraham's circumcising men from his entourage had nothing to do with a physical operation. Rather the act was spiritual—and here Barnabas made a huge leap—and it pointed to Jesus.

Barnabas's argument was as creative as it was bizarre and far fetched. He claimed that Abraham was looking ahead toward Jesus when he performed circumcision. His rationale built upon numerology as it is found in the Greek text of Genesis.[7] The English translator of this letter, Staniforth, decodes it as follows. Abraham was said to have circumcised 318 individuals. Eighteen in Greek includes an iota (I) and an eta (E), that is, IE, which Barnabas took as an abbreviation for Iesus (Jesus). Three hundred is the Greek letter tau (T), which, he said, symbolized the cross. So, Barnabas confidently concluded, Abraham was pointing to Jesus, allegorically speaking. No one would consider advancing such a wild argument today.

It is interesting that Barnabas wanted to preserve the ancient scriptures. He did not advance to the point where he could confidently dismiss them entirely. But he was faced with an immense problem: how to set aside their clear meaning. He resorted to a method of interpretation that had been initially pioneered by the Stoics, who were faced with a similar situation: how to retain the time-honored myths of Hesiod and Homer without taking them literally. The solution was allegory. These stories were meant to convey spiritual truths, not literal ones. From time to time, this had appeared within Judaism. The Jewish philosopher Philo, for instance, had interpreted the various stages of the Exodus through the Sinai not as actual geographical locations but as moments in the soul's ascent to God. He, too, had allegorized the story of the Exodus. So it was a method not without precedent.

Barnabas's line of thought demonstrates the difficulties with allegorical interpretation in general. Rather than starting where we might start, with the text in its social and historical circumstances, allegorical hermeneutics starts with the interpreter and the conclusion that person wishes to draw from the text. Thus the method results in an imposition of meaning on a text, not a derivation from the text. The text is simply a convenient excuse for stating a position already arrived at.[8] It represents circular reasoning.

Barnabas also addressed the question of Sabbath observance. Here, not surprisingly, we find that he insists that the laws with respect to the Sabbath were not meant to be taken literally. The commandment was, of course, to "keep the Sabbath holy" (Exodus: 20:8), honoring the pause God established when he rested from the task of creation. We'd understand this to refer to the Sabbath established at the beginning of creation, with God finishing creation in six days and resting on the seventh day, declaring it holy. So our commemoration of the Sabbath would honor a *past* event. Not so, said Barnabas. In a remarkable interpretive twist, Barnabas asked us to consider that this Sabbath is nothing less than a *future* event. It was not one that existed in the remote past. It is not as if all the days of creation have already passed, including that Sabbath on the seventh day, he argued. He said we are still living in day six and have yet to reach year 7000 (each day being counted as a thousand years). So the Sabbath commandment really pertains to some future age, Barnabas argued.

Again, his point is that Jewish leaders have misunderstood their scriptures, thinking that creation is a done deal. Barnabas reinforced this line of interpretation by quoting a passage from Isaiah where God is portrayed as rejecting "new moons and Sabbaths" (*Epistle of Barnabas* 15 quoting Isaiah 1:13). Barnabas construed this as indicating that the prophets rejected Sabbath observances completely. That differs from our interpretation. We'd likely sense that what they objected to was the improper or insincere observance of the Sabbath.

The writing ended with Barnabas noting that the world was about to share the same fate as Satan: destruction. The end-time was at hand, and he urged his hearers to "be yourselves your own good lawgivers" (*Epistle of Barnabas* 21)—"yourselves," he said, not Moses and not Torah. This comes perilously close to saying that each believer is a law unto themselves.

Whatever we make of Barnabas's position, the intent of his argument was clear: no Jewish covenant ever. The Jewish leaders and people do not understand their own writings. Judaism was for him a religion based entirely on an illusion. It had absolutely no substance. As we have noted, this influential document circulated widely within early Christianity probably among Gentile Christians, in part because of its anti-Judaism sentiments and also because it was widely believed to have been written by Barnabas, one of Paul's traveling companions and, hence, apostolic in his authority.

JUSTIN MARTYR

The charge became more radical. Not only did the Jews misunderstand their own scriptures: in fact, these writings were not intended for them at all. Simply put, the Hebrew Bible and its Greek translation, the Septuagint, wasn't theirs at all. It's entirely a Christian text. So now not only is there no covenant, but Judaism is also devoid of writings. This audacious turn has the effect of robbing Judaism of its core scriptures and, as we shall see, of its heritage as Israel as well. Burton Mack pointed out this shift succinctly when he wrote: "The claim was that Christians were the legitimate heirs of the epic of Israel, that the Jews had never understood the intentions of their God, and that of the story of Israel, if one read it rightly, was 'really' about the coming of Christ".[9]

Paul paved the way for this shift when he claimed that his followers, not the Jewish people, were the true descendants of Abraham through Isaac.[10] This was intended to legitimize the heritage of his Christ Movement and to bypass the tradition from Moses to Jesus. This reinterpretation of Jewish history served the purpose of marginalizing it.

About ninety years after Paul wrote the Letter to the Galatians, an influential Proto-Orthodox writer named Justin Martyr advanced a much stronger claim. Born around the beginning of the second century in what is today the city of Nablus in the West Bank, Justin Martyr was an adult convert to Christianity. Like Augustine after him, he had made his way through Greek philosophy without finding intellectual satisfaction. He wrote extensively in defense of the truth of Proto-Orthodoxy, trying to convince emperors that they should abandon persecution of Christians and, instead, embrace the new religion. This, he said, was the true philosophy. At some point in his career, he moved to Rome and was likely martyred there in the mid 160s.

He set his sights on two opponents: Greek philosophy and Judaism. Only the latter concerns us here. Judaism, he asserted, had no scriptures of its own, and the church alone was the true Israel. This effectively stripped Judaism of its entire theological heritage. His position represented an outstanding tour de force, and he presented it audaciously in the context of "a dialogue" with, of all people, a rabbi, Trypho.

Justin Martyr wasn't just concerned with confiscating Judaism's entire heritage. His objective was much larger, to persuade Romans of the truth of the new movement. To accomplish this, he and other early Proto-Orthodox leaders had to establish that the religion did not represent a new, upstart, or novel message, but was rooted thoroughly in antiquity. We saw this earlier with the task that had confronted the author of the Book of Acts, only a few decades before Justin Martyr. Without a lengthy pedigree, Romans would not be attracted to its message. Some contended that the speculations of such ancient Greek philosophers as Plato and Pythagoras found their fulfillment in Christ. Justin Martyr, however, located the source of all ancient wisdom in the Old Testament, asserting that it reached the height of wisdom in the gospel of Jesus. As Paul had done before him, he tied the emerging church into the heritage of Judaism—without, of course, accepting the latter's beliefs and practices or acknowledging the central thrust of Old Testament writings.

Dating from the 130s, Justin Martyr's "dialogue" with Trypho was really a lengthy treatise or sermon, carefully differentiating the new religion from the old. Whether Trypho was a real rabbi, or a fictional one concocted for purposes of the dialogue, his position reflected what Justin Martyr took to be Jewish criticisms of early Christianity. Eusebius held the opinion that this dialogue represented a real exchange, between Justin Martyr and "Rabbi Tryphon"— "the most distinguished among the Hebrews of the day"—and that the conversation took place at Ephesus.[11] Rabbi Trypho advanced some good questions, but he was never really allowed within the dialogue to offer a rebuttal. So the "answers" remained unchallenged.

REJECTION OF JEWISH CLAIMS

Justin Martyr asserted that the covenant with the Jewish people through Moses was only temporary. This represented a different tack than the one taken in the *Epistle of Barnabas*, which stated that the Jewish people had forfeited the covenant altogether. Here Justin Martyr's account is similar to the one Paul had made almost a century earlier in Galatians, that the Torah was only for a specific period in history. The covenant with the Jewish people had a beginning (Moses) and an end (Jesus). Justin Martyr argued that there were many righteous Jewish individuals prior to Moses—Abraham, Isaac, Jacob, and many others. These individuals, however, were not under the law given by God through Moses, having lived centuries before the giving of the law on Mount Sinai. Yet they will be saved. This showed, he said, that Torah was not necessary for salvation.

He went on to claim that the true Israelites are the Christians, not the Jewish people:

> For the true spiritual Israel, and descendants of Judah, Jacob, Isaac and Abraham (who in uncircumcision was approved of and blessed by God on account of his faith, and called the father of many nations), are we who have been led to God through this crucified Christ. (*Dialogue with Trypho*, chapter 9)[12]

> Christ is the Israel and the Jacob, even so we, who have been quarried out from the bowels of Christ are the true Israelitic race.[13]

So, as Justin Martyr saw it, Christians were the true heirs to all of the promises to Abraham. As children of Abraham through faith, Christians will inherit "the holy land" and will be the means by which all the nations of the world shall be blessed. This cuts out any role for a continuing Judaism, which will not regain the land of Israel. Nor will Judaism be the instrument through which all the nations of the world will be blessed by God.

Finally, Justin Martyr contended that the biblical writings were not really intended for the Jewish community. Only the Christian religion held the key to understanding what they mean. As he observed, "for we believe them [the scriptures]; but you, though you read them, do not catch the spirit that is in them."[15] The method Justin Martyr used to establish these points seems alien to us today and completely unconvincing: selected proof texts, passages torn out of context, and heavy allegorizing, where every person and event is taken as pointing to Jesus. Scholars today would not give this fanciful methodology any credence whatsoever, however influential it was in antiquity. This approach overlooks the central thrust of the Hebrew Bible, which presents Torah as the constitution of the people of Israel, the human obligations of the covenant. Unfortunately, Trypho never got to challenge Justin Martyr's imaginative allegorizing, and so a real debate never emerged.

Justin Martyr did not adopt an historical approach to biblical interpretation, as we might—reading chronologically from Abraham forward, through Moses and the prophets, into the future promises of the end-time kingdom. Rather, he reversed the chronological order. He read back in time, from Jesus into earlier times, allegorizing along the way and then showing how all texts, so understood, pointed to Jesus. This tactic allowed Justin Martyr and the early Christian community generally to ignore the plain meaning of biblical writings and salvage these documents for their movement.

THE VIRGIN BIRTH

An example of Justin Martyr's methodology is provided by the proof text for the virginal conception and birth of Jesus. Some Christian leaders were familiar with problems connected with this portrayal of Jesus' special birth. For one thing, the genealogies in Matthew and Luke differ. They date the birth of Jesus differently, one to the reign of Herod the Great who died in 4 B.C., the other to a census in Judea in A.D. 6. They differ on the visitors, whether shepherds or wise men. And they diverged on what happened immediately after the birth, whether the family escaped into Egypt to avoid Herod's wrath or whether they headed up to Jerusalem as required by Jewish law for purification, circumcision, and the redemption of the firstborn.

Differences weren't the only problem. There was a far greater one. Both narratives contain genealogies, tracing Jesus' ancestry through Joseph, his father, back to King David. That lineage was needed to establish Jesus' potential claim to be a Davidic Messiah. Without descent from David, a messianic claim could not be defended. Alongside these genealogies, however, both Matthew and Luke presented their respective versions of the virgin birth. These accounts both postulate the view that Joseph was not Jesus' father. Rather the Holy Spirit was. This immediately creates a tremendous problem. What, then, are we supposed to make of these genealogies and the supposed descent from David? These are thrown into question. The virgin birth narratives destroy the value of these genealogies. If Jesus' father is not Joseph, why present genealogies that claim he was the link back to David? It is difficult to imagine how belief in a virgin birth can be at all reconciled with Jesus as a Davidic Messiah. The virgin birth story cancels out the possibility of a descent from David since it makes the lineage completely bogus.

Another major problem has to do with citing Isaiah 7:14 as a proof text for the virgin birth. The whole passage from Isaiah is worth noting, for it places the entire matter in the social and historical context of *its* times:

> *Again the Lord spoke to Ahaz, saying, Ask a sign of the Lord your God; let it be deep as Sheol or high as heaven. . . . Then Isaiah said: "Hear then, O house of David! Is it so little for you to weary mortals, that you weary my God also? Therefore the Lord himself will give you a sign. Look, the young woman is with child and shall bear a son, and shall name him Immanuel. He shall eat curds and honey by the time he knows how to refuse the evil and choose the good. For before the child knows how to refuse the evil and choose the good, the land before whose two kings you are in dread will be deserted."* (Isaiah 7:10–16)

Looking at the whole passage makes the context clear. In 734–733 B.C., King Ahaz of Judah was faced with a serious crisis. He was confronted with a coalition of enemies. King Rezin of Aram had formed an alliance with King Pekah of Israel to attack the Southern Kingdom, Judah. Ensconced in the royal palace in Jerusalem, King Ahaz was rightfully concerned. He asked for a sign from God, and this the prophet Isaiah provided. That sign was that before a young woman could conceive and bear a child and before that child would reach the age when he could distinguish right from wrong, the two menacing kings will have backed down. The Hebrew word for "young woman" is *almah*. Clearly the reference had to do with some event that would be forthcoming *at the time of* Ahaz and Isaiah. It was a way of saying that within a few years, the crisis will have disappeared, and that Ahaz should not be worried. It makes no sense whatsoever in context to think of a sign that would come true some seven hundred years later. That would have given King Ahaz no reassurance or comfort at all.

The Hebrew word *almah* (a young woman who may or may not be physically a virgin) is translated in the Greek Septuagint as *parthenos*. This is a much more specific word, indicating a woman who is physically a virgin. Justin Martyr seized upon this Greek translation, ignoring the original Hebrew text, and proceeded to use this proof text. Matthew had made the same move earlier.

Here's where Rabbi Trypho really shone. He raised a surprisingly modern objection, that the passage cited has been shorn of its historical context. He pointed out that this interpretation makes no sense as a sign or word of reassurance that the crisis will soon be averted. Clearly the text has been misapplied. Rabbi Trypho did not stop there, however; he went on to point out that the idea of a virgin birth was not something new, having its origin in Greek mythology. As the following passage makes clear, one such example is Perseus, who also had a virgin birth:

And Trypho answered, "The Scripture has not, 'Behold, the virgin shall con-
ceive, and bear a son,' but, 'Behold, the young woman shall conceive, and bear
a son,' and so on, as you quoted. But the whole prophecy refers to Hezekiah,
and it is proved that it was fulfilled in him, according to the terms of this
prophecy. Moreover, in the fables of those who are called Greeks, it is written
that Perseus was begotten of Danae, who was a virgin; he who was called
among them Zeus having descended on her in the form of a golden shower."[16]

So not only did Christianity face the problem of having misapplied an ancient
scripture: it also had too many virgin births on its hands. If Perseus and others
also had virgin births, this would have the effect of undermining the claim that
Jesus was unique. Trypho also claimed that according to Jewish expectation,
the Messiah will be human.[17] The debate continued, and the fanciful, complex
allegorizing details of Justin Martyr's response need not detain us here. Trypho,
however, succeeded in opening up an intriguing line of thought.

JEWISH AWARENESS OF CHRISTIAN CLAIMS

The importance of Justin Martyr's dialogue is twofold. It served his purpose of
dismissing Judaism, appropriating for Christian purposes the entire Hebrew
Bible. No longer was it the property of Judaism. If Justin Martyr were correct,
they shouldn't even be reading or interpreting it. It wasn't theirs to use. This
dialogue also provides us with important evidence that at least some early
Christians were aware of the way its evolving message was being received by
ancient Jewish leaders. Justin Martyr would not have concocted this series of
debates with a Jewish leader if these did not represent real issues that perplexed
people of the time. The positions were not "straw men"; they constituted important current charges that had to be refuted. His work provides evidence not
only that Jewish leaders were reading what early Christians were writing, criticizing major inconsistencies and providing their followers with counterargu-
ments, but also that Christians were aware of their critical position. These
charges had chiefly to do with the problem for messianic claims about Jesus
generated by the virgin birth theory, the pagan image of the Christ, and the
failure of Jesus so far to fulfill the task of a Jewish Messiah.

CULTURAL APPROPRIATION

By the time of Justin Martyr in the 130s, we have major cultural appropriation.
As far as the Proto-Orthodox Christians were concerned, the church had become the new Temple, and they were the true Israelites. The historic mission

of Judaism—"the light to the nations," the nation through "whom all the families of the earth shall be blessed"—was relocated within the Christian movement. With Sabbath services and festivals rejected, everything that was of value within Judaism was confiscated for Christian use: the covenant, the Hebrew scriptures, as well as the entire Jewish mandate. As these writers saw it, there simply was no purpose in Judaism continuing.

What did these public relations exercises achieve? They probably made no direct impact on evolving Judaism faced with other pressing concerns at the time. They did, however, establish a climate of extreme hostility, the Proto-Orthodox versus their Jewish neighbors. Likely these writings provided reassurance and comfort to Proto-Orthodox believers, indicating that they were chosen by God and destined for eternal life secure in the knowledge that theirs was the one true religion endorsed by God himself. It may also have scared off those who wished to cling, for whatever reason, to ancient Jewish customs and practices.

15

ATTACKING THE JEWISH CONCEPT OF GOD

Dashed religious hopes can create profound anxiety and intellectual dislocation as people begin to ask, what has gone wrong? The destruction of the Temple illustrates this. The Jews believed that surely God would protect his Temple and his holy city, Jerusalem. That was the confident assertion of many of the Psalms, which took comfort in proclaiming that God would protect his people in this place: "For the Lord has chosen Zion; he has desired it for his habitation: 'This is my resting place forever; here I will reside'" (Psalm 132:13–14). The psalmist tells the people to "Pray for the peace of Jerusalem: 'May they prosper who love you. Peace be within your walls, and security within your towers'" (Psalm 122:6–7). Yet, in 70, the unimaginable happened: the destruction of the Temple, the city, and, according to Josephus, over a million Jewish lives. Deep dismay ran throughout the Jewish community. How could this have happened? If Zion (Jerusalem) was God's dwelling place and it had been destroyed, where was God now? Were the promises of protection to be believed?

Difficult questions also existed on the side of the Proto-Orthodox Christians. Important issues had bubbled to the surface, and there were also some significant unmet promises that provoked considerable anxiety. By the 140s, just over a century after Jesus' death, people were asking hard questions about the shape of the new religion.

WHY KEEP THE JEWISH WRITINGS?

For one thing, they asked, why should the Jewish writings be retained? It is important to remember that even by the 140s, there was as yet no Christian

Bible—no "old" versus "new" testament. We need to recognize that what was considered scripture was fluid for centuries. Nor should we imagine that every Proto-Orthodox congregation had easy access to all the writings now included in our Old and New Testaments. Likely they possessed very few, and the ones they did have might very well not have been writings that were eventually included in our New Testament, the precise contents of which were not decided upon until the late fourth century.

In practice, early Christians used the Septuagint, the Greek translation of the Hebrew Bible. They probably differed on what status they accorded it, however, given the distaste the Proto-Orthodox had toward its message. When would they ever have had the opportunity to read it? And why? What purpose would that serve, except perhaps to show that the ancient Jewish scriptures pointed the way to Jesus?

Paul's letters began to be circulated, probably as a collection, but not used by the Ebionites. Different gospels were issued and treasured by different factions within early Christianity. The Proto-Orthodox, Ebionites, and Gnostics all read their own favorites, ignoring the others. There was no common body of literature to which all of the early factions within Christianity subscribed. Each of the various communities gathered around the texts it preferred and that reinforced its "take" on the religion. The process was circular. Each community produced writings that reflected their own point of view. Then they used these writings to bolster their position. Writings with which they disagreed, reflecting the viewpoints of others, were rejected as "false teachings" or "heretical." Thus the Proto-Orthodox rejected the Gnostic scriptures. The Ebionites rejected all of Paul, the Gospels of Luke and John, and the virgin birth portions of Matthew. This really complicated theological debate, for the various factions were not arguing from the same base of evidentiary texts.

Scores of writings survive from early Christianity that were considered authoritative by some communities but did not end up being included in the New Testament. These include dozens of Gnostic writings as well as such influential Proto-Orthodox texts as the *Epistle of Barnabas, 1 Clement,* and the prized romance, the *Acts of Thecla*.[1] The latter writing told the story of the heroic deeds of Thecla who underwent tremendous pain and suffering in her quest to join the new faith. She heard Paul preaching and responded eagerly to his asceticism, rejecting marriage and sexuality. She abandoned her fiancé, defied her family, amazed Paul, fended off a potential rapist, escaped torture, and, after baptizing herself, engaged in a productive Christian missionary career. The work was a first-rate romance, urging women to renounce marriage as a way of entering into the public domain in a leadership capacity. It was the favorite reading of many a Christian in the second century.

Another Proto-Orthodox document that did not get included in the new Testament was the extremely influential *Infancy Gospel of James*.[2] Dating from the midsecond century, this interesting writing explored the special birth of Mary, the mother of Jesus, as well as her exceptional, pure upbringing at home and in the Temple. This document puts forward the concept of the immaculate conception. This concept differs from that of the virgin birth, for it applies to Mary, not Jesus. According to this writing, Mary also had an exceptional birth under mysterious circumstances. When she was twelve, Joseph, a much older widower, became her protector-husband. Four years later, at age sixteen, she became pregnant by the Holy Spirit. The narrative then turns to the birth of Jesus. Mary gives birth in a miraculous way to Jesus in a cave—not in a stable or manger—just outside Bethlehem. The ancient Church of the Nativity in Bethlehem is built over a cave, reflecting this long-standing tradition. This site is still accessible to visitors today.

The *Infancy Gospel of James* substantially advanced the theology of Mary, answering the question of why she, of all the Jewish women of the time, had been chosen by God to be the mother of Jesus. Later documents would build upon this writing. As Jesus became increasingly viewed as divine, Mary became spoken of not only as "Mother of Jesus" but also as "Mother of God," understood as mother of God incarnate. Some, recognizing her closeness to Jesus, referred to her as "Co-Redemptrix," that is, co-redeemer, for her crucial role in salvation history. The *Infancy Gospel of James* almost made it into the canon of the New Testament.

It was not until the late-second century that the idea of a "new" versus an "old" testament emerged. Nor were the contents of what is now known as the New Testament determined until 367. In that year, Bishop Athanasius in Egypt issued a famous letter that listed the twenty-seven books that now make up this collection. The shape of the New Testament was determined politically by the Proto-Orthodox faction favored by Constantine and subsequent Roman emperors. The New Testament was a partisan document that supported one—but only one—faction of early Christianity.

With the proliferation of new writings and the rejection of Torah observance on the part of the Christ congregations, the question naturally arose: Why preserve the Jewish writings at all? What possible Christian use could they reinforce? Actual Proto-Orthodox practices were clearly at odds with the Jewish teachings reflected in these documents. Why create bewilderment among newcomers to the fold? Why expose new, Gentile converts to a body of literature whose central teaching—that of Torah observance—was ultimately to be rejected? Why read or refer to such literature when its primary message had then to be shunted aside or drastically reinterpreted? It simply was not germane to their experience—not the least bit relevant, except with the wildest of intellectual gyrations.

In the previous chapter, we noted how early writers within Proto-Orthodoxy rejected the Jewish interpretation of scripture. They teased out of the texts fanciful allegorical interpretations to explain away the clear requirements of dietary, circumcision, and Sabbath laws. These explanations probably struck many at the time (as they do us) as ridiculous, contrived, and completely unpersuasive. But allegory represented one way of salvaging the Hebrew Bible for Christian purposes.

Others invented links between the Old Testament and the growing body of Christian literature in a desperate attempt to preserve the relevance of the ancient Jewish writings. Were there, they wondered, covert references to Jesus within selected passages of the Jewish writings, especially in the Prophets? Matthew, for instance, had attempted to do this, wrenching a passage in Isaiah from its original historical context to refer to a virgin birth of Jesus. Still others resorted to imaginative devices, suggesting that occurrences in the Jewish writings be seen as "types" or a "foreshadowing" of later Christian events. The crossing of the Red Sea (or Sea of Reeds), for example, could be seen as a type of baptism, the crossing of the Christian convert from death into new life. Moses on Mount Sinai was a type of Jesus on the mount giving his famous sermon as the new Moses. Joshua entering Canaan by crossing the Jordan River was a type of Jesus entering the afterlife. This "recycling of history" approach was also as imaginative as it was arbitrary, and in this, typology did not differ from allegory. But, for some, it preserved the relevance of the Jewish writings: they foretold the Christian message, albeit in an obscure fashion.

All these maneuvers only delayed the inevitable question: Why read the ancient opaque texts at all, especially when newer writings were available?

Around 140, one of the most brilliant Christian minds of the second century, an influential leader named Marcion, proposed a radical strategy for understanding the Jewish scriptures, one that he thought was consistent with the views of Paul. He questioned the assumption that the Christian community needed to retain the ancient Jewish writings at all. His position will be examined shortly.

IN WHAT SENSE WAS JESUS A MESSIAH?

Another issue that bothered Christians midsecond century was how should Jesus be understood *as a Messiah*. The criteria for being the Messiah were clear in Jewish writings. The Messiah was expected to assist God in restoring Israel and Jerusalem to prominence, bringing about the universal worship of the one God, establishing universal peace, ending wickedness, and redeeming the righteous. The Messiah would be instrumental, as God's agent, in inaugurating a new world order. It was not necessary that a Messiah have a special birth, be divine, suffer, or be resurrected any more than it would be necessary for any other just and righteous individual. All these considerations were utterly irrelevant to the

Jewish concept of the Messiah. What was essential was that the world be dramatically changed. Anyone living at the time of redemption would immediately recognize "the after" as fantastically different from "the before."

This hadn't happened. Political reality had failed to live up to religious expectations. The midsecond century was definitely not the messianic era. The world did not bask in universal peace. The worship of the one God did not exist. Israel and Jerusalem were not preeminent—Rome was absolutely triumphant. Because of the destruction caused by the two Jewish wars against Rome (66–70; 132–135), the Temple and its priesthood had been destroyed, the population was reduced, and Jerusalem was proclaimed a Roman city. Lee Levine traces the aftermath of the Second Jewish Revolt against Rome:

> *Aelia Capitolina was built on the site of Jerusalem. The city bore a decidedly pagan character for the next several centuries, and Jews were banned from the city. . . . The end of the Bar-Kokhba hostilities also saw the beginning of an exodus of Jews from their homeland to countries of the Diaspora. For the first time, we read of sages who took up residence in Babylonia. . . . In Palestine, the Jews were forbidden to observe some of their most traditional and basic practices, including prayer, study, circumcision, holiday observance, etc., for a number of years.*[3]

Clearly the messianic era had not yet arrived. Earlier on, in the first century, many had expected Jesus to return any moment, to actualize what he had announced. Leaders in Jerusalem had asked the resurrected Jesus if this was the time when he would "restore the kingdom to Israel" (Acts 1:6). They recognized that while Jesus had announced the Kingdom of God, it had not yet appeared. Fulfillment lay within the future. Time was marching on, however. How long could people cling to the view that redemption was at hand?

The members of the Dead Sea Scroll group had sustained their hope in imminent world transformation for well over a century. That was a remarkable achievement—most millennial sects cannot sustain an unrealized promise for so long. The Dead Sea Scroll community, however, witnessed their dreams dashed as the Romans swept down from the Galilee in 68, crushing Qumran in its path. Burying their scrolls in caves around Qumran, they anticipated that they would survive the temporary Roman setback, and would return to retrieve their precious hoard, and wait for God's triumph to materialize. This never transpired.

Somewhat later, Rabbi Akiva's hopes that Bar Kokhba would be revealed as the Messiah were also dashed in the 130s during the Second Jewish Revolt against Rome. That brave revolt had been decisively defeated by Rome. In the contemporary world, many wonder how long the devoted followers of Rabbi Schneerson will wait for him to return to be unveiled as the Messiah? How long is long enough? This was the same issue that Christians back in the second century faced: How long could they wait, sustaining the expectation, week after week, year after year, that Jesus would return soon to complete what he had announced?

WHERE WAS THE PROMISED KINGDOM?

Christians advanced differing strategies for dealing with the delay of the promised messianic era. Probably some quit the movement, as failing to live up to its promises. This often happens with millennial sects that promise something dramatic on a specific date that fails to materialize: the movement then peters out. This happened to the Christian groups that gathered on the Mount of Olives, east of Jerusalem, on December 31, 1999, in the belief that surely this would be an auspicious time for God to make good on his promises. They were there ready to greet the Messiah at the stroke of midnight, at the dawn of the new millennium, having sold all their possessions back in the United States.

Some second-century Christians continued to say that, eventually, Jesus would return to bring about the Kingdom of God on earth. That is, after all, what he talked about and promised, and they clung to this hope. This represents a "this-worldly" or literal interpretation of the expectation. As the decades passed, enthusiasm for this approach withered. What is the length of a promise that does not materialize? How long can an unmet promise be sustained as a legitimate hope without its eventually being perceived as false?

But there were other ways of coping with the problem of the delayed reappearance. Some began to spiritualize the concept, maintaining that the promised messianic era was not a political entity—not a transformed world after all. On this view, the Kingdom of God came to be located within the hearts and minds of believing Christians. The Kingdom message became reinterpreted as something spiritual—something available to everybody, in the here and now. This meant abandoning the expectation that *the world* would be changed in favor of the view that *people* would be changed. In this view, the Kingdom was a present reality that all could access. There was no need to wait for Jesus to return. Gnostics—the ancient "New Agers"—veered in this direction, contending that "the living Jesus" was available everywhere, for all who search sincerely for insight. For them the Kingdom of God was a present reality. It was just there, waiting for insightful people to discover it.

Others, however, adopted a *supernatural* interpretation. On this view, the Kingdom of God was attainable in an afterlife, in a place or state called heaven, not on earth. Christians would be rewarded with eternal life in a heaven, a supernatural realm, after death. Nonbelievers would be relegated to a hell, either a place of punishment or a state of nonexistence. Thus there was no need for Jesus to return. A supernatural interpretation meant that the dream of a transformed world was abandoned. This was not, however, the biblical expectation at all. The world to come is depicted as a transformation of this earth, and resurrection as a coming back to life on this planet. The supernatural heaven-hell reinterpretation of the Kingdom message *spatialized* the message that was originally *temporal* in nature.

The original concept of resurrection, whether from the Pharisaic or Christian camp, viewed redemption as something that would happen on earth at some *time* in the future, at a point in history when God will make good on his promises to restore the world to its original pristine form, without sin and without evil. Those righteous people who are alive when this happens will automatically be transformed, to suit conditions in the new terrestrial environment. Those who had died—and were righteous—would come back to life, transformed, again to suit the circumstances of the newly created world. Paul set forth this view of resurrection, for instance, toward the end of his letter 1 Corinthians, and, in this, he builds on the traditional Jewish view. Thus, in its inception, the idea of redemption was a temporal one: the righteous will inherit the earth, at some point *in the future*, when God decides to re-create the world. The dead are truly dead, "waiting" for resuscitation by God at some point at the end of time.[4]

The heaven-hell reinterpretation represented a new concept on the Christian scene, one that is not typically found within the biblical narrative. It is a *spatial* concept, locating the afterlife in another dimension, place, or state, which we enter immediately upon death. The origin of this approach lies within Greek philosophy—the works of Plato, Orphism, and the neo-Platonists in particular— or within ancient Egyptian religion, the religion of the pharaohs with its examination and judgment upon the individual soul at death. According to the Egyptian *Book of the Dead,* Osiris and forty-two judges weigh the human soul in accordance with forty-two criteria for admission into the afterlife. This *otherworldly* view is often tied in with a view of human personality as involving an immortal soul, an indestructible soul substance. According to this view, judgment occurs at the time of death, and then the immortal soul is sentenced to a future eternity, either in heaven or hell (or, in some theologies, in an intermediate state called purgatory).

These otherworldly interpretations of the expectation preserved the emphasis on transformation, either spiritually in this life or supernaturally after death. Both reinterpretations, however, abandoned the need for a return of Jesus to transform the world. Thus there was no waiting for Jesus to return and so the problem of the delay was solved. This was not, however, the original biblical expectation. These otherworldly interpretations represented creative solutions to an immense pastoral problem faced by early Christian leaders.

These differing strategies are still at work within contemporary Christianity. Some look for a transformed universe with Jesus the Messiah returning to

Israel—soon, within our lifetimes. This is typical of the theology of Evangelical Christianity. Others look for individuals transformed spiritually or redeemed in a heavenly afterlife, views often found within liberal Protestantism and Catholicism. Contemporary discussion today mirrors the divergence of views found within second-century Christianity regarding the true identity of the Kingdom of God.

As we shall see, Marcion confronted this important problem and offered an innovative, more radical strategy for understanding Jesus as Messiah.

WHO WAS JESUS, REALLY?

Finally, there was growing concern how best to interpret the nature of Jesus. While the earliest gospel, Mark, had focused on the adult mission of Jesus, later ones such as Matthew and Luke claimed a special birth for Jesus. Remarkably, these were the only two writings in the New Testament that put forward virgin birth stories. Mark did not mention it, nor did Paul or the Gospel of John. The idea of a virgin birth was not rooted in Jewish thought—although there were unusual births to women well past menopause—nor was it part of messianic expectation. The Messiah, on most views, was to be fully human, not a God-human hybrid. The virgin birth concept was Gentile in origin. Whatever the intent of the unknown writers of Luke and Matthew, the virgin birth narratives in no way singled out Jesus as unique. Roman emperors, Greek heroes, and ancient Egyptian pharaohs all claimed special births, and these parallels are now well known.

In ancient Egyptian times, for instance, two pharaohs had claimed special divine-human births or "theogamies." In the fifteenth century B.C., Queen Hatshepsut claimed a divine-human origin in a relief in her splendid temple, Deir el-Bahri, near the Valley of the Kings at Luxor. The god Amon is depicted as her father and Queen Ahmose as her mother. Similarly, in the fourteenth century B.C., in the magnificent Temple of Luxor, Amenhotep III is depicted as having a divine-human birth. In this instance, a sequence is presented with an annunciation of an impending special birth; the conception between the god Amon and the human Queen Mutemwiya; the birth; and the presentation. This annunciation-birth-presentation narrative is suspiciously similar to the sequence outlined in the virgin birth story in Luke.

Freke and Gandy as well as Harpur point out many similarities between the special birth of Jesus and the divine-human births of other religious and political figures.[5] These include Attis (a god and virgin mother Cybele); Pythagoras (god Apollo and human mother Parthenis), Caesar Augustus (god Apollo and mother Atia), the Persian religious figure Zoroaster, and many more.

The growing interest in the late first century and early second century in the divine-human birth of Jesus reached its pinnacle in the *Infancy Gospel of James*. Its focus was partly on Mary's special birth under mysterious circumstances as well as the virgin birth of Jesus. Because of her exceptional purity and her own "immaculate" conception, Mary was chosen by God to be the bearer of Jesus. At the very young age of sixteen, according to this document, she gave birth to Jesus. This occurred in such a way that there was no distension of the hymen, so that Mary remained physically a virgin throughout the entire process. In fact, a midwife, Salome, had the temerity to doubt God and conducted a bold postpartum examination. This somewhat lurid document vastly extended the interest raised by Matthew and Luke in the divine birth of Jesus.

This dovetailed with another development. With the growing problems surrounding the messianic status of Jesus and the failure of the world to be changed dramatically as expected, the spotlight shifted to the divine aspect of the person of Jesus. The virgin conception and virgin birth stories paved the way for the development of the God-human. Ancient mystery religions shared similar motifs. The religious figure of the mystery cults was viewed as having a special divine-human birth; as being a God incarnate (a special Son of God); and as suffering, dying, and rising to save mankind. That's the common pattern.

This figure of the God-human was well known throughout the Mediterranean world of the time, and, in various forms, it was the theological underpinning of many Gentile religions of the time. Egyptian religion provided the cult of Osiris, a divine being who suffered, died, and rose from the dead and who granted righteous individuals eternal life. In Greece, Dionysus was the offspring of the god Zeus and the mortal Semele, and he, too, constituted a dying-rising God-man savior. The religion of Mithraism from Persia, focusing on the God-man Mithras, exhibited the same features. These parallels in no way diminished the stature and importance of Jesus. They placed him on a par with other major religious and political leaders of his time. They did not, however, make him unique. Contemporary Christianity may wish to view Jesus as unique in being a divine-human, but this perspective forgets the Mediterranean world into which early Christianity was born. Today we may think of these beliefs as distinctively Christian, but second-century Christians did not. They were exceptionally hard pressed to explain to their non-Christian counterparts why their beliefs were so similar to theirs.

Curiously, the problem in the second century is not *our* problem. We know of no "virgin births." They knew too many. That was *their* problem.

Portraying Jesus as a figure well known to Mediterranean audiences represented a convenient way of speaking about him in a manner that involved no references to Judaism or to the Jewish Messiah. It was timely to substitute this divine-human hybrid image of Jesus for the older view of Jesus as a human Messiah. The Messiah concept necessitated a search through Jewish scriptures, themselves already scorned by Christian writers, for proof texts. It also invited difficult questions and lengthy explanations of why the world had not yet dramatically changed as envisaged in the messianic era. The dying-rising savior Christ God-human was a much easier portrait. It offered all the advantages: no need to probe Jewish scriptures for possible messianic references, and a less-complicated "sell" with a Gentile audience. This shift from Messiah to Christ fitted fortuitously into the de-Judaism initiatives of early Christian authors. Marcion made the significance of this shift in perspective extremely apparent.

So who was Marcion?

MARCION

Marcion was one of the most colorful, engaging, thoughtful, and intriguing figures in early Christianity. His provocative views acted as a prod for forcing Christians to rethink many of the fundamentals of the movement. As Burton Mack puts it,

> *Marcion of Sinope triggered the explosion. . . . As he looked around at his fellow Christians, some things did not make sense. Christians were still trying to be loyal to the Jewish God even after they learned that they did not have to keep his law. But the God who gave the Jews their law could not be the same God who sent his son to proclaim mercy.*[6]

MARCION'S LIFE

Marcion was born around 110 into a Christian family in Sinope, on the northern Black Sea coast of modern Turkey. He became a wealthy businessman, the owner of a fleet of ships, a powerful merchant whose transport vessels helped move goods around the Mediterranean. He was an entrepreneur, not a theologian, and this is important, for he injected a note of reason into the thinking of early Christianity. Like many businesspeople, he cut to the chase. Just prior to 140, he moved to the strategic center of the Roman Empire, the city of Rome itself. During the 130s or 140s, he began to formulate his religious ideas, producing an influential work called *Antitheses,* which exploded some of the comfortable assumptions second-century Christians were fond of making. This writing has, unfortunately, not survived, but his position can be reconstructed from the views of his later opponents. Some sixty or seventy years after Marcion, for instance, the Proto-Orthodox leader Tertullian took the time to write a five-volume work titled *Against Marcion.*[7] What Marcion said made the Proto-Orthodox extremely uncomfortable, for it had the ring of logic to it.

Marcion forced his contemporaries to confront the stark contradictions between the Hebrew scriptures and the writings of Paul. He was impressed by Paul's strong contrast between the slavery of Torah observance and the freedom brought about through Christ. That simplified Judaism, as far as he was concerned. It represented a clear, straightforward religion, one that he could grasp . . . and sell. Being probably the most consistently Pauline thinker who ever lived, he methodically and logically traced the implications of this dichotomy for Christian life. He demonstrated what happens when the abolition of Torah is taken seriously and consistently. His conclusions were astounding. He clearly saw that Paul's religion was new and grasped that it did not make any pretensions of being a Judaism or related to Judaism in any way. He understood exactly where Paul's thought was headed, and he had the audacity to say it out loud. Thus he rejected not only the validity of the Old Testament but also the Jewish concept of God and the view that Jesus was the promised Jewish Messiah.

Marcion's bold claims were not accepted by other Christian communities, and he was excommunicated by the Proto-Orthodox in Rome around 144. This did not stop him from establishing Christian congregations of his own, and he viewed himself as standing in the succession from Paul. If others wished to shy away from the implications of what Paul said, then Marcion's attitude was, so be it. Marcionite Christianity survived in many centers within the Roman Empire for several centuries. Had he not advocated celibacy for his followers, consistent with Paul's ascetic theology, it might have lasted much longer. According to Marcion, marriage was not supported by Paul's writings.

MARCION'S VIEW OF GOD

Marcion began by contrasting two passages—one from the Hebrew Bible and one from the Gospel of Luke. On the one hand, the prophet Isaiah in the Old Testament said, "I am the Lord, and there is no other. I form light and create darkness, I make weal and create woe; I the Lord do all these things" (Isaiah 45:6–7). Here God is portrayed as saying that he created not only good, but evil as well. That simplifies the problem of evil. It is not the result of a Satan or a proclivity toward depravity found within human nature (a wicked impulse, for instance). Rather, as this passage views it, bad things happen as the result of divine agency. God alone is responsible for both good and evil. This is not the usual explanation for evil found in the Old Testament, but it is present in this text of Isaiah.

On the other hand, the Gospel of Luke had Jesus say, "No good tree bears bad fruit, nor again does a bad tree bear good fruit; for each tree is known by its own fruit" (Luke 6:43–44). Marcion interpreted this as affirming that evil can only come from evil, whereas good can only come from good. Thus God cannot be the author of evil, on this view. There must be another source for evil.

Two passages. Two different views. God is both responsible and not responsible for evil. What should be made of these two contradictory positions when lined up side by side in this contrasting fashion? Clearly, Marcion said, there must be two gods.[8] There is the real God who is good and who produces good things. In addition, there has to be an evil God as well, one who produces malevolency. Logic as well as biblical revelation demanded it. The God who created evil was a lesser God and had nothing of the status of the real God. This supreme God was the authentic God, the one who was truly good and responsible for producing good things.

Marcion's next move was interesting, for he squarely tackled the Jewish concept of God—at least as he saw it. He equated the evil God with the Creator God of the Jewish writings. As he read the Jewish scriptures, God was described in harsh, warlike, and highly judgmental terms. This God was strict, stern—a God of law rather than one of love, compassion, and grace. As Tertullian put it, "we know full well that Marcion makes his gods unequal: one judicial, harsh, mighty in war; the other mild, placid, and simply good and excellent."[9] This God arrogantly claimed to be the only God and seemed to lack awareness of a greater divinity. This, of course, ignores the many passages in the Hebrew scriptures that describe God as one of mercy and compassion—for example, "The Lord, the Lord, a God merciful and gracious, slow to anger, and abounding in steadfast love and faithfulness" (Exodus 34: 6); and "But you, O Lord, are a God merciful and gracious, slow to anger and abounding in steadfast love and faithfulness" (Psalm 86:15). But Marcion overlooked these in his haste to stereotype—and renounce—the God of the Hebrew Bible.

The supreme God, however, was the one revealed in Christ. This was truly the real God, a God of love, grace, and compassion who only produced good things. The existence of this God beyond the Creator God was not known, Marcion asserted, until Jesus came. That was Jesus' major role: to reveal to humanity the true nature of the real God. The authentic God was not the one portrayed in the Hebrew Bible, the one Marcion described as full of anger and judgment and causing fear, stress, and anxiety in humans. The real God loves, wants, desires, and embraces all humanity and is in no way responsible for evil or anything vile.

MARCION'S AUTHORITATIVE WRITINGS

Marcion rejected completely all the writings that Christians would later dub the Old Testament. The Jewish scriptures were false writings, presenting an inadequate portrait of God. They reflected the worship of the lower God. Unlike other early church leaders, he maintained that these scriptures were not to be interpreted away through clever allegory or some other fanciful means. They were just to be discarded as incompatible with Christian revelation. They were not to be used or read within a Christian context.

This forthright position cut through the problem created by Paul's rejection of Torah. As we have noted, Paul's views on Torah observance immediately threw into question the validity of the writings of the Hebrew Bible. Now that problem floated to the surface in a dramatic manner. If Torah was not to be observed by Christians and if Torah observance was the central message of these ancient Jewish writings, then why bother to retain and read them at all? That was a good question that perplexed many within the early church. Marcion's position was innovative: just get rid of them. There was no need to allegorize them, spiritualize them, or explain them away.

Marcion also mentioned absurd depictions of deity, if taken literally, in the Jewish writings. He noted God "walking" in the garden, for instance, God "repenting" of some error, God "asking questions" as if ignorant of the answer, and God "uncertain" of situations as if he did not know human conditions and events. All these portrayed God in an unflattering perspective and reinforced Marcion's view that this conception of God was inadequate. This critique reveals a very literal interpretive perspective on Marcion's part. He did not take into account the use of metaphor or other literary devices. Nor did he appear sensitive to the position that all descriptions of God are anthropomorphic by nature, since we are using human language to describe that which is beyond humanity. Even to ascribe goodness to God reflects a human understanding of what "good" means. Later, theologians would tackle the problem of human language used to discuss the divine. Many centuries later, a Christian thinker like Thomas Aquinas would propose that we speak of God only by way of analogy, and even then, based on "proper proportionality," that is, by preserving the proper distance between us and God.

Rejection of the Jewish writings had immediate consequences. It severed, for instance, Christianity from its Jewish roots. All the background writings vanished from the horizon, so there no longer existed a context in which to make sense of the Torah, dietary laws, Sabbath observances, or the festivals referenced within the gospels. This was not a problem for Marcion, however, for all these Jewish references were to be removed from Christian writings as totally irrelevant. Jesus was also detached from his Jewish roots—there was no context for understanding his life and mission within his cultural setting. Again, for Marcion, there was no problem. Just delete any reference to Jesus as a "fulfillment" of Jewish scripture. Christian living, for Marcion, did not involve history lessons. There was absolutely no need to back up and explain the whole historical tradition of Israel in order to grasp the essential nature of Paul's Christ. It just wasn't relevant. In fact, it was very likely that Marcion did not see Jesus as Jewish but as a universal emissary from the one true God speaking to humanity to liberate us from the shackles of ignorance.

On a more practical note, doing away with what became the Old Testament made it easier to attract converts. The required reading list was shorter. Much like Paul, Marcion's followers did not have to devote any time to studying the scriptures of an alien religion. They benefited from a much shorter collection of sacred texts. Gone was the Hebrew Bible, but also many of the writings from the growing Christian library. According to Marcion, many writings—including some now contained within the New Testament—contained false teachings as well and had to be discarded.

For Marcion, there were only eleven authoritative writings. That was his total Bible. All the useful writings, he maintained, derive from Paul. Tertullian informed us that Marcion had ten letters of Paul. But these were edited to eliminate all Jewish references. In addition, he used the Gospel of Luke, which he attributed to Paul—Luke was, he thought, Paul's gospel. Even this, too, was edited. In modern terms, he simply suggested hitting the Delete key to rid texts of troublesome references. And, like many other early Christian leaders, he did not think of these writings as unalterable sacred texts. He was not alone in altering texts: Matthew altered Mark, changing and omitting material, as did Luke. Later scribes also amended texts as they copied them, rendering them more useful to their respective constituencies.[10] In identifying these specific works as his evidentiary base, his authoritative literature, he was probably the first to develop a canon of Christian writings.

To simplify understanding the Christ, Marcion just eliminated passages he found "too Jewish." He downplayed, for instance, Jesus' origins, positioning Jesus instead as an exemplar of all humanity. He removed references to Jesus being in a synagogue or having fulfilled some passage mentioned in the Old Testament. In Paul's Letter to the Galatians, he dropped Abraham as an example of faith. Marcion was consistent: without an Old Testament, there existed no basis for understanding Paul's reference. So no knowledge of Judaism was presupposed in his portrait of Jesus.

Marcion was clear about his de-Judaising motivation. In addition to wanting to "universalize" Jesus, he provided a fascinating additional and telling rationale. Writers such as those who composed the Gospels of Mark, Matthew, and John simply had misunderstood Jesus. They were wrong and, as a result, they produced defective documents. That's why these gospels needed to be discarded. They did not understand the dimensions of Jesus' radical message about the true nature of God or the role of Jesus in securing liberation for all humanity. For Marcion, they also seemed wedded to the Jewish framework emanating from the Old Testament writings. As Tertullian noted, this criticism was applied by Marcion to the leaders in Jerusalem, including James, Peter, and John.[11] None of these early leaders, Marcion thought, understood the message correctly. He gave no credence to the pioneers of the Jesus Movement who knew the Jesus of history and who perpetuated Jesus' practices.

Having dismissed the Jesus Movement from true understanding, Marcion now defended Paul's religion. It was precisely because these Jewishly oriented disciples failed to grasp Jesus' message that Paul was chosen to carry out the task—the new religion of liberation for all humanity. That's why he had been privileged to have a separate and distinctive revelation. Marcion took Paul at his word: his religion was radically new, having a different origin than the movement in Jerusalem and devoid of any attachments to Judaism. That new and unique revelation is what gave Paul authority. For Marcion, the Christ of experience conveyed through Paul was far more important to salvation than the Jesus of history, who had failed to communicate his message successfully. Marcion was clear: his religion grew out of Paul's. It was emphatically not from the Jesus Movement, nor from the teachings of the Jesus of history nor biblical Judaism. That, contended Marcion, was its merit.

Marcion's views confirm how radically different the Jesus and the Christ Movements truly were from each other. In this, he possessed an accurate grasp of the history that had occurred only a century or so before his own times. He discerned the contrast, spoke of it clearly, and grasped the startling innovativeness of Paul's message. Building solely on Paul, he was able to dismiss the entire Jewish heritage, its writings, as well as the perspective of the Jesus Movement and writers who did not fully share Paul's perspective. He reduced the clutter within the writings, stripping away everything that would detract from its central message: the revelation of the real God disclosed by Jesus.

It is questionable, however, whether he came down on the right side of authenticity. As he assessed the situation, everyone within the early Christian movement was wrong—except for Paul. It did not occur to him that the reverse might very well be true, that the other leaders such as James and the author of the Gospel of Matthew got it right and Paul didn't. This latter point represents the stance of the Jesus Cover-Up Thesis, a view Marcion definitely would not have shared. As we have seen, Paul was "the odd man out" when it came to Jesus and Torah observance.

A stripped-down list of authoritative books would have assisted in gaining converts within the Gentile world. Marcion's churches had no Old Testament to master and interpret. Nor did they have conflicting gospel accounts full of Jewish references that might lead one to suspect that there was a Jewish side to Jesus. With a shortened version of Luke's gospel alongside Paul's letters, focus could more easily be placed on the Christ rather than on the Jesus of history. Tertullian saved some of his choicest words for what Marcion did to the Gospel of Luke. He accuses Marcion of "adulterating the Gospel," favoring a "mutilated edition" of this writing. Such treatment, Tertullian says, was "sacrilegious."[12]

MARCION ON THE REAL JESUS

According to Marcion, Jesus was not the Jewish Messiah. He faced the objection squarely that Jesus had not accomplished what a Messiah was expected to do, namely, restore Israel and Jerusalem to prominence and assist in bringing about the messianic era characterized by universal peace and the worship of the one God. That person had yet to come and he was of little interest to Marcion. Again, Marcion's perspective confirmed the way Paul's Gentile cosmic Christ figure differed from Jesus and the Jewish political Messiah. He grasped the contrast clearly.

Jesus, the liberator of humanity from ignorance—that was Marcion's grand vision. The supreme God had sent Jesus into the world to rescue people from the clutches of the Creator God. He revealed the true identity of the real God and proclaimed love, compassion, and grace for all humanity. This message offered people a new hope through an insight into the authentic nature of the Supreme Being.

Marcion also contended that Jesus was not human—he only *appeared* to be human, a view characterized by scholars of early Christianity as "docetic." Jesus was a divine figure who entered the world to liberate humanity from blindness and error, being the teacher and emissary of the supreme deity. Since Jesus was not the Jewish Messiah, he would not be expected to return to fulfill the mandate of such a figure. He had had his day as an historical apparition and, quite frankly, he failed at that time to communicate his message to his earliest associates, who continued to think of him, in Jewish terms, as a potential Messiah. They just got it wrong. After his death, he communicated his new vision to Paul through a new revelation. Paul was the one who got it right.

This de-Judaising of the portrait of Jesus paved the way for alternate reconstructions of the significance of Jesus. Marcion as well as the rival Gnostics generally were content to view Jesus as a teacher of enlightenment. Others found the removal of the Jewishness of Jesus very convenient for promoting their universalizing views of him as the dying-rising savior God. We find that view reflected later in the second century, in the Proto-Orthodox's statement of faith, the Apostles' Creed, with all of the Jewish elements stripped away from this affirmation of belief.

MARCION'S LEGACY

Marcion attracted a considerable following, perhaps because his streamlining position resolved many complex confusions of the 140s. With Marcion, there was no need to read or interpret the Jewish writings, no history lessons, and no necessity to refer to the Old Testament to understand either the Christian faith

or Jesus. The Marcionite movement offered hope of liberation for all humanity without a lot of historical baggage. It constituted a thoroughgoing simpli-
fication of the Christ Movement, building on and advancing the views of Paul
consistently.

Marcion also insisted that members of his churches accept celibacy and refrain from marriage. If Marcion had not insisted on this particular self-limiting
discipline, perhaps his churches, in time, would have rivaled other forms of early
Christianity in size. As it was, the Marcionite movement died out within several centuries and never reached the strength of the Proto-Orthodox or Gnostic Christian communities.

Marcion's critics reacted angrily to his depiction of two gods. About sixty
years later, early in the third century, Tertullian launched a counterattack
against Marcion and Marcionite Christianity. He tried to show the absurdity
of there being two Supreme Beings. He did so on logical grounds: by defining
"God" as a supreme being: "God is the great Supreme existing in eternity, un-
begotten, unmade without beginning, without end".[13]

It would follow from this definition that there cannot be two "supreme"
beings. Hence, there cannot be two gods. It is not clear if this charge really
meets Marcion's view of the two Gods, one of which is inferior to the other.
This Tertullian himself recognized, noting that Marcion held that the creator
God was "unequal" to the supreme God. Marcion's comeback would probably
have been that there really was only one supreme God. The other so-called
God—the creator God—was simply a pretender to the title, not a real God at all.

Marcion's views were partially shared by other communities in the second
and third centuries. The concept of a supreme God beyond a creator God
played an important role in Gnostic thinking. The *Apocryphon* or *Secret Book of
John*, for instance, produced probably in the midsecond century—slightly later
than the time of Marcion—echoed this thought.[14] For the author of this
work, the creator God was an ignorant deity who had created the world without any knowledge of a higher divinity. The world was therefore an imperfect
creation, which is what one would expect from an imperfect divinity. Since it
doesn't constitute humanity's true home, the objective of the Christian lay in
escaping from this prison. As Ehrman notes, this work, the *Apocryphon of John,*
"contains one of the clearest expositions of the Gnostic myth of creation and
redemption, an exposition designed, ultimately, to explain the existence of evil
in the world and the path of escape for those who recognize their plight."[15]
Gnostic churches sought to liberate people from the bonds of this imperfect
world full of evil, disasters, pain, and suffering by focusing on the one true
God. In this, it was similar to the Marcionite congregations. Marcion's single-
minded devotion to Paul, however, set these two movements apart.

With Marcion, we see the contours of a radical de-Judaising of Christianity.
He forced others to draw back from the logical consequences of Paul's extreme

views and to develop a more "centrist," less radical, view of faith fundamentals. In time, in the fourth century, especially after Constantine and Theodosius's favoring of Proto-Orthodox Christianity as the official religion of the Roman Empire, leaders shaped the religion along lines that are more recognizably modern. A canon of authoritative Christian writings, alongside the Septuagint, was developed by the late fourth century. A fuller statement of faith came to light in the Creed of Nicea in the early fourth century. Furthermore, ways of speaking about the divine and human nature of Jesus were thrashed out through the complex formulations of the doctrine of the Trinity.

In short, Marcion served as a major catalyst in shaping subsequent Christianity. He was instrumental in teaching people to view the writings that eventually became the New Testament primarily through the eyes of Paul. This had an enormous impact on the perceptual filter through which the Christian scriptures were interpreted. It helped to obscure the real differences that existed between early Christian leaders—James versus Paul, with the latter as "the odd man out." Paul was seen as the hero of the early Christian movement, while the others were relegated to obscurity and ignominy. Hence very few people today know and recognize the earliest form of Christianity led by Jesus' brother, James. In fact, if it were not for the sensationalism around the recent discovery of the burial ossuary of "James, son of Joseph, brother of Jesus," even fewer would know about James and his leadership in Jerusalem.[16]

This "Pauline prism" also serves to eliminate different views about Jesus within the writings of the New Testament. Matthew's portrait of Jesus, for instance, cannot be reconciled with that of Paul. The Jesus who taught extended Torah observance would hardly be the same Jesus who would authorize Paul to discard Torah completely. These represent two contrasting views of what Jesus stood for and what he wanted his followers to observe. Marcion at least had the merit of recognizing these disparities honestly, but his solution was simplistic. He simply eliminated documents, keeping only Paul's letters and an abbreviated version of Luke, which he attributed to Paul.

Second, he contrasted law and gospel, disparaging the former. The Old Testament is often stereotyped by Christians—then and now—as containing harsh laws from a stern God full of wrath and condemnation. The New Testament, on the other hand, is stereotyped as well, as presenting a God of love, compassion, and mercy. This oft-repeated dichotomy stems from Marcion's teachings and it has several effects. It distorts the teaching and examples of the Jewish writings tremendously—which challenge people to choose wisely and pursue a path of righteousness and social justice. It also serves as blanket permission for Christians to ignore or downplay the impact and significance of the Old Testament.

Marcion failed to take the message of the Old Testament seriously, dismissing these texts. While subsequent Christianity did include the Septuagint along with Christian writings as biblical, its use of these texts differed from that of Judaism. Some read these writings as a foreshadowing of Jesus. Others drew upon the prophets with their emphasis on social justice. Still others mined these and other writings for references to the end-time when the messianic era will eventually occur. The Psalms were read for their universal affirmation of faith, hope, and confidence in God in times of stress, anxiety, and trouble. But the message of Torah observance and the Torah itself (the first five books of the bible)—so central to Judaism—tended to be ignored within Christianity. Marcion's attempt to de-Judaise Christianity largely succeeded, being replaced by a portrait more congenial to a Gentile audience.

In many ways, in practice, Christians since Marcion have been Marcionites, in spite of official church pronouncements to the contrary.

In the long term, Marcion did not succeed in his attempt to promote a "two Gods" approach, and other Christian authors backed away from his attempt to radically disassociate the God of the Old Testament from the God revealed by Jesus. Still, stereotypes persist, with some contending that the God of the Old Testament is a harsh God while the God of the New Testament is one of love. That view, too, divided the unity of God and was a legacy of Marcion's two Gods. For most Christians other than the Marcionites and Gnostics, there is one and only one God, revealed in both sets of scriptures. How the two testaments relate, however, remains a difficult issue.

From Paul through Ignatius of Antioch, the *Epistle of Barnabas,* Justin Martyr, and Marcion, major Proto-Orthodox leaders mounted attacks on Judaism. Why? What are we to make of this pattern of vilification?

16

ANTI-SEMITISM

Leader after Proto-Orthodox Christian leader rose up to denounce the Jews as demonic—as agents of Satan, enemies of the church and of God—a pernicious view that has had massive repercussions for the Jewish people over the ensuing centuries. Proto-Orthodoxy felt compelled to vilify Judaism, its leaders, and its people in its quest for self-identity. We have traced this history of deep antagonism in documents from the late first and early second centuries.

The charges against Judaism were easier said than enforced. Not everyone immediately changed their beliefs or behavior just because some leader or bishop said to do so. There were, of course, the holdouts, the Jesus Movement people, who continued the observance of Torah and thought of themselves as Jewish. They became increasingly marginalized from both Judaism and Proto-Orthodoxy, and for centuries, these Ebionites inhabited a strange no-man's-land between the two evolving religions.

There were people within other ancient communities, the Proto-Orthodox included, who honored at least portions of Torah—circumcision, the dietary laws, Jewish festivals, and participation in Jewish Sabbath services, for instance. These believers were not, as is sometimes said, "Judaisers" or "re-Judaisers" who were backsliding into the ancestral religion. They were, rather, followers of Christ who held the view that Torah obligations were still in effect, despite the radicalizing of Paul's letters and the Book of Acts. They did not understand why Torah and belief in the teachings of Jesus—synagogue and church—could not coexist. That moderate belief and those well-engrained ancient practices did not die easily.

It was not Judaising as a cultural force that was significant. That way of putting the matter presupposes that Paul's Gentile Christ Movement was normative and the Torah-observant form of early Christianity was deviant, a lapsing back into Judaism.

CHRISTIFICATION

The real problem with the early church was "Christification"—the attempt to make the religion conform in all aspects to the Christ teachings of Paul. The "Christifiers" tried to eradicate every other understanding of Jesus, especially the view that he was a human teacher of the Kingdom of God. They covered over that perspective with the message of the divine savior God-human and attacked every other form of early Christianity with this powerful message, Ebionites and Gnostics alike. As far as those who clung to Torah observance were concerned, however, they were upholding the authentic teachings of Jesus and the way it was understood by his earliest followers in Jerusalem. For them, it was Paul's religion with its Christ message that was deviant. It had "Christified" the religion of Jesus.

The church emerged from this Christification process with anti-Semitic attitudes well entrenched. By 150, whatever links that had once existed with Judaism had been broken and a new infrastructure created, both within the Jesus and the Christ Movements. But every now and then, within third- and fourth-century writings, we get glimpses of continued Jewish observances. One remarkable insight comes from 387 in Antioch, that same eastern Mediterranean city that had witnessed the birth of the Gospel of Matthew and from which Ignatius went to his death in Rome. There John Chrysostom became incensed with Christians in his congregation observing Jewish practices. Perhaps they were resting from work on the Sabbath or circumcising their infants or following the dietary laws and so forth. We don't know what triggered his tirade. Whatever set him off, Chrysostom preached eight vicious sermons against the Jews, whom he attacked personally as "vile," "dogs," and "fit for slaughter." He reviled the synagogue, denounced the festivals, and accused Jewish leaders of understanding neither the Torah nor the prophets. Jews were "godless," "mad" and "sick" individuals, he charged.[1] Moreover, he inveighed, the Jews killed God's Son, and, consequently, they do not know the Father. Their prayers are ineffective and their worship null and void.

Chrysostom's hateful words were certainly designed to intimidate members of his own congregation into avoiding Jewish Sabbath observances in the synagogue. Perhaps his vehement language represented a desperate attempt to make them choose decisively, once and for all, between the practices of the two religions. But his forceful sermon was much more than a scare tactic, and his words cannot be whitewashed simply as internal pastoral advice. His words had a much greater impact as they spilled out into the larger community of

Antioch and the surrounding region. Jews and Ebionites alike must have cringed under the weight of this Christian leader's extremely harsh pronouncements. We do not know what effect these sermons had on his followers. Did his congregants abandon their Jewish practices as Chrysostom wished? The consequences for Jews, however, were much more devastating. As James Carroll points out, referring to Chrysostom's sermons, "Such words inevitably led to actions: assaults on synagogues, the exclusion of Jews from holding public office, expulsions."[2]

CHRISTIAN ANTI-SEMITISM

JEWISH RESPONSIBILITY FOR THE DEATH OF JESUS

There are a number of positions that contributed to anti-Semitism within the early church. One prominent view concerns the often-repeated charge that the Jews killed Jesus. Once again, the source of the mischief was Paul. In 1 Thessalonians, his indictment was made clear:

> *For you, brothers and sisters, become imitators of the churches of God in Christ Jesus that are in Judea, for you suffered the same things from your own compatriots as they did from the Jews, who killed both the Lord Jesus and the prophets, and drove us out; they displease God and oppose everyone by hindering us from speaking to the Gentiles so that they may be saved.* (1 Thessalonians 2:14–16)[3]

Paul's language reflects an us versus them orientation. He does not use inclusive language—"us" or "some of us"—as if he himself were part of the Jewish people and blaming others within his ethnic group. Rather his language is "them." *They* killed Jesus. This passage was penned by a person who clearly stood outside the Jewish circle and who wished to defame them, not the Romans. As we have seen, in light of Paul's views on Judaism, it was highly unlikely that he considered himself Jewish when writing his various letters. Nor would he have been perceived by Jews as Jewish.

A few years after Paul, the Gospel of Matthew explicitly blamed the Jewish people for the crucifixion of Jesus: "His blood be on us and on our children" (Matthew 27:25). In this infamous passage, Matthew accused the Jewish people "as a whole"—not only then and not only for two generations (literally, they and their children), but, as it became interpreted, for all time. This "sound bite" shrouded an entire people in blame forever. When this passage is read, or presented in passion plays or a popular film, the historical context is typically omitted. "Just following what the text says" is the usual justification, as if that exonerates what was written in the original text itself. People are left with the general impression that this crowd comprised the Jews of that time. As we have noted, the members of the assembled mob were agitators, rounded up by the Sadducee high priest for the express purpose of convicting Jesus. That paints a somewhat different picture and references the political nature of Jesus' arrest and trial. But the damage caused by one sentence cannot be undone by scholarly biblical exegesis or careful contextual analysis. The problem lies in the written text itself and what it has authorized by way of interpretation over the centuries by people bent on finding biblical support for anti-Jewish sentiments.

Written about 90 or later, some sixty years and several generations after the death of Jesus, the Gospel of John contains many passages that can be construed as anti-Jewish. He talked about Torah as "your law," not "our law," as one would expect from a Jewish writer (John 8:17). Later on he wrote of "their law" (John 15:25). He claimed that "the Jews" persecuted Jesus (John 5:16), and that they even tried to kill him on several occasions (John 5:18, 8:37). He portrayed Jesus as accusing Jews who do not accept him as children of the devil (John 8:44). The impression the Gospel of John conveyed is that all Jews are evil, opposing God's Son, the Christian Jesus. The language John used indicated that the writer of this gospel stood well outside the Jewish family. It represents the language of radical dualism: the forces of evil (Satan, Jews) versus the powers of goodness (Jesus, his followers, Christians).

The tendency to exonerate Roman authorities and to fix the blame on the Jews increased with time as early Christianity moved into the Mediterranean arena. To make converts from the Gentile world, Roman involvement in the crucifixion was reduced to heighten Jewish culpability. This is evident in a popular writing, the *Gospel of Peter*, which was widely read and highly regarded in some circles of second-century Christianity but which was not eventually included in the New Testament.[4] This gospel wrote that after the crucifixion, "the Jews, the elders, and the priests realized how much evil they had done to themselves and began beating their breasts, saying, 'Woe to us because of our sins. The judgment and the end of Jerusalem are near.'"[5] This last phrase echoes a charge that some Christians were later to make, that the destruction of the Temple and Jerusalem represented a punishment by God upon the Jewish people for rejecting Jesus. The Temple, priesthood, and worship had migrated over into the church.

The *Gospel of Peter* showed the Roman procurator, Pontius Pilate, explicitly accusing the Jewish leaders of the killing, saying, "I am clean of the blood of the Son of God; you decided to do this." They bear the full weight of judicial responsibility. Exonerating the Romans and blaming the Jews formed part of the task of the second and third centuries as Proto-Orthodoxy attempted to make converts among Roman citizens. Blaming the citizens for the death of the religion's leader would not have been helpful in this endeavor.

As Jesus increasingly became viewed as a God-human, the charge that the Jews killed Jesus escalated into "the Jews killed God." Around 190, Bishop Melito of Sardis uttered this terrifying accusation in a sermon on the Passover and the sacrifice of Christ.[7] Attacks in this vein continued for centuries. Somewhat later than Melito, John Chrysostom attacked "the Jews" as serving demons because "they slew God."[8]

The New Testament writings cannot be shielded from the charge that they contain anti-Semitic statements. They were not, after all, neutral, a representative cross-section or reference library of early Christianity. Out of a vast array of possible documents, the ones specifically included in the New Testament were written and selected by the Proto-Orthodox leaders with the express purpose of bolstering their understanding of their faith and empowering their community at the expense of other Christian groups. In light of the Proto-Orthodox attack on Judaism and the Jews, it is not surprising that their writings include such self-serving sentiments. Today, some interpreters and commentators are very careful to provide the historical context for these passages, but that in no way diminishes the use made of these texts throughout history in justifying persecution of the Jewish people. That many contemporary Christians, from all denominations, choose not to interpret these texts as reflective of the Jewish people today does not mitigate the fact that these passages still linger on in print, ready to be seized upon by those hostile to Judaism or ignorant of their social and historical contexts.

SUPERSESSIONISM

Another contributing factor to Christian anti-Semitism comes from the view that Christianity has "superseded" or "replaced" Judaism historically and is now heir to all God's promises. This view denies legitimacy to Judaism as a viable religion and deprives the Jewish people of having a covenant with God. They have ceased to be the people of God. There is, on this view, one and only one covenant, namely, that between God and the church. If Judaism has no right to exist, then the next logical question is: What right do the Jewish people have to exist? Some Christian anti-Semitism takes the form of an answer to this question: none whatsoever.[9]

Supersessionism was invented by Paul in his Letter to the Galatians. There he said that followers of Christ should not observe Torah, that its time in history had passed. It once served a purpose—in the time between Moses and

Christ—but now that Christ has come, Torah is obsolete. Hence there is no reason to follow Jewish law, or, for that matter, to be Jewish. Ideally, for Paul, Jews would cease being Jewish and would convert to his new movement. Later on, Justin Martyr also advanced supersessionist views in his *Dialogue with Trypho*. So, too, did Marcion and many other early church leaders. It was important to them that Judaism have no raison d'être whatsoever.

All these leaders could have taken a different stand. They could have said, "We have one covenant; Judaism has another," and left it at that. But that is not the route they chose to take. They adopted a much more aggressive, usurping position. The Jews and Judaism simply had to be displaced. Interestingly enough, we hear no dissenting views within early Christianity. No one arose to champion the cause of Judaism or the Jews among the Proto-Orthodox. They were left to fend for themselves.

Neither the Jewish people nor Judaism withered away, however. Their continuity posed huge problems for Proto-Orthodox theology making replacement claims. How should their continued existence be understood? Why had they not crossed over into the new movement? Why hadn't they embraced the truth of this new religion? Jesus had come to them first—why hadn't they, in turn, flocked to Christ? This led to charges that the Jewish people were simply obstinate, blind to the truth, or just ignorant—just the type of accusations leveled against them in John Chrysostom's sermons.

A DESTRUCTIVE LEGACY

The charges of Jewish collective guilt and supersessionism are both contributing factors to Christian anti-Semitism.[10] This phenomenon has, over the years, resulted in massive destruction of Jewish people: persecutions, killings by crusaders on their way to the Holy Land, expulsions from a large number of European countries, the creation of ghettos, inquisitions, pogroms in Russia and Poland, attacks on Jewish institutions and cemeteries; and, to some extent, Christian anti-Jewish sentiments fed into the Holocaust, which, in addition to killing six million individuals, denuded Europe of Jews and Jewish institutions.[11] Many of these atrocities occurred long after the Proto-Orthodox had managed to achieve reasonable self-definition. What accounts for the *persistence* of such hatred over hundreds of years? Why do these sentiments shout across the centuries in Christian circles, lingering on long after the process of separation and self-definition was over?

Is it just a matter of putting texts in context? Would that allow us to overcome pejorative references to the Jewish people, Christian supersessionist claims, and blaming the Jews for the death of Jesus? Could Christian anti-Semitism be cleared up by honest, straightforward biblical exegesis? This "sorry, it was all a mistake" approach seems impotent in the face of such a powerful historical dynamic.

Moreover, why were early Proto-Orthodox leaders so fearful of Judaism? What was really at stake? None of the contributing factors mentioned above provides an explanation of why Proto-Orthodox Christianity thought it had to attack Judaism in the first place. None of these reasons, moreover, accounts for the *comprehensiveness* of the assault. Let's remind ourselves of the totality of what was rejected or confiscated: Jewish leadership, its texts, its understanding of its own scriptures, oral law, its heritage, its mandate under the covenant, Torah observance, and its understanding of God. Everything it valued either got shredded or transported over into the Christian camp. This wide path of destruction vastly exceeded the requirements for launching a new religion, especially one that in its Proto-Orthodox form originated outside the Jewish family. These considerations do not account for the persistence, strength, and virulence of these angry attacks throughout the centuries by most forms of subsequent Christianity—Catholic, Orthodox, and Protestant.

What is the underlying motivation that propels this continuing anger and hatred? Why the perpetual hostility? The Jesus Cover-Up Thesis takes us into another way of looking at continued Christian anti-Semitism.

$$\boxed{17}$$

THE COVER-UP REVEALED

So, what was the cover-up? How did Jesus the Jew become Christian? The Jesus Cover-Up Thesis explains the transformation. It's time to put all the pieces of the puzzle together and see where it leads us.

PAUL VERSUS JESUS

We began this investigation by looking at Matthew's portrait of the Jesus of history. A dynamic teacher in Galilee, Jesus proclaimed the imminent arrival of the Kingdom of God. That concept, an appealing alternative to the prevailing Pax Romana, unleashed huge expectations that God's sovereign rule would soon be established over the entire world. Jesus practiced Judaism, interpreted Torah, and challenged his followers to a higher righteousness. In a radically innovative manner, Jesus coupled the promise of the Kingdom with the challenge for a stricter observance of Torah.

His followers began to think of him as the potential Messiah. They expected he'd be the Davidic king of a restored Israel, assisting God in bringing about world transformation. The newly minted world of the messianic era would be startlingly different from the sinful and evil world that existed before. Gone would be the emperor, his governors, tax officials, the military, and all the others involved in promoting Roman rule throughout the world. In their place would be the reign of the righteous, rewarded with eternal life, in a splendid new environment. It was a powerful expectation. Members of the Jesus Movement under James, Jesus' brother—like members of the Dead Sea Scroll community—hoped they would live to see the day when the Romans would be swept from power. These occupiers, along with all evil people, would just disappear by a miraculously creative act of God and his Messiah. One day they would wake up to a whole new world.

Yes, that is what they were led to expect would happen: a brand-new world, in fact, an entirely new creation. Not a virgin birth. Not a resurrection. And certainly not the need for a return engagement.

But something strange happened. There was a massive power shift. The religion of Jesus and his earliest followers became upstaged as an imaginative and startlingly new religion entered the arena—Paul's Christ movement. Shunning the Jesus Movement leaders, he crafted his own cult. He took as his source of inspiration mystical communiqués from the Christ—not the teachings of the Jesus of history or the practices of Jesus' earliest followers in Jerusalem. He thought he enjoyed a separate and special pipeline to the divine, receiving different information and insights than others of his time. The mystical Christ, however, a dying-rising savior, shared many of the same characteristics as other figures well known within the Roman world through the cults of Dionysus, Isis, and Mithras. Paul's group was not a form of Judaism but a separate Hellenized religion that paid no attention to the teachings of Torah or Jesus. In fact, his movement denied the ongoing validity of Torah, and this applied across the board, to all human beings, Jews included.

That should have been the end of the matter. They should have remained two separate, parallel religions, each with their own teachings and practices, fending for themselves in the multicultural Hellenistic world. But that was not to be. The religion of Paul became associated with that of Jesus. Why did it not just remain a separate religion? How did it become so confused with Jesus' religion that people today have difficulty recognizing how truly different it actually was? That linkage, we will recall, was the amazing result of the Book of Acts. Years after the death of Paul and James, around A.D. 100, Luke, the gifted creator of both the Gospel of Luke and the Book of Acts, penned one of the most audacious stories of all human history. He brazenly attached Paul's Christ Movement on to the Jesus Movement. This immediately linked Paul's new religion to that of Jesus and, through him, to biblical Judaism. Brushing aside key differences, Acts gave this new Pauline religion legitimacy by forging an impressive pedigree back into ancient times. A non-Jewish movement thereby became grafted on to Judaism.

Ancient roots were vitally important for the proselytizing initiatives of Paul's followers throughout the Roman Empire. Prospective Roman converts demanded a noble ancestry, and the author of the Book of Acts stepped up to the plate to provide the requisite credentials. Acts bent Paul's activities out of shape to make them fit his revisionist history. We recognized that, once we noticed the differences between what Paul said about himself and what Acts wrote about Paul. Acts invented the fiction of the Jerusalem Conference. There James was alleged to have authorized a twofold missionary strategy—one directed to the Jews, which was Torah-observant, and one directed to Gentiles, which was not. Only the Seven Noahide Laws need be observed by the Gentiles.

There is a problem with the history Acts presented. No one knew about this conference. Paul didn't. Nor did the rival teachers with whom he was disputing in his Letter to the Galatians know of this high-level meeting. Similarly, in 1 Corinthians, when discussing dietary food practices, Paul showed no awareness of the food requirements allegedly imposed on the Gentiles by James. These would have restricted the eating of meat slaughtered improperly, containing blood, or prepared in the context of idol worship. For Paul, what one ate was of no consequence; for him, eating did not carry the same religious significance as it did for Jews.

The Book of Acts dovetailed with Luke's pro-Roman agenda, to present the new synthesized movement as a religion ripe for Roman believers. It showcased its values: antiquity and a special birth. It is not surprising that in Luke's gospel we find that Jesus had a virgin birth. This placed him on a par with many Roman emperors and the hero figures of the mystery cults. Luke's readers would have been impressed with these credentials. Luke's gospel also portrayed Jesus as exemplifying the Roman trait of serenity. There Jesus dies without panic or consternation, saying calmly, "Father, into your hands I commend my spirit" (Luke 23:46). This contrasts remarkably with the last gasp of desperation recorded by Matthew—"My God, my God, why have you forsaken me?" (Matthew 27:46). Luke's noble death scenario, worthy of the calm rational Socrates or the serene Cleopatra in the face of death, would have appealed to the Roman audience more than an expression of utter despair at the failure of the whole enterprise.

As Acts presented the history, there was one common origin for the movements with divergent paths—first Jesus, and then, branching out from him, James and Paul. One origin; two missions. While this model for understanding early Christian history has passed into Christian self-understanding, it is simply fictitious. Once we understand Acts' agenda and revisionism, the real model is not one of divergence from a common source, but *convergence*. Luke took two separate religions and spliced them together through the device of the Jerusalem Conference. The truer historical picture, however, would be that of two parallel religions, different in origin, that were then brought together, at least on paper. What Acts did would be comparable to us taking religious movements with different origins such as the Church of Scientology or the Unification Church and then linking them into a common history with such Christian denominations as Methodism or the Baptist Church. Just not credible or persuasive.

It was just that, however—a *literary* synthesis, not descriptive of historical reality. On the ground, there continued to be major differences in beliefs and practices as well as social reality. It just wasn't history. The synagogues of the Jesus Movement and the congregations of the Christ were not suddenly brought together in an ecumenical gesture of goodwill and harmony.

Complex social problems still remained. Members of the Jesus Movement couldn't have socialized with their counterparts in the Christ Movement. Dietary and purity requirements would have prevented this, as well as their perception that Paul's was a non-Jewish, pagan religion. Frustrated by the Christ Movement's claim that it was the authentic heir of Jesus, they would have been deeply angered that their perspective was increasingly ignored. We can hear them asking in a perplexed tone, How did this happen? Why would anyone think we had anything in common?

Members of the Christ Movement would have been equally frustrated. They would have asked, Why can't the Jesus Movement people see the advantages of the Christ religion? They could easily have listed its many benefits. Gentiles could now be brought into the fold of Abraham without having to observe the law. They, too, can now experience the promise of the Kingdom. People can enjoy greater food selection with forbidden items removed. No male circumcision. Couldn't the leaders of the Jesus Movement see, and be impressed by, the huge numbers of converts flocking to their movement? Didn't this sound very much like the fulfillment of the parable of the Sower with its expectation of exponential growth? Didn't this reflect the true will of God?

The Jesus Movement was beleaguered with major problems at a crucial time in history. It experienced a gap in leadership between the murder of James in 62 and the selection of Simeon some years later. It was caught up in the convulsions in Israel during the 60s. And, after 70, it inherited all the problems that Judaism faced after this massive blow delivered by the Romans. The writings that survive from the Jesus and Ebionite movements make it clear that they continued to regard Paul as a false teacher. Over time, they withered away, but that process took centuries. Never did they have sufficient resources or power to counter the growing influence of the Christ Movement. They must have felt that their religion had been hijacked. It had.

Contrast this with the experience of the Christ Movement. It was unaffected by the traumas that plagued the Jesus Movement. It expanded throughout the Diaspora unfettered by the requirements of Torah, the task of reconstruction, or the necessity of adult male circumcision. Bolstered by the credentials established by Acts, this religion gained momentum. Unconstrained by either the Jesus Movement or Judaism, it proclaimed its Roman-friendly message of a Torah-free Christ-focused religion.

CHRISTIFICATION

The makeover of the Jewish human Jesus, teacher of the higher righteousness, into a Gentile, divine God-human, the savior of humanity, is the process I call Christification.

The two realities—the Jewish teacher Messiah claimant and the Gentile Christ savior—have never coalesced properly. There have always been many puzzles. How did Jesus come to be a Christ? Why was Jesus, conceived of as a Christ, considered a Messiah when the expectations for the latter had not been met? How did the teachings of Jesus become obscured by doctrines about the Christ?

None of these dilemmas makes sense without the Jesus Cover-Up Thesis. The explanatory power of this approach unravels the mysteries. While the Christifying religion had a separate origin in Paul's experience, through Acts' creative efforts, it became associated with the heritage and lineage of the Jesus Movement. It wasn't, but all it took to create the illusion was a bit of historical fiction on the part of Acts. The author of Acts told such a wonderful story that we conflate the Christ with Jesus. We relate the Christ Movement with the religion of Jesus. Helpful confusions, the author of Acts would have called it. And yet the evidence was there, all along, for everyone to see: Acts' account of Paul distorts what we know of Paul from Paul himself. Once we recognize this, the deception is unmasked. We begin to see how separate and different the two religions really were and appreciate the marvelous work of Acts in attaching the two.

Acts' masquerade may not have been a bad move historically. It gave the Christ Movement the credentials it required to make headway in the Roman world. Had Christianity been derived from the Jesus Movement instead, it would probably have remained a sect of Judaism, sitting uncomfortably within the Jewish family. It would have waited—decades, centuries, even millennia—for the Messiah claimant to make good on his word. It would also have been relegated to the edges of Judaism, watching while that religion was being reconstructed by the rabbinical sages at Yavneh and subsequent Jewish centers of learning. The Jesus Movement was isolated and bypassed—by Rabbinic Judaism on one side and by the Christifying religion on another. It must have been exceptionally uncomfortable being an Ebionite in the second through fourth centuries, with few friends in either camp.

The Christ Movement occupied a powerful positioning: an attractive Graeco-Roman mystery religion combined with an impressive Jewish pedigree. In this, it successfully buttressed itself effectively against its two main competitors—Judaism and the popular mystery religions. Leaders of the

Christ Movement could congratulate themselves that they enjoyed the best of both worlds—Judaism's respectable ancient lineage but without Torah obligations on the one hand, and mystery religion beliefs and practices on the other. A powerful religious mix.

The new religion denounced, eradicated, or appropriated everything Jewish. Decade by decade, the Christifiers stripped Judaism of its legitimacy and validity—Torah observance, leadership, worship, and understanding of scripture and God. Matthew, Ignatius of Antioch, the *Epistle of Barnabas*, and Justin Martyr swept away this ancient faith, at precisely the same time—post 70, when Jewish leaders were hard at work revamping the religion. The church was the true Israel, heir to all the promises made to Abraham, the Christifiers proclaimed. The Jewish priesthood had been eliminated, replaced by the new Christian ministry. The Temple had become the church, and thus the locus of true worship had been shifted from one institution to the other. The scriptures of the Hebrew Bible had been ransacked and reinterpreted, as pointing directly to Jesus. As far as these early Christifying leaders were concerned, there was nothing left for Judaism and the synagogue to represent. Everything of value had been shifted over to the new religion; the rest was discarded. From the point of view of the Christifiers, it was a mystery why Judaism, the Jewish people, and the Jesus Movement continued to exist at all.

Marcion possessed the clearest grasp into the dynamics of early Christian history. He recognized that Paul had experienced a unique revelation. That insight provided Marcion with the clue concerning what had really happened. Why did Paul have a separate revelation? Why did the others not receive the same information? Marcion had suggested that the followers of the early Jesus Movement failed to grasp the real message. They thought the movement was about the Kingdom of God, an expression of Judaism, messianic in nature, a political alternative to the Pax Romana that would usher in the advent of a whole new world order. What fools, said Marcion. They were dead wrong. That political understanding of Jesus encapsulated a huge misperception. The disciples in Jerusalem—including James—just didn't grasp the importance of the Christ and his cosmic message of liberation.

The effect of the Christification process was to change the character of the religion, from one focused on the teachings *of* Jesus to one *about* the Christ. The contrast is most readily seen when we compare passages from the gospels—the Sermon on the Mount, for instance—with the creeds of Christianity. Three creeds are operative within historic Catholic, Orthodox, Anglican, and Reformation Protestant churches. These authoritative pronouncements consist of the Apostles' Creed, dating from the second century, along with the fourth-century Creeds of Nicea and St. Athanasius. These creeds came to define what is meant by Christianity. Those who assent to these statements are Christians. Those—like the Ebionites, Arians, Gnostics, Nestorians, Monophysites, and many others—are excluded. The creeds represent a defining moment in early Christianity: they crystallize what a believer had to affirm in order to be counted as a "correct" or "orthodox" believer. Even today, the flagship creed, the Nicene Creed, is uttered by the faithful at Mass, the Divine Liturgy, Holy Communion, or the Eucharist in traditional forms of Christianity, usually as a congregational response to the hearing of the word through the reading of scripture.

The Nicene Creed structured the faith on the basis of the doctrine of the Trinity. Drafted under duress during the reign of Emperor Constantine at the Council of Nicea in 325 and later reaffirmed with some additions in 381, this important statement makes no references to the teachings of Jesus, its focus being on who Jesus is thought to be:

> *We believe in one Lord, Jesus Christ,*
> *the only Son of God,*
> *eternally begotten of the Father,*
> *God from God, Light from Light,*
> *true God from true God,*
> *begotten, not made,*
> *of one Being with the Father.*
> *Through him all things were made . . .*[1]

Similarly, the Creed of St. Athanasius focuses on the divinity of Jesus, while also mentioning his humanity:

> *Thus the Father is God, the Son is God, and the Holy Spirit is God. However, there are not three gods, but one God. The Father is Lord, the Son is Lord, and the Holy Spirit is Lord. However, there are not three lords but one Lord. For as we are obliged by Christian truth to acknowledge every Person singly to be God and Lord so too are we forbidden by the catholic religion to say that there are three Gods or Lords.*[2]

Creedal affirmations emphasize the need for correct beliefs about the person of Jesus—who he was, not what he said, did, or taught. In these highly influential statements of faith, the historical Jesus is covered over by layers of hard-fought beliefs about the person of Jesus. These creeds also transform the religion, shifting the emphasis away from the teachings of the historical Jesus to beliefs about Christ—preexistent, creator, God incarnate, having a virgin birth, and so forth. This is consistent with the work of Paul and the efforts of later Christifiers.

Many of these beliefs find expression not only in the creeds, but also in the pages of the New Testament. That collection of documents, however, was reflective of the Proto-Orthodox position and simply reinforces its Christifying stance. It is not a neutral library of early Christian writings, for it ignores documents and stances that represented other points of view. As we now know, other communities such as the Ebionites, Gnostics, and Marcionites had their own favorite writings. The contents of the current New Testament, decided upon by Proto-Orthodoxy in the late fourth century, reflect the writings favored by the one group that became the official religion of the Roman Empire. It contains the writings of Paul plus the books of Luke/Acts. The New Testament, too, is riddled with Christification.

The Christifying religion was *a substitute religion*, however, not that of the founder, if one thinks of the originator of Christianity as Jesus. It became the religion about beliefs about the Christ, not the teachings of Jesus. That became the standard of orthodoxy—what one believed about the Christ, not whether one practiced what Jesus challenged us to do. This new religion grew out of that created by Paul.

The older claim, that Jesus was the Jewish Messiah who would help usher in the end-time, was buried beneath the vastly different superstructure of the dying-rising savior God. The image of Jesus was repackaged as the Christ, another divine-human figure so familiar to the Roman world. The similarities between the portrait of Jesus as it emerged within the Gentile Christian movement and other cults of the time were so close that leaders were hard-pressed to explain the commonalities. Some saw the pagan cults as anticipating the truth of Christianity. That was one way of handling the similarities. Another option, however, was to dismiss the mystery religions as the work of the devil who was busily sowing confusion.

The latter point of view is evident in Justin Martyr's *Dialogue with Trypho*. This treatise reflected what Proto-Orthodox Christians of the 130s believed Jewish leaders were thinking and teaching. In this dialogue, as we have observed, Rabbi Trypho made important charges against the Christian misuse of the passage from Isaiah in support of a virginal conception of Jesus. He also pointed out the many similarities between the Roman and Christian cults of the divine-human. There are simply too many divine-humans and too many virgin births within the Roman world to mark out the Christian movement as in any way unique.

Justin Martyr's response was that the devil invented these non-Christian tales. So, too, had Satan devised figures of previous divine-humans—Bacchus, Hercules, Dionysus, and many others. The whole intent was to confuse Christians. Likewise the mysteries of Mithras arose to create confusion.[3] Clearly Justin Martyr was embarrassed by the similarities between the virgin birth and divine-human tales from his own culture. He concluded with the following words, designed to reassure Trypho: "And when I hear, Trypho," said I, "that Perseus was begotten of a virgin, I understand that the deceiving spirit counterfeited also this."[4]

WHAT *MUST* A MESSIAH DO?

But what of Jesus as the Messiah? Was Paul's Christ a Messiah?

As one scours the writings of Proto-Orthodox Christianity, it is truly re-markable how little its leaders tried to match the Christ with authentic Jewish messianic expectations. It virtually disregarded the criteria, so much so that we begin to suspect that as soon as they latched on to the Christ-figure, they quickly forgot about what it meant to be the Messiah.

It's important to remember how people conceived of a Messiah in the first century. The *Psalms of Solomon,* from the first century B.C., provides the job description. That writing, building on earlier end-time visions of the prophets, had set forth the relevant criteria concerning what a Messiah had to do. The circumstances were as follows. In 63 B.C., the Roman leader Pompey captured Jerusalem. Welcomed into the city, he seized Temple Mount by force, executed the Jewish resisters led by the high priest, and entered the Temple. The *Psalms of Solomon,* an eyewitness document, adhered to the threefold framework es-tablished by Zechariah for the end-time: a period of exceptional evil followed by world transformation and just desserts.

In actions recalling the earlier events of Antiochus Epiphanes, Psalm 2 of the *Psalms of Solomon* lamented the loss of national sovereignty—Romans arrogantly trampling on Temple Mount, "insulting" Jerusalem (*Psalms of Solomon* 2:19). Psalm 17 reminds us of the perpetual covenant with David and then provides us with a "status report" of the situation. The times were clearly evil—devastation, massacres of Jerusalem's inhabitants, exile, worship of false gods, leaders mislead-ing the people. Knowing the end-time scenario, we immediately recognize where this analysis is heading. Following Zechariah's eschatological agenda, the writer of this psalm envisaged that world transformation was about to happen. The Messiah was the righteous Jewish king, a descendant of David, who would assist God in bringing about a radically changed environment. The Messiah must become involved in massive political and religious changes. The world af-ter the work of the Messiah will differ vastly from the world before—Israel pre-eminent, God universally worshipped, evil eradicated, the righteous rewarded, along with universal peace. That's the expectation. That's what other Jewish communities understood by the Messiah—the Dead Sea Scroll group among them. That, too, is what the original followers of Jesus expected, waiting pa-tiently after his death for him to make good on his promises.

Paul, however, changed all that. Paul referred to the Messiah as *Christos. Christos* is the Greek translation of the Hebrew *Mashiach,* but much is lost in translation. Paul advanced his views of the Christ in his Letter to the Philippi-ans, written sometime either in the late 50s or early 60s. The view of the Christ that he presented there is that he was a preexisting being born in human form. He was obedient to God. He died. He was exalted so that all humanity can worship him. Those who become like him in death can attain resurrection (Philippians 2:5–11).

Paul thus focused on who the Messiah was: the *Christos* or Messiah was a dying-rising savior. His task, according to Paul, was to save those who participate in his suffering and death. The focus for Paul was on personal salvation. "Living is Christ," he said (Philippians 1:21), and he stressed he wanted

> *"to know Christ and the power of his resurrection and the sharing of his sufferings by becoming like him in his death, if somehow I may attain the resurrection from the dead."* (Philippians 3:10–11)

A believer lives "in Christ" and so, in life and death is united with Christ. It is because of this mystical unity and also because Christ himself was raised from the dead that the believer can experience resurrection.

Paul probably recognized, however, that this idea of the Christ was insufficient to meet established criteria for being a Messiah. Where was the expected world transformation? Where were the "just desserts"? In some passages, Paul indicated that he expected the Lord Jesus to return. When "the day of Jesus Christ" (Philippians 1:6) arrives, Christ will "hand over the kingdom to God the Father" (1 Corinthians 15:24). At this time, the dead will be resurrected, those who are alive and righteous will assume a "spiritual body," and all evil powers will be destroyed, including death (1 Corinthians 15:20–57).

Thus we see that Paul proposes a two-stage messiahship for Christ. In stage one, the Christ is the savior. He is the dying-rising savior, redeeming those who participate in his suffering and death. That gave a very important present purpose to the Christ figure: he can save. No need to wait for world transformation. In stage two, however, Christ will return to destroy evil, conquer death, and reward the righteous with eternal life. At that time the righteous dead will be resurrected. Then he will be the Messiah in accordance with existing expectations of what a Messiah must accomplish. This second stage has yet to occur.

The development of a two-stage messiahship was Paul's contribution. Clearly Jesus had not fulfilled the requirements for being a Messiah during his life. World transformation had not occurred, and the righteous had not been truly rewarded. So, Paul contended, there had to be a "return" when Christ will reappear to complete the tasks expected of a Messiah. There was, however, no antecedent in Jewish thought for a two-stage messianic operation. If he did bring about world transformation, then he would be the Messiah. If he didn't, then he was just a Messiah claimant. In Paul's case, the Christ was simply a Messiah who is yet to be. He had not yet performed the deeds necessary to qualify as a Messiah. The correct way of describing Paul's Christ, then, is as a Messiah claimant. The Christ of Paul is in the same situation as Bar Kokhba or Rabbi Schneerson, who are also said by some to be prospective Messiahs and who have yet to return.

There are further innovations as Paul reshaped the definition of what it means to be a Messiah.

As we have seen, Paul's savior figure derived from Graeco-Roman mystery religions. Paul placed the Christ's death and resurrection as central to his concept of the Messiah, a notion foreign to all previous Jewish views of the Messiah. Prior to Paul, there was no requirement that the Messiah be resurrected. Nor was it expected that he would act as the "savior vehicle" through whom all humanity will be saved. These represent important new twists on the idea of a Messiah. Paul built his view of the Christ on models found outside Judaism, in the mystery religions of the time. The Christ is like Dionysus or Mithras or many other figures—heroes who die and rise again to save humanity and whose followers can achieve salvation through participation in the hero's life and death. When *Christos* translated *Mashiach,* it transported the concept from a Jewish environment into a vastly different world.

Paul's Christ, even if he were to return, would not fully correspond to Jewish messianic expectations. Some crucial elements were missing in Paul's description of the Christ versus messianic expectations as outlined in the *Psalms of Solomon.* For one thing, Paul's concept ignored the political dimension of the Jewish Messiah. On his approach, the Messiah would not be the Davidic king who governs Israel and assists God in bringing about world transformation. Instead the Christ was a cosmic savior, a spiritual being who preexisted his earthly life and whose only task was to redeem those who participate in his life and death. There was nothing particularly Jewish about him. Paul would probably have argued that he was universalizing the messianic notion, but that wasn't the expectation. The Messiah had to be the Jewish monarch who had come to restore Israel to prominence, overthrow Roman rule, and encourage the return of Jews from the Diaspora. He wouldn't be a universal figure of goodness.

There were other important differences as well. For Paul, the Christ was not primarily human. The expectation, however, was that the Messiah would be human. He would be born, live, and die, but be chosen by God to assist in bringing about a new world order. Paul's concept presented in Philippians was that of a preexisting spiritual or divine being who appears in human form. For Paul, the Christ had to be a divine figure in order to act as a means of salvation, redeeming all who participate in his life and death and eventually overcoming all cosmic forces of opposition to God's will.

Finally, proclaiming the Christ as Messiah now, in advance of world transformation, ignored the end-time dimension of the Jewish expectation. The world before and after Jesus appeared looks very much the same. Paul would probably have argued, however, that at least for the individual who is "in Christ," there were new possibilities for salvation that did not exist before. But on a political level, the world was the same. Israel was still ruled by Rome; the righteous continued to suffer; and the end-time had yet to appear.

So is Paul's Christ a Messiah? Kindly put, Paul "jumped the gun," proclaiming the Christ figure as Messiah when he wasn't that yet.

DOING IN THE WITNESSES

The Jesus Cover-Up Thesis also exposes the deep anchors of Christian anti-Semitism. *The Jesus Cover-Up Thesis contends that early Christianity effectively killed off the historical Jesus.*

The suggestion that Jesus was a human teacher and Messiah claimant is apt to be met today with skepticism or even jeers from many believers who have been taught differently. Part of the hostile reaction to Dan Brown's *The Da Vinci Code*—other than its distorted depiction of the Opus Dei movement—consists of its suggestion that Jesus was human, married Mary Magdalene, and had sexual relations with her. The fact that Jesus was human and that rabbis of the era were supposed to marry just doesn't seem to count. It violates sensibilities of what is appropriate behavior for the divine.

The transformation brought about by the Christification process was so successful that the religion of the historical Jesus was replaced by the cult of the Christ. In so doing, the early church "killed off" the historical Jesus, focusing, instead, on the worship of the Christ. The myth of the Christ was so effective that it is very difficult now to reconstruct the contours of the authentic teachings, sayings, and doings of the historical Jesus. To get at the Jesus of history, we have to leap over Paul and try to peel away the layers of Christifying efforts to see the Jewish, human Jesus underneath. No wonder that the heroic task of twentieth-century biblical scholarship—the quest for the historical Jesus—has proven so difficult. The prism of Paul and the Christifiers stands in the way, blocking our view.

The only witnesses to this transformation were the Jews, as well as Torah-observant Ebionite communities. The latter were quickly marginalized. Paul won the historical debate with James, the brother of Jesus, so much so that for most of Christian history, the role, influence, and authority of James have been overlooked. The earliest followers of Jesus followed Torah, held that he was born naturally, resisted attempts to make him into anything other than a superior teacher, and looked forward to his returning to fulfill the messianic dream. They were eventually condemned as heretics by the majority movement, Proto-Orthodoxy. Leader after Proto-Orthodox leader castigated them and others within their own ranks for continuing to observe Jewish customs, festivals, and laws.

Attitudes on the part of the Christifiers toward these "deviant" forms of the religion solidified over time. In the 130s, Justin Martyr contended that Christians who were Torah-observant were "weak-minded" but harmless so long as they continued their practices privately. He quickly added, however, that those who tried to persuade others to follow the law given through Moses should be shunned.[5] Presumably Justin Martyr hoped these Torah holdouts would die out in time. The Ebionites, on the other hand, probably thought that the growing move to create Christology—elaborate doctrines about the Christ—represented "Christolatry," that is, idolatry, making that which is not divine into deity.

By the turn of the fourth century, however, attitudes had hardened. Look at what Eusebius wrote about the Ebionites:

> The spirit of wickedness, however, being unable to shake some in their love of Christ and yet finding them susceptible of his impressions in other respects, brought them over to his purposes. These were properly called Ebionites by the ancients, as those who cherished low and mean opinions of Christ. . . . With them the observance of the law was altogether necessary, as if they could not be saved only by faith in Christ and a corresponding life.[6]

For Eusebius, the Ebionites were evil in origin, led by the "spirit of wickedness." So much for the original followers of the historical Jesus. According to the Christifiers, they simply got it entirely wrong.

Essentially only the Jews remained witnesses to "the crime." If Christianity had remained Torah-observant, even with reverence for Jesus as a potential Messiah, there would have been no grounds for excluding the movement from the family of Judaism. Belief in a Messiah was not incompatible with Judaism, so long as the messianic candidate eventually succeeds in bringing about the eschatological era.

In the latter part of first century, however, the Jewish community recognized the dangers that stemmed from the Christ Movement. They sensed that members of this group did not observe Torah, dismissed its legitimacy and displayed a growing inclination to speak of Christ in terms befitting divinity. Any one of these positions would have constituted reasonable grounds for disassociating this movement in particular from Judaism. Moreover, members of the Christ Movement—Paul included—had infiltrated synagogues in the attempt to detach the God-fearer segment. Much was at stake and this new aggressive religion had to be confronted.

At some point in either the late first or early second century, Jewish leaders took steps to distance their religion and that of the sectarians. A prayer was added to the Shemoneh Esrei (Eighteen Benedictions):

AGAINST HERETICS: And for slanderers, let there be no hope; and may all wickedness perish in an instant; and may all Your enemies be cut down speedily. May you speedily uproot, smash, cast down and humble the wanton sinners—speedily in our days. Blessed are you HASHEM [God] Who breaks enemies and humbles wanton sinners.[7]

This had the effect of removing sectarians from Jewish synagogues. It also demonstrates the degree to which Jewish leaders were concerned about the growing success of the Christ Movement. After all, Judaism would not have changed the structure of its central prayer, the Amidah or Shimonei Esrei, to include a nineteenth petition against sectarians unless it faced a substantial threat from the new movements.[8]

In his *Dialogue with Trypho*, Justin Martyr demonstrated how aware each community was of the other. In the following passage, Trypho articulated some of his best lines. He expressed utter amazement that Christians expect favors from God when they do not observe his commandments:

Trypho:
Moreover, I am aware that your precepts in the so-called Gospel are so wonderful and so great, that I suspect no one can keep them; for I have carefully read them. **But this is what we are most at a loss about: that you, professing to be pious, and supposing yourselves better than others, are not in any particular separated from them, and do not alter your mode of living from the nations, in that you observe no festivals or Sabbaths, and do not have the rite of circumcision; and further, resting your hopes on a man that was crucified, you yet expect to obtain some good thing from God, while you do not obey His commandments.** *Have you not read, that soul shall be cut off from his people who shall not have been circumcised on the eighth day? And this has been ordained for strangers and for slaves equally. But you, despising this covenant rashly, reject the consequent duties, and attempt to persuade yourselves that you know God, when, however, you perform none of those things which they do who fear God.[9]*

Good question: How do you expect "to obtain good things from God, while you do not obey His commandments"? Arguing on the basis of the ancient scriptures, Rabbi Trypho expressed concern with the lack of Torah observance. While he did not explicitly draw the comparisons, we can imagine him wondering how this new sect differed from the ancient Israelites who had abandoned the covenant with God and had wandered off into Canaanite religion. Or how these new sectarians were really different from other religions of the Hellenized world.

Rabbi Trypho raised other concerns as well—for example, how Jesus

fulfilled the mandate of a Messiah as well as how he was resurrected and ascended into heaven.[10] We have already noted Trypho's observation concerning
the amazing parallels between the virginal conception stories and the divine-
human birth narratives of Jesus alongside Dionysus, Perseus, and Mithras, so
much so that Trypho was amazed that Christians were not embarrassed by the
parallels. Trypho accused Christians of blasphemy, supposing that Jesus was a
preexistent divine being who should be worshipped:

> For you utter blasphemies, in that you seek to persuade us that this crucified
> man was with Moses and Aaron, and spoke to them in the pillar of the cloud;
> then that he became man, was crucified, and ascended up to heaven, and comes
> again to earth, and ought to be worshipped.[11]

Proto-Orthodox church leaders recognized that they could not hide their
escalating Christological beliefs about Jesus from the rabbis. The latter were
well aware of the growing claims being made about Jesus as the Christ, that he
was being spoken of in terms that befit divinity, and that he was worthy of
worship. Early Christianity had created a substitute, counterfeit religion, one
vastly different from that of its founder. We have traced the contrast—from an
original religion that was Torah-observant and that viewed Jesus as a teacher
and Messiah claimant to one that rejected Torah observance and advanced
strong claims about Christ as having a special birth and being a divine-human.

In making this transition, early Christianity effectively killed off the historical Jesus. The Christ of faith became the focal point, belief in whom was
sufficient for salvation. Gone was the covenant between God and the Jewish
people, and Christians were on the cusp of talking in terms of an "old" versus
a "new" covenant—a distinction that emerged in the latter part of the second
century, in the writings of Irenaeus.

The Jews were the only ones around, other than Torah-observant Christians, who recognized what had happened. For a successful crime to take place,
witnesses have to be eliminated. *Guilt at having killed off the historical Jewish Jesus
in favor of a Gentile God-human—along with recognition that the Jews were the witnesses to this act—accounts for the deep roots of Christian anti-Semitism, whether directed against the Jewish people or the religion of Judaism.* The Jews are the only
people whose persistence on the world stage exposes the Christification process for what it was: a cover-up. They and they alone recognize the transformation early Christianity underwent, how it switched the divine Gentile
Christ for the human Jewish Jesus. They're the only ones who could "blow the
cover" off this historical manipulation.

We are familiar that fear and guilt represent powerful emotions that can
drive actions toward the elimination of the offending party, especially when that
party remains visible and present. We see this in contemporary mass media.

Witnesses and informants who come forward to testify against gangs or members of organized crime often face the threat of reprisals. They fear for their lives and those of their family. Some require round-the-clock protection prior to trial in order to guarantee their safety and, even then, live in fear of an acquittal or a revenge slaying by gang or mob associates at some point in the future. In extreme cases, some need to be put into witness protection programs, with changed identities and relocation. Witnesses have good reason to fear retribution from those whom they could potentially expose.

The *Da Vinci Code* follows the same plot line. There was a cover-up by the Roman Catholic Church which allegedly knows that Jesus was married to Mary Magdalene and together they had children who became rulers in Europe. There are witnesses who know the truth and who are charged with safeguarding it, the Priory of Sion. Finally, there is revenge, with the perpetrators of the cover-up (represented by a deranged member of the Opus Dei movement) bent on killing the witnesses so as to avoid exposure of the secret information about Jesus that, allegedly, could destroy the foundations of Christianity. While not history, this story illustrates the lengths to which someone who fears exposure will go to cover up the truth.[12]

We find the same dynamic at work in other stories in contemporary media. Some violent criminals claim that they killed the victims they raped or robbed so that they would not be able testify against them. Perpetrators of some crime, fearful of detection, intimidate, harass, or inflict retribution upon witnesses whose only mistake was having witnessed an event. Witnesses are vulnerable—their only fault having been at the scene of the crime.

According to the Jesus Cover-Up Thesis, the guilt dynamic, lashing out at the witnesses, provides an explanation for the sustained attack on Judaism throughout Christian history. There was "a crime," that is, a transformation of the religion by the Christifiers. There were witnesses, the Jews. There was the psychological need on the part of the Christifiers to eradicate and silence the Jewish witnesses, so as to avoid detection.

Christian anti-Semitism was not a one-time event, by isolated Christian leaders. It represents a sustained assault in ancient, medieval, Reformation, and modern times—from Orthodox, Catholic, and Protestant forms of Christianity. The anti-Jewish sentiment within Christianity is not just a matter of differentiation, of positioning Christianity as distinctive from Judaism—as if the issue were simply how to tell a Democrat from a Republican or a liberal from a conservative. The assault stems from a deeply rooted inner feeling that manifests itself on an ongoing basis. The various contributing factors we noted in the previous chapter for Christian anti-Semitism are simply symptoms of a pervasive underlying guilt.

The root issue is Christification: the supplanting of the Jewish Jesus, the human teacher and Messiah claimant, by a Gentile God-human, savior of humanity. The Jesus

Cover-Up Thesis alone makes sense of the *persistent* attempt to discredit Jewish leaders and their interpretation of their own writings, and to deny the ongoing validity of Judaism as a religion in its own right. From the time of Paul's Letter to the Galatians, the contention has been that Judaism has no right to continue to exist. This thinking is a logical outgrowth of Paul's handiwork—his elimination of Torah observance and his substitution of the Christ of faith for the Jesus of history. The attack, moreover, is rooted in the Christian scriptures, not isolated early church leaders. It is its Christification texts that continue to give power and expression to Christian anti-Semitism today.

The Jesus Cover-Up Thesis also explains why rational attempts to situate biblical texts in historical context do not eliminate the motivation toward anti-Semitism. While statements by church leaders situating strident biblical passages in historical context are helpful, they do not ferret out the underlying root cause of Christian anti-Semitism. The root problem is psychological.

So Jesus did become Christian. But the transformation of the religion and of the portrait of Jesus was not without a harsh price.

✓

EPILOGUE:
THE WAY FORWARD

AN AMAZING VICTORY

In the beverage marketing wars being waged throughout the world, Coca-Cola is faced with a huge number of significant competitors. First of all, its major competitor in the cola category is PepsiCo. In the soft drink category generally, there are other beverages—"uncolas," such as 7Up; cherry-flavored drinks such as Dr. Pepper; orange- and grape-flavored soft drinks; root beer; and local soft drinks. Sports beverages include Gatorade and other products. In the water category are bottled waters and many types of flavored waters. The alcohol category includes beer, wine, coolers, and hard liquors. All of these liquids compete for a "share" of the consumer's throat.

Imagine if Coca-Cola displaced all of these competitors in one fell swoop. That would constitute *the* marketing coup of all time.

That is exactly what Proto-Orthodox Christianity pulled off in the fourth century. It replaced all other brands of Christianity—the Ebionites, Arians, Marcionites, Nestorians, Monophysites, Bardaisanites, and Gnostics, among many others. Most importantly, it was a permanent victory. These nonconforming movements were suppressed and eventually died out, or else they found footholds outside the Roman Empire. They did not regroup to formulate a "comeback" strategy. Christianity also closed down the schools of Greek philosophy—the Platonists, Aristotelians, Stoics, Pythagoreans, Skeptics, Epicureans, and Hedonists whose ancient centers dotted the Mediterranean world. Some of these teachers went into exile, outside the Roman Empire to the east. Gone, too, were the vast temple complexes of the ancient mystery religions—Isis, Dionysus, Mithras, and myriad others. Every major competitor was eradicated by the new Christianity blessed by the Roman emperor Constantine and his bishops at Nicea. The power of these orthodox leaders—backed by Roman imperial might—won the day. In 380, under Emperor Theodosius, it and it alone became the official state religion of the Roman world . . . except for one competitor: Judaism.

What Christianity achieved in the post-Constantine fourth-century era represented the marketing victory of all times. It is especially ironic that a movement that started off as a radical challenge to the Pax Romana succeeded in becoming the official religion of the Roman Empire. This testifies to the remarkable transformation early Christianity underwent at the hands of the leaders of the Christ cult.

This new religion likely would not have succeeded so brilliantly without the Christification process. The church promoted a message rooted in the power of the Christ to confer eternal life on humanity, coupled with an ethical framework that did not include the hard work demanded by the Torah. An ancient ancestry with links through the Jesus Movement to Judaism gave it the advantage of antiquity and venerability. Christ was confidently asserted to be the Messiah without anyone really taking the time to match reality with the posted job specifications. Situated advantageously between Judaism on the one hand and the mystery religions on the other, Proto-Orthodoxy had the religious positioning that clearly represented the winning marketing formula. Within three hundred years of Jesus' death, one form of Christianity—Proto-Orthodoxy, as we have called it—became the official religion of the empire.

But the victory came at a tremendous price. Simply put, the teachings of Jesus himself were smothered by the religion of Paul.

This book has been written for the ordinary reader curious about how Jesus became Christian. In examining writings from the first one hundred years of early Christianity, I have put forward the Jesus Cover-Up Thesis. There are several legs to this point of view. For one thing, it contends that the early church engaged in a *switch,* that is, that Paul's religion became substituted for the religion of Jesus. What we have today in Christianity is largely Paulinity, a religion about the Gentile Christ that covers over the message of the Jewish Jesus of history. Second, it involved a hostile *differentiation,* with scathing attacks by the Proto-Orthodox on anything Jewish. Third, the cover-up resulted in the entrenchment of *anti-Semitism,* directed against Judaism and the Jewish people.

While building on contemporary scholarship, the Jesus Cover-Up Thesis represents my take on what the early church accomplished. Going forward, we need to recover the humanity and Jewishness of Jesus *at the popular level,* not just in academia. This means returning to the original Jewish teacher and Messiah claimant, stripped of all the Christifying elements that have camouflaged this towering figure of history. While scholars may acknowledge these facets of Jesus' life, such historical details have not permeated the consciousness of ordinary people. They still regard Jesus as the divine Gentile and picture him through the Christ figure of Paul. Some readers may bristle at attempts to depict Jesus as less than fully divine. The image of Jesus as a heavenly being has had remarkable sticking power in the popular consciousness. But it's a position that loses much that is of value.

Jesus' own provocative Kingdom message needs to be examined again, as a radical social alternative not only to the Pax Romana but to any society marred by arrogance, self-righteousness, and self-centeredness. His challenge to follow the path of higher righteousness requires observation and not neglect. In other words, we should endeavor to focus again on the message, not the messenger, to visualize him as his earliest followers did, as a rabbi who painted a vision of a better world and who dared us to live in an enhanced manner.

We should also imagine that the writings of Paul and Luke/Acts miraculously disappear from the pages of the New Testament—exactly the opposite of what Marcion would have wished. Some readers may find this unsettling, for these writings make up a good percentage of the New Testament. However, there are good reasons why these attempts to remake the religion should be set aside. Recovering Jesus demands that we jump over Paul and the Christifiers, back to the gospels, and through them to the words that appear to reflect what the Jesus of the 20s likely said to the audiences of his time. This means moving Paul's distinctive religion off its privileged place of honor where it has stood for many centuries.

We should adopt as a sound interpretive principle "as James, so Jesus"— that is, that the best way of trying to grasp the Jesus of history is through his brother James, how he and his group and his successors understood the movement. That has the effect of privileging James, the Jesus Movement, and the Ebionites, a move long overdue. They saw him as human, Jewish, a teacher, and a potential Messiah. When beliefs stray from these attributes of Jesus, we begin to enter Christifier territory.

The Christifiers' rewriting the religion of Jesus as the Christ is not a new phenomenon with respect to biblical and related writings. There is a history of biblical rewriting. The later book of Chronicles in the Old Testament, for instance, rewrote the earlier account of King David in 2 Samuel. This document whitewashed many of David's character flaws. The Book of Jubilees from the second century B.C. rewrote the story of Abraham we find in the biblical book of Genesis in order to heighten Abraham's monotheism. It is in that work that we find the delightful story of how the youthful Abraham smashed the idols in his father's factory, asserting that these material objects have no substance. Several works from the Dead Sea Scroll community also reworked materials from Genesis as well as decoding the words of the prophets to suit their own time and situation. The attempt by Luke/Acts to rewrite early Christian origins is another example of this tendency to make history fit the circumstances of the day.

RECOVERING THE HUMAN JESUS

In the sixteenth century, the Protestant Reformation was fought to bypass centuries of church tradition and go directly back to the message of the Bible. *Sola scriptura* ("scripture alone") was the rallying cry as reformers sought to appreciate anew the perspective of the writers of the New Testament, uncontaminated by the decisions of church councils and the philosophizing of the medieval scholastics. There, within the pages of holy writ, it was hoped, the true and authentic message of Jesus and the early church would come into sharp focus.

The intervening four hundred years, however, have witnessed a remarkable flurry of new insights into the biblical writings themselves. Today we have a better sense of when and where these were composed. How the canon of the New Testament was formed is also better understood. We are now aware of the shaping hand of the Proto-Orthodox faction in deciding which texts to include—and exclude—and the political objectives, both ecclesiastical as well as imperial, this selection reinforced. The New Testament is the creature of this group within the early church, not the other way around, as the Protestant Reformers thought. The authority of the present composition rests on the authority of the Orthodox bishops—St. Athanasius in 367 proclaiming its definitive structure and other leaders who concurred with Athanasius's selection. These are polemical documents that reflect one—but only one—way of being Christian.

For the person interested in how early Christianity developed, we now have access to dozens of writings that were left out of the official canon of the New Testament. For instance, the many Gnostic documents recently discovered augment our knowledge of early Christianity. We are now better able to identify the issues and controversies that divided the fledgling Christian communities around the Mediterranean. Moreover, with the discovery of the Dead Sea Scrolls, we now know more of the pressing political and religious concerns within first-century Judaism, when the Jesus Movement came to light. All these factors give us a better basis upon which to understand the texts of the New Testament than had the reformers of the sixteenth century.

They were overly optimistic that the message of Jesus would shine forth, freed from the clutter and complications of medieval theology. We are now familiar with many of the problems involved in the quest for the Jesus of history—that he wrote nothing and that the sources are later, representing third- or fourth-generation Christian writings. They are also inconsistent in their depiction of Jesus, and both Matthew and Luke take it upon themselves to "correct" Mark, making additions and deletions to suit their own agendas.

But the major problem in unearthing the message of Jesus of the 20s lies elsewhere. It has to do with the effects of Paul and the Christification process engaged in by early leaders of Proto-Orthodoxy as they gravitated toward the Gentile savior message. They battled with the Jesus Movement and the Ebionites while denigrating everything Jewish about Jesus and denouncing Judaism vehemently. We have seen how they did that, decade after decade, in a vocal and vicious manner. The gospels themselves were written after Paul, and, to some extent, they too show evidence of Christification, especially the Gospel of John with its emphasis on the "I am" statements not found in any other characterization of Jesus. So the problem in trying to uncover the historical Jesus lies not just in church tradition within the postbiblical period. The Christification layering process is to be found within the pages of the New Testament itself, with Paul's Christ superimposed on the Jesus of history. That means that as we read the gospels, judgments have to be made along the way concerning what might reflect what Jesus himself actually could have said and did, versus what authors forty to eighty years later wanted him to have said.

We catch glimpses of the authentic Jesus here and there in the gospels. In the sayings of the Sermon on the Mount, for instance, we see Jesus advancing teachings that challenge his audience to a higher excellence in living, based on Torah but exceeding its usual demands. The parables, moreover, propel us into a new dimension, to grasp what life could be outside the parameters of the Pax Romana. We see there, too, an idea of what God's sovereign rule over all humanity might look like, and we can become fascinated by its possibilities: a new life for all, built on caring and compassion, but not neglectful of the duties of Torah.

We do not know enough to speculate about Jesus' daily routine—where he lived, what he ate for breakfast, who cooked, how he planned the day's itinerary, the round of daily prayers, his interactions with local synagogue authorities, the decisions he made, or the sessions he must have held with his closest associates like a rabbi with devoted disciples. Was he vulnerable to the critical reactions of other people? Did rejection bother him? Did he experience stress, regrets, moods, uncertainty, anxiety, dread, fear, and joy? It is even more difficult to get inside the mind of Jesus. What set him off on the path opposing Roman rule? How much of Israel's ancient writings did he know, and how did he become familiar with them? Did he read Hebrew as well as speak Aramaic (and, possibly, Greek)? Did he "buy into" the dream-myth of Israel, that wonderful expectation of a future king who would change the world? Did he envisage himself fulfilling that role, or did he think God would act unilaterally in establishing the new world order?

As fully human, did Jesus experience our range of emotions? Did he have hopes, ambitions, dreams, and disappointments? Was he, in all ways, human? If we think of Jesus as divine, then all is known and Jesus moves through history, towering over life's perplexities and complexities like a being above the fray. In that view, the problems we confront on a daily basis were not his. Everything is preordained, simple, clear—and ever so removed from our world. The price tag of seeing Jesus as divine is that we cannot identify with him, nor he with us, for we do not share the same situation, the same lot in life.

Did he struggle to control his passions? Did he, quite frankly, "lose it" when he attacked the currency converters in the Temple who were pursuing a legitimate business? Did he experience sexual feelings and passions the way we do? Were his temptations in the wilderness at the beginning of his mission handled as easily as the gospels depict? Or were they real temptations? Was it a real interior battle such as we might experience over the right direction for our life? Did he experience doubts and hesitations on the Mount of Olives east of Jerusalem just prior to his betrayal? Did he really sense what might be coming? Did he have qualms, with so much of his mission left undone?

At age thirty, what did he imagine his world would be like thirty years later? If we were conducting an interview with Jesus in his prime, how would he have answered that question? Did he think the future he projected in the parables would be realized within his lifetime? What role did he himself think he'd play? To what extent did his associates—the disciples—share in this vision? How did they spend their days—plying their trades, studying, debating biblical texts, plotting against Rome, listening to a wonderful vision of the coming Kingdom of God, and organizing routines of daily life?

And what of his family, what role did they play—Mary, his mother; Joseph, his father; his four brothers; his sisters; and his cousin John the Baptist? Did they engage in his enterprise and to what extent? And what was the role of his close associate, Mary Magdalene—the follower who, along with several other wealthy women, funded his mission, who went to Jerusalem on his last trip there, who stood vigil with him throughout the hours of his crucifixion, and who went to the tomb on the first day of the week and witnessed it empty?

A work that opens up many of the details of Jesus' human life is James Tabor's *The Jesus Dynasty*. This intriguing book represents an important contribution to recovering what we can now know about the man—his ancestors, his immediate family, and his successors—all set against the complex Jewish and Roman politics of the era. Recognizing that there are many things about Jesus we cannot ever know, Tabor argues for an initial joint baptizing mission between John the Baptist and Jesus "the Baptist." As Tabor reconstructs the scenario, John worked in the North while, early on in his career, Jesus and his disciples operated in Judea, in the South. Their joint campaign was exceptionally ambitious: "Jesus had become a full partner with John the Baptizer and their plan was to arouse the entire country and shake the establishment, both political and religious, during the coming summer and fall months of A.D. 27."[1] In doing this, Jesus and John the Baptist were functioning in many ways like the dual Messiahs expected by the Dead Sea Scroll community—a priestly one (John the Baptist) and a political one (Jesus). The arrest of John the Baptist by Herod Antipas threw this joint enterprise into disarray, and Jesus had to reenvisage his mission.

By careful detective work, Tabor also unveils the prominent role Jesus' brothers exercised within his inner core of disciples. As he writes, "This is perhaps the best-kept secret in the entire New Testament. **Jesus' own brothers were among the so-called Twelve Apostles.**"[2] This represents a startling finding, for early Christian texts tended to cover over the involvement of Jesus' family in his mission. This was due to the desire of the Christifiers to downplay the role of James and the Jesus Movement in favor of Paul's religion; James would have none of the Christ cult beliefs and practices.

Tabor's argument is interesting. He splices together several key strands with the gospel accounts. Joseph, the husband of Mary, disappears from the narrative very early on: he just isn't mentioned. Jesus has several brothers— James, Jude, and Simon being three. Interestingly, these are also the names of three of Jesus' disciples. Tabor hypothesizes that Mary married a second time. After Joseph died, his brother Alphaeus (Clophas) married her. Together they had several children—James, Jude and Simon among them.[3] Hence these three—James, Jude, Simon—would be Jesus' half-brothers as well as being, very likely, members of his inner core group, the twelve disciples.

If Tabor is correct, then truly Jesus' mission was a family business, with his brothers and cousin all playing a major role.

As a human figure, Jesus becomes more accessible to us as a role model struggling with his own path in life as well as the relationship of belief in God to social and political systems of the day. He struggled to convince people of his vision of the Kingdom of God on earth, with foreign rule and evil swept away. We see him engaging the world's superpower of the time, rousing people to awareness and action. A struggling human meeting challenges and overcoming crises is more easily related to than a divine being who does not feel the contradictions and limitations of the human condition and for whom everything is presumed to be easy. Hopes, dreams, ambitions, successes, and failure— all these are the fabric of being human, but not of divinity, for whom all is known and all is possible.

So, too, are disappointments, and Jesus must have experienced many. The execution of his cousin, John the Baptist, must have been a crushing blow— they shared the same hope and vision. There were villages that rejected his message and were inhospitable. There was betrayal by Judas, one of his own core of disciples. Perhaps there was also bewilderment. During his last week in

Jerusalem, he staged a dramatic entrance into the city, riding on a lowly animal and then attacking the currency converters in the Temple. What was this all about? What did he think would happen? Did he imagine that the masses of people there to celebrate Passover would spontaneously rise up in support of his cause? Or did he harbor the belief that God would suddenly appear to intervene in human history, transform the Temple, and evict the Romans from power? What are we to make of that final cry upon the cross—"My God, my God, why have you forsaken me?" Was that a recognition, as he was dying, that the world was not going to be transformed the way he had anticipated? If so, then that, too, is something with which we can identify—dashed hopes, a vision smashed, or a marvelous plan postponed.

And yet that vision survives, as one that challenges each generation to ponder anew the contrast between what is and what might be if only people responded and God acted.

A human Jesus. This is not a modern invention. It is the *original* Jesus. That was precisely how his earliest followers—including his brother—understood him. It is only Paul, the Christifiers, and their successors who thought otherwise.

DISCOVERING THE JEWISH JESUS

Who are the most famous Jews of all time? When asked this question, people typically start with the Bible—Abraham, some suggest, with others adding in Moses and David. Then, skipping over three thousand years of history, they might come up with such suggestions as Madonna (the pop star Madonna, that is), while a few might add Golda Meir, David Ben-Gurion, or Albert Einstein.

Some might eventually say, "Well, of course, Jesus was Jewish, as was Mary, his mother. Oh, and also Mary Magdalene." Others, then, sensing the drift, might add, "And, yes, all of his original twelve disciples were Jewish . . . and his brothers . . . and John the Baptist." These responses, however, are not typically the ones first uttered, coming only after a long pause during which people rack their minds wondering what the correct answers are. These results are not unexpected. For the most part, the people who populate the New Testament just aren't thought of as Jewish. This is ironic. Of all the Jewish males who ever lived, Jesus was by far the most influential. Of all the Jewish women of history, probably Mary the mother of Jesus has had the greatest impact on people. Indeed, the most common Christian prayer uttered on a daily basis throughout the contemporary world is likely the intercessory prayer to the Jewish Mary ("Holy Mary, Mother of God, pray for us sinners now and at the hour of our death"), followed closely by the Lord's Prayer.

Christians today who honor Jesus, Mary, and the other figures of the New Testament writings do not think of them as Jewish. Similarly, Jews today, who do not honor them, also do not think of them as Jewish. They reside in a curious ethnic no-man's-land.

The Jewishness of Jesus lies on the remote margins of Christian imagination, if it exists at all. This is not just a matter of picturing him in our minds as a Jewish rabbi—being circumcised, participating in Jewish prayers, observing the annual round of festivals, studying the Torah, engaging his disciples in discussion and debate, arguing the law with other Jewish leaders, going to the Temple, observing Passover, following the dietary laws, and keeping the Sabbath. All that is integral, of course, to the Jewishness of Jesus and was what he did.

We miss a lot if we do not think of Jesus as Jewish. For one thing, the radical *political* import of Jesus' mission does not emerge—his taking on mighty Rome and its much-touted Pax Romana. The forcefulness of his challenge becomes obscured if we do not place him in the context of his culture and his world. The resilience of this message draws on the depths of Jewish expectations and hopes, that God would one day alter the world for the better. Without an understanding of that expectation, we are ill equipped to appreciate the resonance his message created within the society of the time.

Jesus' message was a much more powerful affront to the foreign rulers than any other Jewish groups mustered, notwithstanding the ambitions of the uncompromising Essenes and militant Zealots. For those who yearned for an end to Roman rule, this represented a different strategic option than that presented by any other group. The Sadducees had opted for accommodation with the Romans; the Pharisees taught; the Essenes separated; the Zealots fought; John the Baptist urged a rededication to Torah; and Paul encouraged assimilation. Only Jesus had the imagination to pose an alternative to Rome and Hellenization: anticipate, prepare for, and participate in the Kingdom of God that was soon to be established on earth.

Did he personally think of himself as the Messiah of Israel, or was that a hope confined just to his later followers who made grand claims about him? We cannot be sure, and the texts appear to ascribe some messianic aspirations to Jesus himself, as King of the Jews. If we do not place him within his Jewish context, then we miss out on the powerful emotions created by these messianic anticipations. We have reviewed the expectations for being a Messiah very carefully—the Davidic ruler over Israel and catalyst for world transformation, ushering in, with God's power, an era of universal peace. If we do not have this criterion firmly in place, then we become susceptible to another description, that of Paul's Christ figure—a different model altogether and, as we have shown, one that derives not from a Jewish context but a foreign Gentile environment.

In addition, if we do not see Jesus, his mother, his brothers, his disciples, and Mary Magdalene as Jewish, then we are more apt to fall prey to the virus of anti-Semitism. Any vilification of Judaism and of the Jewish people represents an attack on these figures of the faith who in their day operated well within the confines of the Jewish family. They were not initiators of a new religion, and they were never, ever Christians. They remained Jewish throughout their lives. These individuals were, however, the victims of the Christifiers who remade the image of Jesus into a Gentile God, stripping him of his Jewish identity and humanity, with powerful consequences that still reverberate today.

Rediscovering the Jewish Jesus should help Christians participate in endeavors to combat contemporary anti-Semitism, whatever its source and whatever form it takes, whether personal, religious, or national. This includes all attacks on the Jewish people, the legitimacy of Judaism, and the right of the Jewish homeland to exist.

Jesus' message was straightforward: keep Torah and plan for the Kingdom of God. Both require action. The practice of Torah requires daily choices, control of attitudes and right behavior, aligning oneself with a pattern of life presented in the books of the Torah and endorsed by Jesus in an extended fashion. The parable of the Talents (Matthew 25:14–30) praises those who made use of what they had been given. The individual who hid his coin was rebuffed. This parable of the Kingdom shows us the need to use all of one's resources imaginatively, much as Esther and Judith did before when they were faced with difficult circumstances. The parable of the Great Judgment (Matthew 25:31–46) validates those who actively respond to the needs of others—welcoming strangers, clothing the naked, and taking care of the sick. They are the ones who will inherit eternal life.

In these astounding parables, the message of the Kingdom of God has nothing to do with an elaborate infrastructure of belief about a Christ figure, worship of Jesus as divine, baptism, communion, belonging to one true church, or assent to creedal statements that precisely affirm the correct Trinitarian formula thrashed out by a committee of select bishops in the fourth century. That superstructure simply does not exist in Jesus' message. It was the creation of the later Christifiers.

As a good Jewish rabbi, Jesus taught his followers a prayer. Matthew embeds this within the Sermon on the Mount (Matthew 6:9–13). Nowhere does one draw closer to the teachings of Jesus than in this prayer, for the themes it articulates points to what was central in his thought. It is a threefold prayer, similar in structure to the central Jewish prayer, the Amidah, to which it bears other similarities—praise, petitions, thanksgiving.

The Lord's Prayer begins with an address: "Our Father in heaven." This opening phrase clearly identifies to whom the prayer is being addressed: God our Father. This positions everyone as children of God. We are all sons of God or daughters of God. All humanity has a common parentage.

The prayer continues with the sanctification of God's name: "Hallowed be your name." This praise requires some decoding. We need to recognize two things: first of all, the word *name* stands for God. Even today many devout Jews use the phrase *HaShem* (the name) when praying to God so as not to say the divine name or to presume undue familiarity with the omnipotent creator and infinite ruler of the universe. We also need to recognize that the ancient English word *hallowed* means "holy." So this phrase in contemporary English might be better rendered, "Holy are you, O God." It's an important statement, for it calls upon the person praying to recognize the utter difference between humanity and God: only God is holy.

The prayer then continues with five petitions. The first two focus on our responsibilities toward God and recognize God's agenda for humanity. The most important petition is uttered first and it has to do with the Kingdom message: "Your kingdom come." This reflects the priority that Jesus places upon this teaching. It is followed by a second petition having to do with making God's will manifest on earth as it already is in heaven: "Your will be done, on earth as it is in heaven." What Jesus means by "God's will" is carefully indicated throughout the Sermon on the Mount. The will of God encompasses the path of higher righteousness, the call to excellence in living, and the blessedness achievable through the attitudes and actions expressed in the beginning portion of the Sermon on the Mount, the Beatitudes—showing mercy, being hungry for righteousness, being eager for spiritual nourishment, and striving to make peace among people and parties in conflict. The prayer makes it clear that the sphere of our actions is terrestrial: "on earth." In uttering these petitions, Jesus asks us to recognize that we have a role to play, working in conjunction with God, to help establish his Kingdom by aligning ourselves with his agenda and establishing the conditions within which the Kingdom will flourish. It is not a prayer that leaves everything up to God: it represents a partnership arrangement, as befits a covenantal relationship. It offers an immense opportunity for humanity—and responsibility—to work to further God's purposes within the sphere of our domain, the world we inhabit. It is emphatically not a petition to flee the world, to avoid the situations with which we are confronted or to abandon current responsibilities toward the world by seeking refuge in an afterlife.

The next segment of the prayer turns to the human agenda. The third petition represents an omnibus prayer for having all one's needs accommodated: "Give us this day our daily bread" —whatever needs are required to get through the day, material, emotional, or spiritual. This petition presupposes confidence in God, that he will provide, and it encompasses a wide territory—whatever we require for life and living. It is wider than just food, which is a metaphor for sustenance. All needs are summed up in this petition—our need for spiritual growth, emotional development, intellectual maturity, and physical requirements are all combined, as well as the hope for salvation or redemption. It calls upon God to provide all these. Nowhere is this clearer than in the desire for eternal life: restoring the dead to life is the prerogative of God, when and how he sees fit. That, too, is part of our needs.

A fourth petition asks for forgiveness but places a condition on our receiving forgiveness, namely, that we have forgiven others: "And forgive us our debts, as we also have forgiven our debtors." Again, there is much that we have to do to be part of God's Kingdom. It recognizes that we will fail in our tasks, as, indeed, others will fail. But it provides for an act of individual will to re-create life so that we are not perpetually imprisoned by victimization to past misdeeds and misfortunes, whether ours or those of others. It is what allows us to move on in life, forgiving and being forgiven, not being stuck because of some incident in the past. In this petition, the person praying recognizes the need to take the first step, to forgive, in order personally to be forgiven.

Finally, there is a fifth plea to be able to avoid periods of dreadful testing and the power of evil: "And do not bring us to the time of trial, but rescue us from the evil one." This refers to times when our inner resources, our spiritual and emotional state and physical abilities, can be stretched to the limit. Help us avoid despair, desperation, and despondency—all the things that remove us from vibrant participation in God's Kingdom and deprive us of the ability to think not only of ourselves, but also of others. It again presupposes confidence that we can trust God to act on our behalf, however he sees fit.

Matthew ends the prayer here. It is short and to the point, encapsulating Jesus' teaching in a succinct fashion. The usual prayer, as it is said today by many, ends with a third section acknowledging God's power and purpose: "For thine is the Kingdom, the power and the glory, for ever and ever. Amen."

This powerful prayer highlights what Matthew has emphasized about the teachings of Jesus in his gospel. It is noteworthy for what it includes—and excludes. It focuses succinctly on two agendas—God's and ours—and it places priority on the Kingdom message and doing God's will. It encapsulates what Jesus encouraged his followers to believe and do.

Furthermore, it is directed not to Jesus, but to God. It is not said "through Jesus" or "in Jesus' name," however much that has become enshrined in later Christian practice. Like the Amidah, a longer prayer with more petitions, this one is addressed directly to God, not through an intermediary. As it makes clear, only God can fulfill the petitions expressed in this prayer.

A valiant Jewish challenger to Rome's imperial power. A potential Jewish Messiah. A teacher with great insight. That was how Jesus' earliest followers in Jerusalem viewed him—Jewish, as they were. This is not a modern invention. It was the *original* view of Jesus.

TIMELINES

EVENTS AND MOVEMENTS

HELLENIZATION

Hellenization in General (Fourth Century B.C.–Sixth Century A.D.)
Hellenization was the spread of the Greek language, values, and culture throughout the Mediterranean world. It was disseminated through the development
of local Greek city-states, governmental influence, laws, troops, religion, philosophy, drama, and customs. It developed from the 330s B.C. onwards after
Alexander the Great conquered the Near East. In its broadest sense, Hellenization includes the pervasive influence of both Greek and later Roman
culture.

Enforced Hellenization: 167–164 B.C.
Antiochus Epiphanes' policy of enforced Hellenization outlawed the practice
of Judaism. This resulted in persecutions of observant Jews, desecration of the
Temple, and the destruction of Jewish sacred texts. The Maccabees led a revolt.
They succeeded in capturing Jerusalem, and the Temple was rededicated in
164 B.C. This is commemorated in the festival of Hanukkah.

Factions Within Judaism As a Result of Hellenization (After 164 B.C.)
After the persecutions of Antiochus Epiphanes, various groups or "parties"
arose within Judaism. These represented different ways of being Jewish in light
of Hellenistic pressures. These included:

- **Sadducees,** who controlled the Temple and commerce, emphasized *accommodation* with the Greeks and Romans.
- **Pharisees** taught Torah and focused on *education* as a strategy for defending the Jewish community against assimilation.
- **Dead Sea Scroll community** (Essenes). Led by a Teacher of Righteousness, this group preferred *separation* to avoid contamination with foreign influences. This movement may have originated in the post-164 period or somewhat later, during the reign of Queen Salome Alexandra, 76–67 B.C. The scrolls themselves date from the first century B.C. through to A.D. 68 when Qumran, the headquarters of this movement, was destroyed. Most scholars identify the Dead Sea Scroll community with the Essenes.
- **Zealots,** who advocated active resistance or *fighting* the occupying forces, originated later than the other groups, in A.D. 6.

The Sadducees, Zealots, and members of the Dead Sea Scroll movement did not, for the most part, survive the first Jewish War against Rome (A.D. 66–70). Only the Pharisees survived the destruction of Jerusalem and the Temple. They became the leaders in reconstructing Judaism after 70.

The Greeks and the Romans (After 63 B.C.)

Rome conquered the Greek Empire including the Near East. The common language remained Greek. In time, the Greek deities were simply given Roman names. The process of Hellenization continued through the city-states, schools, laws, religion, and, especially, through the proliferation of mystery religions. These included the Egyptian cult of Isis, the Greek cult of Dionysus, the Persian religion of Mithras, and many others.

JESUS AND HIS TIMES

Herod the Great (Died 4 B.C.)

The Jewish ruler just prior to the time of Jesus, Herod the Great, had engaged in massive building projects including expansion of the platform of Temple Mount and the rebuilding of the Temple. He also constructed Masada, Herodion, the port city of Caesarea Maritima, and many other sites. He built up Jerusalem as a showcase city for the Roman Empire.

Jesus (5/6 B.C.–A.D. 30)

Jesus was born sometime before 4 B.C. since Herod the Great died in that year. Hence his birth is usually dated to 6 or 5 B.C.

According to the gospels, Jesus was born in Bethlehem (a few miles south of Jerusalem) but grew up in Nazareth (in the Galilee in the north). John the Baptist was Jesus' cousin. John preached and baptized sometime during the mid to late 20s A.D. Jesus had four brothers and at least two sisters.

Jesus' ministry occurred during the late 20s A.D., approximately 27–30. According to the Gospel of Matthew, he promised his hearers that the Kingdom of God was about to be manifest on earth and he challenged them to live a life of higher righteousness (strict Torah observance). He was put to death by the Romans around A.D. 30. (Some say A.D. 33 or several years later.)

EARLY CHRISTIANITY

Jesus Movement (Ebionites)

Jesus' earliest followers, the Jesus Movement, were led by James, Jesus' brother, in Jerusalem from the 30s to the early 60s. They were Torah-observant. They looked on Jesus as human, and expected him to return soon to help establish the promised Kingdom of God on earth. James, Peter, and John were known as the Pillars. Josephus, the Jewish historian who lived from A.D. 37 to about 100, noted that James was killed in 62.

During the First Jewish Revolt against Rome (66–70), this movement may have fled to Pella in what is today northern Jordan, returning after hostilities ceased. James's successor as bishop of Jerusalem was Simeon, another relative of Jesus. Simeon was killed in the early second century.

This expression of the Christian movement continued to exist, but it became increasingly marginalized. They were later referred to as Ebionites or Nazarenes and were shunned by what became mainstream Christianity, Proto-Orthodoxy, as scholars refer to the group that succeeded.

Christ Movement (Proto-Orthodoxy)

The Christ Movement was led by Paul, in the Diaspora. Paul rejected Torah observance and focused his message on the death and resurrection of Christ. Paul never met the Jesus of history, rarely quoted him, and distanced his movement from that of James's. In origins, teachings, and practices, the Christ Movement differed significantly from the Jesus Movement.

Paul wrote letters to fledgling congregations during the 50s and early 60s. These were located in modern-day Turkey, Greece, and Italy. His letters are the earliest Christian writings we have, predating any of the gospels.

Paul and Peter were killed in Rome in the early to mid 60s.

The Christ Movement succeeded, bringing in many converts from a non-Jewish (Gentile) background. As this segment of early Christianity grew in the second through fourth centuries, scholars refer to this movement as Proto-Orthodox Christianity. They were the faction favored by fourth-century Roman emperors and thus became the dominant group. Modern Christianity stems from the Christ Movement/Proto-Orthodoxy.

Gnostic Movement

This form of early Christianity originated sometime during the first century A.D.—we don't know when or how. We know about it not only from the writings of its opponents, but also from the discovery in 1948 of the Nag Hammadi Gnostic writings.

Important writings include the *Apocryphon of John,* the *Gospel of Thomas,* the *Gospel of Mary,* the *Gospel of Philip,* and many others. Unlike the Jesus Movement, which emphasized Torah (law), or the Christ Movement, which focused on faith, the Gnostic Movement stressed *gnosis* ("insight" or "knowledge"). None of the Gnostic writings was included in the New Testament. This form of early Christianity at times rivaled Proto-Orthodoxy. It declined or was suppressed during the fourth century as Proto-Orthodoxy became the favored religion of the Roman Empire.

FIRST JEWISH REVOLT AGAINST ROME (A.D. 66–70)

Qumran, the headquarters of the Dead Sea Scroll movement on the northeastern shore of the Dead Sea, was destroyed by the Romans in 68. Jerusalem was decimated in 70, along with the Temple. Only the Pharisees survived. For the most part, the Sadducees, Dead Sea Scroll community members, and Zealots did not. Masada, the Zealot fortress by the shores of the Dead Sea, was destroyed in 73 or 74. Josephus wrote about this revolt based, in part, on his own eyewitness accounts.

LATER EVENTS

In 313, the Roman emperor Constantine issued the Edict of Milan, which extended toleration to all religions, Christianity included. In 380, Emperor Theodosius declared one form of Christianity—what scholars call Proto-Orthodoxy—the official state religion of the Roman Empire.

In 325, the Proto-Orthodox bishops at the Council of Nicea developed the Nicene Creed as the authoritative expression of the correct faith. In 367, Archbishop Athanasius of Alexandria, Egypt, circulated a letter outlining the twenty-seven books that compose the New Testament.

MOVEMENTS WITHIN EARLY CHRISTIANITY

COMPARISONS: JESUS MOVEMENT VERSUS CHRIST MOVEMENT

The Christ Movement differs in origins, practices and beliefs from the Jesus Movement.

	JESUS MOVEMENT	CHRIST MOVEMENT
LEADER	• James in Jerusalem	• Paul in the Diaspora
ORIGINS	• The historical Jesus	• Paul's personal mystical experience of the Christ • Paul never met the historical Jesus
PRACTICES	• Torah-observant	• Non-Torah-observant
BELIEFS	• Jesus as inspired teacher, resurrected, expected to return to complete the job of Messiah • Political catalyst • Era of universal peace (Kingdom of God)	• Christ as a cosmic figure • Christ: a divine being who has came into the world in human form to save humanity by dying and rising • Those who have faith in Christ can share in his suffering, dying, and rising
	Religion *of* Jesus	Religion *about* the Christ

COMPARATIVE ORIGINS

Two movements had their origin in biblical Judaism:
• Rabbinic Judaism
• the Jesus Movement (Ebionites)

Two movements had separate origins:
• the Christ Movement (Proto-Orthodoxy)
• the Gnostic Movement

The Christ Movement originated with Paul's teachings. The origins of the Gnostic Movement are unknown.

ORIGIN	THROUGH	BECAME
Biblical Judaism	Pharisees	Rabbinic Judaism
	Jesus	Jesus Movement/Ebionites
	Paul	Christ Movement/Proto-Orthodoxy
	not known	Gnostic Movement

CHRISTIAN WRITINGS (IN HISTORICAL SEQUENCE)

There is controversy about the precise dating of some of these writings. In general, for biblical works, I follow the dating suggested by Bart Ehrman in several writings *(The New Testament, Lost Christianities, Lost Scriptures)* and Burton Mack *(Who Wrote the New Testament?)*.

FIRST CENTURY A.D.
50s Paul's Letters (Romans, 1 and 2 Corinthians, Galatians, Philippians, 1 Thessalonians, Philemon)
70s Gospel of Mark
80s Gospel of Matthew
90s Gospel of John

Sometime midfirst century
• Q—the common source used by Matthew and Luke that does not come from Mark

Sometime late first century
• *Didache*
• Letter of James
• Parts of the *Gospel of Thomas*
• Letters attributed to Paul but probably not written by him (e.g., 1 and 2 Timothy, Titus, Ephesians, Colossians, 2 Thessalonians)
• Gospel of Luke, Book of Acts (dates range from the 90s to the 120s)

SECOND CENTURY
100   *Epistle of Barnabas* (late first century or early second century)
110s Ignatius of Antioch's letters
130s Justin Martyr, *Dialogue with Trypho*
140s Marcion's *Antitheses*
150s *Infancy Gospel of James*
after 150
        Apostles' Creed
        Epistle to Diognetus
        Gospel of Peter

THIRD CENTURY
• Tertullian, *Against Marcion* (early third century)
• *Recognitions of Clement* (sometime during the third century)
• *The Homilies of Clement* (sometime during the third century)

FOURTH CENTURY

- Eusebius's *Ecclesiastical History* (early fourth century)
- 367—Athanasius's *Thirty-ninth Festal Letter*—lists the twenty-seven books of the New Testament

TERMINOLOGY

ACTS (BOOK OF). A work written by the same author who composed the Gospel of Luke. Scholars date Luke and the Book of Acts to A.D. 90–125.

AMIDAH. The "Standing" prayer is the central prayer of the Jewish liturgy. It is also known as the Eighteen Benedictions (Shemoneh Esrei), although it now includes nineteen sections. It is made up of three parts. In the first section, the person praying addresses God as the God of Abraham, Isaac, and Jacob, and praises God's might and power, for example, in healing the sick and raising the dead. The middle section includes petitions on behalf of the individual and the people of Israel—for knowledge and insight, repentance, forgiveness, redemption, healing, blessing upon the produce of the earth, for the gathering in of the exiles, justice, destruction of heretics, righteousness, restoration of the Kingdom of David, and for a descendant of David. The last part thanks God for his goodness and mercy.

ANTIOCHUS EPIPHANES. The Greek ruler of the Seleucid Empire from 175 to 163 B.C. In 167 B.C., he attempted to destroy Judaism, outlawing the possession of sacred texts and banning such practices as the dietary laws, circumcision, and observing the Sabbath. He desecrated the Temple in Jerusalem. This occasioned a revolt by the Maccabeans. In 164 B.C., they succeeded in capturing Jerusalem and the Temple, which they purified, instituting the festival of Hanukkah.

ANTI-SEMITISM. A view that singles out for selective condemnation the Jewish people, their religion, and/or their homeland, Israel.

APOSTLES' CREED. An early Proto-Orthodox statement of faith, probably dating at least in part from the second century A.D.

ATHANASIUS. A bishop of Alexandria, Egypt, in the fourth century A.D. In 367, in a document referred to as his *Thirty-Ninth Festal Letter,* Athanasius enumerated the twenty-seven books of the New Testament. This became the standard list. In addition, a creed focusing on the doctrines of the Trinity and Incarnation was attributed to St. Athanasius, although it was probably composed later.

B.C./A.D. "Before Christ"/*Anno Domini* (Latin for "year of our Lord"). Some scholars prefer to use B.C.E. (Before the Common Era) or C.E. (Common Era).

BROTHERS OF JESUS. According to Mark 6:3, and Matthew 13:55, Jesus had four brothers: James, Joses (Joseph), Simon, and Judas.

CANONICAL GOSPELS. The four gospels included in the New Testament. These were the ones selected by Proto-Orthodox leaders by the fourth century for inclusion in the canon of the New Testament. Many other gospels existed that were not included in the New Testament, written from differing perspectives—from Gnostic and Ebionite points of view, for instance.

CHRIST. The Greek word for "Messiah."

CHRIST MOVEMENT. The movement stemming from Paul's teachings about the Christ, which attracted a large Gentile following. In particular, the movement emphasized freedom from the Torah and the role of the Christ as savior. Scholars refer to this movement in the second through fourth centuries as Proto-Orthodoxy, that is, the form of early Christianity that was eventually successful in becoming the official religion of the Roman Empire. Orthodox, Catholic, and Protestant branches of Christianity stem from the Christ Movement/Proto-Orthodoxy.

CONSTANTINE (EMPEROR). An influential fourth-century Roman emperor whose decisions marked a major turning point for early Christianity. In 313, he issued the Edict of Milan, which promulgated tolerance for Christians, removing from them the threat of persecution. In 325, he convened the influential Council of Nicea, which attempted to gain theological consensus regarding the nature of Jesus and his relationship to God the Father.

CREED OF ST. ATHANASIUS. A creed focusing on the doctrines of the Trinity and Incarnation, attributed to St. Athanasius, bishop of Alexandria, who lived during the fourth century A.D. The creed was probably composed later than Athanasius.

DEAD SEA SCROLLS. A collection of important scrolls found in the Dead Sea area of Israel in the late 1940s. Portions of over eight hundred different scrolls (some with duplicates) have been discovered. Some were of books of the Hebrew Bible. Others were writings belonging to the Dead Sea Scroll community itself—*War Scroll, Community Rule, Temple Scroll, Copper Scroll,* interpretations of the prophets, psalms, and interpretations of Jewish law.

DEAD SEA SCROLL COMMUNITY (ESSENES). The name given to the community that lived at Qumran during the first century B.C. and first century A.D., up until 68 when Qumran was destroyed by the Romans. Many scholars, but not all, believe that this community should be identified with the Essenes, who reportedly also lived in the same approximate area.

DEUTERONOMY. The fifth book of the Hebrew Bible or Old Testament.

DIASPORA (JEWISH DIASPORA). As it applies to Judaism, Jews living outside the land of Israel, for example, in Babylonia, Egypt, areas of what is now modern Turkey, Greece, Italy, and other centers around the Mediterranean.

DISCIPLES OF JESUS. Very generally, the followers of Jesus. Twelve individuals are named as the twelve apostles, close associates of Jesus, very likely "the core group." While the lists vary, Matthew (10:2–4) cites them as follows: Simon Peter; Andrew, brother of Simon Peter; James, son of Zebedee; John, brother of James, son of Zebedee; Philip; Bartholomew; Thomas; Matthew; James, son of Alphaeus; Thaddaeus or Lebbaeus; Simon the Cananaean; Judas Iscariot.

EBIONITES. A name given to the Jesus Movement as it evolved in the second through fourth centuries.

ENFORCED HELLENIZATION. The policy of Antiochus Epiphanes outlawing the practices of Judaism, 167–164 B.C., in favor of encouraging everyone to adopt Hellenistic ways.

ENOCH. Several Jewish writings from the second century B.C. and first century A.D., named after Enoch, the seventh descendant of Adam and Eve. Books of Enoch are included in the Pseudepigrapha, a collection of Jewish writings that were never part of the Hebrew Bible but that, in their own day, enjoyed circulation among various Jewish groups.

EPISTLE OF BARNABAS. A Christian writing from the late first century or early second century. While its authorship is unknown, it was attributed to Barnabas, one of Paul's traveling companions.

ESSENES. A Jewish group that inhabited the northwest shores of the Dead Sea during the first century B.C. and first century A.D. The Dead Sea Scroll community is often identified as the Essenes. In addition, there were Essene communities throughout the Galilee and Judea, including a section of Jerusalem known as the Essene Quarter.

FAMILY OF JESUS. This includes his mother (Mary); his father (Joseph); four brothers (James, Joses or Joseph, Judas, and Simon); at least two unnamed sisters; a cousin (whom we call John the Baptist); an aunt (John the Baptist's mother), Elisabeth; and an uncle (John the Baptist's father), Zacharias.

FIRST JEWISH REVOLT AGAINST ROME. A.D. 66–74. Qumran was captured in 68; Jerusalem and the Second Temple were destroyed in 70; Masada fell either 73 or 74.

GENTILES. A Jewish expression for non-Jews.

GNOSTICS, GNOSTICISM. A widespread movement encompassing many differing groups during the first four centuries A.D., united by the belief that *gnosis* (insight or knowledge) was the way of salvation from the evil material prison in which humans have become entrapped. Some Gnostics claimed to be Christians. Others did not. Those Gnostics who were Christians viewed Jesus as a teacher of knowledge. In the late 1940s, at Nag Hammadi in Egypt, a collection of over fifty Gnostic writings were discovered. These included various gospels used by Gnostic Christians but not included in the New Testament (*Gospel of Philip, Gospel of Truth, Gospel of Mary*).

HEBREW BIBLE. A collection of writings that forms the Bible for Judaism and the Old Testament for Protestants. In the Jewish Bible, the writings are arranged into three divisions: the Torah (first five books); the Prophets; and the Writings.

HELLENIZATION. Assimilation into Greek (and later, Roman) culture.

HEROD THE GREAT. The king who ruled Judea in the last three decades of the first century B.C. and who was noted for his large and impressive building projects (e.g., enlarging Temple Mount, Herodion, Caesarea Maritima). He died in 4 B.C.

HILLEL. An important Jewish sage who lived in Jerusalem during the last decades of the first century B.C. and the early decades of the first century A.D. His movement attracted many disciples. The House of Hillel, as his group was known, debated many issues of Jewish law against a rival group, the House of Shammai, and they generally adopted a less strict line of interpretation.

IGNATIUS OF ANTIOCH. An influential early Christian leader, bishop of Antioch on the Orontes, who was condemned to death by the Romans around A.D. 115. On his way to execution in Rome, he wrote letters to various congregations. Seven of these letters survive.

IMMACULATE CONCEPTION. The special conception of Mary, Mother of Jesus, by Anna, her mother, seemingly without male involvement. A prominent theme in the second-century work the *Infancy Gospel of James.*

INFANCY GOSPEL OF JAMES. A writing from around A.D. 150 that talks about Mary's special conception and upbringing as well as Jesus' virginal conception and birth.

ISAIAH. The scroll of the prophet Isaiah contains the words of two or three prophets dating from different times. In general, scholars attributed chapters 1 through 39 to Isaiah, son of Amoz, seventh century B.C. Chapters 40–55 come from a prophet—called by scholars Second Isaiah—who spoke around the end of the Babylonian Exile in the sixth century, around 539 B.C. Chapters 56 to 66 are attributed to a Third Isaiah who lived slightly later than Second Isaiah, shortly after the return of the first exiles, perhaps around 530 to 510 B.C.

JAMES, BROTHER OF JESUS. The leader of the Jesus Movement in Jerusalem from the death of Jesus to his own death in A.D. 62. This group held to Jewish practices while affirming that Jesus was the Messiah who would restore the Kingdom to Israel.

JESUS. 6 or 5 B.C. to around A.D. 30. Teacher, Messiah claimant, and, as a descendant from King David, an heir to the Jewish throne ("King of the Jews"). Taught in the Galilee for the most part in the later 20s. Crucified in Jerusalem around A.D. 30.

JESUS COVER-UP THESIS. This view of Christian origins has three main components. First, it contends that the original message of Jesus and the Jesus Movement, Jesus' earliest followers in Jerusalem, became switched for a different religion, that of Paul's Christ Movement. Second, it advances the view that there was an important shift away from the teachings *of* Jesus to those *about* the Christ. Finally, it proposes a new way of understanding Christian anti-Semitism.

JESUS MOVEMENT. The first followers of Jesus, in Jerusalem, composed of Jesus' family, the eleven remaining disciples, and Mary Magdalene. The movement was led by James until his death in 62. Then, after a brief interruption, it was headed by Simeon until the early years of the second century. The Jesus Movement looked upon Jesus as a messianic claimant to the throne of Israel. In their view, he was fully human and a teacher of Torah. They waited for his return to establish the Kingdom of God he had announced was imminent. Later became known as the Ebionites or Nazarenes.

JOHN (GOSPEL OF). A canonical gospel dated by scholars to the 90s A.D. It was attributed later on to a "John."

JOHN THE BAPTIST (OR BAPTIZER). A cousin of Jesus. Sometime during the mid to late 20s A.D., he immersed Jewish people in the Jordan River as a sign of their personal rededication to the Torah. He was imprisoned and beheaded by Herod Antipas.

JUDAS ISCARIOT. One of the disciples of Jesus, possibly a Zealot, who betrayed Jesus.

JUSTIN MARTYR. A second-century Christian thinker who lived in Rome. In the 130s, he wrote a *Dialogue with Trypho*, about his conversation with a rabbi.

LUKE (GOSPEL OF). A work written by the same author who composed the Acts of the Apostles. Scholars date this composite work to A.D. 90–125. Later sources attribute it to a "Luke." Luke used Mark, Q, and possibly other sources including his own material in writing this work, which was primarily targeted at a non-Jewish or Gentile audience.

MARCION. A second century Christian leader who during the 130s or 140s composed a work entitled *Antitheses*. In it he opposed the concept of God as a harsh judge with that of a loving and merciful deity as revealed by Jesus. Rejecting the Old Testament and using only selected texts he believed came from Paul, his restricted canon stimulated discussion of which Christian texts were authoritative. While condemned by the Proto-Orthodox, his views gained considerable support, and there were many Marcionite churches around the Roman Empire during the second through fourth centuries.

MARK (GOSPEL OF). The earliest of the four canonical gospels. Scholars usually date this writing to around A.D. 70, either just before or just after the destruction of Jerusalem and the Second Temple by the Romans. Later sources attribute it to a "Mark."

MARY MAGDALENE. An important follower of Jesus who helped support his mission financially. She was present at his crucifixion and was a witness to his resurrection. While Proto-Orthodox Christianity downplayed her role, some Gnostic Christians made her out to be the chief apostle.

MARY, MOTHER OF JESUS. The mother of Jesus who was present with him at his crucifixion. According to the New Testament, Mary gave birth to Jesus in Bethlehem, just south of Jerusalem, but raised him in Nazareth, in the north, in Galilee. Jesus had four brothers and at least two sisters.

MATTHEW (GOSPEL OF). The second gospel to be written of the four canonical gospels. Scholars usually date this writing to the 80s A.D. Sources used include Mark and Q as well as Matthew's own material. This gospel was primarily targeted toward a Jewish audience, including those early members of what became Christianity, who observed the laws of Torah.

MESSIAH. According to Jewish belief, the Messiah is a world transformer who helps to overthrow foreign authority, establishes an independent Jewish state, is the Davidic king, and, with God's help, ushers in an era of universal peace, thereby establishing the universal rule of God, the Kingdom of God.

MISHNAH. A writing that brings together the discussions and decisions of Jewish oral law. It was composed by Judah the Prince around A.D. 200 and records the debates of the rabbis and Pharisees before them on the meaning of biblical law. A later collection of oral law tradition was called the Gemara and was compiled around 500 A.D. The Mishnah and the Gemara together make up the Talmud.

MODEL OF THE TWO WAYS. Derived from Deuteronomy 30:15–20, this model sets forth the choice before Israel, either to obey the commandments of God, loving him and walking in his ways, or choosing not to do so. Different consequences are envisaged for each choice: life and prosperity or death and adversity.

NICENE CREED. A creed developed by the Proto-Orthodox bishops meeting at Nicea in 325 representing the agreed-upon statement of faith. Those who assent to it are deemed Christian; those that do not are not considered

Christian. Some additions were made to the creed in 381 at the Council of Constantinople. The Nicene Creed is still regarded as the standard of Christian Orthodoxy.

PAUL. Leader of the Christ Movement in the Jewish Diaspora who attracted a large number of Gentiles to his religion. Paul emphasized Christ as the savior of all mankind, Gentile or Jew, and claimed that members of his movement need not follow Torah. He wrote letters to his early congregations and many of these have survived. He was probably born in the first decade A.D. and likely died in Rome in the early to mid 60s.

PETER. Simon Peter or Cephas was one of the original disciples of Jesus. He probably died in Rome in the early to mid 60s.

PHARISEES. A Jewish group that arose in the midsecond century B.C., shortly after Antiochus Epiphanes' failed attempt to impose Hellenization on the Jewish people. They were primarily teachers, and, in addition to the written law, they treasured the oral law, which helped interpret the written text of the Bible. After the destruction of Jerusalem and the Second Temple, they were the only group of Jews to survive. From them comes Rabbinic Judaism.

PONTIUS PILATE. The procurator or prefect of the Roman province of Judea from A.D. 26 to 36. He presided over the trial of Jesus.

PROTO-ORTHODOXY. The name given by some scholars to Paul's Christ Movement as it expanded throughout the Roman Empire in the second through fourth centuries, eventually becoming the official religion of the Roman Empire.

PSALMS OF SOLOMON. A collection of eighteen psalms or songs composed shortly after the conquest of Jerusalem by Pompey in 63 B.C. Several of the songs describe conditions in Jerusalem as a result of the Roman invasion and look forward to the time of the Messiah when the Kingdom of God will be established. This writing is not the Psalms (of David) found within the Hebrew Bible or Old Testament.

Q. The name given to the material that is common to the Gospels of Matthew and Luke and does not derive from Mark.

SADDUCEES. A Jewish group that originated shortly after the time of Antiochus Epiphanes. For the most part they were the wealthy priestly elite that offered worship in the Temple.

SECOND JEWISH REVOLT AGAINST ROME. An unsuccessful revolt in A.D. 132–135 led by Bar Kokhba.

SEPTUAGINT. The translation of the Hebrew Bible into Greek in the third and second centuries B.C. In time additional works were added to the collection (books such as Judith, Maccabees, Tobit) and some preexisting writings were modified (e.g., the Book of Esther, the Book of Daniel). It is named the Septuagint (the seventy) because it was translated by seventy-two scholars in Alexandria, Egypt. This was the Bible for early Christians and it is the Old Testament for Roman Catholicism.

SEVEN NOAHIDE LAWS. The seven laws that, according to Jewish tradition, are incumbent upon all humanity. These laws derive from the covenant between God and Noah, who represented all humanity after the flood. These laws include abstaining from: food sacrificed to idols, illicit sexuality, eating meat of animals that have not been properly killed, murder, stealing, and cursing God. They also include the injunction to be just.

SHEMA. An important Jewish prayer that starts, "Hear O Israel: the Lord our God, the Lord is one" (Deuteronomy 6:4). It includes Deuteronomy 6:5–9 ("Thou shalt love the Lord your God with all thy heart and with all thy soul and with all thy might. And these words which I command thee this day shall be in thy heart . . ."); Deuteronomy 11:13–21 ("It shall come to pass, if ye shall hearken diligently unto my commandments which I command you this day . . ."); and Numbers 15:37–41 ("The Lord spoke unto Moses, saying: Speak unto the children of Israel, and bid them make fringes in the corners of their garments throughout their generations, putting upon the fringe of each corner a thread of blue. . . ."). Translation by the Rabbinical Assembly of America and the United Synagogue of Conservative Judaism, *Sabbath and Festival Prayer Book*.

SISTERS OF JESUS. According to Mark 6:3, Jesus had at least two sisters (who are not named) and four brothers, who are identified.

TALMUD. A record of discussions and debates among the rabbis relating to interpreting the Torah and Jewish ethics. The Talmud is composed of the Mishnah, which was originally composed around A.D. 200, as well as the later Gemara, compiled around A.D. 500.

TORAH. The written law, found within the first five books of the Bible: Genesis, Exodus, Leviticus, Numbers, and Deuteronomy.

TORAH-OBSERVANT. Those who follow the law (Torah).

VIRGIN BIRTH. The belief that certain individuals, typically emperors or founders of major Graeco-Roman religions, had a human mother and a divine father. Jesus, for instance, was said to have had a virgin birth (Gospels of Matthew and Luke).

ZEALOTS. A Jewish group that originated in the first decade of the first century A.D. that fiercely opposed rule of Judea by foreigners, the Romans.

ZECHARIAH (BOOK OF). One of Israel's prophets. Chapters 1 through 8 come from a prophet of the early Persian period, likely around 520–518 B.C. Chapters 9 to 14 stem from a later prophet, probably during early Hellenistic times.

NOTES

PROLOGUE: A PERSONAL NOTE

1. See "Taking Paul at his Word" and "Paul: A Radical Reassessment." The articles "Plato: Some Inconsistencies," "Sophocles, Oedipus Tyrannus," "Bar-
daisan: On Nature, Fate, and Freedom," as well as a paper on Bultmann are
included in my book, *Hermeneutical Studies: Dilthey, Sophocles and Plato*. An anthology of readings on interpretation theory from ancient allegorical methods
through the medieval and Renaissance/Reformation period into modern
times can be found in my *About Interpretation: From Plato to Dilthey—A
Hermeneutic Anthology.*
2. See also John Wilkinson, *Egeria's Travels.*

1. THE COVER-UP

1. Some scholars prefer to use C.E. (Common Era) for A.D. and B.C.E. (Before the
Common Era) for B.C. I use A.D. and B.C. simply because it is more familiar to
general readers. The death of Jesus is generally attributed to either A.D. 30 or
A.D. 33.

2. CULTURES IN CONFLICT

1. Burton Mack has an excellent description of the various currents thrashing
around the Mediterranean during the Hellenistic period in his *Who Wrote the
New Testament?* Chap. 1, "Clashing Cultures."

2. There are some differences between the Hebrew Bible and the Old Testament. For one thing, for Roman Catholic, Orthodox, and Anglican Christians, the Old Testament is larger than the Hebrew Bible, being based on its Greek translation—the Septuagint. The Septuagint contains Greek translations of the Hebrew Bible plus additional works such as 1 and 2 Maccabees, Judith, and Tobit. In addition, the Septuagint contains longer versions of the books of Esther and Daniel. The shorter Protestant Old Testament corresponds to the Jewish Hebrew Bible. In addition, there are differences in emphasis. Judaism places greatest stress upon the five books of the Torah; Christians focus more on the Prophets.

3. Portions of Ezekiel the Tragedian's tragedy still exist. See James H. Charlesworth, ed., *The Old Testament Pseudepigrapha*, vol. 2, 803–7.

4. Thomas L. Friedman, *The World Is Flat: A Brief History of the Twenty-first Century.*

5. 2 Maccabees was written in Greek between 104 and 63 B.C. and is an abridgment of a five-volume work written originally by Jason of Cyrene. It is included in the Septuagint, the Greek translation of the Hebrew Bible.

6. The covenant with Abraham and his offspring involving the receipt of land for the obligation to circumcise is said to be "an everlasting covenant" (Genesis 17:7, 19). Keeping the Sabbath is said to be "a perpetual covenant," as a "sign forever between me and the people of Israel" (Exodus 31:16, 17). The Psalms understand the covenant through Abraham, Isaac, and Jacob to be "an everlasting covenant" (Psalm 105:9, 10).

7. According to modern scholars, the text of Deuteronomy was edited by priestly redactors at the time of the Babylonian Exile or shortly thereafter (587/586 B.C.). Hence what is projected as "future" is more likely to be interpreted as a "reading back" into the text in the light of history. Whatever the literary history, the point is that the Model of the Two Ways is used to understand historical dynamics.

8. Scholars would remind us that this is more apt to be a retrospective rather than a predictive event.

9. The *Community Rule* IV, 5, G. Vermes, *The Complete Dead Sea Scrolls*, 102.

10. The *Community Rule* IV, 10, Ibid.

3. BEING JEWISH IN A COSMOPOLITAN WORLD

1. An interesting video from the Biblical Archeology Society, "*Where Jesus Walked*," contains footage showing these findings.

2. Translations of the Dead Sea Scrolls as well as introductions to their study are found in Geza Vermes, *The Complete Dead Sea Scrolls*; Robert Eisenman and Michael Wise, *The Dead Sea Scrolls Uncovered*; and Michael Wise, Martin Abegg, Jr., and Edward Cook, *The Dead Sea Scrolls: A New Translation*.

3. *Damascus Document* X and XI. See Vermes, *Complete Dead Sea Scrolls*, 139, 140.

4. Robert Eisenman and Michael Wise, *The Dead Sea Scrolls Uncovered*, 19–23.

5. See Vermes, *Complete Dead Sea Scrolls*, for the view that this group emerged shortly after the time of Antiochus.

6. See Michael O. Wise, *The First Messiah: Investigating the Savior Before Christ*.

7. Especially recommended for an introduction to the views of this group are the three books mentioned in note 2 above as well as: Lawrence H. Schiffman, *Reclaiming the Dead Sea Scrolls: Their True Meaning for Judaism and Christianity*; James C. VanderKam, *The Dead Sea Scrolls Today*; John J. Collins, *Apocalypticism in the Dead Sea Scrolls*; and James H. Charlesworth, ed., *Jesus and the Dead Sea Scrolls*.

8. Vermes, *Complete Dead Sea Scrolls*, and Eisenmann and Wise, *The Dead Sea Scrolls Uncovered* 478.

9. Ibid., 481.

10. For a translation and commentary on 4QMMT, see Eisenman and Wise, *Dead Sea Scrolls Uncovered*, 180–200.

11. Vermes, *Complete Dead Sea Scrolls*, 102.

12. Some contend that some of the scrolls must have originated in the Temple in Jerusalem. See Norman Golb, *Who Wrote the Dead Sea Scrolls?* Others disagree, contending that the eschatological outlook of the library as a whole is unrepresentative of Judaism in the first century A.D. and thus must represent the narrower interests of a sectarian library.

13. The story of the discovery of the Dead Sea Scrolls can be found in many works including Vermes, *Complete Dead Sea Scrolls*, VanderKam, *The Dead Sea Scrolls Today*, and, more conspiratorially, in the popular book by Michael Baigent and Richard Leigh, *The Dead Sea Scrolls Deception*.

14. See Josephus, *The Jewish War*, bk. 7, chap. 8 and 9.

15. Jesus may have been referring to the Dead Sea Scroll community when he said, "You have heard that it was said, 'You shall love your neighbor and hate your enemy'" (Matthew 5:43).

4. THE SECRETS OF HISTORY

1. The dating is that given in Charlesworth, *The Old Testament Pseudepigrapha*, vols. 1 and 2 at the translators' Introductions to each of these writings.

2. See, for instance, John Hagee, *Jerusalem Countdown: A Warning to the World*.

3. In the opinion of many biblical scholars today, the current Book of Isaiah contains the work of three prophets. First Isaiah extends from chapters 1 through 39 and represents the sayings of a prophet who lived during the eighth century B.C. Second Isaiah extends from chapters 40 to 55 and comes from a prophet who lived near the end of the Babylonian Exile, around 539 B.C. Third Isaiah, chapters 56 to the end of the book, represents a slightly later prophet, dating from the early stages of the return, around 515 B.C. For more information,

consult standard introductions to the Old Testament such as those provided by Barry Bandstra (*Reading the Old Testament*) or Lawrence Boadt (*Reading the Old Testament*).

4. Chapters 1–8 of Zechariah date from 520 to 518 B.C., during the time when some exiles were returning from Babylonia and plans were being made for rebuilding the Temple in Jerusalem. The final chapters of Zechariah, chapters 9 through 14, appear to come from a later date, since references are made to Greeks rather than to Persians (see Zechariah 9:13 for instance) and the style differs. Hence scholars think that the latter part of the Zechariah scroll represents the thinking of a prophet who lived in early Hellenistic times.

5. Book II of *Enoch*, chapters 37–71, is referred to as the Book of Similitudes. E. Isaac notes that *Enoch* Book II dates from 105–64 B.C., according to the consensus of critical scholars. See Charlesworth, *The Old Testament Pseudepigrapha*, vol. 1, 7.

6. See Wise, *The First Messiah*, 57.

7. The *Community Rule* XI, 5, Vermes, *Complete Dead Sea Scrolls*, 114, 115.

8. See texts #10 (*The Book of Secrets*) and #88 (*The Secret of the Way Things Are*) in Michael Wise, Martin Abegg, Jr., and Edward Cook, *The Dead Sea Scrolls, A New Translation*, pp. 174–177, 378–390.

9. The *Community Rule* VIII, 15, Vermes, *Complete Dead Sea Scrolls*, 109.

10. The *Damascus Document* VI, 10, Ibid., 132.

11. Ibid.

12. The main exception is the Messiah in *Enoch* Book II who is described as a pre-existing being chosen by "the Lord of the Spirits" to act as the Messiah (*Enoch* 38:2). There is no mention in this work of how the Messiah operates, whether supernaturally from heaven or on earth. There is no suggestion of any incarnation.

13. Christianity, which views Jesus as the Messiah, regards him as having a special birth. Two gospels, Matthew and Luke, make reference to a virginal conception and differ in significant details (e.g., dating, location, visitors). Matthew appeals to the Greek (Septuagint) version of Isaiah 7:14, "Look, the virgin shall conceive and bear a son, and they shall call his name Emmanuel." The original context of Isaiah 7, however, does not necessarily refer to a virgin but to a young woman: the Greek translators made the translation too specific. In addition, the intended referent would have to be someone who was alive during the Syro-Ephraimite War of the eighth century B.C. In context, Isaiah is reassuring King Ahaz of victory by the time a young woman has a son and he grows to the age where he "knows how to refuse the evil and choose the good" (Isaiah 7:16). Later on in this work we will discuss the virgin birth and what it means.

5. THE CHALLENGE OF JESUS

1. For discussions of the dating of the various gospel writings, see standard contemporary introductions to the New Testament such as: Bart D. Ehrman, *The New Testament*; Mack, *Who Wrote the New Testament?* and Steve Mason and Tom Robinson, *An Early Christian Reader*.

2. We could start with Mark, the earliest gospel. But then we would immediately face an important problem. We now know that both Matthew and Luke "wrote over" Mark, correcting, adding, and subtracting information this earlier document presented while retaining much of what he wrote. They appear to have thought that Mark did not quite get the story straight, at least as far as they were concerned. So it's probably best to avoid Mark in presenting Jesus' teachings.

3. This is not to say that *everything* contained in the Gospel of Matthew reflects the Jesus Movement of James. Later followers of the Jesus Movement, it appears, favored a shorter version of Matthew than the one we have. This version omitted the virgin birth narrative, which conflicted with their view that Jesus was human. Unlike our Greek text, their Matthew was written in Aramaic.

4. According to the Gospel of Luke, however, Jesus' birth is to be dated differently. "In those days a decree went out from Emperor Augustus [ruled 27 B.C. to A.D. 14] that all the world should be registered. This was the first registration and was taken while Quirinius was governor of Syria" (Luke 2:1, 2). This census occurred in A.D. 6 but the registration was only for Judea and Syria.

5. See James Tabor, *The Jesus Dynasty*, 141ff.

6. For a translation of the *Infancy Gospel of Thomas* see Robert J. Miller, *The Complete Gospels*, 369–79. See also www.earlychristianwritings.com. A new translation and commentary is forthcoming by Tony Chartrand-Burke, *Evangelium Thomae de infantia Salvatoris*. Corpus Christianorum Series Apocryphorum.

7. For an intriguing account of the political thrust of Jesus' ministry, including the role played by his brothers and cousin, see Tabor, *The Jesus Dynasty*. See also Jeffrey J. Bütz, *The Brother of Jesus and the Lost Teachings of Christianity*, for a study specifically of James, the brother of Jesus who led the Jesus Movement in Jerusalem.

8. See Tabor, *The Jesus Dynasty*, 162–65, for an informative account of the role played by Jesus' brothers within this inner core of disciples. As Tabor writes, "This is perhaps the best-kept secret in the entire New Testament. *Jesus' own brothers were among the so-called Twelve Apostles.*"

9. We know that some of the disciples were married. Peter certainly was (Matthew 8:14). So, too, were some of the other disciples and brothers of Jesus (1 Corinthians 9:5).

10. See Carla Ricci's *Mary Magdalene and Many Others*. chap. 3, "Women and Jesus in the Land of Galilee."

11. A large number of books have appeared on Mary Magdalene as well as an issue of *Newsweek* ("The Mystery of Mary Magdalene," May 29, 2006). See especially such recent publications as: Bart D. Ehrman, *Peter, Paul and Mary Magdalene*; Bruce Chilton, *Mary Magdalene: A Biography*; and Ann Graham Brock, *Mary Magdalene, The First Apostle*.

12. For a study of Judas, see Hyam Maccoby, *Judas Iscariot and the Myth of Jewish Evil*.

13. Or possibly half-brother. See Tabor, *The Jesus Dynasty*, 81.

14. See Ibid. for an examination of Jesus' family and successors, chap. 4, 73–81.

15. *Halakhah* refers to the interpretation of Torah. Usually reserved for the Pharisaic and rabbinic interpretations of Torah, it can be applied by extension to the interpretations of Torah given by the Teacher of Righteousness (of the Dead Sea Scroll community) and by Jesus. An example of halakhah at work is the thirty-nine categories of "work prohibited on the Sabbath" (Mishnah *Shabbat* 7:2).

16. The first half of the commandment—"to love your neighbor"—is found in Leviticus 19:18. The second half—"to hate your enemies"—is not found in the Books of the Torah. The only known ancient source for "hating your enemies" is to be found in the writings of the Dead Sea Scroll community. Jesus may have been familiar with their teachings and may be referring to their movement here. See the opening sections of the *Community Rule* of the Dead Sea Scroll community for loving all that God has chosen and hating all that he has rejected, loving the sons of light and hating the sons of darkness. Vermes, *Complete Dead Sea Scrolls*, 98, 99.

17. Louis Jacobs, *The Book of Jewish Belief*, 98.

18. The *Damascus Document* X, XI, in Vermes, *Complete Dead Sea Scrolls*, 139, 140.

19. See Schiffman's discussion in chapter 17, "The Law of the Sect," in his *Reclaiming the Dead Sea Scrolls*, 273–87.

20. Jesus' rhetorical question would not elicit a uniform "yes, by all means, we'd lift the sheep out of the pit." The Sabbath rules of the Dead Sea Scroll community explicitly prohibit this act.

21. Josephus, *Jewish Antiquities*, book 18, chapter 5, section 2.

6. THE PROMISES OF JESUS

1. There are many studies of the parables of Jesus. See, for instance, John D. Crossan, *In Parables: The Challenge of the Historical Jesus*; Robert W. Funk, Bernard Brandon Scott and James R. Butts, *The Parables of Jesus: Red Letter Edition;* and Robert W. Funk, *Parables and Presence: Forms of the New Testament Tradition*. There are some critical issues in the study of the parables. These include identifying the likely original form of the parable as uttered by Jesus rather than as expounded by later writers for their own purposes; comparing parable

versions in the canonical and noncanonical gospels; examining interpretations of specific parables in the context of Jesus' own time and later times when the gospel writers were producing their texts; as well as identifying parables attributed to Jesus but unlikely to have been spoken by him.

7. JESUS' EARLIEST FOLLOWERS: THE JESUS MOVEMENT

1. If James Tabor is right that Cleophas was the second husband of Mary, after Joseph died, then this Simeon (Simon) would have been Jesus' half-brother. See Tabor, *The Jesus Dynasty*, 289.
2. See Eusebius, *Ecclesiastical History*, bk. 3, chaps. 11, 12, 19, 20, and 32.
3. Eusebius, *Ecclesiastical History*, bk. 4, chap. 5.
4. My favorite introductory work on the history of Judaism is Max I. Dimont, *Jews, God and History*. Part 3 of this work is entitled "Moses, Christ and Caesar," and it provides a wonderful introduction to how Judaism reconstructed itself in the light of necessity, while early Christianity, too, was evolving into a separate religion. See also Lee I.A. Levine, "Judaism from the Destruction of Jerusalem to the End of the Second Jewish Revolt: 70–135 C.E.," in Hershel Shanks, ed., *Christianity and Rabbinic Judaism*.
5. See Bart D. Ehrman, *Lost Christianities*, chapter 5, "At Polar Ends of the Spectrum: Early Christian Ebionites and Marcionites," 95–112.
6. For a translation of the surviving fragments of these works, see Bart D. Ehrman, *Lost Scriptures*, 9–16.
7. For translations of these writings, see Ehrman, *Lost Scriptures*, 191–94.

8. WHAT HAPPENED TO JESUS?

1. The date of the Apostles' Creed is a subject of some controversy. Tertullian (around A.D. 200) quotes a creed very similar to what we know as the Apostles' Creed. See New Advent entry on Apostles Creed: http://www.newadvent .org/cathen/01629a.htm.
2. For this creed and the Nicene Creed as well as information about the Creed of St. Athanasius, see http://www.episcopalchurch.org/visitors_11838_ENG_ HTM.htm.
3. The Greek word for *Christ* translates the Hebrew word for *Messiah*, but it places the concept in a vastly different environment. In brief, it strips the notion of its political connotations, giving it a cosmic dimension instead.
4. Dan Brown, *The Da Vinci Code*.
5. See Michael Baigent, *The Jesus Papers*; his earlier book, Baigent, Richard Leigh, and Henry Lincoln, *Holy Blood, Holy Grail*; and Baigent, Leigh, and Lincoln, *The Messianic Legacy*.

9. THE TROUBLE WITH PAUL

1. See Acts 9:1–9, 22:4–16, and 29:9–18.

2. For more information on the role of the God-fearers in Jewish synagogues within the Diaspora, see John Dominic Crossan and Jonathan L. Reed, *In Search of Paul*, 23ff.

3. In a separate incident, one involving Cephas in Antioch, Paul implicates "the circumcision faction" and "people from James" (Galatians 2:11, 12). But these are not identified as the cause of the disturbances in Galatia.

4. The Seven Noahide Laws were being formulated during the Tannaitic period (200 B.C.–A.D.200), based in part on oral tradition as well as an interpretation of the narrative of Noah in Genesis. E. P. Sanders discusses what constitutes a "righteous Gentile" during early Christianity and concludes that "the later view, that he is one who keeps the seven Noachian commandments, is probably not too far off the mark." E. P. Sanders, *Paul and Palestinian Judaism*, 210.

5. Simcha Jacobovici, in his documentary *The Exodus Decoded*, proposes a date around 1500 B.C. Other dates include the mid 1400s and the mid 1300s. The majority dating for the Exodus is to the early 1200s, that is, to around 1290 or 1280 B.C. There are issues, however, with respect to all these datings.

6. Mason and Robinson, *Early Christian Reader*, 77, fn. g.

7. See such passages as Galatians 1:20, I Thessalonians 2:3, and Romans 9:1 in which Paul has to deal with charges of lying.

8. Bart D. Ehrman introduces this helpful terminology in *Lost Christianities*.

9. Ibid., part 3, "Winners and Losers."

10. Ehrman, *Lost Christianities*, 180.

10. THE BIG SWITCH: CHRIST FOR JESUS

1. The dating of Luke and Acts varies, from approximately the late 80s (Bart Ehrman) to the second half of the second century (Freke and Gandy). Burton Mack dates these writings to the first quarter of the second century. These diverse datings reflect differing views on how quickly the fierce feuds between members of the Jesus Movement and Christ Movement simmered down.

2. We now know much more about the various movements within early Christianity thanks to the important research of Elaine Pagels, Burton Mack, and Bart Ehrman.

3. The passage in Matthew that portrays Jesus as saying to Peter, "Simon Peter answered, 'You are the Messiah,' the son of the living God. And Jesus answered him . . . And I tell you, you are Peter, and on this rock I will build my church" (Matthew 16:16–18) is viewed by most scholars as reflecting issues in Matthew's own time when the Christian community was forming institutions

of its own, separate from those of Judaism. See, for instance, the interesting discussion in Hyam Maccoby, *The Mythmaker: Paul and the Invention of Christianity*, 121, 122. The version in the earlier gospel, Mark (Mark 8:27–33), omits any reference to "building a church." In both contexts, the Peter of the 20s would have been saying that Jesus was the Messiah in its Jewish sense, that is, as a claimant to a throne who would act as a catalyst for world transformation. See also the discussion in Frank W. Beare, *The Earliest Records of Jesus*, 136–40.

4. There was also a third movement—Gnostic Christianity—which also had an origin separate from the Jesus and Christ Movements, along with different beliefs and practices from either. But that is not our story here.

5. Josephus, *The Jewish War*, bk. 4, chap. 3, sec. 2.

6. Another revolt flared up some sixty years later—Bar Kokhba's revolt, A.D. 132–135 The Jewish people were once again defeated by Rome.

7. See, for instance, Bruce Chilton's very readable and informative *Rabbi Paul*.

8. Scholars have long been wary of using Acts as a source of information about Paul. The one reliable source of information on Paul's career and message is his own account, to be found in his authentic letters from the 50s and 60s. Steve Mason and Tom Robinson have already gone a long way toward making this claim when they note, "So for a historical understanding of Paul, his own letters must take absolute priority over the presentation in Acts." *Early Christian Reader*, 306.

9. This could be interpreted either as fourteen years from his first visit to Jerusalem and so seventeen years after his dramatic mystical experience, or it could be fourteen years from that remarkable life-altering event.

10. Bruce Chilton says A.D. 46 (*Rabbi Paul*, 268); Burton Mack says A.D. 48 (*Who Wrote the New Testament?* 103).

11. *The New Oxford Annotated Bible with the Apocrypha* says "about A.D. 55 or slightly earlier" (263 New Testament); Burton Mack in *Who Wrote the New Testament?* says A.D. 52–54.

12. It is interesting, too, that Paul speaks of them as rival teachers, not as "colleagues" as one might expect from members of the same movement. They are positioned as "other." This provides further evidence of distancing his movement from the Jesus Movement, if in fact the rival teachers were members of that group.

13. Josephus, *Jewish Antiquities*, bk. 20, chap. 8.

11. THE JESUS MOVEMENT FADES AWAY

1. For a translation of the *Didache*, see Maxwell Staniforth, trans., *Early Christian Writings*, 187–99, or Ehrman, *Lost Scriptures*, 211–17. Quotations from the *Didache* are from the Staniforth translation.

2. The Amidah (Standing Prayer), or Shemoneh Esrei (Eighteen Benedictions), as it is also called, is an ancient Jewish prayer that goes back to practices prior to

the destruction of the Temple. It would have been said by observant Jews on a daily basis. Ancient tradition has this prayer originating in the time of Ezra, with an additional benediction being added by the sages at Yavneh, in part to counter the growing influence of the early Christian movement. So, although the prayer now contains nineteen benedictions, it is still called the Eighteen Benedictions.

3. Vermes, *Complete Dead Sea Scrolls,* 159, 160.

4. Maccoby, *The Mythmaker,* chapter 11, "Paul and the Eucharist."

5. Timothy Freke and Peter Gandy, *The Jesus Mysteries,* 48, 49.

6. Maccoby, *The Mythmaker,* 110.

7. Ibid., 111.

8. A translation of 4 *Ezra* as well as another work by a Jewish author in the late first century A.D. reflecting on the destruction of the Temple, 2 *Baruch,* can be found in Charlesworth, *The Old Testament Pseudepigrapha,* vol. 1, 517–559 (4 *Ezra*) and pp 615–652 (2 *Baruch*).

9. Levine, "Judaism from the Destruction of Jerusalem," 139, 140.

10. Ehrman, *Lost Scriptures,* 12.

11. For translations of selected portions of these works, see Ibid., 191–200.

12. For a translation of the *Acts of Paul* and the *Acts of Thecla,* see Ibid., 109–21.

13. *Letter of Peter to James* 2:3, Ibid., 192.

14. *Letter of Peter to James* 2:5, Ibid., 192.

12. PAUL THE RADICAL

1. Many Christian churches have moved away from supersessionism. The worldwide Anglican Communion, for instance, rejected this way of understanding Christianity's relationship to Judaism in a 1988 Lambeth Conference document entitled "Jews, Christians and Muslims: The Way of Dialogue." Similarly, in 2000, The United Methodist Church released a position paper entitled "Building New Bridges in Hope: A Commentary on the United Methodist Statement on Christian-Jewish Relations." The United Church of Canada issued an important document in 2003 entitled "Bearing Faithful Witness."

2. The covenant with Noah is said to be with God and "your descendants after you" (Genesis 9:9). The covenant with Abraham, including circumcision, is said to be "an everlasting covenant" (Genesis 17:7). The covenant between God and the people of Israel is not only for those alive at Moses' time, but also for all their descendants (Deuteronomy 5:3—"Not with our ancestors did the Lord make this covenant, but with us, who are all of us here alive today"). Deuteronomy 7:9 notes that God maintains covenant loyalty "to a thousand generations." The laws pertaining to the Sabbath are said to be "in perpetuity" (Exodus 31:16—"Therefore the Israelites shall keep the Sabbath, observing the

Sabbath throughout their generations, as a perpetual covenant") as are the laws pertaining to the observance of Yom Kippur, the Day of Atonement (Leviticus 23:31). God's covenant with David that a descendant of his would always be on the throne of Israel is also said to be in perpetuity: "Your house and your kingdom shall be made sure forever before me; your throne shall be established forever" (2 Samuel 7:16).

3. During one of Paul's infrequent visits to Jerusalem, Paul is informed that many "thousands of believers," have been told "that you teach all the Jews living among the Gentiles to forsake Moses and that you tell them not to circumcise their children or observe the customs." As it turns out, those rumors were accurate. It is exactly what Paul had been saying.

4. Tom Harpur, *The Pagan Christ,* 169.

13. DEMONIZING JEWISH LEADERSHIP AND THE JEWISH PEOPLE

1. For comparisons among Matthew, Luke, and Mark, see Burton H. Throckmorton, Jr., *Gospel Parallels: A Comparison of the Synoptic Gospels.*

2. "Q" refers to the material that is common to Matthew and Luke that does not come from Mark. So it is relatively easy to reconstruct: one strips away Mark from both Matthew and Luke. What remains that is common is Q. There is, however, some residue. This represents material that is only found in Matthew and some material only found in Luke. For ease of reference, scholars call the material that is only found in Matthew—his own material not coming from either Mark or Q— M. Similarly the material that is only found in Luke—his own material not coming from either Mark or Q—is referred to as L.

3. See Anthony J. Saldarini's *Matthew's Christian-Jewish Community* for a discussion of the social context of the Gospel of Matthew.

4. Saldarini emphasizes that this writing represents "an inner Jewish polemic, not an affirmation of Christianity against Judaism" (Ibid., 45).

5. Elaine Pagels, *The Origin of Satan,* 76.

6. Ibid., 84.

7. Staniforth, *Early Christian Writings,* 140.

14. CONFISCATING JUDAISM'S HERITAGE

1. Eusebius, *Ecclesiastical History,* bk. 3, chap. 22.

2. Translations of Ignatius of Antioch's letters can be found in Staniforth, *Early Christian Writings,* 53–112.

3. Incidentally, as the translator points out, this is the first known usage of the noun *Christianity.* Ibid., 75, n. 8.

4. See translation with introductory comments in Ehrman, *Lost Scriptures*, 219–35. A translation with introduction is also provided in Staniforth, *Early Christian Writings*, 155–84.

5. Ehrman, *Lost Scriptures*, 219.

6. As Bart Ehrman points out, the sources for some of these alleged biblical prohibitions are unknown (e.g., not eating the lamprey eel, the octopus, the cuttlefish, and the hyena). See Ibid., 228, nn. 56 and 58.

7. See Staniforth, *Early Christian Writings*, 183, n. 11.

8. For primary texts on allegorical interpretation, with introductions, see Wilson, *About Interpretation*, sec. 1, "Allegorical Hermeneutics," 1–101.

9. Mack, *Who Wrote the New Testament?* 252.

10. Paul allegorized the story of Sarah and Hagar: "Now this is an allegory [referring to Abraham, his two wives and his two sons]: these women are two covenants. One woman, in fact, is Hagar, from Mount Sinai, bearing children for slavery. Now Hagar is Mount Sinai in Arabia and corresponds to the present Jerusalem, for she is in slavery with her children. But the other woman corresponds to the Jerusalem above; she is free, and she is our mother." (Galatians 4:24–26).

11. Eusebius, *Ecclesiastical History*, bk. 4, chap. 18.

12. Justin Martyr, *Dialogue with Trypho*, chap. 9. *Ante-Nicene Library, Vol I*; http://www.ccel.org/fathers2/.

13. Ibid., chap. 135.

14. Ibid., chap. 119.

15. Ibid., chap. 29.

16. Ibid., chap. 67.

17. Ibid., chap. 69

15. ATTACKING THE JEWISH CONCEPT OF GOD

1. For a translation of the *Acts of Thecla*, see Ehrman, *Lost Scriptures*, 113–21.

2. For a translation of the *Infancy Gospel of James*, also called the *Proto-Gospel of James*, see Ibid., 63–72, or Miller, *Complete Gospels*, 380–96.

3. Levine, "Judaism from the Destruction of Jerusalem," 148.

4. See Oscar Cullmann, *Immortality of the Soul or Resurrection of the Dead?*

5. Freke and Gandy, *The Jesus Mysteries*; Harpur, *The Pagan Christ*.

6. Mack, *Who Wrote the New Testament?* 253.

8. For a translation of Tertullian's treatise, *Against Marcion*, see www.newadvent.org/fathers/0312.htm.

9. Tertullian, *Against Marcion*, bk. 1, chap. 2.

10. Ibid., bk. 1, chap. 6.

11. See Bart D. Ehrman, *Misquoting Jesus: The Story Behind Who Changed the Bible and Why*, and *The Orthodox Corruption of Scripture*.

12. Tertullian, *Against Marcion*, bk. 4, chap. 3

13. Ibid., bk. 4, chap. 5.
14. Ibid., bk. 1, chap. 3.
15. A translation of this fundamental text of Gnostic Christianity can be found in Marvin W. Meyer, *The Secret Teachings of Jesus: Four Gnostic Gospels*, 55–87.
16. Ehrman, *Lost Scriptures*, 297.
17. See Hershel Shanks and Ben Witherington III, *The Brother of Jesus: The Dramatic Story and Meaning of the First Archeological Link to Jesus and his Family*. See also Robert Eisenman, *James the Brother of Jesus*; John Painter, *Just James: The Brother of Jesus in History and Tradition*; Bruce Chilton and Jacob Neusner, *The Brother of Jesus: James the Just and His Mission*.

16. ANTI-SEMITISM

1. For a text of St. John Chrysostom's eight sermons, see http://www.fordham .edu/halsall/source/chrysostom-jews6.html. See especially Homily I (Section II, 2—Jews are "dogs"; Section II, 6—Jews are "fit for slaughter"; Section VI, 5—"the godlessness of the Jews and the pagans is on a par"; Section VII, 5— the Jews "slew the Son of your Lord" and "they slew God").
2. James Carroll, *Constantine's Sword: The Church and the Jews*, 191.
3. The editors of the New Oxford Annotated Bible note, "This passage, so critical of the Jews, is held by many scholars to be a later addition to the letter, not only because the anti-Jewish language is not like what Paul writes elsewhere, but especially because the passage introduces an atypical second thanksgiving into the pattern of the letter" (291NT).
4. For an introduction and translation of this work, see Ehrman, *Lost Scriptures*, 31–34. For extended commentary, see Ehrman, *Lost Christianities*, 13–28.
5. *Gospel of Peter* 25, Ehrman, *Lost Scriptures*, 33.
6. *Gospel of Peter* 46, Ibid, 34
7. See translation of Bishop Melito's *On Pascha*: http://www.monachos.net/ pascha/common/melito_pascha.shtml.
8. John Chrysostom, Homily 1, Section 7, 5, "For I am persuaded to call the fasting of the Jews a table of demons because they slew God."
9. Supersessionism is characterized by the Institute for Christian and Jewish Studies as follows:

"According to the supersessionist view, God repudiated the Jewish people for their rejection of Christ. As a result, God's covenantal relationship with Israel was abrogated, to be taken up by the Church; and the Mosaic Law (Torah) was annulled, to be replaced by the law of Christ. Christians inherited all the promises of God to Israel in the Bible; Jews retained all the Bible's prophetic criticism and condemnation. Jewish biblical interpretation was discounted, and the 'Old Testament' was assigned only a provisional validity. Judaism came to be regarded as merely a historical and social entity at best, and, at worst, a dead faith, the victim of a Pharisaic-rabbinic obsession with legalistic piety." See "Supersessionism," The Institute for Christian and Jewish Studies, www.icjs.org/clergy/supersessionism.html.

10. Many works examine the topic of anti-Semitism. James Carroll in *Constantine's Sword* explores the broad sweep of interactions between the church and the Jews over the centuries, culminating in a call for a Vatican III to address some long-standing issues. David Kertzer's *The Popes Against the Jews* traces the Vatican's role in the development of moderm anti-Semitism. Dennis Prager and Joseph Telushkin's *Why the Jews?* raises concerns about renewed anti-Semitism on a worldwide scale. It traces the contours of different types of anti-Semitism including Christian, Islamic, Secular, Leftist, and even Jewish anti-Semitism. In *The Origins of anti-Semitism,* John G. Gager traces the attitudes toward Judaism in Christian and non-Christian circles in antiquity. A classic study is Rosemary Radford Ruether's *Faith and Fratricide: The Theological Roots of Anti-Semitism.* In a more contemporary vein, Phyllis Chesler's *The New Anti-Semitism* examines the various guises that this expression of hatred assumes today. Anti-Semitism is a topic, moreover, that has been addressed by many Christian denominations at the highest levels that, in light of the Holocaust, are trying to eradicate anti-Semitic attitudes from their membership, beliefs, and liturgical practices. Particularly noteworthy is the Roman Catholic statement *Nostra Aetate* ("In Our Time") which tries to overcome the belief that all the Jewish people, then or now, are responsible for the death of Jesus.

11. See John Cornwell, *Hitler's Pope: The Secret History of Pius XII*; Daniel Jonah Goldhagen, *Hitler's Willing Executioners: Ordinary Germans and the Holocaust.* See also Martin Luther's writing, *On the Jews and Their Lies.* Published in 1543, this text advocated that Jewish synagogues should be burned, their sacred texts destroyed, and Jewish property destroyed. He also proposed the expulsion of all Jews from German territory.

17. THE COVER-UP REVEALED

1. For a full text of the Nicene Creed, see http://anglicansonline.org/basics/nicene.html.

2. For a full text in Latin and English of the Creed of St. Athanasius, see http://www.creeds.net/ancient/Quicumque.html.

3. Justin Martyr, *Dialogue with Trypho,* chaps. 69, 70.

4. Ibid., chap. 70.

5. "But if some, through weak-mindedness, wish to observe such institutions as were given by Moses, from which they expect some virtue, but which we believe were appointed by reason of the hardness of the people's hearts, along

with their hope in this Christ, and [wish to perform] the eternal and natural acts of righteousness and piety, yet choose to live with the Christians and the faithful, as I said before, not inducing them either to be circumcised like themselves, or to keep the Sabbath, or to observe any other such ceremonies, then I hold that we ought to join ourselves to such, and associate with them in all things as kinsmen and brethren." Ibid., chap. 47.

6. Eusebius, *Ecclesiastical History*, bk. 3, chap. 27, "The Heresy of the Ebionites."
7. Rabbi Nosson Scherman, *The Complete ArtScroll Siddur Weekday/Sabbath/Festival*, 106 (Hebrew) and 107 (English).
8. I owe this insight to Simcha Jacobovici, President of Associated Producers, Toronto. Associated Producers' projects include *The Lost Tomb of Jesus, The Exodus Decoded, The Naked Archaeologist, Fathers and Sons, Biblical Archeology, James the Brother of Jesus, Impact of Terror, Quest for the Lost Tribes* and many other documentaries that have aired on American, British, and Canadian television.
9. Justin Martyr, *Dialogue with Trypho*, chap. 10. Emphasis added.
10. For the question of how Jesus fulfilled the mandate of a Messiah, see Ibid., chap. 39. For Trypho's discussion of how Jesus was resurrected and ascended into heaven, see Ibid., chap. 63.
11. Ibid., chap. 38.
12. Another example suggested to me by a good friend, Dr. Julio Szmuilowicz, is to be found in *Witness*, an award-winning 1985 film that explores the fear that a young Amish boy and his mother go through after he witnesses the violent killing of an undercover narcotics agent in the train station in Philadelphia. Harrison Ford is "the good cop" who blends in with the Amish community in order to protect the boy and his mother. The killers, however, are relentless in their pursuit of the witnesses to their crime, to eradicate and silence them.

EPILOGUE: THE WAY FORWARD

1. Tabor, *The Jesus Dynasty*, 142.
2. Ibid., 165. Emphasis in the original.
3. Ibid., 79–81, 162–67.

BIBLIOGRAPHY

BIBLE

The New Oxford Annotated Bible with the Apocrypha. New Revised Standard Version, College Edition. New York: Oxford University Press, 1991, 1994.

SECONDARY PRINT SOURCES

Baigent, Michael. *The Jesus Papers.* New York: HarperSanFrancisco, 2006.

———— and Richard Leigh. *The Dead Sea Scrolls Deception.* London: Jonathan Cape, 1991.

————, Richard Leigh, and Henry Lincoln. *Holy Blood, Holy Grail.* New York: Delacorte, 2005.

————, Richard Leigh, and Henry Lincoln. *The Messianic Legacy.* New York: Dell, 1989 reissue.

Bandstra, Barry L. *Reading the Old Testament.* Belmont, MA: Wadsworth, 1999.

Beare, Frank W. *The Earliest Records of Jesus.* Oxford: Basil Blackwell, 1962.

Boadt, Lawrence. *Reading the Old Testament.* Mahwah, NJ: Paulist Press, 1984.

Brock, Ann Graham. *Mary Magdalene, The First Apostle.* Harvard Theological Studies 51. Cambridge: Harvard University Press for Harvard Theological Studies, 2003.

Brown, Dan. *The Da Vinci Code.* New York: Doubleday, 2003.

Bruce, F. F. *The Canon of Scripture.* Downer's Grove, IL: InterVarsity Press, 1988.

Bütz, Jeffrey J. *The Brother of Jesus and the Lost Teachings of Christianity.* Rochester, VT: Inner Traditions, 2005.

Carroll, James. *Constantine's Sword: The Church and the Jews.* Boston: Houghton Mifflin, 2001.

Charlesworth, James H., ed. *Jesus and the Dead Sea Scrolls.* New York: Doubleday, 1992.

———, ed. *The Old Testament Pseudepigrapha.* Vol. 1. New York: Doubleday, 1983.

———, ed. *The Old Testament Pseudepigrapha.* Vol. 2. New York: Doubleday, 1985.

Chesler, Phyllis. *The New Anti-Semitism.* San Francisco: Jossey-Bass, 2003.

Chilton, Bruce. *Mary Magdalene: A Biography.* New York: Doubleday, 2005.

———. *Rabbi Jesus: An Intimate Biography.* New York: Doubleday, 2000.

———. *Rabbi Paul.* New York: Doubleday, 2004.

———, and Jacob Neusner. *The Brother of Jesus: James the Just and His Mission.* Louisville: Westminster John Knox, 2001.

———, and Jacob Neusner. *Classical Christianity and Rabbinic Judaism: Comparing Theologies.* Grand Rapids, MI: Baker, 2004.

———, and Jacob Neusner. *Judaism When Christianity Began: A Survey of Belief and Practice.* Louisville: John Knox, 2002.

Collins, John J. *Apocalypticism in the Dead Sea Scrolls.* London: Routledge, 1997.

———. *The Scepter and the Star: The Messiahs of the Dead Sea Scrolls and Other Ancient Literature.* New York: Doubleday, 1995.

Cornwell, John. *Hitler's Pope: The Secret History of Pius XII.* New York: Viking, 1999.

Crossan, John D. *In Parables: The Challenge of the Historical Jesus.* Sonoma, AZ: Polebridge, 1985.

———, and Jonathan L. Reed. *In Search of Paul.* New York: HarperSanFrancisco, 2004.

Cruse, C. F., trans. *Eusebius' Ecclesiastical History.* Peabody, MA: Hendrickson, 1998.

Cullmann, Oscar. *Immortality of the Soul or Resurrection of the Dead?* London: Epworth, 1958.

Dimont, Max I. *Jews, God and History.* 2nd ed. New York: Signet Classics, 2004.

Donin, Rabbi Hayin Halevy. *To Be a Jew.* New York: Basic Books, 1972.

Duling, Dennis C. *The New Testament: History, Literature and Social Context.* 4th ed. Belmont, MA: Wadsworth, 2003.

Dunn, James D. G. *Jesus, Paul and the Law.* Louisville: Westminster, 1990.

————, ed. *Paul and the Mosaic Law.* Grand Rapids, MI: William B. Eerdmans, 2001.

Ehrman, Bart D. *Lost Christianities: The Battles for Scriptures and the Faiths We Never Knew.* New York: Oxford University Press, 2003.

————. *Lost Scriptures: Books That Did Not Make It Into the New Testament.* New York: Oxford University Press, 2003.

————. *Misquoting Jesus: The Story Behind Who Changed the Bible and Why.* New York: HarperSanFrancisco, 2006.

————. *The New Testament: An Historical Introduction to Early Christian Writings.* 3rd ed. New York: Oxford University Press, 2004.

————. *The Orthodox Corruption of Scripture.* New York: Oxford University Press, 1993.

————. *Peter, Paul and Mary Magdalene.* New York: Oxford University Press, 2006.

Eisenman, Robert. *James the Brother of Jesus.* New York: Penguin Books, 1997.

———— and Michael Wise. *The Dead Sea Scrolls Uncovered.* Rockport, MA: Element, 1992.

Eusebius. *Ecclesiastical History.* Translated by C. F. Cruse. Peabody, MA: Hendrickson, 1998.

Friedman, Thomas L. *The World Is Flat: A Brief History of the Twenty-First Century.* New York: Farrar, Straus and Giroux, 2005.

Freke, Timothy, and Peter Gandy. *Jesus and the Lost Goddess: The Secret Teachings of the Original Christians.* New York: Three Rivers, 2001.

————. *The Jesus Mysteries: Was the "Original Jesus" A Pagan God?* New York: Three Rivers, 1999.

Funk, Robert W. *Parables and Presence: Forms of the New Testament Tradition.* Minneapolis: Fortress, 1982.

————, Bernard Brandon Scott, and James R. Butts. *The Parables of Jesus: Red Letter Edition.* The Jesus Seminar. Sonoma, AZ: Polebridge, 1988.

Gager, John G. *The Origins of Anti-Semitism.* London: Oxford University Press, 1983.

Golb, Norman. *Who Wrote the Dead Sea Scrolls?* New York: Scribner, 1995.

Goldhagen, Daniel Jonah. *Hitler's Willing Executioners.* New York: Alfred A. Knopf, 1996.

Gray, Patrick T. R. *Leontius of Jerusalem: Against the Monophysites: Testimonies of the Saints and Aporiae.* New York: Oxford University Press, 2006.

———, ed. *The Defense of Chalcedon in the East (451–553).* Leiden, The Netherlands: E.J. Brill, 1979.

Hagee, John. *Jerusalem Countdown: A Warning to the World.* Lake Mary, FL: Frontline, 2006.

Harpur, Tom. *The Pagan Christ.* Toronto: Thomas Allen, 2004.

Harris, Stephen L. *The New Testament: A Student's Introduction.* 4th ed. New York: McGraw-Hill, 2002.

Jacobs, Louis. *The Book of Jewish Belief.* West Orange, NJ: Behrman House, 1984.

Kertzer, David I. *The Popes Against the Jews: The Vatican's Role in the Rise of Modern Anti-Semitism.* Toronto: Random House Canada, 2002.

Kloppenborg, John. *The Formation of Q: Trajectories in Ancient Wisdom Collections.* Philadelphia: Fortress, 1987.

Knox, John. *Marcion and the New Testament.* Chicago: University of Chicago Press, 1942.

Levine, Lee I. A. "Judaism from the Destruction of Jerusalem to the End of the Second Jewish Revolt: 70-125 C.E.," in Hershel Shanks (ed.), *Christianity and Rabbinic Judaism: A Parellel History of Their Origins and Early Development,* pp 125–149.

Ludeman, Gerd. *Paul: The Founder of Christianity.* Amherst, MA: Prometheus Books, 2002.

Maccoby, Hyam. *Judas Iscariot and the Myth of Jewish Evil.* New York: Free Press, 1992.

———. *The Mythmaker: Paul and the Invention of Christianity.* San Francisco: Harper & Row, 1986.

Mack, Burton L. *The Lost Gospel: The Book of Q and Christian Origins.* New York: HarperSanFrancisco, 1993.

———. *Who Wrote the New Testament?* New York: HarperSanFrancisco, 1993.

Mason, Steve. *Josephus and the New Testament.* Peabody, MA: Hendrickson, 1992.

———, and Tom Robinson. *An Early Christian Reader.* Toronto: Canadian Scholars' Press, 1990.

McDonald, Lee M. *The Formation of the Christian Biblical Canon.* Peabody, MA: Hendrickson, 1995.

————, and James A. Sanders, eds. *The Canon Debate.* Peabody, MA: Hendrickson, 2002.

Meyer, Marvin W. *The Secret Teachings of Jesus: Four Gnostic Gospels.* New York: Random House, 1984.

Miller, Robert J. (ed.) *The Complete Gospels.* Sonoma, AZ: Polebridge, 1992, 1994.

Pagels, Elaine. *Beyond Belief: The Secret Gospel of Thomas.* New York: Random House, 2003.

————. *The Gnostic Gospels.* New York: Vintage Books, 1979.

————. *The Origin of Satan.* New York: Random House, 1995.

Painter, John. *Just James: The Brother of Jesus in History and Tradition.* Minneapolis: Fortress, 1999.

Prager, Dennis, and Joseph Telushkin. *Why the Jews?* New York: Touchstone, 1983, 2003.

Räisänen, H. *Paul and the Law.* Tübingen, Germany: Mohr, 1983.

Ricci, Carla. *Mary Magdalene and Many Others.* Minneapolis: Fortress Press, 1994.

Ruether, Rosemary Radford. *Faith and Fratricide: The Theological Roots of - Anti-Semitism.* New York: Seabury, 1974.

Sabbath and Festival Prayer Book. Published by The Rabbinical Assembly of America and The United Synagogue of Conservative Judaism, 1973.

Saldarini, Anthony J. *Matthew's Christian-Jewish Community.* Chicago: University of Chicago Press, 1994.

Sanders, E.P. *Paul and Palestinian Judaism.* Minneapolis: Fortress Press, 1977.

————. *Jesus and Judaism.* Minneapolis: Fortress, 1987.

Scherman, Rabbi Nosson, trans. *The Complete ArtScroll Siddur: Weekday/Sabbath/Festival.* 3rd ed. Brooklyn: Mesorah, 1997.

Schiffman, Lawrence H. *Reclaiming the Dead Sea Scrolls: Their True Meaning for Judaism and Christianity.* New York: Doubleday, 1995.

Segal, Alan. *Rebecca's Children: Judaism and Christianity in the Roman World.* Cambridge: Harvard University Press, 1986.

Shanks, Hershel, ed. *Christianity and Rabbinic Judaism: A Parallel History of their Origins and Early Development.* Washington, DC: Biblical Archeology Society, 1992.

————, and Ben Witherington III. *The Brother of Jesus: The Dramatic Story and Meaning of the First Archeological Link to Jesus and His Family.* New York: HarperCollins, 2003.

Skarsaune, Oscar. *In the Shadow of the Temple: Jewish Influences on Early Christianity.* Downers Grove, IL: InterVarsity, 2002.

Staniforth, Maxwell, trans. *Early Christian Writings.* Revised translations, introductions, and new editorial material by Andrew Louth. London: Penguin Books, 1968 and 1987.

Tabor, James D. *The Jesus Dynasty: The Hidden History of Jesus, His Royal Family, and the Birth of Christianity.* New York: Simon & Schuster, 2006.

Throckmorton, Jr., Burton H. *Gospel Parallels: A Comparison of the Synoptic Gospels,* 5th ed. Nashville: Thomas Nelson Publishers, 1992.

VanderKam, James C. *The Dead Sea Scrolls Today.* Grand Rapids, MI: William B. Eerdmans, 1994.

Vermes, Geza. *The Complete Dead Sea Scrolls in English.* London: Penguin Books, 1997.

————. *Jesus the Jew: A Historian's Reading of the Gospels.* Philadelphia: Fortress, 1973.

Wenham, David. *Paul: Follower of Jesus or Founder of Christianity?* Grand Rapids, MI: William B. Eerdmans, 1995.

Wilkinson, John. *Egeria's Travels.* Oxford: Aris & Phillips, 1999.

Wilson, Barrie A. *About Interpretation: From Plato to Dilthey—A Hermeneutic Anthology.* Bern: Peter Lang, 1989.

————. *The Anatomy of Argument.* Lanham: University Press of America, 1980 and 1986.

————. *"Big Fish:* Understanding Historical Narrative." Forthcoming in *The Journal of Religion and Popular Culture,* Spring 2008.

————. "Dreamchild and Biblical Studies." Forthcoming in *The Journal of Film and History,* 2006.

————. *Hermeneutical Studies: Dilthey, Sophocles and Plato.* Lewiston, NY: Mellon, 1990.

————. *Interpretation, Meta-Interpretation and Oedipus Tyrannus.* Berkeley: Center for Hermeneutical Studies, 1980.

————. "Paul: A Radical Reassessment." Paper presented to the 4th Annual International Conference on Arts and Humanities, Honolulu, Hawaii, January

2006. Published in *Proceedings of the 4th Annual International Conference on Arts and Humanities,* Honolulu: 2006, 6539–6552.

————. "Taking Paul at his Word." Paper presented to the American Academy of Religion, Eastern Division Meetings, Quebec City, May 2006.

————. *"What's a Messiah To Do?"* Paper presented at the 5th Annual International Conference on Arts and Humanities, Honolulu, Hawaii, January 2007. Published in *Proceedings of the 5th Annual International Conference on Arts and Humanities.* Honolulu, 2007, 5843–5858.

Wise, Michael O. *The First Messiah: Investigating the Savior Before Christ.* New York: HarperSanFrancisco, 1999.

————, Martin Abegg Jr. and Edward Cook. *The Dead Sea Scrolls: A New Translation.* San Francisco: HarperSanFrancisco, 1996.

INTERNET RESOURCES

Chrysostom, John. *Adversus Judaeos.* See translation from *John Chrysostom: Eight Homilies Against the Jews [Adversus Judaeo], Patrologia Greaca,* vol. 98 at http://www.fordham.edu/halsall/source/chrysostom-jews6.html.

Justin Martyr. *Dialogue with Trypho.* Philip Schaff, *ANF01 The Apostolic Fathers with Justin Martyr and Irenaeus.* Grand Rapids, MI: Eerdmans, 2001 reprint. http://www.ccel.org/ccel/schaff/anf01.toc.html.

Luther, Martin. Selections from *On the Jews and their Lies* (1543). See http://www.jewishvirtuallibrary.org/jsource/anti-semitism/Luther_on_Jews.html.

Melito of Sardis. See translation of *On Pascha* based on the 1979 English translation of S. G. Hall, Oxford; updated and revised by M. C. Steenberg, Oxford, 2002. http://www.monachos.net/pascha/common/melito_pascha.shtml.

Pope Paul VI, *Nostra Aetate,* proclaimed by Pope Paul VI on October 28, 1965. http://www.vatican.va/archive/hist_councils/ii_vatican_council/documents/vat-ii_decl_19651028_nostra-aetate_en.html.

Tertullian. *Against Marcion.* See www.newadvent.org/fathers/03121.htm.

FILM REFERENCES

Biblical Archeology Society *Where Jesus Walked.* 2005.

Simcha Jacobovici. *The Exodus Decoded.* 2006.

INDEX

❧